T4-ADN-262

# Religion
in the Age of
Enlightenment

# Religion in the Age of Enlightenment
Volume 2

Editor
*Brett C. McInelly, Brigham Young University*

Book Review Editor
*Kathryn Stasio, Saint Leo University*

Editorial Board

Patricia Bruckmann, *University of Toronto*
Kevin L. Cope, *Louisiana State University*
Jeremy Gregory, *University of Manchester*
Richard P. Heitzenrater, *Duke Divinity School*
David Hempton, *Harvard Divinity School*
Phyllis Mack, *Rutgers University*
Scott Mandelbrote, *Peterhouse, Cambridge University,* and
*All Souls College, Oxford University*
David Paxman, *Brigham Young University*
Isabel Rivers, *Queen Mary, University of London*
Muriel Schmid, *University of Utah*
Laura M. Stevens, *University of Tulsa*
Michael F. Suarez, *University of Virginia*
Norman Vance, *University of Sussex*

# Religion
### in the Age of
# Enlightenment
### Volume 2

Editor, Brett C. McInelly
Book Review Editor, Kathryn Stasio

AMS Press, Inc.
New York

Volume 2
# Religion in the Age of Enlightenment
ISSN: 1947-444X

Set ISBN-10: 0-404-63310-2
Set ISBN-13: 978-0-404-63310-3

Vol. 2 ISBN-10: 0-404-63312-9
Vol. 2 ISBN-13: 978-0-404-63312-7

**Copyright © 2010 AMS Press, Inc.**

All rights reserved. No part of this publication may be reproduced in any form without the permission of the copyright holder.

All AMS books are printed on acid-free paper that meets the guidelines for performance and durability of the Committee on Production Guidelines for Book Longevity of the Council on Library Resources.

Editorial and production services provided by the BYU Humanities Publication Center.

AMS Press, Inc.
Brooklyn Navy Yard, 63 Flushing Avenue–Unit #221
Brooklyn, NY 11205-1073, USA
*www.amspressinc.com*

MANUFACTURED IN THE UNITED STATES OF AMERICA

# Contents

**Preface**

**Articles**

1     Samuel Johnson at Prayer
*Elizabeth Kraft*

19    Religion in the Age of Enlightenment: Putting John Wesley in Context
*Jeremy Gregory*

55    "If God . . . see fit to call you out": "Public" and "Private" in the Writings of Methodist Women, 1760–1840
*Joanna Cruickshank*

77    "Improving the *present* moment": John Wesley's Use of the *Arminian Magazine* in Raising Early Methodist Awareness and Understanding of National Issues (January 1778–February 1791)
*Barbara Prosser*

103   Allegiance, Sympathy, and History: The Catholic Loyalties of Alexander Pope
*Steven Stryer*

131   More Light? Biblical Criticism and Enlightenment Attitudes
*Norman Vance*

153   Jonathan Edwards's Metaphors of Sin in Indian Country
*Joy A. J. Howard*

177   Holy Land Travel and the Representation of Prayer in the Enlightenment
*Michael Rotenberg-Schwartz*

209   Theological Enlightenments and Ridiculous Theologies: Contradistinction in English Polemical Theology
*David Manning*

243   "Chastisements of a Heavenly Father": The Meaning of the London Earthquakes of 1750
*Christopher Smyth*

277   Porn, Popery, Mahometanism, and the Rise of the Novel: Responses to the London Earthquakes of 1750
*Samara Anne Cahill*

303   Reading Diderot's *La Religieuse* as an Evangelical Novel
*Muriel Schmid*

323   Enlightenment Sermon Studies: A Multidisciplinary Activity
*Bob Tennant*

## Reviews

343 *Heart Religion in the British Enlightenment: Gender and Emotion in Early Methodism*
Dustin D. Stewart

349 *Bodies of Thought: Science, Religion, and the Soul in the Early Enlightenment*
Robin Runia

353 *Peripheral Wonders: Nature, Knowledge, and Enlightenment in the Eighteenth-Century Orinoco*
Laura Miller

357 *Enlightenment and Modernity: The English Deists and Reform*
Scott Breuninger

361 *Fellow-Feeling and the Moral Life*
Patrick Mello

365 *Anna Letitia Barbauld: Voice of the Enlightenment*
Robert K. Lapp

369 *Trauma and Transformation: The Political Progress of John Bunyan*
Jeffrey Galbraith

375 *Walls and Vaults: A Natural Science of Morals (Virtue Ethics according to David Hume)*
Christopher Fauske

379 *Art and Religion in Eighteenth-Century Europe*
Karen Bryant

383 *Revolutionary Spirits: The Enlightened Faith of America's Founding Fathers*
Kevin L. Cope

## Index
389

## Submissions Policy
398

# Preface

Volume 2 of *Religion in the Age of Enlightenment* brings together the work of both established and up-and-coming scholars from a variety of fields of study and helps to solidify *RAE*'s thematic and methodological scope. Looked at collectively, their work spans more than a century, from the late seventeenth to the early nineteenth centuries, and the varied topics and approaches demonstrate the rich possibilities for the study of religion during the Enlightenment.

Volume 2 includes a number of articles by scholars who take as their subject matter some of the more prominent personalities and influential figures of the eighteenth century. Elizabeth Kraft, for example, examines the prayer habits of Samuel Johnson, and Jeremy Gregory studies the life and times of John Wesley, suggesting that Wesley, who lived through most of the eighteenth century, and held and expressed views on a range of topics and issues, in addition to religion, may tell us as much about the historical and cultural context in which he lived as that context might tell us about him. Steven Stryer considers Alexander Pope's Catholic loyalties and alleged Jacobite sympathies through the lens of his poetry, arguing that Pope used his verse to expound principles that undergirded his own faith—sympathy, toleration, charity—principles he believed might overcome the Catholic-Protestant divide and help unite his countrymen. Joy A. J. Howard turns her attention to colonial America and Jonathan Edwards, suggesting the ways his theological views were modified by his experiences ministering among Native Americans, while Muriel Schmid reads Diderot's *La Religieuse* as an evangelical novel, exhibiting a Protestant-like faith predicated on a personal relationship with God and a firm belief in the saving power of Christ.

Several articles examine equally prominent eighteenth-century "movements," broadly defined. For example, two scholars study aspects of the Methodist revival. Joanna Cruickshank intervenes in the long-standing debate regarding gendered "separate spheres" by looking at the experiences of eighteenth- and early nineteenth-century Methodist women as they navigated between their "private" religious experiences and "public" ministry. Barbara Prosser suggests that the *Armenian Magazine* evidences Wesley's interest in promoting civic responsibility among his followers by informing them of social and political issues, in addition to attending to their spiritual welfare. Such social and political awareness, Prosser contends, anticipated nineteenth-century developments as Methodists became more socially and politically involved. David Manning reconsiders the whole idea of "the Christian Enlightenment" by examining the limits of theological contradistinction and polemic in an age of ever-increasing religious pluralism.

Michael Rottenberg-Schwartz focuses on the movement of people through space. Specifically, he examines the ways prayer was represented in narratives depicting travel to the Holy Land, arguing that such narratives created a space wherein piety and religious devotion might coexist with the kind of intellectual curiosity typical of Enlightenment thinking. Christopher Smyth and Samara Anne Cahill study planetary movements by offering unique insights into the ways the London earthquakes of 1750 signified in the English imagination.

Finally, two contributors offer insights into two mainstays of religious scholarship, biblical criticism and sermon studies. Norman Vance provides an insightful overview of the history of biblical criticism since the Enlightenment, questioning whether such criticism has delivered on its promise of illuminating our understanding of the Bible, while Bob Tennant calls for more interdisciplinary cooperation among scholars interested in the eighteenth-century English sermon.

I am also pleased to note that the concluding section of *RAE* has been significantly expanded in this volume, including nearly a dozen reviews of the most recent scholarship relevant to *RAE*'s scope and focus.

Besides the contributors to this volume, I wish to thank Professor Melvin J. Thorne of the BYU Humanities Publication Center and his student editors for their help with copyediting, design, and the layout of this volume. I also wish to thank *RAE*'s editorial board and especially Kathryn Stasio, *RAE*'s book review editor. Finally, I express my appreciation to Gabe Hornstein, President of AMS Press, and David Ramm, Editor-in-Chief at AMS, for their continued support of eighteenth-century studies generally and *RAE* specifically.

*Brett C. McInelly*
*Brigham Young University*

# Samuel Johnson at Prayer

*Elizabeth Kraft*

Samuel Johnson's life was punctuated by prayer. In this essay, I will examine Johnson's prayer practice in terms of both meaning and behavior. Johnson's *Dictionary of the English Language* provides clear and succinct evidence in Johnson's own words of what he understood prayer and the act of praying to be. Of the two definitions of *prayer* and the seven definitions of *to pray* included in the *Dictionary*, the first in each category concerns religion and simply states that the noun and the verb are the same. According to Johnson the first meaning of *to pray* is "to make petitions to heaven"; the first sense of *prayer* is, likewise, a "petition to heaven." Indeed, Johnson does not define any of the other words commonly used for prayer in the eighteenth century (e.g., *adoration, praise, thanksgiving,* and *confession*) with the word *prayer,* whereas the first sense of *petition* is "request; intreaty; supplication; prayer."[1] Clearly, to Johnson, *prayer* and *petition* are synonymous. The

---

A version of this paper was written for and presented at the *Johnson at 300 Houghton Library Symposium* at Harvard University, August 27–29, 2009. I would like to express my appreciation to Thomas Horrocks, the conference organizer, to Howard Weinbrot, the chair of my panel, to the other panelists, Steven Scherwatzky, Michael F. Suarez, S.J., and Alvaro Ribeiro, S.J., and to the conference participants who asked questions and offered constructive advice, particularly Lisa Berglund, Helen Deutsch, and Michael Bundock. I also extend my gratitude to the two anonymous readers of this essay for their helpful suggestions toward revision for publication in *Religion in the Age of Enlightenment*.

primary point of prayer is to beseech heaven or "the supreme power; the sovereign of heaven."[2]

In a 1765 journal entry, Johnson records a vow that implicitly elaborates the definition of *prayer* as petition. It reads, "To consider the act of prayer as a reposal of myself upon God and a resignation of all unto his holy hand."[3] These words may seem a repudiation of the notion of prayer as petition, but, in fact, they articulate the petitioner's role in a way consistent with theological discussions Johnson knew well. To repose upon God is to "rest in confidence,"[4] to consider all prayer answered prayer. As Robert South (1634–1716) puts it, "Our prayers are sometimes best answered, when our desires are most opposed."[5] Johnson himself had earlier articulated the premise in his 1749 *Vanity of Human Wishes* wherein the narrator advises the "Inquirer" as to proper objects of hope and fear:

[P]etitions yet remain,
Which Heav'n may hear, nor deem Religion vain.
Still raise for good the supplicating voice,

---

1. *The Oxford English Dictionary* (*OED*) lists seven separate definitions of the term as used in a religious context during the eighteenth century. Prayer is "a solemn request to God, a god, or other object of worship; a supplication or thanksgiving addressed to God or a god"; "the action, act, or practice of praying"; in the plural, "requests to God or a god to bless and protect someone; (hence) good wishes"; "a particular text or form of words used when praying"; "religious worship, esp. of a public nature, of which praying forms a principal part (as *morning prayer, family prayers,* etc.) *one's prayers* n. one's private, individual devotions"; "*R. C. Church.* In *pl.* among recusant Catholics (as a code word)" for *mass;* or "the object of a request or appeal; something prayed for or entreated." For a discussion of the relationship of the *OED* and Johnson's *Dictionary,* see Penny Silva, "Johnson and the *OED,*" *International Journal of Lexicography* 18 (2005): 231–42.

2. Samuel Johnson, *Dictionary of the English Language*, 2nd ed. (London: W. Strahan, 1755–56), s.v. "heaven."

3. R. D. Chapman, ed., *Life of Johnson* (Oxford: Oxford University Press, 1980), 352; E. L. McAdam Jr. and Donald and Mary Hyde, eds., *Diaries, Prayers, and Annals*, vol. 1 of *The Yale Edition of the Works of Samuel Johnson*, ed. Herman W. Liebert et al. (New Haven: Yale University Press, 1958), 97. James Boswell transcribed this passage from a journal that Johnson eventually burned. For the circumstances of this transcription, see the introduction to *Diaries, Prayers, and Annals*, xviii. All subsequent references to both *Life* and *DPA* are to these editions and are cited parenthetically in the text.

4. *Dictionary of the English Language,* s.v. "to repose."

5. Robert South, "Sermon III: A Discourse against Long Extempore Prayers," *Sermons Preached upon Several Occasions*, vol. 2 (London: H. Lintot, 1737), 103.

But leave to Heaven the measure and the choice.
Safe in his power, whose eye discerns afar
The secret ambush of a specious pray'r;
Implore his aid, in his decisions rest,
Secure whate'er he gives he gives the best.[6]

As early as 1766, Johnson entertained the notion of writing discursively about the practice of prayer. On March 2 of that year, he records in his diary that he "thought of writing a small book to teach the use of the Common Prayer" (*DPA* 103). Again, during Lent of 1768, he records a prayer that "may be said before or after the entrance into bed, as a preparative for sleep," and observes afterward "When I transcribed this Prayer, it was my purpose to have made this Book a Collection" (*DPA* 93, 118). In the year of his death, Johnson spoke again of such a project with Boswell, Dr. Adams, and others. Clearly his thinking on the topic had evolved considerably, he having said, "I have thought of getting together all the books of prayers which I could, selecting those which should appear to me the best, putting out some, inserting others, adding some, and prefixing a discourse on prayer" (*Life* 1293). When "two or three" of the company began "pressing him to execute this plan," Johnson grew agitated and demanded that the importunities cease. He continued, "Do not talk thus of what is so aweful. I know not what time God will allow me in this world. There are many things which I wish to do" (*Life* 1293). Boswell considers Johnson's posthumously published *Prayers and Meditations* (despite the absence of the "discourse") to be the fruition of this plan, proving, in Boswell's words, "that amidst all his constitutional infirmities, his earnestness to conform his practice to the precepts of Christianity was unceasing, and that he habitually endeavoured to refer every transaction of his life to the will of the Supreme Being" (*Life* 1293).

Johnson's discomfort in this discussion about prayer stands in stark contrast to the moment some months before when he awakened in the middle of the night to discover that he had suffered a "paralytic stroke." Here, he reacts with amazing presence of mind. He is alarmed by "a

---

6. Samuel Johnson, "Vanity of Human Wishes," in *The Complete English Poems*, ed. John David Fleeman (New Haven: Yale University Press, 1971), 92.

confusion and indistinctness in [his] head," but by his own account, this alarm provokes a prayer "to God, that however he might afflict my body, he would spare my understanding" (*Life* 1241). This response is not unusual. Many religious people, faced with trouble and confusion, pray likewise for help, relief, comfort, understanding, and mitigation. Yet Johnson's prayer, it seems, served a dual purpose—to petition God for help as well as to mentally test the extent of Johnson's loss of capacity. Johnson said, "This prayer, in order to try the integrity of my faculties, I made in Latin verse. The lines were not very good, but I knew them not to be very good, and concluded myself to be unimpaired in my faculties" (*Life* 1241). McDonald Critchley calls the prayer composition an "intelligence test of a most unusual type."[7] Although Johnson's biographer John Hawkins says that Johnson merely tried to repeat the Lord's Prayer and failed, the following lines have been identified as the verses Johnson composed and deemed inferior:

> Summe Pater, quodcunque tuum de corpora Numen
> Hoc statuat, precibus Christus adesse velit:
> Ingenio parcas, net si mihi culpa rogâsse
> Qua solum, potero parte, placer tibi.[8]

Frances Burney said that Johnson composed this prayer internally and then tried to speak and found he could not do so.[9] Whatever the case, the anecdote is arresting and somewhat perplexing. We, who tend to regard Samuel Johnson as a sincerely religious man, have to ask ourselves: What is prayer to one who at a moment of mortal crisis composes lines addressed to "heaven" or "the supreme power" in an attempt at self-diagnosis? What kind of a "petition" or even a "reposal" is that? To answer, it is necessary to pay close attention to Johnson *at*

---

7. McDonald Critchley, "Dr. Samuel Johnson's Aphasia," *Medical History* 6 (1962): 28.

8. "Almighty Father, whatever thy holy power may decide about this body, may Christ consent to attend to my prayer: spare my mind and may it not count as a fault to have asked to please thee with the only part by which I shall be able to do so." Niall Rudd, trans. and ed., *Samuel Johnson: The Latin Poems* (Lewisburg, PA: Bucknell University Press, 2005), 72.

9. Charlotte Barrett, ed., *Diaries and Letters of Madame D'Arblay*, vol. 1 (Philadelphia: Carey and Hart, 1842), 332.

prayer—not simply at this crucial moment but throughout the course of his lifelong engagement with prayer.

Where did Samuel Johnson pray? When did he pray? How did he pray? And why did he pray? Determining the first two matters is relatively easy, as reliable biographical information abounds. Johnson prayed at home and in church regularly, and occasionally (in both senses of the word) in the homes of others. Boswell reports that in 1732, when Johnson was serving as an usher in the Market-Bosworth school in Leicestershire, he "officiated as a kind of domestick chaplain" in the home of Sir Wolstan Dixie, the patron of the school, "so far, at least, as to say grace at table" (*Life* 60–61). His diaries record two occasions on which he visited the death chambers of friends. On one of these occasions he visited Hester Thrale's mother, Hester Maria Salusbury. In this instance, his prayer was brief: "God bless you, for Jesus Christ's sake" (*DPA* 157). The more well-known of these visitations is to faithful family friend Kitty Chambers, which he describes movingly in his diary entry for October 18, 1767:

> I desired all to withdraw, then told her that we were to part for ever, that as Christians we should part with prayer, and that I would, if she was willing, say a short prayer beside her. She expressed great desire to hear me, and held up her poor hands, as she lay in bed, with great fervor, while I prayed, kneeling by her, nearly in the following words.
>
> Almighty and most merciful Father, whose loving kindness is over all thy works, behold, visit, and relieve this thy Servant who is grieved with sickness. Grant that the sense of her weakness may add strength to her faith, and seriousness to her Repentance. And grant that by the help of thy Holy Spirit after the pains and labours of this short life, we may all obtain everlasting happiness through Jesus Christ, our Lord, for whose sake hear our Prayers. Amen. (*DPA* 116–17)

The Yale edition glosses this prayer as "one of Johnson's most affecting" (*DPA* 117n). In her foreword to *Johnsoniana*, Robina Napier remarks on the "tender pathos" of this final meeting.[10] Boswell introduces the scene as "affecting and solemn" and presents a moral at the conclusion of his quotation: "By those who have been taught to look upon Johnson as a man of a harsh and stern character, let this tender and affectionate scene be candidly read; and let them judge whether more warmth of heart, and grateful kindness, is often found in human nature" (*Life* 385–86). After citing the entire passage, Thomas Carlyle exclaims, "Tears trickling down a granite rock!"[11] Elton Trueblood similarly comments, "Here is one of the truly noble scenes of our history—the leading man of letters of his nation and century kneeling in humble faith by the bedside of his mother's servant."[12]

These responses to Johnson's prayer with Catherine Chambers illustrate the general critical use to which Johnson's prayers have been put from Boswell onward. The tendency has been to deduce character traits and psychological states from Johnson's prayers—the content and the occasions for which they were composed. Of course, we are tempted to read the prayers biographically, in large part because of the circumstances of their first publication. In November 1785, the young clergyman George Strahan published Johnson's *Prayers*, honoring Johnson's last wishes. The volume, however, also included Johnson's *Meditations*, or diary entries, many of which had to do with his mental and physical health. As Michael Bundock has pointed out, "Strahan's role in the publication was . . . somewhat controversial" on several counts, not least of which was the startling juxtaposition of the pious prayers and the coarse self-reflections, as when, for example, "a solemn prayer" on one page is followed on the next by a record of Johnson's nocturnal "'flatulencies.'"[13] Yet, the association of Johnson's prayers with his more

---

10. And wishes an artist had been there to draw it! Robina Napier, *Johnsoniana: Anecdotes of the Late Samuel Johnson, LL.D.* (London: George Bell and Sons, 1884), v.

11. See Thomas Carlyle's review of Croker's edition of James Boswell's *Life of Johnson* in *Fraser's Magazine*, May 1832, 379–413; rpt in James T. Boulton, ed., *Samuel Johnson: The Critical Heritage* (London: Routledge, 1995), 432–43; 443.

12. Elton Trueblood, *Dr. Johnson's Prayers* (New York: Harper, 1947), xiii. Quoted by J. Ellsworth Kalas, *Preaching About People: The Power of Biography* (St. Louis: Chalice Press, 2004), 75.

13. Michael Bundock, "The Making of Johnson's *Prayers and Meditations*," *The Age of Johnson* 14 (2003): 83, 81; Bundock, "Johnson's *Prayers and Meditations*," 87.

mundane self-commentary was firmly established. In 1958, when Yale again published the prayers along with the diaries and annals in volume one of *The Works of Samuel Johnson*, the decision was predicated on the reading of the prayers as "autobiographical" and "intimate" reflections of Johnson's inner life (*DPA* xi).

Prayer is indeed an intimate act, but for Johnson it was also an act of spiritual discipline done in Christian community, whether in church or at home. In 1961, Chester F. Chapin made this point regarding the prayer we have just examined. Though the prayer for Catherine Chambers was "extemporaneous," he points out, "an important part of the prayer itself is not original with Johnson but is taken *verbatim* from prayers in the Service for the Visitation of the Sick in the Book of Common Prayer."[14] To Chapin, the fact that Johnson combines two prayers from that service into the prayer he prays with his friend suggests Johnson's "thorough assimilation of prayer-book phraseology."[15] I would go further and posit that Johnson had thoroughly assimilated the actual prayers and had (quite likely) verbatim knowledge of many of them.[16] In both its occasion and its content, then, the prayer for Catherine Chambers alerts us to aspects of Johnson's prayer practice that are matters of principle, not simply reflections of individual taste or personal need. It is to these aspects—the how and the why—of Johnson at prayer that I turn now.

The first point about *how* Johnson prayed is that he prayed deliberately. It is clear from his diaries and letters that he set aside five days a year to address God in prayer at home and/or in church: New Year's

---

14. Chester F. Chapin, "Johnson's Prayer for Kitty Chambers," *Modern Language Notes* 76 (1961): 216–17.

15. Ibid., 218.

16. Boswell's anecdote regarding Johnson's early memorization "when he was a child in petticoats" of a collection from the Common Prayer is just one of many stories attesting to the rapidity and accuracy with which Johnson retained verbatim knowledge of what he read. See *Life*, 30. Given Johnson's prodigious memory, it would be surprising to discover that he did not know by heart the prayers he uttered regularly or heard often. Interestingly, one early satirical critic on *Prayers and Meditations* complained that "most of what are called Dr. Johnson's prayers, in Mr. Strahan's book, are in reality only slight alterations from the liturgy of the Church of England, adapted to his own particular situation at the time of penning them." *A Poetical Epistle from the Ghost of Dr. Johnson, to His Four Friends: The Rev. Mr. Strahan, James Boswell, Esq., Mrs. Piozzi, J. Courtenay, Esq. M. P.* (London: Harrison and Co., 1786): 6n line 40.

Day, March 28 (the anniversary of his wife's death), Good Friday, Easter Sunday (on which he also took communion), and September 18 (his birthday). He also prayed at the undertaking of new tasks—as he began the *Rambler*, for example, or as he prepared to study law, philosophy, or religion (*DPA* 96–97, 57, 62).[17] On these and other occasions, he composed prayers that he then used. These two verbs—*composed* and *used*—are Johnson's consistent way of referring to his prayer practice, whether at home or in church. For example, on January 1, 1767, Johnson writes, "About one in the morning composed a prayer and prayed" (*DPA* 112). The next day, he "rose before 9, trifled. . . . Used the new prayer both night and morning" (*DPA* 113).

This particular prayer is characteristic in its mode of address, its elevated language, and its petitionary content:

> Almighty and most merciful Father, in whose hand are life and death, as thou hast suffered me to see the beginning of another year, grant, I beseech thee, that another year may not be lost in Idleness or squandered in unprofitable employment. Let not sin prevail on the remaining part of life, and take not from me thy Holy Spirit, but as every day brings me nearer to my end, let every day contribute to make my end holy and happy. Enable me O Lord to use all enjoyments with due temperance, preserve me from unreasonable and immoderate sleep, and enable me to run with diligence the race that is set before me, that after the troubles of this life, I may obtain everlasting happiness through Jesus Christ, our Lord, Amen. (*DPA* 111–12)

Johnson's use of the metaphor of life as a race is somewhat uncharacteristic for his prayers. Indeed, he told Boswell, "I do not approve of figurative expressions in addressing the Supreme Being; and I never use them" (*Life* 1293). As this metaphor is a biblical one (Ecclesiastes 9:11; 1 Corinthians 9:24), and as it appears in the *Book of Common Prayer*'s Collect for the fourth Sunday in Advent and the third Sunday in Lent, in Johnson's view, it would not displease the Lord.

---

17. In November 1752 and March 1766, Johnson composed a prayer to be used at the undertaking of any new study (*DPA* 48, 103).

Easter Sunday generally provoked Johnson to make elaborate preparations in terms of resolutions and prayers that he recited at home and at church. Here, as in the distrust of metaphor in prayer noted above, Johnson reflects on the teachings of the Church of England, particularly those of Anglican divine Robert South, whose sermons on the sacrament focus entirely on the theme of "preparation."[18] On Easter morning, 1766, for example, Johnson "Took my Prayer book to tea, drank tea, planned my devotion for the church" (*DPA* 107). Easter Day, 1777, finds him as often (though not always) on that day of the year, "at Church early" where he "prayed over my prayer and commended Tetty and my other Friends" (*DPA* 265). He had made no resolutions that year, but as the service continued, he "wrote with my pencil in my common prayer book" a few Latin phrases that focused his mind for the receiving of the sacrament: *vita ordinanda, biblia legenda, theologiae opera danda, serviendum et laetandum, scrupulis obsistendum*—phrases that recall his general Easter resolutions to live an ordered life, read the scriptures, study theology, and fight off "religious scruples" (*DPA* 266).[19] After jotting his notes in his prayer book, Johnson "went to the altar having I believe, again read my prayer." He "then went to the table and communicated, praying for some time afterwards, but the particular matter of my prayer I do not remember" (*DPA* 266).[20] His diary for 1765 records perhaps most clearly Johnson's deliberate approach to prayer: "At church I purpose," he writes, "before I leave the pew to pray the occasional prayer, and read my resolutions. To pray for Tetty and the rest; the like after Communion. At intervals to use the collects of fourth after Trinity, and first and fourth after Ephiph. And to meditate." The next line reads, "3 p.m. This was done, as I purposed but with some distraction. I came in at the Psalms, and could not well hear. I renewed my resolutions at the altar" (*DPA* 94). Even on his travels, Johnson maintained

---

18. See Gerard Reedy, S. J., *Robert South (1634–1716): An Introduction to His Life and Sermons* (Cambridge: Cambridge University Press, 1992), 88–106 (on South's attitude toward language); 107–22 (on South and the sacrament).

19. See, for example, the next Easter's resolutions (*DPA* 289) and the next (*DPA* 297). For "religious scruples" see *DPA*, 105–8n.

20. Though this year seems to have been a particularly troubled year for Johnson, it is not unusual for him to record imprecise remembrance of his thoughts, prayers, and meditations during this most intense of religious exercises. See *DPA*, 108, 131.

his devotional schedule; in September 1775, on his tour in France with the Thrales, Johnson composed a prayer during a restless birthday eve and used it the next morning on a visit to the church of Notre Dame in Calais (*DPA* 228).

Johnson's prayer practice no doubt attests to his personal piety, sincerity, and devotion, but its nature also marks it as a theological commitment to the Church of England's forms of worship in contradistinction to those practiced by other Protestant sects. The Methodist movement within the Church of England fought the Church's censure of extempore prayer.[21] The Presbyterians' laxity with regard to prayerful utterance provoked Johnson's complaint to Boswell in 1769 that they "have no public worship . . . no form of prayer in which they know they are to join" (*Life* 424).[22] In this conversation, Johnson goes on to recommend that Boswell read Bishop South's sermons on prayer in which we find an energetic defense of "*premeditation of thought*" in prayer as well as an endorsement of "a set form of prayer, to guide our devotions by."[23] South also demands succinct rather than prolix prayers and, while recognizing that "mental or inward prayer" is sometimes acceptable, he reads the scriptural injunction to prayer as indication of the "necessity of *vocal prayer*."[24] Johnson seems to have followed all of these strictures in that he participated in public prayer and used set prayers even in his private devotions.

---

21. On this point, see Philip Davis, *In Mind of Johnson: A Study of Johnson the Rambler* (Athens: University of Georgia Press, 1989), 204–5.

22. Johnson seems to have been more sensitive to the difference between Presbyterian and Episcopalian practice than many of his time, including—perhaps most especially—Boswell, "whose religious choices," according to James J. Caudie, "were always contextually conditioned" and about as significant as "the choice between buying a Ford or a Chevrolet." William Gibson and Robert G. Ingram, eds., "Boswell and the Bi-Confessional State," in *Religious Identities in Britain, 1660–1832* (Aldershot, UK: Ashgate Publishing, 2005), 121.

23. South, "Sermon III," 108. On Johnson's intellectual engagement with the advice of South (and William Law) regarding the development of good mental habits and behaviors, see Paul K. Alkon, "Robert South, William Law, and Samuel Johnson," *SEL: Studies in English Literature, 1500–1900* 6 (1966): 499–528.

24. Robert South, "Sermon IV: A Discourse Against Long Extempore Prayers," *Sermons Preached upon Several Occasions*, vol. 2 (London: H. Lintot, 1737), 140.

Johnson also accommodated South's demand for modesty, discretion, respect, brevity, and premeditation of thought in his private prayers. Here, too, his habits of "composing" and "using" prayers suggests that he concurs with South's opinion of the extempore prayer, though he would not state such an opinion with what he described as South's "violence, and sometimes coarseness of language" (*Life* 913). Both these characteristics might be noted in the following diatribe by South against "this intoxicating, bewitching cheat of extempore prayer . . . the devil's master-piece and prime engine to overthrow our church by."

> For I look upon this as a most unanswerable truth, that whosoever renders the public worship of God contemptible amongst us, must in the same degree discredit our whole religion. And, I hope, I have also proved it to be a truth altogether as clear, that this extempore-way naturally brings all the contempt upon the worship of God, that both the *folly* and *faction* of men can possibly expose it to; and therefore, as a thing neither subservient to the true purposes of religion, nor grounded upon principles of reason, nor lastly suitable to the practice of antiquity, ought by all means to be cast out of every sober and well ordered church; or that will be sure to throw the church itself out of doors.[25]

Peter Barclay, in a 1713 address to the people of Scotland, more temperately argues for set prayers and an understanding of "praying by the spirit" as consistent with premeditated worship. He also describes the manner by which each worshiper can address the divine presence in the public setting with private concerns and with his or her own (ideally pre-formulated) words:

> When therefore we meet together to worship God, it is usual with us for every particular Person as he first comes into the Pew in the Church, before he takes his Seat, to fall on his Knees

---

25. South, "Sermon III," 118–19.

to put up his private Pray'rs for the Assistance of God's Grace and Holy Spirit to enable him to offer him acceptable Service.[26]

As not everyone can be expected to compose prayers of the sort Barclay premises, he includes two brief prayers, one of which (or one of "like Forms," followed by the Lord's Prayer) should be recited while kneeling, before one pays "Civilities to your Neighbours . . . provided that you have come in before the Worship is begun."[27]

Johnson's practice of "composing and using," then, conforms to Anglican precepts. Yet, certain of his private prayers discomfited George Strahan as he prepared to publish Johnson's *Prayers and Meditations*. In fact, the Yale edition of *Diaries, Prayers, and Annals* notes two occasions on which Strahan altered Johnson's language to disguise or soften reference to religious doubts or "scruples" (*DPA* 297, 300). Perhaps more significant however, in terms of Johnson's prayer practice, is Strahan's lengthy objection to the practice of praying for the dead. Johnson himself sometimes noted that he did so conditionally. "I hope I did not sin," he says of his prayer for Tetty on Easter 1753; on Easter 1764 he further says, "I did so only once that it might be lawful for me" (*DPA* 53, 79). He seems wistful when responding to Boswell's claim that the Episcopal Church of Scotland liturgy includes a prayer for the dead: "Sir, it is not in the liturgy that Laud framed for the Episcopal Church of Scotland: if there is a liturgy older than that, I should be glad to see it" (*Life* 472). Strahan states unequivocally that this practice of praying for the dead, "though it has been retained by other learned members of our church, her Liturgy no longer admits, and many, who adhere to her communion, avowedly disapprove."[28] Although Strahan absolves Johnson of any belief in purgatory, he nevertheless feels that prayers focused on the dead are "the vain oblations of superstition," though "the least unamiable, and most incident to a good mind."[29] Indeed Strahan's

---

26. Peter Barclay, *A Letter to the People of Scotland in Order to Remove Their Prejudice to the Book of Common Prayer* (London: John Morphew, 1713), 15.
27. Ibid., 15–16.
28. George Strahan, preface to *Johnson's Prayers and Meditations*, 2nd ed. (London, 1785), x–xi. Hester Piozzi and William Cowper were also disturbed by the prayers for the dead. See Bundock, "The Making," 88–89.
29. Ibid., xn, xii.

sense that in this practice Johnson leaned uncomfortably toward Roman Catholicism is underscored by Boswell's account of a conversation about Purgatory. "What do you think, Sir, of Purgatory, as believed by the Roman Catholicks?" Johnson responds,

> Why, Sir, it is a very harmless doctrine. They are of opinion that the generality of mankind are neither so obstinately wicked as to deserve everlasting punishment, nor so good as to merit being admitted to the society of blessed spirits; and therefore that God is graciously pleased to allow of a middle state, where they may be purified by certain degrees of suffering. You see, Sir, there is nothing unreasonable in this. (*Life* 425)

And he continues, "If it be once established that there are souls in purgatory, it is as proper to pray for *them*, as our brethren of mankind who are yet in this life" (*Life* 425).

This topic leads us to our final question: why did Johnson pray? Certainly it is a religious duty to attend public worship and to pray with others of one's faith. And obviously, as the case we have just discussed illustrates, even public prayer allowed Johnson to address spiritual and emotional needs that were not strictly met by the liturgy to which he subscribed. Johnson's famous "scruples" are paradoxically another reason for his piety. As Jack Lynch has argued, Johnson was a highly rational man who did not turn away from difficult intellectual challenges to his faith. These challenges, however, never eroded Johnson's belief because he practiced that belief. As Johnson knew, Lynch asserts, "only rigorous spiritual exercise can ward off encroaching unbelief"; for, essentially, belief is a "matter of discipline . . . not entirely something that happens to you, but at least partly under the control of the will."[30] And Johnson also prayed, apparently, as an example. According to Boswell, Johnson revealed that he "went more frequently to church when there were prayers only, than when there was also a sermon, as the people required more an example for the one than the other; it being much easier for

---

30. Jack Lynch, "Samuel Johnson, Unbeliever," *Eighteenth-Century Life* 29 (2005): 12, 16.

them to hear a sermon, than to fix their minds on prayer" (*Life* 479).[31] I do not think that this statement should be misconstrued (as certainly it could be) as evidence of spiritual pride. By the time Johnson spoke thus to Boswell, he was a famed moralist; his presence at church would have been remarked; his demeanor during prayer observed. Having, as he put it, fallen "into an inattention to religion or an indifference to it," around the age of nine, and become a "*talker* against religion" at the age of fourteen, Johnson was rationally persuaded to return to religious observance by the perusal of William Law's *Serious Call to a Devout and Holy Life* (*Life* 50–51). There is no theme more dominant in Law's book than that of religious hypocrisy in those who ostentatiously and rigorously observe public prayer while privately pursuing vice. It is only when we have "a devout spirit, and habit of mind in every part of our common life" that prayer can be of benefit to us or at all pleasing to God.[32] As Law puts it early on, "There can not anything be imagined more absurd in it self, than *wise* and *sublime*, and *heavenly* Prayers added to a life of *vanity* and *folly*, where neither *labour* nor *diversions*, neither *time* nor *money*, are under the direction of the wisdom and heavenly tempers of our Prayers."[33]

It seems reasonable to believe that Johnson wished his churchgoing to be exemplary in the sense of Law's *Serious Call*, evidence of a sincere effort to live a devout life. I think, however, it was also evidence of how to participate in public worship despite handicaps that would seem to prevent it. By his own admission, the reason Johnson spent his youthful Sundays reading "in the fields" rather than at church services was because of "having bad eyes and being awkward about this" (*Life* 50). His defective hearing was also a problem. The liturgy, of course, can be followed without acute hearing, as the congregants' responses can guide if the reader's words are indistinct. Johnson often could not hear

---

31. In "The Prayer Book and the Parish Church: From the Restoration to the Oxford Movement," Jeremy Gregory observes that "eighteenth-century parishioners much preferred to attend a Sunday service with a sermon and found a service without preaching tedious." Charles Hefling and Cynthia Shattuck, ed., *The Oxford Guide to the Book of Common Prayer* (Oxford: Oxford University Press, 2006), 97.

32. William Law, *Serious Call to a Devout and Holy Life* (London: William Innys, 1729), 228.

33. Ibid., 6.

the sermons, however, so when he attended services where sermons were delivered, he developed the habit of concentrating on the prayers, both the liturgical prayers and his precomposed private prayers. On occasion, he would compose prayers during sermons that he could not hear well and repeat them "mentally" (i.e., silently) until the liturgical prayers resumed (*DPA* 52–53, 97). In other words, forced by physical infirmity to rely on prayer rather than sermons for his devotions, Johnson discovered that public prayer can become a matter of individual psychology.

Ramie Targoff has explored Anglican divine Richard Hooker's focus on the "efficacy" of public prayer "in producing spiritual ease and heightening devotional affect among the members of the congregation."[34] Of course, Johnson was quite familiar with Hooker's *Laws of Ecclesiastical Politie*, as its status as one of the major sources of the *Dictionary*'s "illustrations" clearly demonstrates. In a well known passage from this work, Hooker explains how public prayer "transforms . . . [the] inward nature" of those who participate:

> By this means there stealeth upon them a double benefit; first because that good affection, which things of smaller account have once set on work, is by so much the more easily raised higher; and secondly in that the custom of seeking so particular aid and relief at the hands of God doth by a secret contradiction withdraw them from endeavoring to help themselves by those wicked shifts, which they know can never have his allowance, whose assistance their prayer seeketh.[35]

Johnson's deliberate and dedicated approach to prayer seems to support Hooker's sense that the cadences and content of the *Book of Common Prayer* can so work their way into the mind that individuals will resign themselves to divine guidance almost imperceptibly. Samuel Ogden,

---

34. Ramie Targoff, *Common Prayer: The Language of Public Devotion in Early Modern England* (Chicago: University of Chicago Press, 2001), 56.

35. Quoted in Targoff, *Common Prayer*, 56 (though I have truncated her quotation inasmuch as she goes on to discuss the apparent hypocrisy of public prayer as the secret manipulation by which natures are transformed). In Johnson's case, there can be no question of hypocrisy.

whose sermons both Johnson and Boswell admired, wrote of prayer as "an employment of the greatest use, having a natural tendency to amend the heart." It is, as well, "a reasonable service, and one of the natural means of moral and religious improvement."[36] For Ogden, as for Hooker and for Johnson, the true benefit of prayer lies in its ability to transform the petitioner, rather than in its power to procure the petition.

In a sense, then, our tendency—from Boswell onward—to read Johnson's prayers as evidence of his psychological state has been correct, but not for the reasons we have thought. Speaking to God in prayer became Johnson's psychology. All of his "scruples," fears, and doubts were, in the end, no match for the deliberateness of a lifetime of prayer. Faced with death, Johnson set about ordering his affairs. One of his final acts, as we have noted above, was to make arrangements for his prayers to become available to the public in print, for use or for example in composing prayers of their own. Johnson composed, used, and recorded his last prayer on December 5, 1784:

> Almighty and most merciful Father, I am now, as to human eyes it seems, about to commemorate for the last time, the death of thy son Jesus Christ, our Saviour and Redeemer. Grant, O Lord, that my whole hope and confidence may be in his merits and in thy mercy: forgive and accept my late conversion, enforce and accept my imperfect repentance; make this commemoration [of] him available to the confirmation of my Faith, the establishment of my hope, and the enlargement of my Charity, and make the Death of thy son Jesus effectual to my redemption. Have mercy upon me and pardon the multitude of my offences. Bless my Friends, have mercy upon all men. Support me by the Grace of thy Holy Spirit in the days of weakness, and at the hour of death, and receive me, at my death, to everlasting happiness, for the Sake of Jesus Christ. Amen. (*DPA* 417–18)[37]

---

36. Samuel Ogden, *Sermons on the Efficacy of Prayer and Intercession* (Cambridge: J. Woodbyer, 1770), 10.

37. The editors explain that Strahan deleted the reference to conversion in the fear that the term might be misinterpreted, as indeed it has been, forgetting that one of the defini-

He knelt and used the prayer "previous to his receiving the Holy Sacrament in his apartment" (*Life* 1391).[38] This prayer, like all of Johnson's prayers, is a petition and a reposal; and, in a pleasing symmetry from one who so often remembered the dead in his yearly devotions, the prayer offers remembrances of the living from beyond the grave.

---

tions in Johnson's *Dictionary* is, "change from reprobation to grace, from a bad to a holy life" *DPA*, 418n.

    38. *Life*, 1391. See also Bundock, 88.

# Religion in the Age of Enlightenment: Putting John Wesley in Context

*Jeremy Gregory*

Wesley's long life (1703–91) spanned almost the whole of the eighteenth century, and any attempt to understand him undoubtedly needs to include some sense of the period in which he lived. There have, of course, been many attempts to evoke Wesley's context, whether broadly defined—as in the thousands of books and scholarly articles that have been written about the era in general, ranging from the economy, politics, and society to cultural, intellectual, and religious matters (and much else besides), or in the various studies that have more directly positioned Wesley, and early Methodism, within his, and its, time. Most obviously these include some of the biographies of Wesley, of which the most impressive and successful to date is Henry Rack's *Reasonable Enthusiast: John Wesley and the Rise of Methodism*, which made particular efforts to locate Wesley within his age.[1] But what was that age like? In 1938, as part of the celebrations marking the bicentenary of Wesley's conversion, the amateur historian J. H. Whiteley published *Wesley's England: A Survey*

---

A heavily edited version of this essay was published in *The Cambridge Companion to John Wesley*, ed. Randy Maddox and Jason Vickers (Cambridge: Cambridge University Press, 2009).

1. Henry Rack, *John Wesley and the Rise of Methodism*, 3rd ed. (London: Epworth Press, 1989; repr., 2002). I am grateful to Henry Rack and Geordan Hammond for their comments on this chapter.

*of XVIIIth Century Social and Cultural Conditions*, which, drawn from secondary sources and aimed at a Methodist readership, rather unsatisfactorily attempted a sweeping survey of England during Wesley's lifetime. It covered topics as diverse as population growth, government, law and order, class contact, language, education, and religion (here oddly hardly mentioning Wesley himself), but without really giving the reader a coherent sense of the period. Nevertheless, Whiteley rather astutely recognized that "the difficulties of the project are manifold, for this is a century of England's story whose details are surprisingly contradictory and elusive."[2]

Neither have professional historians writing since 1938 been able to reach a general consensus on how we should understand Wesley's context, and indeed, at present they are probably more divided than they have ever been about how to conceptualize the period when Wesley was alive. Their debates are critical since they have a crucial bearing on how we should judge Wesley's significance, what he stood for, and what he achieved. For example, did he "revive" religion at a time when, as many historians have asserted (and Methodist scholars have often assumed), spiritual and religious concerns were ebbing away,[3] or rather did he build on and develop what some more recent scholars see as an existing vibrant and pastorally dynamic religious culture?[4] Should he be viewed as opposing or extending the Church of England?[5] Was he "anti-Enlightenment,"[6] or was he actually part of a wider Enlightenment trend?[7] Answers to

---

2. J. H. Whiteley, *Wesley's England: A Survey of XVIIIth Century Social and Cultural History* (London: Epworth Press, 1938), 11.

3. John Kent, *Wesley and the Wesleyans* (Cambridge: Cambridge University Press, 2002).

4. Jeremy Gregory, "The Making of a Protestant Nation: 'Success' and 'Failure' in England's Long Reformation," in *England's Long Reformation, 1500–1800*, ed. Nicholas Tyacke (London: UCL Press, 1998), 307–33.

5. Frank Baker, *John Wesley and the Church of England* (London: Epworth Press, 1970).

6. E. P. Thompson, *The Making of the English Working Class* (London: Penguin, 1963); Roy Porter, *The Creation of the Modern World: The Untold Story of the British Enlightenment* (New Haven: Yale University Press, 2000).

7. Bernard Semmel, *The Methodist Revolution* (London: Heinemann, 1973); David Bebbington, *Evangelicalism in Modern Britain: A History from the 1730s to the 1980s*

questions such as these (let alone questions about whether Wesleyan Methodism "saved" England from having a French-style revolution[8]) are only possible if we have as full an understanding as possible of the period in which Wesley lived. Indeed, Wesley's life and works might indicate ways in which the current rival, even contradictory, views of what the eighteenth century was like can to some extent be reconciled and reconfigured. Our studies of Wesley should therefore take account of his context since, by examining Wesley, we might also gain a clearer sense of his age. As someone who lived as long as he did; who traveled, wrote, and said so much (he has perhaps left more of a written record than any other person who lived in the eighteenth century); and who had views and opinions about almost all aspects of his times, Wesley can illuminate his context as much as it can shed light on him,[9] and this suggests that he ought to be of value to a wider group of historians than just scholars of the movement associated with his name.

Put simply and boldly, did the eighteenth century mark the founding of modern England/Britain, where the forces of change—signposted by the Glorious, the Agricultural, the Industrial, and the French revolutions (all of which have been used as reference points for Wesley/Methodist studies)—helped to transform the time in which Wesley lived into the modern era? Historians who think that it did have emphasized topics such as the rise of parliamentary government and the development of political parties,[10] agricul-

---

(London: Unwin Hyman, 1989), 20–74; David Hempton, *Methodism: The Empire of the Spirit* (New Haven: Yale University Press, 2005), chapter 2.

8. Elie Halevy, *The Birth of Methodism in England*, trans. B. Semmel (Chicago: Chicago University Press, 1971); idem, *A History of the English People in the Nineteenth Century*, vol. 1, *England in 1815* (London: Ernest Benn, 1949). For an overview of the debates his work has engendered, see G. W. Olsen, ed., *Religion and Revolution in Early Industrial England: The Halevy Thesis and Its Critics* (Lanham, MD: University Press of America, 1990). See also John Walsh, "Elie Halevy and the Birth of Methodism," *Transactions of the Royal Historical Society*, 5th ser., 25 (1975): 1–20.

9. Maldwyn Edwards, *John Wesley and the Eighteenth Century: A Study of His Social and Political Influence* (London: Allen & Unwin, 1933).

10. B. W. Hill, *The Growth of Parliamentary Politics in England, 1689–1742* (London: Allen & Unwin, 1976). See idem, *The Early Parties and Politics in Britain, 1688–1832* (London: Macmillan, 1996).

tural change,[11] urbanization and industrialization,[12] the growth of the middling sort,[13] the birth of a consumer society,[14] new kinds of print culture,[15] and the advance of progressive ways of seeing the world (represented by a scientific outlook),[16] as well as the Enlightenment and the "Age of Reason,"[17] where religion and the churches played an increasingly marginal role in political, cultural, and social life—all this leads some scholars to see the period as the start of secularization.[18]

This view of the eighteenth century as one dominated by modernizing changes was implicitly shared by most historians who wrote in the nineteenth and the first three-quarters of the twentieth centuries,[19] whatever their own political and religious standpoints, and it has influenced the ways Methodist scholars have understood Wesley's context. In 1909, for example, W. J. Townsend, as part of his contribution to *A New History of Methodism*, with a brief similar to this chapter, contrasted the period when Wesley was born (which, Townsend said, "was so different . . . from the England of today as

---

11. J. D. Chambers and G. E. Mingay, *The Agricultural Revolution, 1750–1880* (London: B. T. Batsford, 1966).

12. Peter Mathias, *The First Industrial Nation: An Economic History of Britain, 1700–1914* (London: Methuen, 1969).

13. Paul Langford, *A Polite and Commercial People: England, 1727–1783* (Oxford: Oxford University Press, 1989).

14. Neil McKendrick, John Brewer, and J. H. Plumb, eds., *The Birth of a Consumer Society: The Commercialization of Eighteenth-Century England* (London: Europa, 1982).

15. G. A. Cranfield, *The Development of the Provincial Newspaper, 1700–1760* (Oxford: Clarendon Press, 1962).

16. R. E. Schofield, *Mechanism and Materialism: British Natural Philosophy in an Age of Reason* (Princeton: Princeton University Press, 1970).

17. Roy Porter, *The Enlightenment* (Basingstoke: Macmillan, 1990).

18. Alan D. Gilbert, *Religion and Society in Industrial England: Church, Chapel and Social Change, 1740–1914* (London: Longman, 1976); Roy Porter, *English Society in the Eighteenth Century* (London: Allen Lane, 1982).

19. This view implicitly owed much to Thomas Babington Macaulay, *History of England from the Accession of James II (1848)*, in particular the famous third chapter, which measured the social improvements in England in the early nineteenth century against the situation in 1685 and influenced other classic Whig interpretations of the age such as W. H. Lecky, *A History of England in the Eighteenth Century*, 3 vols. (1904–1913), which was cited by Townsend.

to be scarcely recognisable"[20]) with the period when he died. He emphasized progress in economic, social, political, and cultural life from around 1760, which anticipated something like the modern world, with Methodism intimately responding to—and helping to create—the agents of change. In Townsend's view, for example, the Methodist connection could not have developed without a better road network, while improvements in lighting allowed Methodist evening services to flourish; conversely, he maintained that Methodism itself helped to transform social, cultural, and economic attitudes and behavior.[21]

Similarly, in 1965 in the first volume of *A History of the Methodist Church in Great Britain*, Sir Herbert Butterfield, regius professor of modern history at Cambridge and an authority on the period (as well as being a Methodist and, for much of his life, a lay preacher), contributed an essay on "England in the Eighteenth Century."[22] For someone who had risen to fame with his iconoclastic *The Whig Interpretation of History* (1931),[23] Butterfield offered here a very Whiggish reading of the age, seeing the eighteenth century as increasingly more like the twentieth (for him the seventeenth century was "a strange, violent, fantastic, baroque world"[24]) and emphasizing "modern" developments in a wide range of spheres and activities, from the creation of the Bank of England to new technologies, better transport links, the rise of political consciousness, and precursors to the theory of evolution.[25]

Perhaps above all, and of consequence in a book on Methodism, Butterfield emphasized that this was the significant period in what he termed "the Great Secularisation."[26] Historians who have come to

---

20. W. J. Townsend, "The Times and Conditions," in *A New History of Methodism*, ed. Townsend, Workman, and Eayres (London: Hodder & Stoughton,1909), 2 vols., 1:77–133, and ibid., "English Life and Society, and the Condition of Methodism at the Death of Wesley," 1:335–78 (quote at 82).

21. Townsend, 1:80, 342, 370–74.

22. Herbert Butterfield, "England in the Eighteenth Century," in *A History of the Methodist Church in Great Britain*, ed. R. E. Davies and E. G. Rupp (London: Epworth, 1965), 1:3–33.

23. Herbert Butterfield, *The Whig Interpretation of History* (London: G. Bell & Sons, 1931).

24. Butterfield, "England in the Eighteenth Century," 4.

25. Ibid., 3, 10, 11, 21, 33.

26. Ibid., 6.

similar conclusions have done so from a variety of perspectives. Some have viewed these as generally positive developments,[27] while others have bemoaned what they have considered to be the loss of an organic community (something on which historians from both the left and the right have concurred).[28] And—of import for Wesley studies—most historians have tended to agree that religion (for better or worse) was by and large of less importance in the eighteenth century than it had been in previous periods.[29]

However, some alternative interpretations have challenged this view of the eighteenth century as witnessing the birth of modernity and secularization (and looking forward to the nineteenth and twentieth centuries), and have claimed that the period in which Wesley lived was more marked by continuities with the sixteenth and seventeenth centuries. Religion, the churches, and traditional orders such as the crown[30] and aristocracy[31] still dominated, and older ways of seeing the world, influenced by Reformation paradigms and ways of thought (clearly vital for Wesley), still controlled habits of mind and patterns of behavior.[32] A number of historians have also argued that the social and economic developments of the time were less transformative than was once thought and that, in most regards, these changes were accom-

---

27. Porter, *Creation of the Modern World*. Actually Porter's attitude to the place of religion in the Enlightenment was more complex than some of his publications suggested: see his "The Enlightenment in England," in Porter and M. Teich, eds., *The Enlightenment in National Context* (Cambridge: Cambridge University Press, 1981), 1–18 for a more nuanced picture.

28. See E. P. Thompson, "The Moral Economy of the English Crowd in the Eighteenth Century," *Past & Present* 50 (1971): 76–136; Peter Laslett, *The World We Have Lost* (London: Methuen, 1965).

29. See C. J. Sommerville, *The Secularization of Early Modern England: From Religious Culture to Religious Faith* (Oxford; Oxford University Press, 1992).

30. Ian Christie, *Stress and Stability in Late Eighteenth-Century Britain* (Oxford: Clarendon, 1984).

31. John Cannon, *Aristocratic Century: The Peerage of Eighteenth-Century England* (Cambridge: Cambridge University Press, 1984).

32. See, above all, J. C. D. Clark, *English Society: 1688–1832* (Cambridge: Cambridge University Press, 1985); also Tony Claydon, *Europe and the Making of England, 1660–1760* (Cambridge: Cambridge University Press, 2007); and Gregory, "Long Reformation" (see note 4).

modated within long-established forms of organization and behavior.[33] Despite undoubted advances in agriculture and industry and a marked population growth, these were, it is now often maintained, more evolutionary than revolutionary in character, and many of the qualitative changes relating to quantitative growth, it is contended, happened in the nineteenth rather than in the eighteenth century (and thus after Wesley's death).[34] Other historians have reassessed our understanding of "the Enlightenment," demonstrating that, in England at least, Enlightenment values could go hand in hand with religion.[35] The "secularization thesis," which could be taken for granted even by someone as interested in religion as Butterfield[36] and which deemed the eighteenth century the crucial step on the ladder, has now been criticized from several directions: secularization's start has been delayed until the nineteenth or even the twentieth centuries;[37] some have argued that in England this process only occurred in the 1960s (ironically at just the time when Butterfield was writing)[38] and others have denied that it has

---

33. Ann Kussmaul, *A General View of the Rural Economy of England, 1538–1840* (Cambridge: Cambridge University Press, 1990); Mark Overton, *Agricultural Revolution in England: The Transformation of the Agrarian Economy, 1500–1850* (Cambridge: Cambridge University Press, 1996).

34. Roderick Floud and Donald McCloskey, eds., *The Economic History of Britain since 1700*, 2 vols. (Cambridge: Cambridge University Press, 1981); N. F. C. Crafts, *British Economic Growth during the Industrial Revolution* (Oxford: Oxford University Press, 1985); Maxine Berg, *The Age of Manufactures, 1700–1820: Industry, Innovation and Work in Britain* (London: Fontana, 1985).

35. Porter, "England"; Bebbington, *Evangelicalism*; idem, "Revival and Enlightenment in Eighteenth-Century England," in *On Revival: A Critical Examination*, ed. Andrew Walker and Kristin Aune (London: Paternoster Press, 2003), 71–86; and Hempton, *Empire of the Spirit*, 32–54. My take on this is that rather than seeing "Enlightenment" and "Evangelicalism"/"Enthusiasm" as polarities, we should acknowledge that what we might term "Enlightenment" might include certain "Evangelical" qualities and vice versa.

36. See his *Christianity and History* (London: Bell, 1949); *Christianity in European History* (Oxford: Oxford University Press, 1951); *Christianity, Diplomacy and War* (London: Epworth Press, 1953); *Writings on Christianity and History*, ed. C. T. McIntire (Oxford: Oxford University Press, 1979).

37. Owen Chadwick, *The Secularisation of the European Mind in the Nineteenth Century* (Cambridge: Cambridge University Press, 1975).

38. Callum Brown, *The Death of Christian Britain: Understanding Secularisation, 1800–2000* (London: Routledge, 2001).

happened at all.[39] What was once assumed to be the "inevitable" trajectory not only of Western European but of world history looks less convincing in the early twenty-first century when religion can be viewed as being at the center of world affairs. Taken together, these reassessments of the period in which Wesley lived amount to a thorough revisionism of the modernizing and secularizing view of the age (although, of course, not all historians who subscribe to one part of the revisionist program necessarily agree with all of it, and they might be surprised to see their names linked together here).

Although a number of historians, writing on different topics, have contributed to this revised view of the period, the most overt and comprehensive revisionist statement continues to be J. C. D. Clark's highly influential *English Society, 1688–1832: Ideology, Social Structure and Political Practice during the Ancien Regime*.[40] This made a powerful case for a wholesale rejection of the modernizing agenda and stressed the central role of the monarchy, the aristocracy, and the Church of England throughout Wesley's lifetime and beyond. Clark applied the concept of the "confessional state"[41] (which had been used by historians of early modern Europe, and in particular Germany, to denote the interplay of religion and state building from the sixteenth to the eighteenth centuries, where a state had a single confession of faith, established by law, to which the whole population conformed[42]) to England between the Restoration and the constitutional changes of 1828–1832. In particular, he argued that the political and hegemonic power of orthodox Anglicanism meant that the only real political radicalism in the period could be expressed through heterodox theology (thereby challenging

---

39. David Nash, "Reconnecting Religion with Social and Cultural History: Secularization's Failure as a Meta-narrative," *Cultural and Social History* 1 (2004): 302–25.

40. 1985, revised edition 2000 with amended chronology extending backwards to 1660 and new subtitle: *Religion, Ideology and Politics during the Ancien Regime*.

41. J. C. D. Clark, "England's Ancien Regime as a Confessional State," *Albion* 21 (1989): 450–74.

42. For example, Heinz Schilling, *Konfessionskonflikt und Staatsbildung: Eine Fallstudie über das Verhältnis von religiösem und sozialem Wandel in der Frühneuzeit am Beispiel der Grafschaft Lippe* (Gutersloh, 1981). For an analysis of the Germanic comparison, see Andrew C. Thompson, "Early Eighteenth-Century Britain as a Confessional State," in *Cultures of Power in Europe during the Long Eighteenth Century*, ed. Hamish Scott and Brendan Simms (Cambridge: Cambridge University Press, 2007), 86–109.

*Religion in the Age of Enlightenment*

the idea of secular political advances). For Clark, the Church's dominant place within the political and social life of the country was strengthened by the Test Acts of 1673 and 1678, which ensured that to hold political office or to be an MP it was necessary to be a member of the Church of England. Although, as some of Clark's critics have emphasized, sections of the English population did not conform to the Church,[43] he is nevertheless surely right to argue that the centrality of the Church's legal position had a profound impact on political and social life; the State, English universities, army, and civil service were Anglican strongholds, and in the localities clergy were often JPs and as such were responsible for the administration of local government. In this regard, perhaps a more accurate description of the Church's position is not Clark's "confessional state" so much, as he himself has suggested, as an Anglican hegemony, which is indicative of the ways the Church (although its position was contested) effectively dominated and sought to marginalize those who challenged its social and political role. Many Churchmen believed that the interests of Church and State were in fact inseparable and interdependent and that enemies of the Church were also enemies of the State. Clark might have also emphasized that those who see the eighteenth century as forward-looking do not always appreciate how the memory of the 1640s and '50s, when "the world was turned upside down," continued to frighten the majority of the political nation for a century and a half after 1660. Not for nothing did Wesley's opponents accuse him of reviving Civil War "Enthusiasm," particularly since his grandfather had been a regicide.[44] A good indication of the interdependence of Church and State can be seen in the Church's response to the Jacobite rebellions of 1715 and 1745, when the vast bulk of the clergy

---

43. Penelope Corfield, "Georgian England: One State, Many Faiths," *History Today* (April 1995): 14–21.

44. *Enthusiasm No Novelty; Or the Spirit of the Methodists in 1641 and 1642* (London: printed for T. Cooper, 1739); George Lavington, *The Enthusiasm of Methodists and Papists Compared*, 3 parts (London: printed for J. and P. Knapton, 1749–51); A. T. Blacksmith (sometimes attributed to John Witherspoon), *Enthusiasm Delineated: Or, the Absurd Conduct of the Methodists Displayed in a Letter to the Rev. Messieurs Whitefield and Wesley* (Bristol, England: printed for the author and sold by T. Cadell, 1764); S. Roe, *Enthusiasm Detected, Defeated; With Previous Considerations Concerning Regeneration, the Omnipresence of God, and Divine Grace, &c* (Cambridge, 1768).

and the Church's hierarchy supported the Hanoverian regime. In 1745 Archbishop Thomas Herring of York (later archbishop of Canterbury) played a crucial role in forming the Yorkshire association to defend the regime and to raise money for the government (Wesley himself took a strong pro-Hanoverian stand).[45] Again, too, in the decade immediately after Wesley's death, the Church was a staunch defender of the government during the French Revolution,[46] believing that threats to the state would also be destructive to the Church and to true religion generally (leading one to wonder whether it was really the Church rather than Methodism that saved England from having a revolution along French lines).

The revisionist interpretation, and particularly Clark's full-blown statement, has provoked both assent and controversy,[47] and since the late 1980s, the debate has continued with scholars arguing both for and against modernity and tradition and disagreeing over the place of religion within the age. Those who have discerned modernity in the period have expanded their fields of enquiry, and exciting work has been

---

45. *The Works of John Wesley (1787–91)*, vol. 20, *Journal and Diaries III: Edited by W. Reginald Ward (Journal) and Richard P. Heitzenrater (Diaries)* (Nashville, TN: Abingdon Press, 1991), 90–94.

46. Robert Hole, *Pulpits, Politics, and Public Order in England, 1760–1832* (Cambridge: Cambridge University Press, 1990).

47. For some discussion and criticisms, see Joanna Innes, "Jonathan Clark, Social History, and England's Ancien Regime," *Past & Present* 115 (1987): 165–200, and the reply by Clark, ibid., 117:195–207; the special number of *Albion* 21 (1989) that was devoted to Clark's interpretation; G. S. Rousseau, "Revisionist Polemics: J. C. D. Clark, and the Collapse of Modernity in the Age of Johnson," in *The Age of Johnson*, ed. P. J. Korshin (1989), 421–50; Roy Porter, "English Society in the Eighteenth Century Revisited," in *British Politics and Society from Walpole to Pitt*, ed. Jeremy Black (Macmillan, 1990); the articles by Clark, Porter, and Black in *The British Journal for Eighteenth-Century Studies* 15 (1992): 131–49; and Frank O'Gorman, "Eighteenth Century England as an Ancien Regime," in *Hanoverian Britain and Empire*, ed. Stephen Taylor, Richard Connors, and Clyve Jones (Woodbridge, 1998), 21–36.

done on concepts of sociability and politeness,[48] the periodical press,[49] clubs and coffee houses,[50] cultural history,[51] popular politics,[52] crime,[53] sexuality,[54] the body and medicine,[55] consumerism,[56] and gender and women's history.[57] Many of these topics are frequently studied within the paradigm of the "public sphere," and many have important bearings on early Methodism, given Wesley's nous of consumerist techniques, use of printed media, and interest in science and medicine, as well as the role of Methodist societies as religious clubs and the prominence of women in early Methodism, although historians of Methodism are only

---

48. For example, Clive T. Probyn, *The Sociable Humanist: The Life and Works of James Harris 1709-1780: Provincial and Metropolitan Culture in Eighteenth-Century England* (Oxford: Clarendon, 1991); Lawrence E. Klein, *Shaftesbury and the Culture of Politeness: Moral Discourse and Cultural Politics in Early Eighteenth-Century England* (Cambridge: Cambridge University Press, 1994).

49. Hannah Barker, *Newspapers, Politics, and Public Opinion in Late Eighteenth-Century England* (Oxford: Oxford University Press, 1998).

50. Peter Clark, *British Clubs and Societies 1580-1800: The Origins of an Associational World* (Oxford: Oxford University Press, 2000); Markman Ellis, *The Coffee-House: A Cultural History* (London: Weidenfeld & Nicolson, 2004); Brian Cowan, *The Social Life of Coffee: The Emergence of the British Coffee House* (New Haven: Yale University Press, 2005).

51. John Brewer, *The Pleasures of the Imagination: English Culture in the Eighteenth Century* (London: HarperCollins, 1997).

52. Douglas Hay and Nicholas Rogers, *Eighteenth-Century English Society: Shuttles and Swords* (Oxford: Oxford University Press, 1997).

53. Robert Shoemaker, *Prosecution and Punishment: Petty Crime and the Law in London and Rural Middlesex, c. 1660-1725* (Cambridge: Cambridge University Press, 1991).

54. Karen Harvey, *Reading Sex in the Eighteenth Century: Bodies and Gender in English Erotic Culture* (Cambridge: Cambridge University Press, 2004).

55. For example, Roy Porter, *Flesh in the Age of Reason* (London; Allen Lane, 2003); Porter, *Disease, Medicine and Society in England, 1550-1860* (Basingstoke: Macmillan, 1987).

56. John Brewer and Roy Porter, eds., *Consumption and the World of Goods* (London: Routledge, 1993); John Brewer and Ann Bermingham, eds., *The Consumption of Culture, 1660-1800: Image, Object, Text* (London: Routledge, 1995); John Brewer and Susan Staves, eds., *Early Modern Conceptions of Property* (London: Routledge, 1995).

57. Hannah Barker and Elaine Chalus, eds., *Gender in Eighteenth-Century England: Roles, Representations and Responsibilities* (Harlow: Longman, 1997); Michele Cohen and Tim Hitchcock, eds., *English Masculinities, 1660-1800* (London: Longman, 1999); Hannah Barker and Elaine Chalus, eds., *Women's History, Britain, 1700-1850, an Introduction* (London: Routledge, 2005).

now beginning to take these findings on board.[58] On the other hand, since the mid-1980s a number of publications have confirmed aspects of Clark's interpretation of the age, if not necessarily agreeing with all his conclusions.[59] Reviewing some of this seemingly contradictory scholarship over fifteen years ago with a question that has not yet been resolved, W. A. Speck not surprisingly asked: "Will the real eighteenth century stand up?"[60] How far, he wondered, was it a period of secularization and change, anticipating the modern world, and how far was it a more traditional and religious society, with links to the early modern period?

These different interpretations of the eighteenth century not only have a bearing on how we understand Wesley's context, but they also affect how historians have viewed Wesley himself. Despite the advances of the revisionist viewpoints, the perhaps still-overriding understanding of the eighteenth century is both modernizing (in political, social, economic, intellectual, and cultural terms) and secularizing, and this continues to influence the ways in which Wesley and Methodism are regarded. In broad terms, Wesley and Methodism have often been seen as "countercultural," going against the dominant Enlightenment, this-worldly, and areligious—if not irreligious—trajectories of the day.[61] Townsend in 1909, for example, viewed Wesley as a heroic individual who stood outside the degeneracy of the age (seeing him indeed almost as the sum of human perfection, in ways

---

58. But see Henry Abelove, *The Evangelist of Desire: John Wesley and the Methodists* (Stanford, CA: Stanford University Press, 1990) for Wesley and consumerism; Deborah Madden, *"A Cheap, Safe and Natural Medicine": Religion, Medicine and Culture in John Wesley's Primitive Physic* (Amsterdam, NY: Rodopi, 2007) for Wesley and medicine; Phyllis Mack, *Heart Religion in the British Enlightenment. Gender and Emotion in Early Methodism* (Cambridge: Cambridge University Press, 2008) for Methodism and gender; and Barbara Prosser, "'An Arrow From a Quiver.' Written Instruction for a Reading People: John Wesley's *Arminian Magazine* (January 1778–February 1791)" (unpublished University of Manchester PhD thesis, 2008) for Wesley and print culture.

59. See the works cited under footnote 82.

60. W. A. Speck, "Will the Real Eighteenth Century Stand Up?" *Historical Journal* 34 (1991): 203–6.

61. Mark Noll, *The Rise of Evangelicalism: The Age of Edwards, Whitefield, and the Wesleys* (Downers Grove, IL: Intervarsity Press, 2003).

that the modern historian or biographer would be wary).[62] But within this framework, historians have differed over whether Wesley (and Methodism) represented a backward-looking force, a throwback to an age of faith,[63] or whether he was more forward-looking, encouraging new social communities (such as the development of a working class)[64] and, with his stress on "the religion of the heart," anticipating movements such as Romanticism.[65]

Alternatively, one of the consequences of the revisionist standpoint is that it has made it possible to see Wesley as part of, rather than apart from, the dominant habits of thought and behavior of his era. If religion was much more central to the age than the secularization (hypo)thesis would have it, then Wesley looks less like a reaction to the period in which he lived and more like a child of his time. Clark has indeed underlined Wesley's Tory politics and pro-establishment views in order to demonstrate the strengths of the confessional state. He highlights the fact that the Wesley who attacked the spiritual and pastoral shortcomings of the established Church nevertheless shared many of its social and political assumptions.[66] Clark's view of Wesley as an insider within the confessional state has, however, been criticized by David Hempton, who has emphasized Wesley's radicalism and the conditional nature of his submission to the Georgian polity;[67] such conflicting views are indicative of the ways in which Wesley himself has been positioned within rival views of the period.

In reaching their various conclusions about the nature of the eighteenth century, historians have sometimes used (albeit often fairly selectively) evidence written by Wesley himself—particularly from his *Journals*, which seemingly give an eyewitness commentary over a

---

62. Townsend, "The Times and Condition," 80.
63. This seems to be the thrust of Kent's *Wesley and the Wesleyans*.
64. R. F. Wearmouth, *Methodism and the Common People of the Eighteenth Century* (London: Epworth Press, 1945); Gilbert, *Religion and Society in Industrial England*.
65. Frederick C. Gill, *The Romantic Movement and Methodism: A Study of English Romanticism and the Evangelical Revival* (London: Epworth Press, 1937).
66. Clark, *English Society*, 235–39.
67. David Hempton, "John Wesley and England's *Ancien Régime*," in *The Religion of the People: Methodism and Popular Religion c. 1750–1900* (London: Routledge, 1996), 77–90.

period of fifty-five years on the age in which he was living—as source material to underpin and support their interpretations. The *Journals* provide us with all kinds of information on Wesley's world, and the extraordinarily rich 160-plus-page "General Index" to the Ward and Heitzenrater bicentennial edition gives a stunning indication of the encyclopedic coverage of what Wesley observed and recorded,[68] including the state of the roads, the landscape, the weather, and the villages and towns he visited. Wesley presents us with a view from someone who lived through the agricultural and industrial changes of his time as well as, of course, comments on the religious temper of the day. The *Journals* are so crammed full of information about eighteenth-century life (and as such ought to be mandatory reading for all historians of the period) that it is tempting to see Wesley's comments and observations almost as a neutral documentary on his times, furnishing the historian with clear-cut evidence about what the eighteenth century "was really like," although the fact that Wesley's words have been used to bolster rival interpretations of the period indicate that the *Journals* are so packed with detail that it is possible to find almost anything in them. And of course the *Journals* are not unbiased evidence. Like any other source, they come from a particular perspective (often with an axe to grind and a point to make), and they were generally written up some time after the events he describes.[69] Moreover, as in other areas of his word and deed, Wesley's commentary on his times can seem somewhat contradictory. This in itself should make us complicate and nuance our interpretations of the age. Rather than seeing the period in terms of either/or—either "modern" or "traditional"—we might (as John Walsh has suggested for Wesley himself, whom he has termed as having a "both/and" personality[70]) see that his context was able to accommodate and combine,

---

68. The comprehensive general index (compiled by John Vickers) is at the end of *The Works of John Wesley* (1787–91), vol. 24, *Journal and Diaries VII: Edited by W. Reginald Ward (Journal) and Richard P. Heitzenrater (Diaries)* (Nashville, TN: Abingdon Press, 2003), 546–711.

69. See W. R. Ward's insightful introduction to vol. 18:1–119.

70. John Walsh, *John Wesley, 1703–1791: A Bicentennial Tribute* (London: Dr. Williams's Trust, 1993), 12.

in ways that historians are only now coming to recognize, some of the apparently conflicting tendencies of the century.

In Wesley we can therefore find aspects of both the "traditional" and the "modernizing" eighteenth centuries (arguably he was influenced by, and furthered, both the Reformation and the Enlightenment). He helps us recognize that the binary polarities with which we have been inclined to discuss the period are rather misleading. In particular, there has been an inclination—perhaps encouraged by Clark's revisionist manifesto—to align religion with the forces of tradition and continuity. But, as Roy Porter suggested, we should not view those perennial concerns of the historian, continuity and change, as being necessarily in antagonism.[71] "Traditional" priorities such as religion could be agents of change and innovation (as evidenced by the rise of Methodism),[72] and new genres and ways of behaving, such as periodicals and clubs, could be vehicles for older concerns (as in the *Arminian Magazine* and the "Holy Club"). Wesley, and the movement he helped to found, arguably demonstrates these seeming paradoxes in spades.

Historians' uncertainty about the feel and shape of the period in which Wesley lived is also reflected in the fact that it sometimes seems as if historians are writing about two different eighteenth centuries, not only in terms of its essence and defining features, but in terms of when it began and ended. In recognition of the fact that it makes no real sense to say that the eighteenth century started abruptly in 1700 or 1701 and finished suddenly in 1800 or 1801, historians' accounts of the period often start in either in 1714[73] (which is not very satisfactory for our purposes since this was eleven years after Wesley was born), 1760,[74] or even as late as somewhere in the 1780s (as in Vic Gatrell's unabashedly modernist study of eighteenth-century satire[75]), and in

---

71. Porter, "English Society," 32–33.
72. See Robert Ingram, *Religion, Reform and Modernity in the Eighteenth Century: Thomas Secker and the Church of England* (Woodbridge: The Boydell Press, 2007).
73. For example, W. A Speck, *Stability and Strife: England, 1714–1760* (London: Arnold, 1977).
74. I. R. Christie, *Wars and Revolutions: Britain, 1760–1815* (London: Arnold, 1982).
75. Vic Gatrell, *City of Laughter: Sex and Satire in Eighteenth-Century London* (London: Atlantic, 2006).

this case often go on into the nineteenth century, so that the eighteenth century appears to be broken into two: before and after 1760 or c. 1780. In *A History of the Methodist Church*, Butterfield saw changes on most fronts accelerating with increasing velocity after about 1780, using the metaphor of a tidal wave to indicate that the world after 1780 was qualitatively different from the world before.[76] But stopping, or starting, the period then, or in 1760, makes little sense for people like Wesley who lived through these divides.

In part to avoid these difficulties and ambiguities, and to make sense of the eighteenth century as a whole, historians—again largely following J. C. D. Clark's lead—have increasingly found the concept of the "long eighteenth century" useful, which has the eighteenth century begin in 1688–89 or even 1660 and continue well into the nineteenth century, to c. 1832 and beyond.[77] In its chronology, the concept of "the long eighteenth century" has the merit of encouraging scholars of the period to encompass both late seventeenth-century and early nineteenth-century developments, and while the validity of this periodization will no doubt continue to be debated, it seems to make sense for someone like Wesley, whose parents—both central figures in his life—were born in the 1660s, whose own wide-ranging theological and religious authorities often came from the last decades of the seventeenth century, and whose own immediate followers, as well as some of the practices that he advocated (such as dual allegiance to the Church and the Methodist societies)[78] continued for several decades after his death.

---

76. Butterfield, "England in the Eighteenth Century," 23.

77. Frank O'Gorman, *The Long Eighteenth Century: British Political and Social History, 1688–1832* (London: Arnold, 1997) has enshrined the concept of "the long eighteenth century" in a book title; see also Wilfrid Prest, *Albion Ascendant: English History, 1660–1815* (Oxford: Oxford University Press, 1998). The eighteenth-century seminar in London went from 1688 to 1848.

78. See Gareth Lloyd, *Charles Wesley and the Struggle for Methodist Identity* (Cambridge: Cambridge University Press, 2007); idem, "'Croakers and Busybodies': the Extent and Influence of Church Methodism in the Late 18th and Early 19th Centuries," *Methodist History*, xlii (2003): 20–32; Frances Knight, *The Nineteenth-Century Church and English Society* (Cambridge: Cambridge University Press, 1995), 23; and the discussion of the 1851 census by John Wolffe, *The Religious Census of 1851 in Yorkshire* (York: Borthwick Institute, University of York, 2005).

What is clear, whether or not historians accept the implications of the revisionist approach to the eighteenth century as typified by Clark's work, is that our knowledge of eighteenth-century Britain has deepened and become more nuanced over the past twenty years or so. This is important for Wesley scholars who sometimes tend to be so concerned with what might be considered "insider" debates within Wesley and Methodist studies (largely dominated until very recently by academics who were themselves Methodists) that they (perhaps understandably) ignore how the scholarship concerning Wesley's context has changed. There has been a vast explosion of research, which has opened up a much more multifaceted set of interpretations of the time, meaning that some of our conventional understandings of the period (on which much Wesleyan and Methodist scholarship is still premised) have been challenged or modified.[79] Scholarly work on many aspects of Wesley's context (whether religious, political, social, economic, cultural, or intellectual) has unearthed a much more complex society than often used to be recognized. For instance, historians have recently paid far more attention to the different political, social, economic, and religious contexts of the various parts of Britain, Ireland, and the North American colonies than they did in the 1960s, when Butterfield could use the word "England" almost as shorthand for Scotland and Ireland[80] (this is of some significance for Wesley, who traveled widely throughout the British Isles and spent twenty-two months in the new colony of Georgia, which for the rest of his life became a benchmark for discussing matters as diverse as the weather and slavery[81]).

---

79. For a shortcut to some of this explosion of scholarship, see the bibliography in Jeremy Gregory and John Stevenson, *Britain in the Eighteenth Century, 1688–1820*, 2nd ed. (London: Routledge, 2007).

80. Hugh Kearney, *The British Isles: A History of Four Nations* (Cambridge: Cambridge University Press, 1989); Alexander Murdoch, *British History, 1660–1832: National Identity and Local Culture* (1998); Murray Pittock, *Inventing and Resisting Britain: Cultural Identity in Britain and Ireland, 1685–1789* (Basingstoke: Macmillan, 1997); and Jim Smyth, *The Making of the United Kingdom, 1660–1800: State, Religion, and Identity in Britain and Ireland* (London: Longman, 2001).

81. For Wesley's time in Georgia, see Geordan Hammond, "Restoring Primitive Christianity: John Wesley and Georgia, 1735–1737" (unpublished University of Manchester PhD thesis, 2008).

A challenge for scholars of John Wesley is to place him within these richer and fuller interpretations of his times, and the rest of this chapter will highlight three key areas where recent research has made significant alterations to the ways in which Wesley's England has been understood: the state of the Church of England, the relationship between Anglicanism and dissent, and the nature of the British Enlightenment.

Perhaps the most obvious way in which our knowledge of Wesley's context has changed has been the transformation in our understanding of the eighteenth-century Church of England and the place of religion more broadly in the period.[82] Older histories viewed this not only as an age of secularization (as we have already seen) but also as a nadir in the history of the Anglican Church.[83] The ills most often flagged for adverse comment (and which have frequently been cited as explanatory factors in the rise of Methodism) include pluralism, which meant that the clergy were frequently nonresident in their parishes; the issue of tithes, which led to disputes between clergy and those who were not members of the church and antagonism from parishioners who resented clergy gaining from improvements in agricultural production; the increasing gentrification of the clergy, which supposedly distanced clergy from the great majority of their parishioners; and a slothful attitude to pastoral

---

82. Contributions to this reassessment: J. Walsh, C. Haydon, and S. Taylor, eds., *The Church of England, c. 1689–c. 1833: From Toleration to Tractarianism* (Cambridge: Cambridge University Press, 1993); Mark Smith, *Religion in Industrial Society: Oldham and Saddleworth, 1740–1865* (Oxford: Oxford University Press, 1994); Judith Jago, *Aspects of the Georgian Church: Visitation Studies of the Diocese of York, 1761–1776* (Madison, NJ: Farleigh Dickinson University Press, 1996); Jeremy Gregory, *Restoration, Reformation, and Reform, 1660–1828: Archbishops of Canterbury and Their Diocese* (Oxford: Oxford University Press, 2000); J. Gregory and J. S. Chamberlain, eds., *The National Church in Local Perspective: The Church of England and the Regions, 1660–1800* (Woodbridge: Boydell Press, 2003); W. M. Jacob, *The Clerical Profession in the Long Eighteenth Century, 1680–1840* (Oxford: Oxford University Press, 2007); Robert G. Ingram, *Religion, Reform and Modernity in the Eighteenth Century: Thomas Secker and the Church of England* (Woodbridge: Boydell Press, 2007).

83. See in particular C. J. Abbey and J. H. Overton, *The English Church in the Eighteenth Century*, 2 vols. (London: Longmans, Green and Co., 1878); John Stoughton, *Religion in England under Queen Anne and the Georges, 1702–1800*, 2 vols. (London: Hodder and Stoughton, 1878); and J. H. Overton and F. C. Relton, *The English Church from the Accession of George I to the End of the Eighteenth Century, 1714–1800* (London: Macmillan and Co., 1906).

work, which left their parishioners bereft of pastoral care.[84] Cathedrals received particularly bad press as being centers of torpor, if not scandal.[85] At the level of high politics, bishops have been blamed for slavishly following the priorities of government ministers (even sacrificing the Church's own interests if necessary) and for being voting fodder for the government in the hopes of securing ever more lucrative preferment. At the local level, parish clergy have been criticized for bowing to the requirements of the local elite.

In short, the eighteenth-century Church of England has frequently been a byword for lax standards and pastoral negligence, indicating an institution that had fallen far short of the ideals of the church of the sixteenth, seventeenth, and even nineteenth centuries.[86] In this scenario, Wesley (and Methodism) has been seen as a backlash against the pastoral stagnation of the established Church, as well as a countercultural throwback to an age of religious fervor and excitement. It is, however, worth stressing that much of the pessimistic history of the eighteenth-century Church of England has been written, both in the nineteenth and in much of the twentieth centuries, from what has been called a "Methodist perspective,"[87] with Wesley's criticisms of the Anglican Church being cited as proof of the shortcomings of that institution—although his negative comments were often taken out of context and generally were not balanced by the affection that Wesley could feel toward it, and in particular its liturgy.[88]

---

84. For modern restatements of these ills, see E. J. Evans, "Some Reasons for the Growth of English Rural Anti-Clericalism, c. 1750–c. 1830," *Past & Present* 66 (1975): 84–109; W. R. Ward, "The Tithe Question in England in the Early Nineteenth Century," *Journal of Ecclesiastical History* 16 (1965): 67–81.

85. Even Norman Sykes denigrated eighteenth-century cathedrals. See *Church and State in England in the Eighteenth Century* (Cambridge: Cambridge University Press, 1934), 415–16.

86. Peter Virgin, *The Church of England in an Age of Negligence: Ecclesiastical Structure and Problems of Church Reform, 1700–1840* (Cambridge: Cambridge University Press, 1989).

87. The phrase is J. H. Plumb's, *In the Light of History* (London: Allen Lane, 1972), 37.

88. See Frank Baker, *John Wesley and the Church of England* (London: Epworth Press, 1970); Jeremy Gregory, "'In the Church I will live and die': John Wesley, the Church of England, and Methodism," in *Religious Identities in Britain, 1660–1832*, ed. William Gibson and Robert Ingram (Aldershot: Ashgate, 2005), 147–78.

For many nineteenth-century Churchmen keen to dwell on the inadequacies of the eighteenth-century Church against which they measured their own successes, Wesley's Methodism was seen as an explicable, if regrettable, reaction against the prevailing lethargy of the age.[89] Norman Sykes (an Anglican cleric and later dean of Winchester) in the first half of the twentieth century developed a more positive portrayal of the eighteenth-century Church.[90] Sykes pointed out that the Church was more efficient as an organization, and its clergy more hardworking as individuals, than had previously been recognized. To a certain extent the criticism of earlier historians could be shown to be based on the biased opinions of the Church's opponents or the result of anachronistic expectations that judged the eighteenth-century Church by late nineteenth-century standards. Indeed during the last twenty-five years or so, there has emerged what might be called a revisionist school of historians whose detailed work, particularly on what the Church was doing at the local and diocesan level, has modified and in some cases reversed the more negative opinions of some of their predecessors. Rather than dwelling on the failures and shortcomings of the established Church, they have highlighted instead its successes and its strengths and have argued that in many respects the Church was more effective then than at any time since the Reformation.[91] And, perhaps surprisingly for someone who is often seen as one of the Church's sternest critics, as late as 1787 Wesley could preach: "It must be allowed that ever since the Reformation, and particularly in the present century, the behaviour of the Clergy in general is greatly altered for the better . . . Insomuch that the English and Irish Clergy are generally allowed to be not inferior to any in Europe, for piety, as well as for knowledge."[92]

Yet, as might be expected with historical fashions, revisionism has been followed by a post-revisionism,[93] which is wary of some of the

---

89. See, for example, Abbey and Overton, *English Church*, 2, 57–59.
90. Sykes, *Church and State*.
91. See the works cited under footnote 82.
92. John Wesley, "On Attending the Church Service," in *The Works of John Wesley, Sermons*, III, ed. Albert C. Outler (Nashville, TN: Abingdon Press, 1986), 470. This sermon is a defense of the efficacy of the Church, even when clergy might be deemed unworthy.
93. M. F. Snape, *The Church of England in Industrialising Society: The Lancashire Parish of Whalley in the Eighteenth Century* (Woodbridge: Boydell Press, 2003); Donald

upbeat claims of the revisionists and is concerned that they are ironing out some of the real structural and pastoral problems faced by the Church in this period. W. R. Ward (himself a Methodist), for instance, warned over fifteen years ago that in his opinion the fashionable rehabilitation of the eighteenth-century Church was going much faster than the evidence warranted.[94] There is at the moment a debate between optimists and pessimists about the state of the Church in the eighteenth century, which Wesley scholars need to take into account.

Some recent scholars have in fact maintained that, far from being a corrupt and inefficient institution, the Church had begun to reform itself long before the administrative reforms of the nineteenth century got underway and had already begun to clamp down on abuses such as pluralism and nonresidence, and others have suggested that the Church of England clergy remained more in tune with popular mores than has often been supposed.[95] Although historians used to argue that industrialization and urbanization were twin problems for a Church that supposedly did better in a rural context,[96] we can certainly exaggerate the ways in which these two developments were necessarily detrimental to the life of the Church. It is, for example, often suggested that the Church in the eighteenth century failed to build new churches to meet the growth of the towns, and the impression is sometimes given that apart from the 50 New Churches Act of 1711, which attempted to build new places of worship in newly populated districts of London (and only actually built ten), little was done until the church-building explosion of the nineteenth century. In actual fact, some of the newly smart urban centers such as Bath, Warwick, York, and Newcastle provided a rich environment for the Church: in all these towns, and in many others, churches were either recently built or refurbished, congregations were

---

A. Spaeth, *The Church in an Age of Danger: Parsons and Parishioners, 1660–1740* (Cambridge: Cambridge University Press, 2000).

94. W. R. Ward, review of John Gascoigne, *Cambridge in the Age of the Enlightenment: Science, Religion and Politics from the Restoration to the French Revolution* (Cambridge: Cambridge University Press, 1989), in *History* 73 (1990): 497.

95. Smith, *Religion in Industrial Society*.

96. Gilbert, *Religion and Society*.

large, and clergy benefitted from the pleasures of urban society.[97] And in parts of Lancashire (the area that witnessed the greatest upsurge in population and in which industrialization was furthest developed, placing the greatest strain on its resources) the Church, through its use of newly built chapels of ease, was able to accommodate a greater percentage of the population at the time of Wesley's death than it had in 1740.[98] Even in Manchester, whose population growth in the last thirty years of the century astounded contemporaries, the Church was not negligent in providing new places of worship; eight new churches were built in the city, including St. Peter's, designed by the architect James Wyatt.[99]

Wesley sometimes blamed the pastoral failings of the Church on the bishops,[100] who, it is often asserted, were frequently out of touch with their dioceses, being more involved with the House of Lords than with their diocesan clergy. But the image we have had of bishops who were negligent of their dioceses is in many ways a misleading one. Despite their involvement in politics, it is clear that the Church had many conscientious diocesans who took care to monitor the clergy under their control and to provide pastoral oversight. Of course there were exceptions, and because there was no system for retirement, elderly bishops might lose a grip on their task, but modern research at the diocesan and local level has revealed much more active leadership than previous historians assumed.[101] For instance, despite the often-held view that archbishops of Canterbury in the eighteenth century were by and large unconcerned with the well-being of the Church, several of them during Wesley's lifetime were outstanding administrators: Thomas Tenison (1695–1715), William Wake (1715–37), Thomas Secker (1758–68), John

---

97. Peter Borsay, *The English Urban Renaissance: Culture and Society in the Provincial Town 1660–1770* (Oxford: Oxford University Press, 1989).
98. Smith, *Religion in Industrial Society*.
99. Chris Ford, Michael Powell, and Terry Wyke, eds., *The Church in Cottonopolis: Essays to Mark the 150th Anniversary of the Diocese of Manchester* (Lancashire and Cheshire Antiquarian Society, 1997).
100. *Arminian Magazine* (1781): 492–93 for slurs on some of the people they ordained.
101. See in particular Jago, *Aspects of the Georgian Church*; Gregory, *Restoration, Reformation, and Reform*; and the essays in Gregory and Chamberlain, eds., *The National Church in Local Perspective*.

Moore (1783–1805),[102] and a number of other diligent bishops. One of the consequences of research into the diocesan archives has been the uncovering of correspondence between bishops (or their officials) and the parish clergy, which indicates that bishops were more in contact with their subordinates than used to be supposed. In particular, much recent research has used the extensive replies written by clergy to the questions asked by the bishops as part of their (usually) triennial visitation of their diocese. These not only provide us with remarkable information concerning the Church's role in individual parishes (such as its personnel, the number of services offered and who attended, and how often children were catechized), but they also provide information concerning the number of Catholic and Protestant dissenters in the parish and the number of inhabitants.[103] As yet, no one has attempted to collate the evidence from all the dioceses over the century, but some preliminary conclusions can be attempted.

    What do we know about the parish clergy in this period (about whom, as individuals, Wesley could be both scathing and admiring)? Much of the writing about the parish clergy in the eighteenth century has been based on literary evidence and has focused on the stereotypes of a clergy divided into the extremes of the fox-hunting parson and the woefully poor curate, but modern studies have indicated that most

---

    102. Gregory, *Restoration, Reformation and Reform*.
    103. For examples of published visitation returns and related material, on which much of the following paragraphs are based, see Patricia Bell, ed., *Episcopal Visitations in Bedfordshire, 1706–1720*, Bedfordshire Historical Record Society 81 (2002); John Fendley, ed., *Bishop Benson's Survey of the Diocese of Gloucester, 1730–50*, Gloucestershire Record Society 13 (2000); K. Wyn Ford, *Chichester Diocesan Surveys, 1686 and 1724*, Sussex Record Society 78 (1994); Jeremy Gregory, ed., *The Speculum of Archbishop Thomas Secker, Church of England Record Society* 2 (1995); John Guy, ed., *The Diocese of Llandaff in 1763*, South Wales Record Society 7 (1991); S. L. Ollard and P. C. Walker, eds., *Archbishop Herring's Visitation Returns, 1743*, Yorkshire Archaeological Society Record Society, 4 vols., (1928–30); Elizabeth Ralph, ed., *Bishop Secker's Diocesan Book*, in *A Bristol Miscellany*, ed. Patrick McGrath, Bristol Record Society 27 (1985); Mary Ransome, ed., *The State of the Bishopric of Worcester, 1782–1808*, Worcestershire Record Society, n.s., 6, (1968); idem, *Wiltshire Returns to the Bishop's Visitation Queries, 1783*, Wiltshire Record Society 27 (1971); W. R. Ward, ed., *Parson and Parish in Eighteenth-Century Surrey: Replies to Bishops' Visitations*, Surrey Record Society 34 (1994); and W. R. Ward, ed., *Parson and People in Eighteenth-Century Hampshire: Replies to Bishops' Visitations*, Hampshire Record Society 13 (1995).

clergy fell well between these extremes. By and large the clergy was a graduate profession, and the vast bulk of those who were ordained had been to Oxford (as had Wesley), Cambridge, Trinity College, Dublin, or one of the Scottish universities.[104] This matched the Church's desire to have a learned ministry, and in its propaganda it liked to contrast this fact with the supposedly unlettered status of its dissenting rivals (this criticism would be leveled at Wesley's lay preachers, which explains in part why Wesley was so keen to stress that his preachers should undergo rigorous programs of reading and study). It is true that, as the century progressed, an increasing percentage of clergy came from what might be broadly called the gentry ranks, but the wholesale gentrification of the clergy can be exaggerated. A significant number of clergy (perhaps well over a quarter) even at the time of Wesley's death came from rather more humble origins and were less likely to have been out of touch with ordinary parishioners than the pessimistic interpretation suggests; an increasing number had fathers (as had Wesley) who had also been clergy. Certainly a large number of parishes, as a consequence of pluralism, were staffed by curates, and some of these lived up to the image of the poorly paid lumpen proletariat, but many were at the early stages of their career and would move on to more settled and lucrative employment. Beneficed clergy (those in permanent employment) were either vicars or rectors, the distinction being that rectors (since they received the tithes on all produce within the parish) were likely to be richer than vicars, who only received "small" tithes (usually just on the minor products of the parish). The lot of those who were most poorly remunerated was somewhat bettered during the course of the century through Queen Anne's Bounty (established in 1704), which diverted funds from government resources and raised extra money to make a significant improvement to the less well-endowed parishes.[105]

As far as the pastoral work of the clergy is concerned, it is of course impossible to generalize, depending as it did on the inclinations of indi-

---

104. There has been some important revisionist work on the state of the universities in this period. See Lucy S. Sutherland and L. G. Mitchell, eds., *The History of the University of Oxford v. The Eighteenth Century* (Oxford: Oxford University Press, 1986).

105. For an up-to-date discussion of the clerical profession that synthesizses much of the available research, see Jacob, *The Clerical Profession*.

viduals (although it is clear that bishops were not content with the most minimal pastoral cover). There are examples, to be sure, of negligent clergy (Wesley was always keen to point these out in his *Journals* and elsewhere), but by and large the pastoral dedication of the parish clergy is more impressive than the traditionally hostile picture would suggest. The broad results of the visitation surveys indicate that services were regularly given on Sundays (with the pattern of two services being more frequent in the north and west, and one service in the south and east)[106] and that the laity was generally happy to attend, as long as there was a sermon. The furnishings of many eighteenth-century churches, and especially those that were refurbished or newly built in the period, confirmed the ascendant place of the pulpit (and sermon) within the interior of the church. St. Ann's in Manchester (built in 1711 from a donation by Lady Ann Bland) had a massive fifteen-foot-high pulpit (from which Wesley preached in 1738).[107] The dominance of the pulpit within the Church, and especially the three-decker pulpit (which figured prominently in the satirical prints of Hogarth, who also, of course, satirized the Methodist preacher), was much derided by nineteenth-century Church reformers, who accused their forebears of neglecting the sacrament, but it is indicative of the central role given to the sermon and "the word" more generally within eighteenth-century religious life. To a large extent this reflects the influence of the Reformation on the piety of the eighteenth-century Church, and indeed a number of scholars have argued that the chief pastoral aim of eighteenth-century clergy was to continue the work of the Reformers, initiating parishioners into the fundamental message of the Reformation and educating them out of popery and superstition.[108]

---

106. See F. C. Mather, "Georgian Churchmanship Reconsidered: Some Variations in Anglican Public Worship, 1714–1830," *Journal of Ecclesiastical History* 36 (1985): 268–69.

107. Wesley, *Journal* 18: 230.

108. See Jeremy Gregory, "The Eighteenth-Century Reformation: The Pastoral Task of Anglican Clergy After 1689," in *Church of England*, ed. Walsh, Haydon, and Taylor, 67–85; idem, "The Making of a Protestant Nation: 'Success' and 'Failure' in England's Long Reformation," in *England's Long Reformation*, ed. Tyacke, 307–33; Jonathan Barry, "Bristol as a Reformation City, c. 1640–c. 1780," in *Long Reformation*, ed. Tyacke, 261–84; Gregory, *Restoration, Reformation, and Reform*.

The visitation returns indicate that clergy were involved in catechizing children, although this was usually only for part of the year, and clergy admitted to their superiors that sometimes parents were reluctant to send their children.[109] Another common complaint made by the clergy was the reluctance parishioners had in taking Holy Communion, but whether this was because they devalued the sacrament or they felt unworthy to receive it is not clear. The returns also show a broad difference between rural and urban parishes. In the towns, it was much more common to find weekday services being offered and attended, and some of the larger urban centers had communion once a month and sometimes every Sunday. In rural parishes, by contrast, clergy found it hard to take parishioners away from the agricultural routine, and in many rural parishes weekday services had long since died out. The visitation returns additionally demonstrate the wider role of the Church and the clergy in the life of the parish. Clergy frequently had the role of supervising the local school, managing charitable funds, and organizing relief for the poor and as such played a vital role within the parish community. Within these patterns of pastoral provision, Wesley, during his only period as a parish priest while in Savannah, Georgia, can be regarded as something of a model incumbent. He held three services each Sunday, offered the sacrament on a weekly basis and on holy days, held two weekday services, and catechized as a regular part of his pastoral practice.[110]

Recent scholarship has also emphasized the ways in which, long before Wesley's "conversion" in May 1738, Anglicanism had itself been undergoing a movement of renewal and reform. This was witnessed most obviously in the creation of the religious societies (from about 1678, first in London, then elsewhere), the societies for the reformation of manners (flourishing from the 1690s), the Society for the Promotion of Christian Knowledge (SPCK) in 1698, and the Society for the Propagation of the Gospel in Foreign Parts (SPG) in 1701 (all of which Wesley was influenced by and drew on), but can also be seen

---

109. Gregory, *Restoration, Reformation, and Reform*, 223–26.
110. Hammond, "Restoring Primitive Christianity," 104, 161–64, 171–73, 351–58.

in efforts at Church reform.[111] The SPCK fostered a range of activities, including establishing a corresponding society for pooling and collecting information on the Church's work in the localities, encouraging the development of parish libraries, and, increasingly, publishing and disseminating religious tracts and pamphlets as a way of spreading religious education (something that Wesley would also do). During its first thirty years, it also had a special role in encouraging the establishment of charity schools.[112] The SPG reveals the extent to which the Church in the eighteenth century can be considered to be a missionary Church; its mission was not only to its English parishioners, but also to those in its colonies (Wesley was to be an SPG missionary to Georgia).[113] Another example of the Church's links with religious groups outside the British Isles was the various funds organized by the Church for the support of Protestants in Europe who were suffering from persecution by Roman Catholics.[114] Wesley himself, of course, had contacts and links with a broader European religious context—as revealed, for example, by his

---

111. J. Spurr, "The Church, the Societies, and the Moral Revolution of 1688," in *Church of England*, ed. Walsh, Haydon, and Taylor, 127–42; Craig Rose, "The Origins and Ideals of the SPCK, 1699-1716," idem, 172–90; Tina Isaacs, "The Anglican Hierarchy and the Reformation of Manners, 1688-1738," *Journal of Ecclesiastical History* 33 (1982): 391–411; Gillian Wagner, "Spreading the Word: The Church and SPG in North America: Thomas Coram and Anglicanism in New England," *Journal of the Canadian Church Historical Society* XLV (2003): 65–76; S. Taylor, "Bishop Edmund Gibson's Proposals for Church Reform," in *From Cranmer to Davidson: A Church of England Miscellany, Church of England Record Society*, ed. S. Taylor, 172–86; R. A. Burns, "A Hanoverian Legacy? Diocesan Reform in the Church of England, c. 1800-c. 1833," in *Church of England*, ed. Walsh, Haydon, and Taylor, 265–82; idem, "English 'Church Reform' Revisited, 1780–1840," in *Rethinking the Age of Reform: Britain, 1780-1850*, ed. Arthur Burns and Joanna Innes (Cambridge: Cambridge University Press, 2003), 136–62. For ways in which some of these influenced Wesley, see Rack, *Reasonable Enthusiast*, 119, 239, 354, 361, 362.

112. Craig Rose, "'Seminarys of Faction and Rebellion': Jacobites, Whigs, and the London Charity Schools, 1716-1724," *Historical Journal* 34 (1991): 831–55.

113. See Hammond, "Restoring Primitive Christianity," 324–26. Although the SPG paid Wesley's salary, he was not a typical SPG missionary under the authority of the bishop of London and the Society. He was licensed by the Georgia Trustees and served as a volunteer missionary.

114. Sugiko Nishikawa, "The SPCK in Defence of Protestant Minorities in Early Eighteenth-Century Europe," *Journal of Ecclesiastical History* 56 (2005): 730–48.

visit to the Moravian community at Herrnhut within a few weeks of his "conversion" experience.[115]

In all these areas of concern the Church showed itself rather adept at raising funds for its activities and was particularly successful in getting money from the laity for its ventures.[116] The SPG and the Corporation for the Sons of the Clergy (which supported the widows and the children of deceased clergy) elicited money through annual concerts and services at St. Paul's Cathedral.[117] The ways in which the Church was able to extract money from the laity point to one of the most important developments within the Church of England in this period—what has been termed the laicization of religion.[118] It is this feature, rather than the conventional stress on this being an age of secularization, that is the hallmark of the Anglican history of the time. Most histories of the Church concentrate either on the Church as an institution or on the clergy, but it needs to be recognized that (in part as a consequence of the Reformation) a considerable emphasis was placed by clergy on the role of the laity (and it could be argued that Wesley's use of lay preachers was extending this to its logical conclusion). Although as yet there are only a few studies of lay piety, what is emerging is a considerable body of people who not only attended the services provided by the Church, but who also wanted to help the Church in other ways and to participate in debates about religion more generally.[119] Several members of the aristocracy, such as the Duke of Newcastle, the Earl of Dartmouth, and Lady Betty Hastings were pious defenders of the Church. Not many lay people, of course, were like Samuel Johnson, who wrote sermons, but the general support for the Church—not only in the fund-raising activities mentioned above and in the regular payment of tithes, but also in

---

115. On wider European links, see W. R. Ward, *The Protestant Evangelical Awakening* (Cambridge: Cambridge University Press, 1992).

116. W. M. Jacob, *Lay People and Religion in the Early Eighteenth Century* (Cambridge: Cambridge University Press, 1996), 155–85.

117. Jeremy Gregory, "Preaching Anglicanism at St Paul's, 1688–1800," in *St Paul's: The Cathedral Church of London, 604–2004*, ed. Derek Keene, Arthur Burns, and Andrew Saint (New Haven and London: Yale University Press, 2004).

118. Sykes, *Church and State*, 379.

119. Jacob, *Lay People*; Mark Goldie, "Voluntary Anglicans," *The Historical Journal* 46 (2003): 977–90.

donations to individual parish churches (most of which dated from the medieval period and were increasingly in need of repair)—is impressive and certainly challenges the view that the Church was increasingly marginal to the life of parishioners. It has also been an axiom of much writing on the Church in the eighteenth century that it had lost its hold over the lower orders (who were thus ready to follow Wesley).[120]

Certainly in this period—as perhaps in all periods—signs of disaffection can be shown, particularly toward individual clergy and over particular grievances. But this did not mean that the Church as an institution had lost its place in the hearts and minds of ordinary parishioners. The famous Church-and-King riots of the early 1790s, which among other things mobbed the dissenter and radical political thinker Joseph Priestley's house in Birmingham and burned his laboratory (in July 1791, four months after Wesley died), were not very edifying, but indicate that the Church could still inspire popular loyalties.

This review of the scholarship on the Church of England suggests that we should view Wesley's relationship to the Church in which he was born, ordained (by John Potter, then bishop of Oxford and later archbishop of Canterbury), and, so he claimed, lived and died, in more subtle ways than traditional accounts of the rise of Methodism would have it.[121] Methodist scholarship is usually premised on the given fact of a moribund and ineffective established Church, but it may be that Wesley (and his brother) is himself evidence of a lively Anglican culture and that much of what has been considered to be Methodist innovation should perhaps be seen as emerging from within an Anglican Church that was itself experimenting with developments in pastoral care.[122]

It is, however, often said that one of the clearest testimonies to the failure of the Church in the eighteenth-century pastoral sphere was the existence of dissent and especially of Methodism (sometimes labeled "new dissent"). If the Church was as successful as some of the more optimistic judgments would have us believe, it can reasonably be asked, Why did nonconformity exist and why did Methodism develop? It is worth stressing that these factors in themselves are not a necessar-

---

120. Gilbert, *Religion*; Snape, *The Church*, 195.
121. See Baker, *John Wesley and the Church of England*.
122. Gregory, "In the Church I will live and die," 162–64.

ily useful guide to the successes or failures of the eighteenth-century Church. In the first place, by the 1730s several contemporaries were noticing a decline in "old dissent" (Presbyterians, Congregationalists, Baptists, and Quakers) because many erstwhile dissenters had by now conformed to the Church of England, including some (like Thomas Secker, a future archbishop of Canterbury) who had initially contemplated becoming nonconformist ministers.[123] The reasons given for the decline in old dissent were varied: some held the internecine wranglings over doctrine responsible; some pointed to the ways in which the confessional state severely limited opportunities for nonconformists to have significant political, social, and educational positions if they remained outside the Church; and others blamed the decline of old dissent on the effects of the Toleration Act, which supposedly weakened the backbone of nonconformity.[124] Whatever the reason, it is clear that the Church gained from winning over some former dissenters and as a consequence the challenge of nonconformity weakened.

Second, it is necessary to emphasize here that Methodism should at least in the first instance be seen as a movement from within the Church of England, rather than as a dissenting movement operating outside it. Wesley, himself the son of the rector of Epworth, remained a member of the Church of England throughout his life (as did George Whitefield and Howell Harris), and although he could be sharply critical of contemporary practice, his energies were devoted to reforming the Church from within. It is curious that the now-lively scholarship on the Church and the prolific research into Wesley have been kept remarkably separate; future study would benefit from bringing these research strands together. Significantly, the revisionist approach to the Church has seldom brought Methodism into its purview, except to argue that Wesley's criticisms of the shortcomings of that institution were frequently exaggerated and to suggest that in many parts of the country the emergence of Methodism was rather later, and the number of adherents

---

123. See Michael Watts, *The Dissenters*, vol.1 (Oxford: Oxford University Press, 1978).
124. Richard Brown, *Church and State in Modern Britain, 1700–1850* (Routledge: London, 1991).

rather smaller, than a triumphalist Methodist reading would have it.[125] Wesley's efforts to keep the movement he founded within the Church—by encouraging his followers to attend both Church services and the Methodist meetings and insisting that Methodist meetings should not clash with the times of church services—may not have been respected, or even put into practice, by all of his followers; yet at least until his death in 1791, Methodism was more of an Anglican than a dissenting phenomenon.[126]

If recent scholarship has provided a much more upbeat picture of the state of the Church of England (which at the very least complicates easy explanations of the rise of Methodism as a direct counter to Anglican pastoral negligence), what can be said about the relationship between the Church and dissent? One feature of Wesley's context that needs to be highlighted here (and which arguably does not feature prominently enough in Clark's analysis of the confessional state) is the Toleration Act of 1689, often seen as a concomitant of the Glorious Revolution, which maintained the establishment position of the Church while giving limited concessions to nonconformists. The act, although contested by some clergy who wanted it either repealed or extended, nicely summed up the position of the Church of England throughout the eighteenth century as established yet (at least in comparison with other periods and churches in Europe) broadly tolerant of at least some at least of its rivals.[127] Yet, although commonly known as the Toleration Act by contemporaries and later historians, it was originally entitled an "act for exempting their majesties' Protestant subjects dissenting from the Church of England from the penalties of certain laws," which indicates that it was less tolerant than has sometimes been suggested. Protes-

---

125. See, for example, the essays by Jeremy Gregory, William Gibson, Colin Haydon, and William Jacob in Gregory and Chamberlain, eds., *The National Church in Local Perspective*.

126. On this, see David Wilson, "Church and Chapel: Parish Ministry and Methodism in Madeley, c. 1760–1815, with Special Reference to the Ministry of John Fletcher." (University of Manchester PhD thesis, 2010).

127. See James Bradley, "Toleration and Movements of Christian Reunion, 1660–1789," in *The Cambridge History of Christianity*, vol. vii, *Enlightenment, Reawakening and Revolution, 1660–1825*, ed. Stewart J. Brown and Timothy Tackett (Cambridge: Cambridge University Press, 2006), 348–70.

tant dissenters could only legally worship in unlocked meetinghouses, providing they had been licensed and their minister subscribed to the Thirty-Nine Articles of the Church of England except those concerning baptism and Church government, and the act clearly proscribed Roman Catholic worship and Unitarianism. One of the issues that would involve Wesley was whether Methodist meetings should be registered under the act, which he strongly resisted, arguing that his followers were not dissenters; although a number of clergy insisted on calling them such (but, significantly, others were not sure how to categorize them), Wesley liked to boast that he brought people to the Church.[128] The act became important for the self-definition of the Church as one which was charitable and enlightened (at least compared with its competitors) and saw persecution of dissent as a hallmark of popery. And although evidence can be found of mobs stoning and harrying dissenters (and early Methodists) and pulling down their meetinghouses, clergy at least had to work within a framework where they persuaded rather than persecuted nonconformists back into the fold.

It is this frame of mind that in part explains why clergy were so eager to publish their views in print as a way of competing with, rather than persecuting, nonconformists. Clergy do seem to have generally treated Protestant dissenters with respect. The vicar of St. Lawrence, Thanet, for instance, reported to Archbishop Moore with some pride in 1786: "I must do all my parishioners, both the Church of England, and likewise the Dissenters, the justice to say that they attend the public worship of God on the lord's day, at the Church and at the meeting house, with great punctuality, regularity and decency."[129] This statement is interesting in that this particular clergyman not only had a positive view of dissenters, but also saw both Anglicans and nonconformists as his parishioners, lingering evidence of the view that the Church of England had a responsibility for the entire nation.

What was of more concern to Anglican clergy was the apparently growing sector of the population who did not attend any form of religious worship (for which the Toleration Act itself was widely suspected; by not insisting that parishioners went to Church of England

---

128. Wesley *Journals* 20, ed. Ward and Heitzenrater, 370; idem, 22:447.
129. Quoted in Gregory, *Restoration, Reformation, and Reform*, 232.

services, it may have encouraged them to attend no place of worship at all), and it was against this group that the Church might join in with the dissenters. This shared pastoral purpose can be witnessed by Anglicans working with dissenters in the societies for the reformation of manners (in the 1690s and early eighteenth century) and educational projects such as charity schools.

If scholars of John Wesley could benefit from giving greater attention to the Church of England, which would locate him more firmly within his century than the countercultural interpretation would have it, there are also other ways in which Wesley can be placed more centrally into recent eighteenth-century scholarship with profit. One of the most significant historiographical developments during the past twenty years has been to widen and complicate what might be meant by "the Enlightenment." Traditional scholarship, heavily based on a French model of the Enlightenment, viewed it as an anti-religious force,[130] and in this portrayal Wesley, and Methodism more generally, could be portrayed as a counter-Enlightenment backlash.[131] More lately, scholars working on British history have argued that the Enlightenment was not necessarily antireligious, and Roy Porter argued that in the English Enlightenment, piety and reason could work in tandem.[132]

Other research has also indicated that it has been too simple to place English Enlightenment figures—such as John Toland—within an antireligious camp. Although Toland was certainly critical of the Church and the clergy, his attacks were in fact based on what he con-

---

130. Classic studies of the Enlightenment include Paul Hazard, *European Thought in the Eighteenth Century* (Harmondsworth: Penguin, 1965); Peter Gay, *The Enlightenment: An Interpretation* (London: Weidenfeld and Nicolson, 1967), esp. vol. 1, *The Rise of Modern Paganism*.

131. See Thompson, *Making of the English Working Class*.

132. Roy Porter, "The Enlightenment in England," in *The Enlightenment in National Context*, ed. R. Porter and M. Teich (Cambridge: Cambridge University Press, 1981), 1–18. However, in some of Porter's later and more extended considerations of the themes, he tended to see the Enlightenment as a secularizing force: Roy Porter, *The Enlightenment* (Basingstoke: Macmillan, 1990); idem, *Enlightenment: Britain and the Creation of the Modern World* (London: Penguin, 2001). See also Sheridan Gilley's pioneering article, "Christianity and the Enlightenment: An Historical Survey," *History of European Ideas* 1 (1981): 103–21.

sidered to be religious principles.[133] Moreover, Wesley himself can be put into an Enlightenment framework, complicating the view of him as "anti-" or "counter-" Enlightenment.[134] The lynchpin of his theology—Arminianism and universal redemption—endlessly reiterated in his correspondence, his *Journals*, and his sermons, was not only the dominant theology of the Church of England (again indicative of the fact that we need to understand Wesley as an Anglican), but its central premises can be understood as chiming in with the Enlightenment emphasis on optimism, human potential, perfectibility, and the essential equality of humankind.[135] Likewise, Wesley's emphasis on evidence and experience can be seen as echoing Enlightenment traits. This is not to say that Wesley was directly influenced by Enlightenment thought (he was frequently hostile to those classically labeled as Enlightenment figures, such as Voltaire, and there has been a long-standing debate about how far he was "Lockean")[136] or that we need to speak of a zeitgeist, but it is to argue that there was at least an elective affinity between his central concerns and those usually viewed as belonging to the Enlightenment. It can also be argued that the whole thrust of Wesley's religious message was—in Enlightenment fashion—the centrality of experience and feeling. But if Wesley put great emphasis on sensation and empiricism, he was—again in Enlightenment fashion—keen to ensure that the experience was a

---

133. Justin Champion, *Republican Learning: John Toland and the Crisis of Christian Culture, 1696–1722* (Manchester: Manchester University Press, 2003). See also his *The Pillars of Priestcraft Shaken: The Church of England and its Enemies* (Cambridge: Cambridge University Press, 1992).

134. Justin Champion, *Republican Learning: John Toland and the Crisis of Christian Culture, 1696–1722* (Manchester: Manchester University Press, 2003). See also his *The Pillars of Priestcraft Shaken: The Church of England and its Enemies* (Cambridge: Cambridge University Press, 1992).

135. For suggestions of the links between Arminianism, Methodist theology, and Enlightenment thought, see Semmel, *Methodist Revolution*, 87–109. Semmel, however, argued that Wesleyanism should be seen as a liberalizing force. I think we can agree that there are affinities between Methodism and the Enlightenment without forcing it necessarily into a liberalizing framework.

136. See Frederick Dreyer, "Faith and Experience in the Thought of John Wesley," *American Historical Review* 88 (1983): 21–50; John C. English, "John Wesley and the Anglican Moderates of the Seventeenth Century," *Anglican Theological Review* 51 (1969): 203–20.

genuine one and that the convert was neither deluded nor fabricating their feelings (this needed to be tempered by scripture and by reason, in a characteristically eighteenth-century balance).[137]

Wesley's concern with experience and feeling should in any case be understood as part of an eighteenth-century emphasis on empiricism and sentiment (seen in such a typically eighteenth-century virtue as benevolence) rather than as what might be thought to be a full-blooded Romanticism.[138] Furthermore, as indicated earlier, Wesley was fascinated by developments in natural philosophy and medicine and kept abreast of the latest research, which he took pains to disseminate to his followers.[139]

More broadly, and crucially for our understanding of Wesley's context, his seeming ability to hold together faith and reason (although how far he did so in synthesis or in tension is a matter for debate) can be seen as part of a wider pattern of the age.[140] Jane Shaw in her *Miracles in Enlightenment England* has demonstrated how a larger range of commentators were able to balance "religious enthusiasm" with "reason," and her reading incorporates elements of the supernatural into an Enlightenment worldview that clearly challenges older models of an Enlightenment hostile to religious sensibilities.[141] Studies such as this are beginning to uncover a religious eighteenth century, which makes it clear that characterizations of this as "the Age of Reason" have led to an unwarranted neglect of the religious impulses and drivers of the period. Recent research into all manner of topics, ranging from the art to literature, travel writing, and even the foreign policy of the time have argued

---

137. Rex Dale Matthews, "'Religion and Reason Joined': A Study in the Theology of John Wesley" (unpublished Harvard University PhD dissertation, 1986).

138. And even "Romantic" writers may have placed more stress on "reason" than is sometimes suggested: see Jon Mee, *Romanticism, Enthusiasm and Regulation: Poetics and the Policing of Culture in the Romantic Period* (Oxford: Oxford University Press, 2003).

139. See Laura Bartels Felleman, "The Evidence of Things Not Seen: John Wesley's Use of Natural Philosophy" (unpublished Drew University PhD dissertation, 2004); Madden, "*Cheap, Safe and Natural Medicine*"; Prosser, "Arminian Magazine."

140. See Henry Rack, "A Man of Reason and Religion? John Wesley and the Enlightenment," *Wesley and Methodist Studies* 1 (2009): 2–17.

141. Jane Shaw, *Miracles in Enlightenment England* (New Haven: Yale University Press, 2006). See also Robert Webster, "Methodism and the Miraculous: John Wesley's Contribution to the Historia Miraculorum" (unpublished Oxford University PhD thesis, 2006).

for the need to bring back the religious framework and imperatives that have been marginalized by conventional scholarship.[142] It may indeed have been that Wesley made such an impact on his age not because his context was irreligious, but because it was already suffused with religious concerns.

---

142. See Clare Haynes, *Pictures and Popery: Art and Religion in England, 1660–1760* (Aldershot: Ashgate, 2006); Claydon, *Europe and the Making of England*.

# "If God . . . see fit to call you out": "Public" and "Private" in the Writings of Methodist Women, 1760–1840

Joanna Cruickshank

In 1770, the renowned Methodist leader Mary Bosanquet (later Fletcher) published a letter of advice she had written to a young woman named Elizabeth Andrews. Amidst a flood of detailed advice about the life of faith, including recommendations about spiritual disciplines, reading matter, and marriage, Bosanquet urged her young friend:

> Strive to be little and unknown; and remember that our Lord lived thirty years in private, and only three in publick, and that the word of God allows a woman, professing godliness, no adorning but that of a meek and quiet spirit. Strive, I say, to be little and unknown; yet if God, on any occasion, see fit to call you out into more publick action, then also say, *Thy will be*

---

This article was completed during a Fellowship at the Oxford Centre for Methodism and Church History, at Oxford Brookes University. I am very grateful to the Centre for this opportunity and to Peter Forsaith and William Gibson for their generous assistance during the fellowship. Early research for the article was undertaken during a British Academy Visiting Fellowship at Manchester University. Gareth Lloyd at the Methodist Archives and Research Centre and Jeremy Gregory at Manchester University were both enormously helpful during this time.

*done*, and embrace, with a ready mind, whatever your Saviour pleases.[1]

Bosanquet's advice to Andrews mapped a complicated path by which a godly woman could negotiate the two worlds of private life and "publick action." Women who emulated Jesus must make every effort to be "little and unknown," but if the divine will directed otherwise, they must equally strive to obey.

These strictures point to two features in the writings of Mary Bosanquet Fletcher and her circle: first, that these writings contain a myriad of references to "public" and "private"; second, that the two concepts often appear to be the focus of powerful emotions, such as longing, anxiety, joy, or relief. This aspect of Methodist women's writings is particularly significant, given the long-standing debate over the gendered nature of the public and private "spheres," which has dominated scholarship on gender in eighteenth- and nineteenth-century British society over the last twenty-five years. Examining what these terms meant to these Methodist women challenges a number of key assumptions in this debate, particularly in relation to notions of privacy. It also sheds light on a group of women whose voices remain largely unheard in histories of this period.

For historians of gender, the debate over the concept of "separate spheres" will hardly need introducing. Within the history of eighteenth- and nineteenth-century Britain, the debate has most recently focused around the claims of Catherine Hall and Leonore Davidoff in their book *Family Fortunes: Men and Women of the English Middle Class, 1780–1850*, first published in 1987.[2] Hall and Davidoff argued that in the latter part of the eighteenth century, a powerful association between spiritual devotion, domesticity, and femininity on the one hand, and worldliness, work, and masculinity on the other, led to the emergence of a strong, gendered distinction between the public and private spheres. Women were increasingly confined to private, domestic

---

1. Mary Bosanquet, *A Letter to Elizabeth A—ws, on Her Removal from England* (James Bowling: Leeds-Bridge, 1770), 12.
2. For a second, revised edition, which addresses criticisms of their claims, see Leonore Davidoff and Catherine Hall, *Family Fortunes: Men and Women of the English Middle Class, 1780–1850*, 2nd ed. (London: Routledge, 2002).

spaces, while men went out into the public realm of work and politics. Hall and Davidoff argued that this view was fostered within the growing Evangelical movement, but was quickly adopted (and adapted) by the English middle class more broadly, as a central part of its class identity.[3]

Since the publication of *Family Fortunes*, almost every aspect of Hall and Davidoff's claims has been both applauded and challenged. In perhaps the most wide-ranging critique, Amanda Vickery argued that their claims were based on an unrepresentative selection of sources, an outdated and unsubstantiated model of class formation, and an inaccurate understanding of the relationship between evangelicalism and the middle class.[4] Other historians, many more sympathetic to Hall and Davidoff's arguments, have called for a more detailed investigation of eighteenth- and nineteenth-century understandings of the public and private sphere, drawing on a broader range of sources.[5] Recent scholarship has argued for the existence of a third, or "social" sphere, in which women developed a strong presence during this period, through religious, philanthropic, and missionary activity.[6] Historians such as Susan Thorne have argued that the notion of "separate spheres" was central to evangelical women's enthusiastic participation in overseas missions, which was justified on the basis of the "heathen" need for the "civilisation" that women could provide.[7] Other research has suggested that during this period significant numbers of women in England participated actively and without apparent censure in the "public" world

---

3. See Hall and Davidoff, *Family Fortunes*, 450–54.

4. Amanda Vickery, "Golden Age to Separate Spheres? A Review of the Categories and Chronology of English Women's History," *The Historical Journal* 36, 2 (1993): 383–414.

5. For example, Jane Rendall, "Women and the Public Sphere," *Gender & History* 11, 3 (November 1999): 475–88; and Lawrence Klein, "Gender and the Public/Private Distinction in the Eighteenth Century: Some Questions about Evidence and Analytic Procedure," *Eighteenth-Century Studies* 29.1 (1995): 97–109.

6. For example, Linda Wilson, *Constrained by Zeal: Female Spirituality amongst Nonconformists, 1825–1875* (Milton Keynes: Paternoster, 2006); and Alison Twells, *The Civilising Mission and the English Middle Class, 1792–1850: The "Heathen" at Home and Overseas* (Houndmills: Palgrave Macmillan, 2009).

7. Susan Thorne, *Congregational Missions and the Making of an Imperial Culture in Nineteenth-Century England* (Stanford: Stanford University Press, 1999), 89–120. See also Twells, *The Civilising Mission*.

of business.[8] Hall and Davidoff have, in turn, published a number of thoughtful responses and additions to their work.[9]

The long-running nature of this debate means that while the concept of "separate spheres" may still be a significant category in both research and undergraduate teaching, it has been argued almost to the point of intellectual exhaustion and certainly to the point where historians complain that it is no longer very interesting.[10] Reviewing the debate in 2005, Jane Rendall concluded that recent scholarship had "tried to look away from such polarities towards the overlapping and fluidity of public and private worlds, and minor shifts, in degree rather than kind."[11] Throughout this debate, however, while religion has been identified as a major factor in the construction of notions of public and private, Methodism has received very little attention, in spite of its crucial role in the development of evangelical piety and practice.[12] This article therefore focuses on the writings of Methodist women, arguing that there are still fruitful questions to be asked about the concepts of "public" and "private" in the eighteenth and early nineteenth centuries, particularly in relation to religious conviction and discourse.

## *Public and Private in Fletcher's Circle*

Mary Bosanquet Fletcher (1739–1815) was perhaps the most prominent of a large group of women who played significant roles in

---

8. Hannah Barker, *The Business of Women: Female Enterprise and Urban Development in Northern England, 1760–1830* (Oxford: Oxford University Press, 2006).

9. See particularly Leonore Davidoff, "Gender and the 'Great Divide': Public and Private in British Gender History," *Journal of Women's History* 15.1 (Spring 2003): 11–27 and the introduction to the second edition of *Family Fortunes*.

10. Amanda Vickery noted in 1993 that "separate spheres" remained the dominant category for teaching undergraduates about the history of gender during the eighteenth and nineteenth centuries, and my own experience would suggest this is still true. "Golden Age to Separate Spheres," 393.

11. Jane Rendall, "Women and the Enlightenment in Britain c.1690–1800," in *Women's History: Britain, 1700–1850*, ed. Hannah Barker and Elaine Chalus (London: Routledge, 2005), 10.

12. For a recent work that does engage with Methodism in relation to the public/private binary, see Brett C. McInelly, "'I had rather be obscure. But I dare not': Women and Methodism in the Eighteenth Century," in *Everyday Revolutions: Eighteenth-Century Women Transforming Public and Private*, ed. Diane E. Boyd and Marta Kvande (Newark: University of Delaware Press, 2008).

the development and spread of the Methodist movement in the late eighteenth and early nineteenth centuries. Fletcher was unusual on a number of counts. Expelled from her upper-class family at a young age because of her Methodist convictions, she quickly became a leader of Methodist classes, set up an orphanage and home for the indigent, established Methodist societies in the various places she lived, took up itinerant preaching, and published a number of very popular tracts. Famous in her own right, she gained further status later in life as the wife (and soon widow) of John Fletcher, an Anglican priest of renowned saintliness. After her husband's death in 1785, Fletcher remained living in the vicarage of his parish in Madeley, where she was given authority to appoint the curate, maintained her preaching ministry, mentored younger women preachers, and corresponded with a huge range of people around Britain.[13]

While Mary Fletcher's activism was in some ways extraordinary, it was echoed on a smaller scale by many of the women associated with Methodism during this period. Women made up the majority of Methodists throughout the movement's early years and were involved in the leadership of the movement through class and band leadership, evangelism, visiting the sick, teaching children, and sometimes preaching, though this was officially discouraged after 1803.[14] As Phyllis Mack has recently noted, however, "The response of secular scholars to this well-known fact of Methodist history has been to insist on the centrality of feminine (or anti-masculine) elements in the movement while almost totally ignoring the thinking and behaviour of actual women."[15] This lack of attention to women's experience cannot be explained by a paucity of sources. Like their male counterparts, Methodist women

---

13. For a good introduction to Fletcher's life, see Gareth Lloyd, "Introduction," *Asbury Theological Journal* 60.3 (Fall 2006), 1–5.

14. See David Hempton, *Methodism: Empire of the Spirit* (New Haven and London: Yale University Press, 2005), 5.

15. Phyllis Mack, *Heart Religion in the British Enlightenment: Gender and Emotion in Early Methodism* (Cambridge: Cambridge University Press, 2008), 19. Mack's own work is groundbreaking in its attention to the actual experiences of early Methodist women. Other works on early Methodist women include Paul Chilcote, *Her Own Story: Autobiographical Portraits of Early Methodist Women* (Nashville, TN: Kingswood Books, 2002); and Earl Kent Brown, *The Women of Mr Wesley's Methodism* (New York: Edwin Mellen Press, 1989).

wrote enormous amounts, particularly personal journals and letters. Many of these are preserved in archives around the world, including a collection of hundreds of letters, journals, and notebooks written by Mary Fletcher and her circle, held in the Methodist Archives and Research Centre in Manchester. This collection provides a rich source for examining Methodist women's use of the language of private and public.[16] These women represented several generations of Methodist women, from a very few who had been part of the early growth of Methodism in the 1740s, to those who came to adulthood after John Wesley's death in 1791. They also came from a wide variety of social backgrounds, from domestic servants to nobility.

The terms "public" and "private," along with a host of related terms, appear throughout the writings of Fletcher's circle and even a quick survey of the relevant texts will reveal that the terms are not used either according to fixed definitions, or always in straightforward binary opposition. This is not surprising. In his brief survey of eighteenth-century uses of the term "public," Lawrence Klein identified an array of such uses, which were "always complex and sometimes contradictory."[17] Klein did conclude, however, that "what people in the eighteenth century most often meant by 'public' was sociability as opposed to solitary life (which was 'private'). 'Sociability' here meant involving the company of others in a range of different settings and combinations."[18] As Klein noted, this distinction could be drawn according to two specifications, "perceptibility" and "accessibility." The terms could distinguish between matters that were exposed to a broad group of people and those that were known only by one or a few, and/or between matters that were open to participation by a broad group and those that were accessible only to one or a few. For the most part, Methodist women's uses of the language of private and public do not neatly conform to Klein's two categories, but his definitions are very useful in teasing out the subtleties in the way this language was used.

---

16. The women whose writings are held in this collection either corresponded with or were known to Mary Fletcher and/or the female companions who shared her house over the years, so I refer to them broadly as "Fletcher's circle."

17. Klein, "Gender and the Public/Private Distinction," 103.

18. Ibid., 104.

## Called Out

The first main context in which the terms "private" and "public" are used in the writings of Fletcher's circle is in discussions of women's ministry, by which I mean their religious activities in service of others. For example, an unnamed servant of Mary Fletcher wrote to friends soon after Fletcher married: "my Dear Mistress ... [h]as savaral sort of meetings some publick and some private."[19] Sarah Boyce, who had received John Wesley's personal approval as a preacher, wrote late in life of her attempts to awaken Methodists to more zeal: "For more than twelve months I warned the people both in publick and private but I seemed to most as one that mocked."[20]

The distinction being drawn in these instances appears to be primarily one of audience, or "accessibility," in Klein's terms, with "public" contexts being those that were open to all and "private" those accessible only to a restricted few. John Wesley seems to have distinguish Methodist meetings along such lines when he wrote:

> That part of our economy, the private weekly meetings for prayer, examination, and particular exhortation, has been the greatest means of deepening and confirming every blessing that was received by the word preached, and of diffusing it to others, who could not attend the public ministry; whereas, without this religious connection and intercourse, the most ardent attempts by mere preaching have proved of no lasting use.[21]

Here again the distinction between public and private seems to refer to those who could attend: the general attendance at the "public ministry" in contrast to the selected group who attended the "private weekly

---

19. This letter is unsigned and undated, but the contents make it clear that it was written by one of Bosanquet Fletcher's servants to a friend, soon after the Fletchers had married. MA 6.9/21, Fletcher/Tooth Collection (F/T). Methodist Archives and Research Centre (MARC). Here and elsewhere I have preserved the original spelling and usage of the sources used.

20. Sarah Boyce to Mary Tooth, 12 October 1828. MA 1.12/1, F/T. MARC.

21. John Wesley, *A Plain Account of Christian Perfection* (London: Epworth Press, 1952), 94–95.

meetings" of class and band.[22] Wesley's comments also make clear the association between, on the one hand, the activities of "prayer, examination, and particular exhortation" with private meetings, and, on the other, the practice of "preaching" with the "public ministry."

Understood in these terms, Wesley's encouragement of class and band meetings provided new opportunities for women to minister in "private" contexts. Women made up the majority of class members in almost all places and were often involved in class leadership.[23] In this context, some women were given an unusual degree of spiritual authority over men. Anne Conibear, a class leader in Gloucester, wrote to Mary Fletcher of her husband: "My dear Mr C with whom I have ever met here was very solicitous to be one in my class, saying, he married me that I might be his guide & leader to heaven, & he wou'd not be parted so I give him a share giving out the hymn &c."[24]

In Methodist women's discussions of ministry, however, the terms "private" and "public" appear most commonly as a focus of anxiety or frustration, marking a boundary beyond which female ministry became controversial. A preacher named Diana Thomas wrote to Mary Tooth, who assisted Fletcher's ministry during the final years of her life: "It is much Imprest upon my mind that you will meet with opposition in your publick labours as some men are much against Women Exercising in any publick way, I know this from Experience."[25] Sarah Boyce, who repeatedly clashed with male preachers over the extent of her ministry, wrote "They own they cannot hinder me from publick speaking—because Mr Wesley took me in as a preacher—but I am denied the pulpit—I may exort in the meetings but take no text ... here was a woman here that had been a publick speaker for some years—but she is not suffered to speak now."[26] Her description confirms that disapproval of women's preaching was identified with the "publick" nature of the activity, though, as her references to pulpit and biblical text make clear,

---

22. For a good overview of the structure of bands and classes, see Hempton, *Empire of the Spirit*, 78–79.
23. Ibid., 78.
24. Anne Conibear to Mary Fletcher, 12 November 1792. MA 2.1/15, F/T. MARC.
25. Diana Thomas to Mary Tooth, 12 February 1816, MA 7.3/4, F/T. MARC.
26. Sarah Boyce to Mary Tooth, 26 January 1841. MA 1.12/9, F/T. MARC.

there were also other issues involved in defining what was legitimate women's activity and what was prohibited.

The issue at stake was not, of course, the presence of women in religious meetings, however accessible these meetings were. Rather, the issue was women ministering in this context through preaching or praying out loud, activities that made them highly visible to such general audiences. To use Klein's terms, the combination of accessibility and perceptibility meant that women's behavior—not simply the contexts in which they acted—was defined as public. For example, writing to Fletcher, a Methodist woman preacher in Leeds described a young protégé of hers, Miss Rhodes, who was "now in Derbyshire, & acting in a public Charrecter in some measure, I believe."[27]

The Methodist women in Fletcher's circle defended their call and thus their right to act in "a public Charrecter," but their comments show that such ventures could be costly. Sarah Boyce's experience of increasing restriction on her activity by the Methodist preachers reflected the well-documented broader development of increasing resistance to women preaching within the movement.[28] But the pressures on women were not merely external, as seen in a letter Diana Thomas wrote to Fletcher in 1808:

> Perhaps you will wonder I do not say anything respecting my being calld out in publick. Oh my Dear Sister none but God knows the Exercise of my mind—many times when I presume to Stand up for my God & his cause and to indeavour to speak to poor sinners I think I shall not be able—but the Lord hitherto supported me. I trust I am not deciev'd—when I say I can appeal to him that knows my heart that my sole motive is his Glory and the Good of my poor fellow creatures Souls.[29]

Such anxieties were not suprising, when one considers Fletcher's exhortation to women to "strive to be little and unknown," quoted at

---

27. Sarah Crosby to Mary Fletcher, 22 April 1799. MA 2.5A/13, F/T. MARC.

28. See Gareth Lloyd, "Repression and Resistance: Wesleyan Female Public Ministry in the Generation after 1791," *Proceedings of the Wesley Historical Society* 55.3 (2005): 101–14.

29. Diana Thomas to Mary Fletcher, 10 January 1808, MA 7.3/2, F/T. MARC.

the beginning of this article. Jesus had set an example of humility for all Christians to follow, and such humility was directly associated with "private" life. For devout women, this general principle was further reinforced by the biblical command to be meek and quiet. By contrast, "public" behavior, as understood by these women, required one to draw attention to oneself. It therefore not only challenged social norms, but brought with it spiritual dangers. Women like Diana Thomas must be very sure that their "sole motive" was the glory of God and the good of others, not self-aggrandizement. For many of the women in Fletcher's circle, then, the division between private and public was experienced in powerful ways, both through the resistance of others and their own anxieties.

The complicated nature of the perceived division between public and private, and Methodist women's negotiation of this division, emerges most clearly in letters written by Fletcher about her own ministry. In 1771, Fletcher wrote to John Wesley, to ask advice on her conduct, because she had been criticized by a local preacher for the extent of her ministry. She wrote that after she and her companion Sarah Ryan ran what she called "little kind of prayer meetings" at their orphanage in Laytonstone, the meetings became so popular that people began inviting them to their houses. Soon they were holding two or three meetings a week, with hundreds attending.[30] The same thing had happened in Yorkshire. These people, Fletcher assured Wesley "would not go near a preaching house."

Recently, however, a local preacher had argued that it was unscriptural for a woman to address such meetings. As a consequence, Fletcher had curtailed her conduct somewhat. She noted that while ministering in Yorkshire:

> I believe I am calld to do all I can for God & in order thereto when I am askd to go with B. Taylor to a prayer meeting in any private house to as many as there Room will hold that I may do it, may both Sing—pray—& Converse with ym Either peticularly or in Generals according to ye Number. Likewise when Brother Taylor goes to preach in Little

---

30. Mary Bosanquet to John Wesley, 1771. MA 13.1/67, F/T. MARC.

Country places in a private house after he has done I believe I may speak a few words to ye people & pray with ym.

Twice it has happened thro ye zeal of ye people that they gave out ye meeting in a preaching house because they had no private house that would hold ye people not one half quarter of ym when I came I was sorry but could not tell what to do so B. Taylor preached & I afterwards spoke to ym. (above 100s of carnal were there & my heart yearned over ym. I fear my Master shd say their blood will I require of you).[31]

In this account, the distinction between private and public is crucial to Fletcher's understanding of appropriate behavior for herself as a woman. This distinction is drawn, however, not on the basis of audience—both contexts are clearly open to all who wish to attend—but on the basis of place. In a "private" house, she felt herself free to speak and pray with the people, but in a "preaching house" she felt far more constrained. Her account demonstrates how carefully she sought to negotiate this distinction. She repeatedly uses the words "little" and "private" to describe the contexts in which she is speaking—and she avoids the use of the words "preach" and "public" to describe her activities. Nonetheless, she emphasises that she thinks such distinctions are unimportant in the light of the much greater consideration of saving souls.

This account contrasts in significant ways with a description of the same period and activities that Fletcher wrote thirty years later. This time she was writing to Mary Baritt Taft, a younger female preacher, who had an itinerant ministry and preached from the pulpit of Methodist chapels.[32] Whereas Fletcher had written to Wesley that she had held "little" prayer meetings in Laytonstone, to Taft she wrote simply that during these years "I held publick meetings & a society was formed & a way made for the preachers—when I was in Yorkshire for near 14 years I went about a good deal & had many meetings both there & in other

---

31. Bosanquet to Wesley, 1771. MA 13.1/67, F/T., MARC.
32. For an example of this, see Sarah Crosby to Mary Fletcher, 22 April 1799. MA 2.5A/13, F/T., MARC.

parts."[33] Clearly, the emphasis on the "publick" nature of these meetings is quite different from her depiction of these years in her letter to John Wesley.

The accounts differ significantly in other ways: in the first account, Fletcher describes herself as accompanying Brother Taylor, who is depicted as taking the primary role; in the second, Fletcher's emphasis on her own agency in traveling and conducting meetings is striking. In her letter to Taft, Fletcher went on to give a description of the role she had taken up in Madeley. In the preaching barn she had built, she met with classes, and preached throughout the week. She explained to Taft that she usually spoke from a text or as she said "expounding, taking a part or whole of a Chapter & speaking on it."[34] As this makes clear, she was not simply telling the story of her own experience or urging spiritual change —which were less fraught types of speaking implied in her account to Wesley—but preaching in the sense considered most authoritative, explaining and applying Scripture.

The differences between the two accounts may be explained as a matter of strategy: in defending her practices to John Wesley, Fletcher depicted herself as seeking to conform wherever possible to acceptable boundaries for female ministry, whereas in her letter to a fellow woman preacher, Fletcher wrote far more frankly. Alternatively, the differences may be seen as a result of changes over time. Later in her life, with forty years of preaching experience behind her, Fletcher may have felt far more confident of the appropriateness of her actions than she had as a young woman in her early thirties. Whatever the explanation, the two accounts provide clear evidence of the significance of the private/public distinction in Fletcher's mind, and the minds of those to whom she was writing, in relation to women's ministry.

Less obviously, however, these accounts point to the complicated relationship between Methodism, space, and contemporary understandings of public and private. Leonore Davidoff has noted that during the eighteenth and nineteenth centuries, the built, or man-made, environment of Britain changed radically, as many new types of buildings

---

33. Mary Bosanquet Fletcher to Mary Taft, 28 November 1803. MA 37.8, F/T. MARC.
34. Ibid.

were constructed, and much communal and individual activity moved inside.[35] Davidoff notes that this occurred "mainly as a result of the establishment of—or major transformation in—a variety of institutions: nationally based scientific societies, business concerns, voluntary associations, and the bureaucratic state operating at local, regional and national levels."[36] These changes related in complicated ways to understandings of "public" and "private," as a variety of new buildings became associated with behavior understood as public—activities associated with the state and the market. Other behaviors, such as washing, sleeping, and breast feeding, were increasingly moved behind closed doors.[37]

Surprisingly, though Davidoff and Hall give such a central role to religion in constructing the meanings of these new spaces, Davidoff does not mention religious institutions in her account of the changes that occurred in the built environment itself. Methodism undoubtedly played a role in these processes of change, as chapels proliferated across the English landscape during the late eighteenth and nineteenth centuries. The implications of this development for gender roles has been examined by Deborah Valenze in her insightful study of women preachers associated with nineteenth-century Methodist sectarian groups. She describes how Methodist sects, such as the Primitive Methodists and Bible Christians, adopted and expanded the early Methodist practice of holding preaching and prayer meetings in domestic settings. In this "cottage religion," she argues, the family home was not understood as a private space, in the way later Evangelicals might construct it. Rather, it was "the locus of economic and social relations intrinsic to labouring life, and no distinction between home and work, or work and life, obtained."[38] In her account, the story of Methodist chapel-building is a story of the increasing restriction of women's ministry within the movement: the building of chapels was part of the institutionalization

---

35. Davidoff, "Gender and the Great Divide," 13–15.
36. Ibid., 15.
37. Ibid., 14.
38. Deborah M. Valenze, *Prophetic Sons and Daughters: Female Preaching and Popular Religion in Early Industrial England* (Princeton: Princeton University Press, 1985), 22.

of Methodism and went hand-in-hand with the process of limiting women's ministry in such "public" arenas.[39]

Valenze is not primarily concerned with the women of mainstream Wesleyan Methodism, but the writings of Fletcher's circle both confirm and qualify the broad narrative she describes. In Mary Fletcher's 1770 account of her ministry in Yorkshire, she repeatedly refers to the country homes in which she spoke as "private" houses. This suggests a sense of the family home as a private space which, according to Valenze, rural sectarian Methodists did not share. This may indeed also have been the case for the inhabitants of the "Little Country places" that Fletcher visited in Yorkshire. Nonetheless, by emphasising the "private" nature of these spaces, Fletcher justifies her practice of addressing large mixed audiences. Her description is evidence that the Methodist practice of meeting for prayer and preaching in family homes problematized any simple notion of the home as "private" space, but identifying homes in this way could have created a protected space for women to minister in unconventional ways.

Valenze's argument, that such opportunities declined as Methodist activity became focused on the chapel, remains largely convincing. Nonetheless, as the quotes above make clear, Methodist women did not simply passively respond to such changes, but by their actions they, along with Methodist men, were involved in them, as they contributed to a longer process of transforming the relationship between religious activity, gender, and notions of public and private. Some women created new spaces in which they could minister to "public" audiences. In Madeley, Fletcher constructed a "preaching barn," where she met with small, single-sex "classes" as well as preached to large crowds of men and women. Fletcher's adopted daughter, Sarah Lawrance, held meetings for men, women, and children in houses in the industrializing town of Coalport, until numbers became too large. Then, as Fletcher recounted, a friend donated the use of "a large part of his Warehouse wh is divided off by a partition & she has put in it a seat for herself & many Benches . . . you wd scarce believe what vast Congregations attend from miles

---

39. Valenze, *Prophetic Sons and Daughters*, 274–81.

round."⁴⁰ Other women, like Sarah Boyce and Mary Taft, rejected the gendered division of public and private, insisting on the right to preach in chapels. Women like Fletcher and Boyce were unusual, but the fact that Boyce and other women were being invited to preach in a London chapel in 1828 demonstrates that the "public" places of institutionalized Methodism were still not entirely closed to women's ministry.⁴¹

These findings suggest that Methodism expanded the spaces for women's ministry in a way that was more significant and more enduring than has generally been recognized. Wesleyan Methodism relied to an unusual extent on "private" meetings, which allowed new opportunities for devout women to speak, pray, and lead. It also inspired some women with the conviction that they had been "called out" to more "public" behavior. In a recent account of women's religious practices between 1700 and 1850, Anne Stott notes the prominence of women in eighteenth-century Methodism, but claims that after the Methodist Conference officially discouraged female preaching in 1803, "female preaching remained a dead issue with the Wesleyans until the twentieth century."⁴² Noting these Methodist women's experiences in the first half of the nineteenth century not only suggests more significant resistance to the Conference's decision by individual women preachers, but also Methodist congregations who welcomed their "public labours," until well into the 1830s.

## *In My Room Alone*

The second main context in which Methodist women used the terms "private" and "public" was in discussions of their personal spiritual development. For example, in 1778, an unnamed domestic servant recounted that she had met with John Wesley to discuss the state of her soul. "He encouraged me to press forward," she reported "and expect

---

40. Mary Fletcher to "John," nd. MA 37.2, F/T. MARC.
41. Sarah Boyce was invited to preach in Harts Lane Chapel in London in 1828, but because she was ill a Miss Berger took her place. See Sarah Boyce to Mary Tooth, 12 October 1828. MA 1.12, F/T. MARC.
42. Anne Stott, "Women and Religion," in *Women's History: Britain, 1700–1850*, 107.

to meet God in every means of Grace, both publick and private."[43] In Wesleyan terms, "means of grace" referred not only to the sacraments of the Lord's Supper and baptism, but also prayer, fasting, hearing, or reading the Bible and "religious conversation."[44] Clearly, most of these activities could take place in a variety of places and could involve any number of people, from one person to a large crowd. Wesley's distinction between the two categories of "means of grace" may simply echo his use of the distinction discussed above, with "private" means of grace meaning those that occurred in the restricted access of class and band meetings, and with "public" means of grace meaning those that occurred among the broad congregations of church, chapel, or open-air preaching.

This distinction does not, however, fully account for the use of the terms by Methodist women describing their own and others' spiritual practices. Mary Tooth recorded that Mary Fletcher's personal notebook contained a plan for each day's prayers, which included four times of "private" prayer, one session of prayer with Tooth, and a time of "family prayer" with the household.[45] Tooth wrote of the times that Fletcher prayed with her: "Many of these times have become seasons of peculiar advantage: *my* soul has cause to praise the Lord for her private, social, and public exercises."[46] In an account of the life of a faithful local Methodist, Mary Tooth wrote approvingly:

> No business ever interrupted his devotional exercise & to secure time for private intercourse with heaven he was always an early riser & never failed to secure the two first hours of the morning for that purpose & again the same in the evening in his closet to be shut up with God alone . . . family worship was always most

---

43. Unnamed servant woman in Nancy Marshall to Mary Fletcher, 1778. MA 33.1, F/T. MARC.

44. See Richard P. Heitzenrater, "Means of Grace," in *Historical Dictionary of Methodism*, ed. Charles Yrigoyen Jr. and Susan E. Warrick (Lanham, Md.: Scarecrow Press, 1996), 138–39.

45. Mary Tooth, *A Letter to the Loving and Beloved People of the Parish of Madeley and its Vicinity who have lost a Friend to Piety in the Death of Mrs Fletcher* (Shiffnal: A. Edmonds, 1816), 23.

46. Ibid., 21.

strictly attended to by him, twice every six days in the week & three times on the Lord's day.[47]

In these comments, "private" devotion appeared to mean that which took place individually and alone: in Klein's terms, behavior that was both imperceptible and inaccessible. These writers distinguished such "private" devotion variously from "public," "social," and "family" devotional activity.

For Mary Fletcher, nothing was more important for spiritual growth than individual prayer, which she described as "the first and greatest of all means."[48] To a Mrs Dalby, who had asked for advice on gaining sanctification, she wrote: "As to the manner of seeking [holiness], I have always found private prayer the truest touchstone. I do not mean, it was never well with me when prayer was difficult; no, that is not the mark; but when I *labour* most in prayer, I get most forward."[49] In an undated letter to a friend, apparently written toward the end of her life, she commented:

> You observe you cannot kneel—neither can I hardly for half an hour together sometimes but for a quarter—but when I lean Back in my Chair in my Room alone I find it a Season of near approach to the Saviour & have Liberty to plead for a Closer walk with God.[50]

Other women referred to prayer alone as "secret" rather than "private" prayer. The autobiography of Hester Rogers, a contemporary of Mary Fletcher's with a reputation for saintliness, contained multiple references to times of "secret prayer," which she found a great blessing.[51] Of one overwhelming experience of God's love, she wrote, "In secret and

---

47. Mary Tooth, Account of George Perks, MA 33.3, F/T. MARC.
48. Mary Fletcher to Mrs. Smith, nd. MA 37.4, F/T. MARC.
49. Mary Fletcher to Mrs. Dalby, 26 December. 1792. *Methodist Magazine* 41 (1818): 688.
50. Mary Fletcher to unknown, nd. MA 13.1/52, F/T. MARC.
51. For examples, see Hester Rogers, *The Experience of Mrs H. A. Rogers* (Bristol: R. Edwards, 1796), 4, 30, 37, 39, 42.

in public, I am filled with his presence; and constrained to cry, enlarge my heart to make thee room!"[52]

Such times alone were spent not only on prayer, but also on reading and reflection. A young housemaid, newly employed away from home, wrote to Mary Tooth:

> I have much time for reading and self medetation for the people I live with ... are out a great deale so I take my prarer Book and go hup stares and shut the door and fall dowen on my nees and power out my soule unto God ... I wish some times I lived in a very quiet place by my self where I should do nothing but read and pray.[53]

Both John Wesley and Mary Fletcher encouraged Methodist women to read widely, including, if possible, the lives of exemplary Christians, history, natural philosophy, arithmetic, and commentaries on scripture.[54] For the purposes of devotional reading, of course, scripture was the primary text.

Such activities required both space and time to be alone, something that many women struggled to find. A young woman preacher named Sarah Jenkins wrote after a visit to London that her first week there "was, I think, one of the most unpleasant ones I ever spent in my life, I was a stranger to solitude. . . . how uncomfortable I passed the time, when I could not get so much as two minutes alone."[55] The redoubtable Sarah Boyce, returning from a preaching tour of London wrote:

> I praised my Lord when I set my feet in my quiet humble Cottage. Here I could be alone with my Lord. And have time for reading prayer and wrighting. This I was cut of from in almost every place. I know not how it is with you. But I am not comfortable in my mind if I have publick means every day if I have not quiet retirement two.[56]

---

52. Ibid., 42.
53. Unnamed to Mary Tooth, 1822. MA 2.10/1, F/T. MARC.
54. See Bosanquet, *A Letter to Elizabeth A—ws*, 17–18, and John Wesley, "A Female Course of Study," *Arminian Magazine* 3 (November 1780): 602–4.
55. Sarah Jenkins to Mary Tooth, 8 March 1825. MA 4.4/4, F/T. MARC.
56. Sarah Boyce to Mary Tooth, 12 October 1828. MA 1.12/1, F/T. MARC.

This desire for time and space alone thus cut across divisions of class and age, being expressed by women from the elderly, upper-class Fletcher to the middle-aged minister's daughter Hester Rogers and the unnamed housemaid.

This space and time alone was identified by women in Fletcher's circle as "private," or by terms such as "secret" or "retirement." Importantly, "private" in this context was not understood in a simple binary with "public," but could also be contrasted with "social" or "family" activity. This latter distinction alerts us to the fact that "privacy," in this sense, was not at all the same thing as "domesticity." This becomes abundantly clear in Fletcher's final letter to the Methodist community in Madeley. Here (as elsewhere), she recommended the advantages of singleness, noting that this state allowed much more control of that "most precious talent" of time:

> Engaged in a family, there is not only the business, (which is seldom lessened thereby,) but there is that attachment to the partner and children which often takes up those moments which should be devoted to retirement. Again, if you are led to cry to God in public, to visit the sick, or in any way to save souls from perdition, you have not to ask leave of man. —How many in this respect are kept back from usefulness.[57]

In this description, family and marriage are seen as a potential hindrance to certain types of both public and private religious activity. This applies to both men and women—the passage is addressed to all those who are single.

Davidoff and Hall note that evangelical Christianity "demanded private space for individual introspection" and that "this could present problems for women concerned with the everyday tasks of running a household and bringing up children."[58] They note that women often worried about the effect of marriage on their spiritual lives. Yet they mention this only briefly as a minor tension within their broader picture of Evangelicalism as a movement that idealised domesticity. I

---

57. Joseph Entwistle, ed. *A Legacy to the People of Madeley by the late Mrs. Mary Fletcher* (London: Thomas Cordeaux, 1819), 71.

58. Davidoff and Hall, *Family Fortunes*, 90.

suggest that the writings of these Methodist women present a somewhat different aspect. These women wrote of a desire for a "private" aloneness that was experienced not primarily as a duty "demanded" of them, but as a deep longing. The women themselves would have denied that this time was spent simply in introspection: reading and prayer were activities intended to direct the mind outwards, at God and one's duty to others, as much as inwards, in self-examination. And clearly, as Fletcher's tracts outlined, the value of such privacy could be placed in direct opposition to domesticity.[59] This finding supports Phyllis Mack's recent argument, that marriage and domesticity were not idealized by early Methodist women, but were affirmed by Methodist male preachers, who relied on the emotional and practical support of a wife to sustain their demanding work.[60]

## *Methodism, Gender, and Separate Spheres*

The writings of Mary Fletcher and her circle provide significant evidence of the complicated nature of the relationship between religion, notions of "public" and "private," and the choices and behavior of women in late eighteenth- and early nineteenth-century England. In particular, these writings make clear that to understand the complexities of this relationship, we need to take seriously the distinctive beliefs and practices of different religious cultures, even within the broad category of "evangelicalism." This article has identified some of the ways in which Methodist women used the language of "public" and "private," noting that in relation to religious ministry, Fletcher's circle experienced the division between public and private behavior as both meaningful and formidable. Religious authorities—such as other Methodist preachers—and religious convictions—about godly behavior— contributed to women's anxieties about transgressing this boundary. Nonetheless, religious convictions led women to undertake "public labours" well into the nineteenth century, in spite of increasing resistance.

---

59. Fletcher's thoughts on the spiritual value of singleness for women are laid out in more detail in her tract *Jesus, altogether lovely: or a Letter to some of the Single Women in the Methodist Society*. 2nd ed. (Bristol, 1766).

60. Phyllis Mack, *Heart Religion*, 298–99.

In addition, I have demonstrated that the women of Fletcher's circle used the language of "public" and "private" in discussing individual spiritual development. In this context, women focused on privacy as a deeply desirable state, understood as time and space alone for prayer, reading, writing and self-examination. This understanding of privacy was not the same as, and could exist in tension with, domesticity.

What broader conclusions can be drawn from these findings? In the first place, this study demonstrates the importance of considering more closely the relationship between space and religion, in relation to debates about gendered "separate spheres." Late eighteenth- and early nineteenth-century Methodists were involved in religious activities that focused on different spaces from those evangelicals who remained staunchly Anglican. Although Methodist chapels came to take on many of the characteristics of Anglican churches, including the restrictions on women's participation, these differences must be taken into consideration in understanding how both "public" and "private" behavior was defined. Both the "private" and "public" spaces of Methodism offered increased opportunities for women's participation. The effect of this was enduring. In Flora Thompson's memories of village Methodism in the 1880s, women spoke of their spiritual experiences to mixed audiences in the local meeting house, which was a domestic home during the week.[61]

Second, the writings of Fletcher's circle demonstrate that the language of "public" and "private" could be used in a variety of related but distinct ways. The two terms were not always used in binary opposition to one another, but could be part of a larger group of related concepts. This demonstrates the danger of treating "public" and "private" as straightforward and binary terms, and so it may be more appropriate to talk of "publics" and "privates" during this period. The meaning of the two terms, and particular women's relationship to these concepts, can only be understood in context of women's lives and choices. In the case of Methodism, the writings of Fletcher's circle suggest that many Methodist women felt anxious about a particular type of "public" behavior and longed for a particular type of "private" space. However,

---

61. See Flora Thompson, *Lark Rise to Candleford* (London: Penguin, 1945), 214–15.

as Fletcher herself exhorted these women, obedience to God should override such emotions.

Methodist women took this seriously. In 1799, a young woman named Catherine Rhodes wrote to Mary Fletcher of a dream that she had, after giving up her practice of itinerant preaching because of her attachment to "a retired Life." Rhodes dreamed that she had developed leprosy and was told that if she did not get out of Leeds, she would be covered with it. "Immediately," she wrote, "I felt as if moved by an invisible power out of the Place, and found myself in a Country Village, in a pure air speaking of the new Birth and Salvation to all that I came near."[62] At the time she wrote the letter, she had returned to preaching and been away from home for seven months.

Finally, this analysis of Methodist women's language and behavior needs to be placed within a longer chronology. Early Methodist women's "public" activity provides an important context for evangelical women's activism in the second half of the century, identifying the latter not only as an attempt to extend the domestic virtues of women into the public sphere, but also as part of an existing, though minority, evangelical tradition of women's "public" religious behavior. It is significant in this regard that Mary Fletcher's autobiography was immensely popular in the second half of the nineteenth century, going through twenty printings after her death.[63] More broadly, the Methodist emphasis on solitary prayer, reading, and reflection point to a valuing of individual intellectual and spiritual development among evangelical women that must be factored into longer chronologies of feminism. To return to the theme of the built environment, the quotes above suggest that the space which many Methodist women craved, as a consequence of their particular spirituality, was not the domestic parlor, but a room of one's own.

---

62. Catherine Rhodes to Mary Fletcher, 18 February 1799. MA 6.5/5, F/T. MARC.
63. Gareth Lloyd, "Introduction," 3.

# "Improving the *present* moment": John Wesley's Use of the *Arminian Magazine* in Raising Early Methodist Awareness and Understanding of National Issues (January 1778–February 1791)

Barbara Prosser

In March 1747, when defending the Methodist practice of lay preaching, John Wesley announced: "I am not careful for what may be an hundred years hence. He who governed the world before I was born shall take care of it likewise when I am dead. My part is to improve the present moment."[1] The same thought was apparent thirty years later when counseling Ann Bolton: "Whatever our past experience has been, we are *now* more or less acceptable to God as we more or less improve the *present* moment."[2]

That "*present* moment" lay within an era of change; finding its place and role within the shifting ideologies was an emergent, vibrant religious movement. The *Arminian Magazine*, a monthly periodical delivered into every Methodist society—accompanied with a demand for it to be read—had been started by the founder of this movement in January 1778 as a religious retort to indefensible criticism by the Calvinistic press. Within a few years the magazine had changed its character to become an interactive miscellany comprising motivat-

---

1. John Wesley to "John Smith," 25 March 1747, *The Letters of John Wesley* (hereafter *JWL*), 2:94.
2. 24 January 1778, in *JWL*, 6:297.

ing accounts of religious lives; emotive death bed scenes; relevant, practical correspondence; no-nonsense sermons; disturbing accounts of the preternatural; minutiae of medical advances and cures; up-to-date horticultural practices; stories of adventure and providential events; geographical and travel information; poetry; and much more, as well as extracts from religious works and observations upon issues and developments within the Methodist movement both at home and abroad. It was John Wesley's project; he selected all the material and "extracted" or abridged that which he did not actually write. It was his tool to relay significant material that he believed his movement needed as it moved into the nineteenth century without him. The *Magazine*, sold at six pence per copy, would be read either individually or more likely collectively within the societies. By dealing with issues not usually considered by the run-of-the-mill Methodists, many of whom would have been illiterate, the *Arminian Magazine* directed readers from their relatively narrow personal concerns regarding their own spirituality to an awareness of not only current social and political issues but also of their responsibilities as citizens of the nation.[3]

In order to "improve the present moment" the Methodists first had to appreciate the late eighteenth-century context through their Arminian mindset. Arminianism had the potential to encourage the individual to take ownership of his or her spiritual life by deciding for Christ through individual faith, to promote confidence and self-worth by acquiring assurance of that salvation given through grace, to encourage social and political awareness through compassionate concern for others and through the necessity of evangelism, and to recognize accountability in the light of potential loss of that salvation. Such beliefs held the momentum of Wesleyan Methodism and were in tune with enlightened values of "the present moment," such as individualism; liberty of conscience; civil and religious toleration; inclusivity; an optimistic emphasis on human physical, intellectual, and spiritual progress; and an increasing awareness of and involvement in political and social issues.

---

3. For an overview of the magazine and its transformation, see Barbara Prosser, "'An Arrow from a Quiver': Written Instruction for a Reading People: John Wesley's *Arminian Magazine* (January 1778–February 1791)" (PhD thesis, University of Manchester, 2008).

Any endorsement of enlightened thinking, however, referred only to its potential and gave no guarantee. Such possible vibrant principles were tempered not only by the intense discipline of Wesleyan Methodism, of both an organizational and personal nature under the paternal, if not all-controlling, eye of Wesley, but also by the symbiotic mixture of these principles with traditional Christian values and beliefs. Tension was possible between the established acceptance of the depravity and ignorance of man and an optimism for his self-improvement. There was also tangible strain between providential control and individual free will, the acknowledgment of the preternatural and recognition of scientific advances. There was also possible tension between individual needs and communal demands plus a difference of opinion over the significance and role of the Enlightenment's champion—reason.

John Wesley believed reason held no value in the production of faith, hope, or love but was "a faculty of the human soul" which, assisted by the Holy Spirit, enabled understanding of the individual's present state and acted as a guide for all the many roles and judgments taken on the road to Christian Perfection.[4] "It is no part of my design to save either learned or unlearned men from the trouble of thinking," Wesley wrote in 1765. "On the contrary, my intention is to make them think, and assist them in thinking."[5] A similar intention was spelled out to Joseph Benson in October 1771: "You want me to *think for you*," he chided. "That is not my design. I would only *help you to think*."[6] The sustained help he offered the membership for the final fourteen years of his life came via his monthly *Arminian Magazine*.

When the proposals for it were written on 14 August 1777, Wesley was clear in his intentions: "This work will contain no news, no politics." He confirmed his thoughts on 18 October: "We agree," he confirmed to Walter Churchey, "that no politics shall have a place in the *Arminian Magazine*."[7] As already noted, the original motive for beginning the literary venture was to enable a theological retort to the critical

---

4. Sermon VI, *Arminian Magazine* (hereafter *AM*), 4:574ff.
5. Preface to *Explanatory Notes upon the Old Testament* (1765), in *The Works of John Wesley* (hereafter *JWW*), 14:267.
6. 11 October 1771. *JWL*, 5:281.
7. *JWL*, 6:283.

Calvinistic press and, as such, would have primarily a narrow, focused remit. Wesley always claimed to feel personally inadequate in dealing with issues relating to the nation, recording in 1768, "I am no politician; politics lie quite out of my province."[8] However, although he instructed his preachers not to preach on anything "political," apart from supporting the monarch from scurrilous attacks,[9] his own published writings of the decade prior to the introduction of his *Magazine* give a very different impression.[10]

The amount of Wesleyan publications relating to political issues decreased significantly once the medium of his monthly miscellany was on hand, through which he could address the readers in their familiar homes and societies.[11] Once the *Magazine* changed its character from a theological periodical, it became an instrument, if not the main instrument, for engaging the movement and encouraging awareness of issues ostensibly outside of the immediate Methodist movement. These included deliberations upon the nature of true government and the impact upon the nation of such issues as the war with America, Catholicism, the current justice system, and the increasing horror of slavery. Through the information given via the *Magazine*, such issues ceased to be hypothetical or irrelevant and became real concerns of the movement.

Leon O. Hynson argues that Wesley as a young man followed the views of the Divine Right of Kings, passive obedience, and nonresistance to the government, based upon the scriptural teaching of Romans chapter 13, verses 1–5, colored by his strict Anglican upbringing in a

---

8. *The Present State of Public Affairs* (December 1768). In this tract, Wesley pointed out the difficulties of becoming involved in political life. These included the difficulty of being objective, of having accurate information as a basis for decision making, and of being able to analyze events coldly without passion.

9. "How Far Is It the Duty of a Christian Minister to Preach Politics?," *AM*, January 1782, 5:151.

10. See footnote 21 together with *Thoughts Concerning the Origin of Power* (1772); *Thoughts on the Present Scarcity of Provisions* (1773).

11. *An Estimate of the Manners of the Present Time* (1782), and a letter to William Pitt on taxation and suicide (1784), *JWL*, 7:234–36. Henry D. Rack, *Reasonable Enthusiast: John Wesley and the Rise of Methodism* (London: Epworth, 1989), 490.

disciplined home and by his own reading.[12] Such opinions were greatly changed in later life by the reading of William Higden's *A View of the English Constitution* (1709), which portrayed a pragmatic view of government rather than a blind observance of loyalty and obedience. Wesley continued to hold that the supreme authority of the English government was divinely vested in the reigning monarch, to whom the people should owe allegiance, but his concept of valid government became a more enlightened one in which human liberty was protected and religious liberty was guaranteed.[13] The monarch was accountable to God, so if the rights of the people were threatened then, he argued, they must be at liberty to protect them.[14]

Via the *Arminian Magazine* Wesley enabled the early Methodists to move on from local and familiar concerns to consider such writings as Robert Boyle's late seventeenth-century "Thoughts upon Government," which highlighted the significance of wise government, the necessity of giving due respect to those in authority, and the responsibility of making the monarch accountable. Underpinning this was the necessary aptitude of both subject and ruler for having reasoned judgment as the following excerpts elucidate: "A monarch may command my life or fortune; but not my opinion. . . . It is no breach of loyalty to question the prudence of a governor."[15] Such was the advice distributed to the ordinary Methodist via the *Arminian Magazine*.

To illustrate his point to the readers, Wesley inserted into the *Magazine* many easily assimilated historical examples of what he considered to be good government, primarily originating from what would have undoubtedly been unfamiliar geographical areas. Acknowledging historical significance for present and future application and benefit was a genre of the enlightened "present moment." "The advantages found in history," David Hume noted, "seem to be of three kinds, as it amuses

---

12. "Human Liberty as Divine Right: A Study in the Political Maturation of John Wesley," *Journal of Church and State* 25 (1983), 57–85. Wesley's readings included George Berkeley's *Of Passive Obedience* and John Jackson's *The Duty of Subjects toward Their Governors*.
13. "Of Human Liberty," Extracted from a Late Author, *AM*, 8:258ff.
14. *Free Thoughts on the Present State of Public Affairs* (1768), *JWW*, 11:14–33.
15. *AM*, 8:630.

the fancy, as it improves the understanding, and it strengthens virtue."[16] Wesley's use of this approach, used often throughout the *Magazine*, came to its preeminence in the realm of encouraging appreciation of true government, inserting in total thirty-three significant case studies exemplifying indispensable qualities of wise government, namely justice, compassion, and the protection of individual liberty. These were shrewdly emphasized by alternative illustrations of vulnerability and deceit among others in authority.[17] These inclusions were filtered through a Christian stance, which in many cases took precedence over

---

16. David Hume, "Of the Study of History" (1741), in *Essays Moral, Political and Literary*, vol. 2, cited by Roy Porter, *Enlightenment: Britain and the Creation of the Modern World* (London: Penguin, 2000), 230.

17. "A Short Account of King Henry the VIII's Queen," *AM*, 3:492, (misuse of power); "A Remarkable Decision of Charles the Fifth," *AM*, 7:612 (justice); "A *late* Memorable Event," *AM*, 8:34 (attempted assassination of a Polish monarch illustrating justice, compassion, protection of liberty, and vulnerability); "Lord Guilford Dudley to Lady Jane Gray both under Sentence of Death for High Treason," *AM*, 8:337 (vulnerability); "The Character and Prayer of Prince Eugene," *AM*, 8:582 (compassion); "A Genuine Copy of King Henry the VIII for a Day's Provision for one of his Queens," *AM*, 8:584 (misuse of power); "The Remarkable Speech of the Great Czar of Muscovy Peter 1 to King WILLIAM 111 when He Met Him at Utrecht," *AM*, 8:633 (vulnerability); "A Fair Revenge" [Galianus], *AM*, 9:226 (justice); "Fine Courage" [Malcolme King of the Scots], *AM*, 9:226 (justice); "Conjugal Affection" [Vespasian] *AM*, 9:280 (justice); "Brotherly Love" [Emperor Augustus], *AM*, 9:280 (compassion); "Rare Fidelity" [King of Cochin–Portugal], *AM*, 9:333 (justice); "A Generous Enemy" [Emperor Conrade], *AM*, 9:334 (justice and protection of liberty); "A Noble Instance of Generosity" [Charlemagne], *AM*, 9:334 (justice and protection of liberty); "The Death of Richard the First," *AM*, 9:454 (justice, compassion, and protection of liberty); "Impartial Justice" [King Thodoric the Great], *AM*, 9:455 (justice); "Righteous Judgement" [Thomas More], *AM*, 9:456 (justice); "Patience of Reproof" [Augustus Caesar], *AM*, 9:456 (justice); "Intrepidity and Obedience" [incorruptible judge under Henry IV], *AM*, 9:456 (justice); "Reproof Well Given, and Taken" [Philip, King of Macedon], *AM*, 9:457 (justice and protection of liberty); "The Remarkable Clemency of Julius Caesar," *AM*, 9:514 (justice); "A Happy Thought" [Emperor Rodolph], *AM*, 9:515 (justice); "Covetousness Well Rewarded" [Lewis XI], *AM*, 9:516 (justice); "King Alfred's Dying Words to His Son," *AM*, 9:564 (justice and compassion); "Treachery Punished" [Emperor Aurelianus], *AM*, 9:566 (justice); "A Proper Return for an Injury" [military anecdote], *AM*, 9:622 (justice); "A Turkish Story," *AM*, 10:550 (justice); "Warning Given in Vain" [assassination of the Duke of Guise in the reign of Henry III of France], *AM*, 11:44 (vulnerability); "An Example of Historical Narration" (Roman government), *AM*, 11:320; "The Real Character of Epicurus," *AM*, 11:321 (compassion); "Anecdote of Peter the Great, Czar of Moscovy," *AM*, 12:434 (justice and compassion); "A Full Account of the Attempt to Assassinate the King of Poland" ELA, *AM*, 13:419ff. (vulnerability); "Filial Affection Rewarded" [Frederick of Prussia], *AM*, 14:104 (compassion).

historical accuracy and objectivity, Wesley himself acknowledging in 1776 that, "wholly to divest one's self of prejudice and partiality is indeed a difficult thing."[18]

The issue of loyalty to the divinely appointed crown was topical in the latter half of the eighteenth century in respect of the war against and eventual loss of America. Wesley had been sympathetic at first to the claims of the colonists, but, by 1775, had publicly changed his mind in tandem with the American call for independence, which conflicted with his view of the monarchy. He believed in a just war but his article "On War," inserted into the *Magazine* in December 1781, was an attempt to dispel the influence of pro-war views relating to America as expressed in another periodical, the *Sherborne Journal*. The positive response from the *Magazine*'s readers to his comments showed that they had indeed deliberated on his views and consequently encouraged him to include a far more analytical evaluation the following month.[19] "The Cause and Cure for War" took the form of explicit indictments against the Americans, the French, the Spanish and the Dutch, accusing them of entering into war on monetary grounds, which was in defiance of the Christian teachings of loving enemies and resisting temptations of avarice, ambition, and anger. Hence it was via his *Magazine* that Wesley not only raised knowledge of current affairs but set them within a Christian context.

Wesley was outspoken about developments in the New World and published many tracts independently of his *Magazine*.[20] Once

---

18. Preface to *Concise History of England*, in *JWW*, 14:289.
19. *AM*, 5:39.
20. *Free Thoughts on the Present State of Affairs* (1768); *Thoughts upon Liberty* (1772); *Thoughts upon Slavery* (1774); *Letter to the Monthly Review* (30 November 1774), in *JWL*, 6:126; *A Calm Address to our American Colonies* (1775); *Some Observations on Liberty* (1776); *A Seasonable Address to the More Serious Part of the Inhabitants of Great Britain, respecting the Unhappy Contest between Us and Our American Brethren: with an Occasional Word Interspersed to Those of a Different Complexion By a Lover of Peace* (1776); *A Calm Address to the Inhabitants of England* (1777); *A Serious Address to the People of England, with regard to the state of the Nation* (1778); *A Compassionate Address to the Inhabitants of Ireland* (1778); *The Late Work of God in North America* (1778); *An Account of the Rise and Progress of the American War* (1780); *Reflections on the Rise and Progress of the American Rebellion* (1780); *An Account of the Conduct of the War in the Middle Colonies Extracted from a Late Author* (1780); *Reflections of the Rise and Progress of the American Rebellion*

the situation had settled down, however, he did use his periodical to justify one of his most controversial tracts, *A Calm Address to the American Colonies*, published in September 1775. This publication was written to explain his dramatic turn of opinion in favor of the government's position regarding the war. Its impact had been phenomenal, with forty thousand copies sold in three weeks, the government itself having ordered the distribution of copies outside city churches.[21] Other main periodicals had printed the work, with fourteen opposing tracts appearing throughout October to the spring of 1776.[22] In the *Magazine* for November 1789, some fourteen years after the initial impact of the tract, Wesley published personal correspondence of October 1779 that demonstrated unmitigated support for his contribution to the debate.[23] The eulogizing about Wesley's tract by itinerant Samuel Wells, confided originally to Wesley but now exhibited to the membership, provided an opportunity for personal reflection upon past events and hopefully vindication of the aged founder's involvement in the national affairs.

It was essentially the effect of the American situation upon individual Methodists that truly concerned Wesley and that the *Arminian Magazine* was instrumental in highlighting to its readers. In 1783 there were seventy Methodist preachers in America caring for almost four thousand members.[24] Through the reports, readers may well have been transported thousands of miles away in their mind's eye, but the issues under consideration were issues that they were dealing with at home and as such would have been received with understanding and sympathy.

It was through the reading of personal correspondence that Methodists at home came to see how their American counterparts were, in spite of their newfound independence, still reliant upon the support

---

(1780); *An Extract from a Reply to the Observations of Lieut. Gen. Sir William Howe, in a Pamphlet Entitled, Letters to a Nobleman* (1781); *An Extract of a Letter to the Right Honourable Lord Viscount Howe on his Naval Conduct in the American war* (1781).

21. Allan Raymond, "'I Fear God and Honour the King': John Wesley and the American Revolution," *Church History* 45 (1976), 322.

22. Donald. H. Kirkham, "John Wesley's 'Calm Address': The Response of the Critics," *Methodist History* 14 (1975), 13–23.

23. *AM*, 12:613 (DXIII).

24. Frank Baker, "John Wesley and America," *Proceedings of the Wesley Historical Society* 44 (1984): 125.

and guidance from themselves and Wesley in particular.[25] In December 1785 the *Magazine* was used to justify the ordination of ministers in America, a matter that was already controversial at home. The *Magazine* included the significant letter of September 1784 entitled "To Dr Coke, Mr. Asbury and our Brethren in North-America"[26] in its entirety, which outlined Wesley's plan for the future Methodist organization in the New World, thus not only raising awareness of what was an inevitable development in America but one that would have a bearing on Methodism at home. Correspondence of November 1782, chosen for inclusion by Wesley as late as December 1790, from respected itinerant Thomas Taylor stationed in East Florida, prophetically noted concern as to the plight of Methodists following independence in the Methodist centers of Savannah and Charleston.[27] Such correspondence brought issues of a wider, fresher Methodism right into the hands and imaginations of second generation members back home.

Wesley also used his *Magazine* to clarify opinion regarding Catholicism. While he advocated liberty of worship in theory, he balanced this with an exploration and warning of a possible conflict of interest in relation to primary allegiance to the Crown, a conflict that was absent in Methodism. Wesley personally opposed Catholic doctrine, especially in relation to meritorious works, praying to saints, transubstantiation, and purgatory, as seen in the moving account of "The Experience of Mrs. A. B.," whose struggle from Catholicism into Methodism was given in detail in the *Magazine* issue for September 1789.[28] Wesley also believed in true Enlightenment fashion "that every man had a right to worship God according to his own conscience."[29] In July 1749 he had written *A Letter to a Roman Catholic* urging toleration between the Church of

---

25. Rev. Devereux Jarrau, Virginia, to John Wesley, 29 June 1773, *AM,* 9:397 (CCCXCIX); Rev. Francis Asbury to John Wesley, Halifax, North Carolina, 20 March 1784, *AM,* 9:680 (CCCCX).

26. *AM,* 8:602–604.

27. Thomas Taylor to John Wesley, 1 November 1782, *AM,* 13:610 (DXLVIII). Taylor had written to Wesley in April 1768 requesting more itinerants for America. Wesley printed and circulated it among his preachers and leading laymen and at the 1769 Conference called for volunteers.

28. *AM,* 12:414ff.

29. "A Disavowal of Persecuting Papists," *AM,* 5:197.

England and Catholicism,[30] and his *Letters* reveal his early toleration of the faith.[31] In his *Magazine*, Wesley instructed his members to accept a similar stance. He was strongly influenced by the example of the lives of individual Catholics, namely Gregory Lopez[32] and Gaston de Renty,[33] both of whom he believed were rare and exceptional examples of Christian perfection.[34] Accounts of the life of Gregory Lopez appeared in the *Magazine* in 1780,[35] along with other exemplar Catholic lives of Armelle Nicolas[36] and Julius Palmer.[37]

Wesley used the *Magazine* to identify individuals who remained steadfast to their faith when facing persecution, and this included Protestants[38] and Catholics alike. His treatment of the Catholic Mary Queen of Scots was colored by his reading of *An Inquiry into the Proofs of the Charges Commonly Advanced against Mary Queen of Scotland*, after which he accepted that her innocence on all charges was proven.[39] He consequently came to revile Elizabeth I who, he believed, had ruled unjustly and denied individual liberty.[40] This tension of

---

30. *JWW*, 10:80–86. See also *A Short Method of converting all the Roman Catholics in the Kingdom of Ireland*, in *JWW*, 10:129–33.

31. John Wesley to John Newton, 9 April 1765, in *JWL*, 4:293.

32. Wesley saw Lopez (b 1542) as one who had an uninterrupted sense of the divine and assurance. Wesley first published this in his *Christian Library* but revised it for the *Arminian Magazine* omitting one chapter by accident.

33. Wesley published a "Protestantised" extract of De Renty's, life (358 pages abridged to 67) in 1741, with subsequent editions published in 1746, 1760, 1778, 1788, 1796 and 1802.

34. Eamon Duffy, "Wesley and the Counter-Reformation," in *Revival and Religion since 1700*, ed. C. Mathew and J. Garnett (London: Hambledon, 1993). See also "A Narrative on the Death of the Hon Fr N\_\_\_\_t, Son to the Late \_\_\_ \_\_\_" ("The Second Spira"), *AM*, 6:24ff.

35. *AM*, 3:249ff.

36. *AM*, 3:19ff. Born September 1606 in Bretany France. The account reveals perseverance and faith amid difficulties.

37. "Sometime Fellow of Magdalene College; burnt at a place called The Sand-Pitts, in Newbury, about the 16th Day of July 1556," *AM*, 4:481ff.

38. "An Instance of Disinterestedness" [Dean of Waterford persecuted under James II], *AM*, 9:669. "A Providential Escape of the Protestants in Ireland, from Queen Mary's Persecution," *AM*, 9:670.

39. See 11 May 1761, in *JWW*, 3:54; 5 May 1768, in *JWW*, 3:319; 6 November 1769, in *JWW*, 3:383; 24 May 1780, in *JWW*, 4:182; and 5 February 1786, in *JWW*, 4:326.

40. See 13 March 1747, in *JWW*, 2:49.

opposing sensitivity for the two women pervaded several articles in the *Magazine*.[41] He also included an account eulogizing the "sacred loyalty" of Flora MacDonald to the Young Pretender, since she helped him make his escape to Catholic France.[42]

However, in Wesley's mind Catholicism itself was a major threat to the security of England. Hynson refers to Wesley's mistrust of Roman Catholics as his "blind spot," but argues that to criticize him for this is anachronistic as it fails to take into consideration the social and political context of "the present moment."[43] John Bossy has shown that the years 1700 to 1770 were not a time of shrinkage of the Catholic faith amid the legal restraints of 1700,[44] but rather three quarters of a century of modest growth. In fact, there was around a thirty percent increase, and not within the rural gentry but in the urban lower and middling class. In 1767 a Parliament census of Catholics in England and Wales totaled 69,376. Bossy argues that due to underestimation and inaccuracies, the number was likely to be around 80,000.[45]

Eamon Duffy offers many reasons for this growth, including the availability of accessible instructional material, simplicity of mission, the emphasis on faith rather than reason, priests becoming independent itinerant instructors, the provision of medical help, lay charity, and a strong emphasis on conversion.[46] Educated Catholics also had their

---

41. "The Last Letter of Mary Queen of Scots, to Queen Elizabeth," *AM*, 9:557; "A very Particular Account of the Execution of Mary Queen of Scots: by an Eye-Witness," *AM*, 9:139; "Anecdote of Queen Elizabeth," *AM*, 13:46.

42. "An Account of the Escape of the Chevalier after the Battle of Cullodon," AM, 13:533ff.

43. Leon O. Hynson, "From Revolution to Revolution," *Methodist History* 43:4 (July 2005): 253.

44. William III's "Act for the Further Preventing the Growth of Popery" (1700) made Catholic worship and conversion illegal; forbade the education of Catholic children abroad; demanded an oath of allegiance; disqualified the buying of real estate and ordered the paying of twice the land tax as Protestants. However the Act was not enforced. Paul Richardson, "Serial Struggles, English Catholics and their Periodicals, 1648–1844" (PhD thesis, University of Durham, 2003), 50.

45. John Bossy, *The English Catholic Community 1570–1850* (London: Darton, Longman and Todd, 1975), 184–85. See also Eamon Duffy, "'Poor Protestant Flies' Conversions to Catholicism in Early Eighteenth Century England," *Studies in Church History* 15 (1978): 289ff; Richardson, "Serial Struggles," 2003.

46. Duffy, "'Poor Protestant Flies.'"

own periodicals from around 1722, printed in the vernacular from 1758 through to the end of the century.[47] There were obvious parallels with the Methodist movement, and as there was also successful proselytizing in all classes,[48] it was important to Wesley that his readers were made aware of the religious and political impact of such a faith upon their nation, and potentially these readers were via the *Arminian Magazine*.

Once the French became involved in America following the battle of Saratoga in 1777, Wesley's general concern became more focused, for he feared the Catholics with respect to revolution and hence took an openly anti-Catholic stance. Savile's Relief Act (1778) was designed to remove penalties upon Catholics imposed by Parliament in 1700.[49] In order for these to come into force, Catholics were required to take an oath to renounce the Pretender, the temporal jurisdiction of the Pope, and the doctrine implemented by the Council of Constance in 1411 that "no faith was to be kept with heretics." Wesley's difficulty, which led to use of the *Magazine* as his weapon of attack, was that in his eyes the oath was meaningless.[50]

The last two decades of the century highlighted the increasing use of written instruction as a weapon of persuasion regarding this topic, with Wesley and his opponents opting to reach the wider audience through the published tract and secular press as well as their religious magazines.[51] Wesley continued to repudiate Roman Catholicism by publishing *Popery Calmly Considered* in 1779,[52] and by going to the *Public Advertiser* in January 1780, to justify the principles of another nationwide tract (of which many believed he was the author), *An Appeal from the Protestant Association, to the People of Great Britain*. In this tract,

---

47. Richardson, "Serial Struggles," 53–55; John R. Fletcher, "Early Catholic Periodicals in England," *Dublin Review* 198 (1936): 284–310.

48. Duffy, "'Poor Protestant Flies,'" 304. Conversions were encouraged through marriage, employment and housing needs, educational opportunities and the proximity of the Mass in large Church of England parishes.

49. Conditions being to relax the persecution of priests and schoolmasters, to allow Catholics to buy and transfer land, but government and military offices, entry into Oxford and Cambridge, and the vote still eluded them.

50. "Anecdote of Arius," *AM*, 13:607.

51. Richardson, "Serious Struggles," 63.

52. *JWW*, 10:140–58. This was appreciated by the Calvinists, see Charles Wesley to John Wesley, 23 April 1779, *AM*, 12:387 (CCCCXCIX).

religious toleration was defended but the probability of Catholic loyalty to the government was refuted. Concern was also shown at the growing number of Catholics in the nation, Wesley noting with alarm, "and they are increasing daily."[53] Significantly, the Calvinistic *Gospel Magazine*, Wesley's hated competitor, printed his justification in its entirety in February 1780, following their own "History of the Inquisition."[54]

The media battle continued in the context of the Gordon Riots of June that year, when Father O'Leary, a Capuchin friar of Dublin, denigrated what he believed to be Wesley's fanatical and seditious stand in a series of six letters to the secular *Freeman's Journal*. Once Wesley was aware of this, he defended himself fiercely on two occasions but then desisted.[55] O'Leary subsequently published all six letters nationwide in one text. In December 1780, Wesley justified his stand again, and returned criticism of O'Leary by relating the whole yearlong debacle to the readers of the *Freeman's Journal*.

Wesley did not turn to his own *Magazine* in relation to this affair until May 1781 and with good reason. In March that year, *The Monthly Review* had printed a defense of O'Leary's criticism and in relation to Wesley had observed: "This *thrust* is well aimed; how the old *prize-fighter* will be able to parry the blow, we know not. He hath had long practice on the stage; and hath minded his hits as much as any man. Arrah! My dear honey, he may be too hard for you yet!"[56] This presumably motivated Wesley to turn to his *Magazine* to reach his members in order to ensure they had the correct information from which to make their judgements. He audaciously reprinted his January 1780 letter to the *Public Advertiser*,[57] followed six months later by his letter to the *Freeman's Journal*, together with his two letters of defense.[58] He also began a series of articles that repudiated central aspects of Catholicism and would have left the reader in no two minds regarding the issue.

---

53. *JWW*, 10:159–61.
54. *Gospel Magazine* (February 1780): 86.
55. The *Freeman's Journal* began in the 1750s and ceased publication in 1924 when it merged with the *Irish Independent Newspaper*. For Wesley's replies, see *JWW*, 10:162–73.
56. *Monthly Review* 64 (March 1781): 237.
57. *AM*, 4:239.
58. *AM*, 4:295.

In April 1782, "A Disavowal of Persecuting Papists"[59] defended his stand against Catholicism but opposed any form of physical persecution of individuals. "I would not hurt a hair of their head," he protested, but added, "I would not use the sword against them, nor put it into their hands, lest they should use it against me; I wish them well, but I dare not trust them."[60] As if to make his point, the *Magazine* became the vehicle in which he illustrated the persecution administered by the Catholic Church.[61] These examples followed exemplar accounts of the dedication and martyrdom of those who opposed the Catholic faith in the sixteenth century, printed in the February 1782 issue.[62] "Some Particulars concerning the Council of Constance Held November 1414" printed in the May 1785 issue illustrated the extravagance of the Catholic Church, whilst reminding the readership that this was the very Council which issued the infamous canon that Catholics should not mix with heretics.[63]

Wesley's use of his periodical in order to convince the readership of his views can be seen in correspondence to Peard Dickenson in April 1788: "I really think it will be proper to publish something in the *Magazine* on that idle Popish conceit of 'Consecrated Ground.'"[64] He did so in the October, describing the practice as "a mere relic of Romish Superstition."[65] He also condemned the "devil's subtlety" of image worshipping in the August 1789 issue.[66] The twin hatreds of absolute power and the Catholic Church were easily identifiable in the *Magazine* as late as November 1790, when an anecdote highlighted the arrogance of Louis XIV in the context of a teenager being persecuted at the hands

---

59. March 1782, *AM*, 5:197.
60. *JWW*, 10:173.
61. "An Account of the Massacre of Paris: translated from the French of M. Bossuet, Bishop of Paris" (1572), *AM*, 7:316ff.; "The History of the Inquisition," *AM*, 8:261; "Of the Inquisition," *AM*, 9:165ff.; "An Account of the Sufferings of Cyrillus Lucasis," *AM*, 13:537ff.
62. "Some Account of Mr. Patrick Hamilton" (burned at the stake 1527), *AM*, 5:93; "Some Account of Mr. Wishart" (who preached in the open air due to being denied the Catholic Churches, and who was martyred February 1546), *AM*, 5:95.
63. *AM*, 8:271.
64. *JWL*, 8:57.
65. "Thoughts on the Consecration of Churches and Burial Grounds," *AM*, 11:541.
66. "The Origin of Image-Worship among Christians," *AM*, 12:437.

of the Jesuits for placing his loyalty to Christ above that of the French monarchy.[67]

The call for personal liberty and rights in Enlightenment England heightened awareness of what was increasingly being seen as ineffective, unjust, and illogical penalties for criminal acts,[68] and this concern was mirrored in the *Magazine* through Wesley's selected inclusions. During the war with America, the situation had become more highlighted in that transportation had ceased, prison ships had been introduced, and the Penitentiary Act in 1779 regulated imprisonment.[69] In 1783, when peace came, the situation became intolerable, especially with the increased rise in crime caused by the lack of employment after the war, and the shifting population due to industrialization. The first convicts left Britain for Botany Bay in 1786, followed in 1788 by the establishment of the prison colony of New South Wales.

Wesley was well aware of inhuman prison conditions due to his lifelong commitment to the spiritual and material welfare of prisoners in Oxford and Newgate jails.[70] He raised the issue of penal reform at the 1778 conference and used the *Magazine* to highlight the situation and encourage the visiting of the condemned in spite of personal danger, criticism, and ridicule.[71] Wesley's underlying belief in penal reform stemmed from his Arminianism. All men had original sin; hence guilt for actions transcended age, sex, or class, and affected rich and poor; all had the choice of repentance and salvation, and all would stand at a much more important judgment day. Recognizing the universality of

---

67. "The Anecdote of Loewis the XIV," *AM*, 13:605.

68. Michael Ignatieff, *A Just Measure of Pain: The Penitentiary in the Industrial Revolution, 1750–1850* (London: Macmillan, 1978), 20.

69. The Act provided for the construction of two jails in the London area to house criminals who would have been transported in order to serve sentences up to two years. Prisoners were to have single cells, regular meals, and uniforms and be involved in hard labor.

70. See 19 September 1738, in *JWW*, 1:158; 8 November 1738, in *JWW*, 1:163; 6 February 1740, in *JWW*, 1:262; 11 January 1742 , in *JWW*, 1:351; 4 September 1742 , in *JWW*, 1:396; 10 July 1744, in *JWW*, 1:468; 20 November 1767, in *JWW*, 3:303; 8 November 1784, in *JWW*, 4:291; 26 December 1784, in *JWW*, 4:294; 23 December 1786, in *JWW*, 4:357.

71. (Charles Skelton), *AM*, 2:92; (Alexander Mather), *AM*, 3:153; (Silas Told) *AM*, 10:72ff; (Sarah Peters), *AM*, 11:67ff; (Joseph Pescod), *AM*, 11:70ff.

sin enabled him to accept the possibility of change within the prisoner. Wesley was in tune with the reformers like John Howard, who called for humanitarian treatment for all inmates, complained of the moral and physical state of the jails, the inequality and bias of the justice system, the length and complexity of trials, and the inhuman treatment of prisoners of war.[72]

Wesley did not use his periodical to attack politicians over penal reform, nor did he resort to the popular press, but rather gave accounts that encouraged the readers to raise their awareness, understanding, and concern about this important issue both at home and abroad. Aspects of the cause such as verified examples of corruption in the courts, imprisonment for religious observance, inhuman prison conditions and unjust executions enabled the readers to think outside of their normal daily routine to issues involving justice and fairness at a higher level. The readers could also catch a glimpse of Wesley's own method of evangelizing the condemned criminal and were able to read moving accounts of last-minute conversions.[73]

---

72. John Howard, *The State of the Prisons in England and Wales with Preliminary Observation, and an Account of Some Foreign Prisons Dated 5 April 1777* (Abingdon: Professional Books Ltd, 1977).

73. "An Address to Prisoners and Captives" (last minute conversions), *AM*, 4:213; "French Mercy Exemplified in the Case of Monsieur Isaac Lefevre" (religious observance), *AM*, 5:34; "in the Case of Mr. Peer Mauru" (religious observance), AM, 5:88; "A Most Remarkable Story" (inhuman prison conditions and executions), *AM*, 6:40; "A Discourse of God's Judgements" (providential justice), *AM*, 7:215ff.; "A Singular Instance of Justice in a Turkish Magistrate" (religious observance), *AM*, 7:662; "A remarkable Punishment for Murder" (providential justice), *AM*, 8:213; "Of Judge Jefferies, on the Trial of Mr. Richard Baxter, in the Court of King's-Bench" (religious observance), *AM*, 8:321; "An Uncommon Murder" (providential justice), *AM*, 9:278; "Murder Discovered" (religious observance), *AM*, 9:335; "An Account of the Behaviour of Three Malefactors, Who Were Executed at Reading, in Berkshire, on the 25th of March Last" (last minute conversion), *AM*, 9:428; "French Liberty: or an Account of the Prison of Bicetre in France, Extracted from a Series of Letters" (inhuman prison conditions and executions), *AM*, 9:448; "Some Account of the Life and Death of Thomas Ramsey Executed at Wexford Nov 20th 1784" (last-minute conversion), *AM*, 9:485; "A Letter from a Person Who Was an Eye-Witness of the Death of the Rev. M. Rochette, and the Three Noblemen Who Were Executed with Him at Thoulouse, the 19th of February 1762, for Professing the Protestant Religion" (religious observance), *AM*, 10:78; "An Anecdote of the Count de Lauzun" (inhuman conditions), *AM*, 11:29; Joseph Pescod (April 12; last-minute conversion), "An Account of John Wynn, who was executed at Bedford April 4 1785," AM, 11:69ff.; "The Punishment of Homicide" (inhuman conditions), *AM*, 11:270ff.; "On the Manners of the Times" (perjury), *AM*,

The *Magazine* was used by Wesley to highlight the reliability of the true justice of God in the face of so much human injustice.[74] Numerous examples were given, including a series of abridged anecdotes from "Mr. Reynold's book, entitled, '*God's Revenge against Murder and Adultery*,'"[75] which appeared from 1787 to 1788 over a twenty-month run. Six stories of intrigue, infidelity, and hateful conspiracies alternating from France, Italy, Spain, and Portugal stressed the certainty of divine justice over moral evil. Perjury, a crime of private judgment, was described as "at once a most daring insult upon the Omnisciency, Justice, and Mercy of Almighty God, and his government of the world; and a most shocking violation of the natural rights of mankind."[76]

Wesley commented upon issues relating to penal reform in the *Magazine* because of the injustice of the present system, and the possibility of individual repentance and change. He did not attack those responsible, but remained one step away by raising Methodist awareness of the facts, leaving the members to exercise individual judgment as to what responses could be made to improve the present situation. This was a practice he would not repeat when faced with another injustice, that of slavery.

It was not until 1807 that Parliament abolished the slave trade in the British Empire. Wesley's editorship of the *Magazine* coincided with an increased enlightened, humanitarian awareness and concern about the practice with which England was profitably involved. Margaret T. Hogden has argued that in the eighteenth century, two contrasting views were held with regard to primitive man; one derived from the sixteenth century held that civilization itself was corrupt, hence primitive races were idolized as the "noble savage." The alternative view was that primitive man was associated with all that was unimprovable and degenerate. Hodgen argues that Wesley's writings suggest that he

---

12:496; "An Remarkable Account of a Murder, for which an Innocent Man Was Nearly Condemned upon Circumstances" (religious observance), *AM*, 14:42ff.

74. Malcolm Gaskill, "The Displacement of Providence: Policing and Prosecution in Seventeenth- and Eighteenth-century England," *Continuity and Change* 2 (1996): 341–74.

75. *AM* 10: 266ff.

76. "Remarks on the Nature and Design of an Oath (By Dr. S),"*AM*, 4:211. See also "On the Manners of the Times," *AM*, 12:496.

regarded primitive man within the latter view[77] and if this is correct, she argues that Wesley must have suppressed his views in the context of slavery so that "African culture was presented as on a parity with that of civilised man."[78] Conversely, T. W. Madison notes that Wesley's attitude to the Negro was based not only in theological and ethical tenets encompassing universal salvation and Christian love, but through an anthropological perspective, which enabled him to see Negroes as intelligent, honest human beings corrupted by social influences, refuting the idea that Europeans were civilizing them through slavery.[79]

Wesley's strength of feeling toward the individual Negro and the practice of slavery is not something that can be categorized so conveniently, neither was it a knee-jerk reaction to contemporary developments, but was born out of reason and experience. He had spent time in Georgia (1736–37) where slavery was illegal until 1751, and although sheltered from any dealings with the slave trade he was influenced by such works as Godwin Morgan's *The Negro's Advocate* (1680).[80] His *Journal* is evidence of the openness in his dealings with black slaves in South Carolina, where he not only included them in his ministry but in education, leading him to declare on his return to England on 3 February 1738: "A few steps have been taken towards publishing the glad tidings to the African and the American Heathen."[81] Back in England, his concern continued via correspondence, evangelism, baptism, and by practical aid, such as the collection for Indian schools in Georgia.[82]

---

77. Margaret. T. Hogden, "The Negro in the Anthropology of John Wesley," *Journal of Negro History* 19 (1934): 308–23 at 308.

78. Ibid., 321.

79. T. W. Madison, "John Wesley on Race: A Christian View of Equality," *Methodist History* 2 (1964): 24–34.

80. Godwin Morgan, Church of England minister, served in both Virginia and Barbados, and called for the religious education of African slaves. His first text was entitled *Negro's and Indian's Advocate*. This was followed in 1681 by his *Proposals for the Carrying on the Negro's Christianity*.

81. *JWW*, 1:84. See also 31 July and 2 August 1736, in *JWW*, 1:40; 23 November 1736, in *JWW*, 1:42; 23 April 1737, in *JWW*, 1:48; 27 April 1737, in *JWW*, 1:49; 2 December 1737, in *JWW*, 1:61; 26 December 1737, in *JWW*, 1:70 and 7 January 1738, in *JWW*, 1:72.

82. 1 March 1756, in *JWW*, 2:354; 28 January 1757, in *JWW*, 2:391; 17 January 1758, in *JWW*, 2:433; 29 November 1758, in *JWW*, 2:464; and 8 August 1767, in *JWW*, 3:294.

In May 1772 Anthony Benezet wrote to Granville Sharp, "My friend John Westly promises he will consult with thee about the expediency of some weekly publication, in the newspapers on the origin, nature, and dreadful effects of the slave trade."[83] In August that year Wesley read Benezet's *Historical Account of Guinea*, through which he obtained factual evidence of "that execrable sum of all villainies, commonly called the Slave Trade,"[84] and it was that which encouraged him to enter the debate publicly between 1774 and 1776.

There is no political comment in Wesley's *Journal* regarding the practice of slavery during the final decade of his life and very little concerning individual Negroes, although evidence suggests that some Methodist societies were racially integrated as early as 1780.[85] There were also hopeful signs among American Methodism where in 1780 the first Conference proclaimed its opposition to the practice and in 1784 required all Methodists to abandon connections with the slave trade and to free all slaves in their possession. In England, however, although public opinion was increasingly hostile, the final decade of Wesley's life was characterized by an increase in the practice of "trading in man."[86]

During these final years, the *Arminian Magazine* transmitted Wesley's instruction regarding the issue. These instructions included the example of Charles Wesley, together with ordinary members of the Bristol society playing their part in educating and supporting individual slaves and an illustration of providential protection for slaves during a sea voyage. He also included a popular legend of adventure, romance, desertion, and humiliation, which illustrated the callousness and inhumanity of the practice, and vibrant correspondence between those involved within America, which condemned such conduct.[87]

---

83. Brycchan Carey, "John Wesley's Thoughts upon Slavery and the Language of the Heart," *Bulletin of the John Rylands University Library of Manchester* 85, nos. 2–3 (2003):274.

84. *An Historical Account of Guinea Situation, Produce, and the General Disposition of Its Inhabitants, with an Enquiry into the Rise and Progress of the Slave Trade, Its Nature and Calamitous Effect*, 12 February 1772, in *JWW*, 3:453.

85. 8 May 1780, in *JWW*, 4:180; 5 March 1786, in *JWW*, 4:327.

86. *AM* 6:98ff. See details in Nicholas Hudson, "'Britons Never Will be Slaves': National Myth, Conservatism, and the Beginnings of British Antislavery," *Eighteenth Century Studies* 34 (2001): 560–76.

87. "An Extract from the Depositions of William Floyd, of the City of Bristol, Mariner, and Little Ephraim Robin-John, and Ancona Robin Robin-John, of Old Town, Old

One account given to the readers, which described how a white seafarer had been protected from violence at the hands of Negroes whose relations had been transported, deserves further analysis. The remarks of the protector, who was a Negro himself, were undoubtedly said ahead of their time and must surely have caused the early Methodists to think deeply not only about the intolerance and injustice of the slave trade but prejudice in general. "You must not kill a man that has done no harm, only for being white," the assailants were told. "This man is my friend: my house is his fort: I am his soldier, and must fight for him; you must kill me before you can kill him."[88]

Benezet's hope that Wesley would engage himself in media coverage of the plight of the slaves came to fruition through the *Magazine*. Wesley included his friend's correspondence from May 1774 in the January 1787 issue. The correspondence contained his own *Thoughts on Slavery*, which Benezet praised. In his letter, Benezet also criticized the Virginian legal system, and emotionally described the plight of slaves.[89] By forwarding Benezet's letter, Wesley was not only sharing valuable information throughout the movement but personalizing the cause of abolition.

Another personalization of the cause concerned the case of James Somerset, a runaway slave. It was not uncommon for domestic slaves to take advantage of a visit to England and escape from their masters. They were subsequently baptized and, having godparents, believed themselves to be free. This had been denied in a legal judgment of 1729 but forty years later Granville Sharp published a refutation of the ruling.[90]

James Somerset was the property of Charles Stewart, a customs officer from the then British Colony of Boston, Massachusetts. He had been brought to England in 1769 but escaped in 1771. Once recaptured

---

Calabar, on the Coast of Africa," *AM*, 6:98ff.; "To_____, from an English Merchant, Giving an Account of the Adventures of His Voyage," *AM*, 8:411; "The History of Inkle and Yarico," *AM*, 8:588; "An Extract from a Letter from a Person in Maryland to His Friend in Philadelphia," *AM*, 8:648.

88. "An Account of an African Negro; Taken from Capt. Seagrove's Journal of His Voyage to Guinea," *AM*, 7:45

89. *AM*, 10:44 (CCCCXII).

90. *A Representation of the Injustice and Dangerous Tendency of Admitting the Least Claim of Private Property in the Persons of Men, in England, etc.* (1769).

he was imprisoned on a ship bound for another British colony, Jamaica, but Sharp intervened and demanded that he be brought before the Lord Chief Justice for a definitive ruling. The case was first called on 24 January 1772 but was adjourned until the following month. During the adjournment Somerset's cause was adopted by many as evidenced by the raising of donations for his legal representation, which resulted in a discharge on 22 June 1772.

Wesley gave a full account of this case, giving all the detailed arguments of the defense and prosecution in the August and September 1787 issues of the *Arminian Magazine*.[91] He also recorded the judgment of James Somerset with the following comment: "[The above is inserted, for the information of those whom it may concern—for the satisfaction of all who are friends to the liberties of mankind—and for the credit of the laws of this most favoured country]."[92] The timing of these insertions, which were now fifteen years out of date, was not coincidental and initiated a concerted effort from Wesley to highlight the situation in the coming year.

The decision of 1772 gave an impetus to the antislavery cause, it being estimated that over fourteen thousand slaves then in England were affected by the ruling.[93] By the summer of 1787, the "Committee for the Abolition of the Slave Trade" came into being with Sharp as its chairman and William Wilberforce its spokesperson in Parliament, encouraged by William Pitt, the Prime Minister. It is not surprising that this was the very time Wesley wished to revitalize interest in his Methodist body concerning the Somerset case. Wesley totally supported the Committee, writing on 27 August and 30 October to offer encouragement against what he saw as inevitable opposition from those involved in the trade.[94]

In April 1788 the *Magazine* brought the issue home to the readership through describing the commitment to the cause by one strongly Methodist area, Manchester. Previous accounts of the Manchester societies, written in early 1783, had appeared in the *Magazine* in

---

91. *AM*, 10:437ff.
92. *AM*, 10:545.
93. Warner, *William Wilberforce*, 43.
94. John Wesley to Thomas Clarkson, August 1787, *JWL*, 8:6; John Wesley to Granville Sharp, 11 October 1787, *JWL*, 8:16.

December 1786 and had recorded instances of wild enthusiasm.[95] The April 1788 edition balanced these accounts by stressing reason and accountability. It recorded a resolution that was specially convened to abolish trading in slaves because it infringed the principles of "liberty, justice, and humanity." Although the Methodist society recognized just how economically significant the trade was to the area, it viewed the practice as "highly impolitic as well as inhuman." The Manchester members decided to attract the attention of Parliament through petitions; hence a resolution, which was reprinted in the *Arminian Magazine*, requested that a circular letter on behalf of the meeting be sent to the mayor or other chief magistrate of every principal town throughout Great Britain. The resolution also expressed the need to "extend information on this important subject to every part of *Europe*." In conclusion, the resolution offered a motion of thanks for the Abolition Committee, which received one hundred guineas from them to continue their work.[96]

Why Wesley included the Manchester resolution in his *Magazine* was clear. It was a practical example of action against an evil practice and, as such, he probably hoped for imitation from elsewhere. It also balanced claims of enthusiasm and held individual members accountable, revealing the potential held within a collective body. In the May issue, Wesley included the above-mentioned circular letter in its entirety,[97] and by so doing he encouraged the whole of the movement to take individual if not collective action against the practice.

In July and August, as if to encourage them further, the readership received a shocking, anonymous account entitled "A summary view of the Slave Trade,"[98] in which the reality of the practice was highlighted with appalling clarity in facts and figures. The second installment printed in August turned the attention to the dreadful condition of

---

95. *AM*, 9:666.
96. "Resolutions of the Society for the Purpose of Effecting the Abolition of the Slave Trade Composed Dec 29$^{th}$ 1787," *AM*, 11:208.
97. "On the Slave Trade. To \_\_\_\_\_" dated 1 January 1788, *AM*, 11:263.
98. *AM*, 11:379ff.

existing slaves and toward the hope that "a foundation will be laid for a general emancipation at last and for a conversion to Christianity."[99]

Via the correspondence in the *Magazine*, the readers received educative information regarding the slavery question during the remainder of the editorship. The letters from America and Antigua were sources of valuable information regarding not only the missionaries, but the physical, spiritual, and political development of the Negroes, "a people," wrote Jonathan Bryan from New York in 1772, "born as free as ourselves, and whose minds are as capable of improvement as our own; yet are kept in worse than Egyptian bondage."[100] The correspondence, although dated, kept the issue of slavery alive while enveloping national developments.

On 12 May 1789 Wilberforce spoke for three and a half hours in the Parliamentary debate on the slave trade, appealing not to passions but to reason. "Sir, the nature and all the circumstances of the Trade are now laid open to us. We can no longer plead ignorance. We cannot evade it. We may spurn it. We may kick it out of the way. But we cannot turn aside so as to avoid seeing it."[101] By the use of his *Magazine*, Wesley made sure that the membership did not turn a blind eye but saw the evil and consequences of the practice and hopefully would also take action to eradicate it. Personal details of fellow Methodists would have helped them to do this.

In August 1789 a letter from John Baxter, dated 10 June 1779, described not only the inhuman conditions facing the Negroes in Antigua but their determination to follow the Christian faith. They were, Baxter claimed, "exposed to want, even of water to drink, and have nothing allowed them to eat but a pint of horse-beans a day!" However, despite this, he optimistically continued, "I hope their extremity is

---

99. *AM*, 11:440.
100. Jonathan Bryan, New York to John Wesley, 1 April 1772, *AM*, 8:167 (CCCLXII); Mr. Francis Gilbert, Antigua to John Wesley, 18 June 1763, *AM*, 5:384 (CCXLVI); Richard Boardman, New-York to John Wesley, 4 November 1769, *AM*, 7:163 (CCCXXIII); Richard Boardman to John Wesley, 2 April 1771, *AM*, 8:113 (CCCLVI); Anthony Benezet, Philadelphia to John Wesley 23 May 1774, *AM*, 10:44 (CCCCXII).
101. Gareth Lean, *God's Politician: William Wilberforce's Struggle* (London: Darton, Longman & Todd, 1980), 50.

God's opportunity; for they seem ripe for the gospel. Six hundred of them have joined our society."[102] In June 1790 a variety of accounts in the *Magazine* raised the profile of the issue within Methodism. An American source noted the numeracy skills of a slave who was "a native of Africa, and can neither read nor write." What is significant is that the correspondent proudly continued, "The slave is the property of Mrs. Coxe. His name is Thomas Fuller," giving the individual the respect he deserved as a named man, not as a slave.[103] In August, Baxter again reported optimistic news. "There is a great outward reformation among the Negroes, and a desire to be thought religious." As if to substantiate his claim, he further announced that "near thirty coloured persons ... receive the Lord's Supper, and their number increases."[104]

As if to give balance to the argument, Wesley had, just two months earlier, included a moving testimony of a Methodist Negro in Antigua, which revealed his plight as head of a Christian family in slavery.[105] Methodism offered such slaves a sense of community and an extended kin, and as such, the account would have brought the issue right into Methodist homes back in England. It bore out the message of *On the Slave Trade*, a poem written by an anonymous slave and included in the *Magazine* in September 1790. The poem reminded the reader that, although the abuse of the human body was possible, the mind and more importantly the soul were still free.

> Still in thought as free as ever,
> What are *England's* rights, I ask,
> Me from my delights to sever,
> Me to torture, me to task?[106]

William Wilberforce first proposed legislation in 1791. Wesley wrote what was to be his last letter to benefit the cause on the 26 February, just four days before his death, and in which he remarked that on that very

---

102. *AM*, 12:439 (CCCCCI).
103. "An Account of an Extraordinary Negro Slave, in Maryland: by Dr Rush, of Philadelphia," *AM*, 13:156.
104. Mr. John Baxter, Antigua to John Wesley, 10 June 1782, *AM*, 13:439 (DXXXVIII).
105. "The Experience of Samuel Paynter, a Negroe of Antigua," *AM*, 13:307.
106. "On the Slave Trade," *AM*, 13:502.

morning he had been shocked by reading about the "villany" of the practice, as reported in "a tract, wrote by a poor African."[107]

Ultimately, via the *Arminian Magazine* John Wesley was able to enlighten his readers and raise the intellectual, ideological, and emotional horizons of the early Methodists, especially on issues that they did not need to be involved with on a daily basis. Many of the issues he brought to their attention were carried on behind closed doors, thriving on the ignorance of ordinary men. The first readers of the *Magazine* might never experience government office and would rarely go to war or see the shores of America, Antigua, or Rome. They might never be intimate friends with Catholics, never experience the injustice of a foreign jail, or the conditions of capture, torture, confinement, and humiliation of a slave. However, they could become increasingly "enlightened," sensitive, and informed through the deliberation of informative, thought-provoking commentaries and personal accounts.

In the pages of the *Arminian Magazine* lay the seeds of that spirit of Methodism that transported the political conscience of the movement into the nineteenth century. This spirit, energized through individual assurance and the quest for sanctification, together with an overriding belief in universal salvation, was bolstered by contemporary enlightened thought. Such energy would be seen clearly in the missionary zeal of the movement in generations to come. In an age of increasing literacy the Wesleyan words and choice of material had informed, guided, and encouraged the movement to be politically knowledgeable and accountable, to see beyond the Methodists' own individual world and as such would, in time, make Methodism a force to be reckoned with in the realms of political life. John Wesley would not be accompanying them on this particular journey, but his conviction that individuals held the potential to improve their own "present moment" would inevitably be realized.

---

107. *JWW*, 13:127.

# Allegiance, Sympathy, and History: The Catholic Loyalties of Alexander Pope

Steven Stryer

King Charles the Second was too much a Libertine, and too much an Encourager of Wit for him; King William the Third was too much a Socinian. But tho' he has without Mercy condemn'd the Reigns of the foremention'd Monarchs, he is graciously pleas'd to pass over in silence that which comes between them.... We find what that is which so happily reconcil'd him to it, and that was the Dispensing Pow'r, which was set on foot in order to introduce and to establish Popery, and to make it the National Religion. Now I humbly conceive that he who Libels our Confederates, must be by Politicks a Jacobite; and he who Libels all the Protestant Kings that we have had in this Island these threescore Years, and who justifies the Dispensing Pow'r so long after we are freed from it . . . must, I humbly conceive, derive his Religion from St. Omer's, as he seems to have done his Humanity and his Criticism; and is, I suppose, politickly setting up for Poet-Laureat against the coming over of the Pretender.

—John Dennis, *Reflections Critical and Satyrical, Upon A Late Rhapsody, Call'd, An Essay Upon Criticism* (1711)[1]

---

1. J. V. Guerinot, *Pamphlet Attacks on Alexander Pope, 1711–1744: A Descriptive Bibliography* (London: Methuen, 1969), 3–4.

The charges leveled by John Dennis against the young author of *An Essay on Criticism* are characteristically hyperbolic: Alexander Pope is disparaged as a historical partisan whose loyalties (to the Catholics James II and his son the Pretender) and antipathies (to the Protestants Charles II and William III) are determined entirely by his allegiance to the Church of Rome. Dennis claims that in comparing the classical writers to absolute monarchs,[2] Pope had hinted his approval of James's suspension of the operation of the penal laws against Catholics in defiance of Parliament—in contrast with his explicit rejection later in the poem of the libertinism of Charles's reign[3] and of the Whiggish political doctrines and Protestant religious heterodoxies under William's rule.[4] As we shall see, Pope's view of the seventeenth-century past is more nuanced than Dennis's remarks would suggest. Yet these comments, however exaggerated, do underscore a series of associations crucial to the poet's work, linking Pope's steadfast loyalty to the persecuted English Catholic minority to which he belonged with his allegedly Jacobite political sympathies and his judgments on English history.

Dennis draws together the accusations of political and religious disloyalty through his reference to the evasion of the penal laws by English Catholic families who sent their children over to France to be educated at the Jesuit College of St. Omer; there they came under the protection of the same absolutist French monarchy that had sheltered and supported the exiled Stuarts ever since their flight from England in 1688. The association of Catholicism with treason and tyranny evoked here was one that Pope's political enemies within the Walpole ministry would repeatedly draw upon in the decades to come. For instance, in

---

2. "But tho' the Ancients thus their Rules invade, / (As Kings dispense with Laws Themselves have made)" (lines 161–62). All references to Pope's poems in the text are drawn from the standard one-volume Twickenham edition, John Butt, ed., *The Poems of Alexander Pope* (London: Methuen, 1963).

3. "In the fat Age of Pleasure, Wealth, and Ease, / Sprung the rank Weed, and thriv'd with large Increase; / When Love was all an easie Monarch's Care; / Seldom at Council, never in a War" (lines 534–37).

4. "The following Licence of a Foreign Reign / Did all the Dregs of bold Socinus drain; / Then Unbelieving Priests reform'd the Nation, / And taught more Pleasant Methods of Salvation; / Where Heav'ns Free Subjects might their Rights dispute, / Lest God himself shou'd seem too Absolute" (lines 544–49).

1733 one anonymous, pro-government pamphleteer charged that under the leadership of Pope's friend and mentor Bolingbroke, the Opposition was "doing the JACOBITES dirty Work for them; and not only raising the Hopes, but encreasing the Number of Votaries among us to Popery, and a Popish Pretender . . . in this malignant Opposition to our happy protestant Government," while seeking to foment discontent with the Walpole administration, "which the Papists always view'd with terror; as the Nation's Security, and the great Bulwark against all their Attempts in favour of the Pretender."[5] The defeat of the Protestant succession, the pamphlet warned, would result in the subjugation of "a numerous, powerful People, to the illegal, arbitrary Sway of a bigoted Tyrant."[6]

Pope was constantly shadowed by such charges about the subversive spiritual, political, and historical loyalties of English Catholics. In order to refute them, he staked his own claim to a faith defined instead by wide human sympathies; this faith manifested itself not in theological controversy but in acts of practical charity toward all fellow Christians.[7] The clearest statement of this religious position occurs within Pope's November 1717 letter to his friend Francis Atterbury, the Anglican Bishop of Rochester, who had sought to convert Pope to the Church of England following his father's death. In the course of rejecting the proposal, Pope explained that at the age of fourteen, he had read

> a collection of all that had been written on both sides in the reign of King James the second: I warm'd my head with them, and the consequence was, that I found my self a Papist and a Protestant by turns, according to the last book I read. I am afraid most Seekers are in the same case, and when they stop, they are not so properly converted, as out-witted. You see how little glory you would gain by my conversion. And after all, I verily believe your Lordship and I are both of the same religion,

---

5. *The Conduct of the Ministry Compared with its Consequences: or an Impartial View of the Present State of Affairs* (London, 1733), 47, 48.

6. Ibid., 22.

7. For Pope's adoption of the medieval Catholic belief in the divinely ordained dispensing of riches by the wealthy to the poor, see Katherine Quinsey, "Satire, and Providence, and Pope," in *Sublimer Aspects: Interfaces Between Literature, Aesthetics, and Theology*, ed. Natasha Duquette (Newcastle: Cambridge Scholars Publishing, 2007), 20–39.

if we were thoroughly understood by one another; and that all honest and reasonable christians would be so, if they did but talk enough together every day; and had nothing to do together, but to serve God and live in peace with their neighbour.[8]

Even as he insists on his loyalty to the faith of his birth, the sympathies that Pope professes here are not narrowly sectarian, but broadly human in their openness toward "all honest and reasonable christians." Throughout his life Pope remained true to this ideal, repeatedly shifting attention away from doctrinal disagreements toward an ethos of practical virtue, which he believed ought to unify people of all faiths. As he wrote to Henry Brooke two decades later, on 1 December 1739, "I sincerely worship God, believe in his revelations, resign to his dispensations, love all his creatures, am in charity with all denominations of Christians, however violently they treat each other. . . . I hate no sect, but I hate uncharitableness in any sect."[9] Pope's parenthetical reference in *An Essay on Criticism* to the constricting prejudices through which "Wit, like Faith, by each Man is apply'd / To one small Sect, and All are damn'd beside" drew the criticism of his fellow Catholics,[10] yet he persisted in this view, urging in Epistle III of *An Essay on Man* (1733–34), "For Modes of Faith, let graceless zealots fight; / His can't be wrong whose life is in the right: / In Faith and Hope the world will disagree, / But all Mankind's concern is Charity: / All must be false that thwart this One great End, / And all of God, that bless Mankind or mend."[11] In addition to upholding the value of tolerance, Pope repeatedly condemned all instances of its violation, observing to Joseph Spence that "There never was anything so wicked as the Holy Wars" and lamenting to his fellow Catholic John Caryll that "This miserable age is so sunk between animosities of party and those of religion, that I begin

---

8. George Sherburn, ed., *The Correspondence of Alexander Pope*, 5 vols. (Oxford: Clarendon Press, 1956), 1:453–54. For Pope's familiarity with the debates between Catholics and Protestants in James II's reign, see also Joseph Spence, *Observations, Anecdotes, and Characters of Books and Men Collected from Conversation*, ed. James M. Osborn, 2 vols. (Oxford: Clarendon Press, 1966), 1:204.
9. Sherburn, *Correspondence*, 4:207.
10. Lines 396–97. For the criticism, see Sherburn, *Correspondence*, 1:118, 126–27.
11. Lines 305–10.

to fear most men have ... faith enough to hinder their salvation."[12] As he declared to Sir William Trumbull in the midst of the Jacobite rising of 1715, "Quiet in the state ... like charity in religion, is too much the perfection and happiness of either, to be broken or violated on any pretence or prospect whatsoever: Fire and sword, and fire and faggot are equally my aversion. I can pray for opposite parties, and for opposite religions, with great sincerity."[13]

The expression of such broad-minded and peaceful sentiments was, of course, prudent given the always tenuous legal position of English Catholics; but in Pope's case they appear to have reflected not merely a genuine dislike of zealotry but a resistance to doctrinal orthodoxy of any sort. He remarked to Spence shortly before his death that his projected "ethic work in four books" would have included one book devoted to "government, both ecclesiastical and civil—and this was what chiefly stopped my going on. I could not have said what I *would* have said without provoking every church on the face of the earth, and I did not care for living always in boiling water."[14] The content of one completed section of this work, the *Essay on Man*, has led many readers, both in his own day and in ours, to suspect Pope of inclining by the 1730s toward a Bolingbroke-inspired deism rather than the ecumenical Christianity that he professed.[15] Whatever the truth of such claims, as Thomas Woodman has demonstrated through a careful reading of the textual evidence, Pope "not only espoused the very broadest definition of his religion but also ... was 'lapsed' or at least lax as far as its practice went."[16] Moreover, the poet readily joked about Catholic practices and beliefs in his correspondence with both Protestants and fellow Catholics,

---

12. Spence, *Observations*, 1:242; Sherburn, *Correspondence*, 1:220.

13. Sherburn, *Correspondence*, 1:324.

14. Spence, *Observations*, 1:134.

15. On the fraught relationship between Pope's supposed deism, his Christian beliefs, and his Catholic identity, see Brean S. Hammond, *Pope and Bolingbroke: A Study of Friendship and Influence* (Columbia: University of Missouri Press, 1984), 105–6, 113–14, 175; Brian Young, "Pope and Ideology," in *The Cambridge Companion to Alexander Pope*, ed. Pat Rogers (Cambridge: Cambridge University Press, 2007), 118–33; and G. Douglas Atkins, "Pope and Deism: A New Analysis," *Huntington Library Quarterly* 35 (1972): 257–78.

16. Thomas Woodman, "Pope: the Papist and the Poet," *Essays in Criticism* 46 (1996): 224.

as when he pleaded to Lady Mary Wortley Montagu in October 1716 that "Unless you write to me, my wishes must be but like a poor Papists Devotions to seperate Spirits; who, for all they know or hear from them, either may or may not be sensible of their Addresses," or when he wrote teasingly to his coreligionists Teresa and Martha Blount on 1 August 1715, "Ladies,—It having been the practise of good Catholiques in times of Persecution, to fly to the Protection of the Virgin Mary, and I not being very well acquainted with her, am obliged in the same circumstance to apply to the most heav'nly Virgins I know."[17]

Beneath Pope's humorous gallantry here lies a more serious desire to differentiate his own character as "an unbigoted Roman Catholic"[18] from the specter of Roman Catholicism that haunted English Protestant imaginations: the church as a persecuting force, as exemplified historically in the Spanish Inquisition, the reign of "Bloody" Mary, and, more recently, Louis XIV's revocation of the Edict of Nantes. Pope's awareness of these looming historical precedents can be sensed beneath his reaction to the intensified enforcement of the anti-Catholic penal laws following Queen Anne's death in August 1714, when the situation was inverted, with the English government now in the role of the persecutor and Pope himself among the persecuted. Writing to Caryll, he declared that "if all Roman Catholics had ever had" the humane spirit of his friend, "it had been well for all others; and we had never been charged with so wicked a spirit as that of persecution"; and he expressed the hope "that our own people may live as quietly as we shall certainly let theirs, that is to say, that want of power itself in us may not be a surer prevention of harm, than want of will in them." He then went on to carefully distinguish the religious community to which he belonged from the Catholic Church in its more menacing aspect on the Continent: "It is indeed very unjust to judge of us in this nation by what other members of our communion have done abroad. Our Church Triumphant there is very different from our Church Militant here (if I may call that a Church Militant which is every way disarmed)."[19] Similarly, when fellow Catholics complained about his attacks on the medieval

---
17. Sherburn, *Correspondence*, 1:363, 310–11.
18. Ibid., 1:151.
19. Ibid., 1:241.

church in *An Essay on Criticism*, his response was to insist that the "bigotries" and "superstition" of "some ages after the subversion of the Roman Empire ... is too manifest a truth to be denied, and does in no sort reflect upon the present Catholics, who are free from it."[20] It was the Catholic inhabitants of the besieged city of Barcelona, not their English coreligionists, whose expectation of receiving "Angels from heaven to their assistance" provoked Pope's scorn in a letter to Edward Blount on 27 August 1714: "May I venture to say, who am a *Papist*, and to say to you who are a *Papist*, that nothing is more astonishing to me, than that people so greatly warm'd with a sense of Liberty, should be capable of harbouring such weak Superstition, and that so much bravery and so much folly, can inhabit the same breasts?"[21]

In remarks such as these, we can hear Pope's strenuous efforts both to articulate a principled basis for his own faith and to disavow the darker impulses of persecution and superstition which his countrymen associated with it. His verbal maneuvering on this subject confused many of his readers, as he playfully acknowledged in a letter to Martha Blount: "Every one values Mr. Pope, but every one for a different reason. One for his firm adherence to the Catholic Faith, another for his Neglect of Popish Superstition."[22] However, his impulse here is in fact one not of self-contradiction but of balance, as he seeks to reconcile loyalty to his church with commitment to his own values of moderation and tolerance. Taken as a group, his statements on his faith enact this search for balance, with one statement qualifying another and laying out the limits within which the first continues to hold true: he can both declare himself (to Louis Racine) ready to submit "all my Opinions to the Decision of the [Catholic] Church" and describe himself (to Atterbury) as "not a Papist, for I renounce the temporal invasions of the Papal power, and detest their arrogated authority over Princes, and States"; just as he can both promise his fellow Catholic Caryll that "in regard to the determinations of the [Catholic] Church ... I shall prove a submissive disciple" and avow to Swift that he is "as sincere a well-wisher ... to

---

20. Ibid., 1:127.
21. Ibid., 1:246–47.
22. Ibid., 1:269.

the [Anglican] church establish'd, as any minister in, or out of employment, whatever; or any Bishop of England or Ireland."[23]

But what then was the motive for such "firm adherence to the Catholic Faith," coexisting as it did alongside not merely "Neglect of Popish Superstition," but firm disavowal of (or at least indifference to) so much of Catholic doctrine and practice? Certainly Pope does not appear to have believed that his salvation depended upon remaining steadfast in the faith: Spence reports that when a Catholic friend asked him on his deathbed "whether he would not die as his father and mother had done, and whether he should send for a priest," he replied, "I do not suppose that is essential, but it will be right, and I heartily thank you for putting me in mind of it."[24] And more worldly concerns would only have pushed him away from the church—as Pope observed in response to Atterbury's attempt to convert him, "As to the *temporal* side of the question. . . . It is certain, all the beneficial circumstances of life, and all the shining ones, lie on the part you would invite me to."[25] The anti-Catholic penal laws had been accumulating steadily since the reign of Elizabeth and expanded during Pope's lifetime in response to the Glorious Revolution and the Jacobite invasion of 1715, along with Jacobite conspiracies in 1716, 1719, and 1722. By these laws he was denied a university education, forced to pay punitive taxes, barred from entering the professions or holding government office, forbidden from keeping arms or purchasing or inheriting land, required to live at ten miles' distance from London, and, after the Jacobite rebellion of 1715, compelled to give up his horse. Anticipation of a second Jacobite rising in 1745 appears even to have kept him from seeking medical attention in London during his last illness.[26] While the Catholic disabilities were

---

23. Ibid., 4:416; 1:454, 128; 3:81.
24. Spence, *Observations*, 1:268.
25. Sherburn, *Correspondence*, 1:454.
26. For detailed accounts of the development of the penal laws, their effects on Pope, and his reactions to them, see John M. Aden, *Pope's Once and Future Kings: Satire and Politics in the Early Career* (Knoxville: University of Tennessee Press, 1978), 3–33; and Paul Gabriner, "The Papist's House, the Papist's Horse: Alexander Pope and the Removal from Binfield," in *Centennial Hauntings: Pope, Byron and Eliot in the Year 88*, eds. C. C. Barfoot and Theo D'haen (Amsterdam: Rodopi, 1990), 13–63. I have drawn on both for my own summary here.

not always enforced, the persistent threat of their enforcement loomed over Pope, and throughout his poems and letters he voiced his resentment of these persecutions. Calling himself "a Slave among a nation of free men," he confessed bitterly to Lady Mary Wortley Montagu: "I can never think that Place my Country, where I can't call a foot of paternal Earth my owne."[27] He also frequently indicated his keen awareness of the verbal attacks such as Dennis's to which his faith left him open, writing to Caryll on 1 May 1714 that "I have also encountered much malignity on the score of religion," and to Swift on 20 June 1716, "I suffer for my Religion in almost every weekly paper."[28]

And yet despite all these disadvantages—and despite his lack of specific attachment to the doctrines of his church—Pope steadfastly refused the appeals to convert that came not only from Atterbury, but from two other Anglican clergymen and close friends, Swift and Warburton. Pope jocularly turned aside the former's "Proposal of giving me twenty Guineas to change my Religion," and, according to Spence, refused the latter's entreaties to "conform with the religion of your country" despite his acknowledgment that "The persecution allowed and encouraged so much by the Church of Rome . . . looked like the sign of a false church."[29] The reasons that Pope cited for rejecting each of these appeals do little to clarify his true motivations: to Swift he responded with an extended joke starting from the premise that "it will be better worth my while to propose a Change of my Faith by Subscription, than a Translation of Homer," while he told Warburton "there was but two reasons that kept him from it: one, that the doing so would make himself a great many enemies, and the other that it would do nobody else any good."[30] This last statement seems less a forthright explanation than a polite deflection, in which Pope characteristically shifts the grounds of discussion from questions of theology to those of the conduct of life. But his response to Atterbury's effort is more revealing, and leads us into the crucial connection between Pope's faith and his attitude to the past, both personal and national. For in order to explain

---

27. Sherburn, *Correspondence*, 1:384–85.
28. Ibid., 1:220, 342.
29. Ibid., 1:199; Spence, *Observations*, 1:156.
30. Sherburn, *Correspondence*, 1:199; Spence, *Observations*, 1:156.

his reasons for staying true to the religion of his birth despite all the disadvantages which it brought him, Pope invoked not points of doctrine but human loyalties across both time and place—to his mother who still lived after the death of his father and to the wider English Catholic community to which he belonged.[31] After expressing his gratitude for Atterbury's concern for "both my spiritual and my temporal advantage," he continued:

> It is true, I have lost a parent for whom no gains I could make would be any equivalent. But that was not my only tye: I thank God another still remains (and long may it remain) of the same tender nature.... For she, my Lord, would think this separation more grievous than any other.... Whether the change would be to my spiritual advantage, God only knows: this I know, that I mean as well in the religion I now profess, as I can possibly ever do in another. Can a man who thinks so, justify a change, even if he thought both equally good? To such an one, the part of *Joyning* with any one body of Christians might perhaps be easy, but I think it would not be so to *Renounce* the other.[32]

Pope's most impassioned comments about his Catholicism emerge out of such vows of sympathy with and loyalty to his fellow Catholics—to the members who comprised the body of the church, rather than to the church as an institution. As Pope explained self-deprecatingly in *A Letter to a Noble Lord* (1733), he remained a Catholic because of these personal attachments, and not out of any theological conviction: he was "a private Person, under Penal Laws and many other disadvantages, not for want of honesty or conscience, but merely perhaps for having too

---

31. Howard Erskine-Hill points out that both John Caryll and his uncle, the Jacobite Secretary of State Lord Caryll, embodied for Pope this virtue of loyalty, as well as the larger dichotomy of his own religious position: that "commitment to a principle, and to one side, must be complemented by a generous and open attitude to people of other persuasions"; however, for Pope, Erskine-Hill notes, "it was the fidelity itself, rather than what was (for the Carylls) its *object*, that assumed the quality of an absolute value." See *The Social Milieu of Alexander Pope: Lives, Example and the Poetic Response* (New Haven: Yale University Press, 1975), 66–67, 71, 92–94, 98–99.

32. Sherburn, *Correspondence*, 1:453.

weak a head, or too tender a heart."[33] The human obligations implied in this "tenderness of heart" begin, as we have seen, as a form of filial piety, a reluctance to give pain to his parents; elsewhere he recalled to Spence that while he was working on the *Iliad* translation early in his career, Lord Oxford "used often to express his concern 'for my continuing incapable of a place' [a government sinecure, for which Pope was ineligible because of his religion], which I could not make myself capable of without giving a great deal of pain to my parents—such a pain indeed as I would not have given to either of them for all the places he could have bestowed upon me."[34]

But these loyalties also extended beyond Pope's parents to encompass the entire English Catholic community to which he belonged. Pope's own roots in this community, if not necessarily deep (his father had been a convert to the church), were broad and firm, beginning with his early education by priests at home and at Catholic schools at Twyford, Marylebone, and Hyde Park Corner, and his residence as a child in Hammersmith and Binfield—two areas known for their concentration of Catholics, including (around Binfield) the Catholic gentry families who would become his lifelong patrons and friends: the Dancastles, Englefields, Blounts, and Carylls.[35] It was in order to reconcile a quarrel between two of those families, the Petres and the Fermors, that Pope was urged by John Caryll to write *The Rape of the Lock*; as Howard Weinbrot has shown, the poem seeks to guide the tiny community of English Catholic aristocrats away from self-destructive infighting toward a spirit of peaceful interdependence.[36]

Pope's opposition to such divisions among his fellow Catholics resulted partly from his sense that a community already so assailed by

---

33. Rosemary Cowler, ed., *The Prose Works of Alexander Pope*, vol. II: *The Major Works, 1725–1744* (Hamden: Archon Books, 1986), 454.

34. Spence, *Observations*, 1:98.

35. On Pope's education, see Spence, *Observations*, 1:8–10; and James King, "'I Never Learned Anything at the Little Schools': Pope's Roman Catholic Education," in *Education in the 18th Century*, ed. J. D. Browning (New York: Garland, 1979), 98–122. On Hammersmith and Binfield, see Gabriner, "The Papist's House, the Papist's Horse," 23–24, 62.

36. Howard D. Weinbrot, "Fine Ladies, Saints in Heaven, and Pope's *Rape of the Lock*: Genealogy, Catholicism, and the Irenic Muse," in *Augustan Subjects: Essays in Honor of Martin C. Battestin*, ed. Albert J. Rivero (Newark: University of Delaware Press, 1997), 150–75.

outside forces could not afford internal strife as well, whether the cause was social or spiritual; he wrote to Caryll in frustration that "besides the small number of the truly faithful in our Church, we must again subdivide, and the Jansenist is damned by the Jesuit, the Jesuit by the Jansenist, the strict Scotist by the Thomist, &c."[37] Consequently, his own affirmations of sympathy and loyalty were strongest at those moments when external pressures threatened to dissolve the unity among English Catholics. Most memorably, in the midst of the renewed enforcement of the penal laws that followed the Jacobite rising of 1715 and precipitated his family's removal from the house that they owned at Binfield in Windsor Forest (through Protestant relatives who held the title in trust for them) to rented accommodations in Chiswick, Pope lamented to Caryll the plight of the English Catholic community: "The misfortunes of private families, the misunderstandings of people whom distresses make suspicious, the coldness of relations whom change of religion may disunite, or the necessities of half-ruined estates render unkind to each other." His response to these dangers was to bind his fate ever more tightly to those of his embattled friends and neighbors:

> If it were generous to seek for alleviating consolations in a calamity of so much glory, one might say that to be ruined thus in the gross, with a whole people, is but like perishing in the general conflagration, where nothing we can value is left behind us. . . . I write this from Windsor Forest, of which I am come to take my last look and leave of. We here bid our papist-neighbours adieu, much as those who go to be hanged do their fellow-prisoners, who are condemned to follow 'em a few weeks after.[38]

Pope's loyalty to an embattled Catholic community is not limited to his own time; it stretches backwards through the centuries, shaping the views of English history that he expresses throughout his poetry. Yet in these passages, he also shows himself as ready to condemn the persecutions and superstitions of his church in the past as he was to

---

37. Sherburn, *Correspondence*, 1:126.
38. Ibid., 1:335–37.

resist its religious and political orthodoxies in the present. In order to describe his own stance toward the church, simultaneously both critical and loyal, Pope turned again and again (as a kind of implicit response to those darker precedents of Inquisition and persecution) to the Catholic ideal represented by Erasmus two hundred years earlier. In *Satire* II.i Pope described himself as being "Like good Erasmus in an honest Mean, / In Moderation placing all my Glory," and he declared in a letter to Swift that he was "of the Religion of Erasmus, a Catholick; so I live; so I shall die."[39] As Chester Chapin has argued, Erasmus (himself a Catholic priest) exerted a powerful shaping influence on Pope as "an exemplar of an enlightened Christianity, an apostle of moderation, tolerance, charity, and a foe to bigotry, obscurantism, and sectarian animosity"; the two men shared a tendency "to exalt . . . whatever in religion tended to unite Christians, and to minimize or deplore whatever divided them."[40] These positions of Erasmus had provoked the outrage of his fellow Catholics, just as the passage in *An Essay on Criticism* in which Pope praised him as "that great, injur'd Name, / (The Glory of the Priesthood, and the Shame!)" was to do.[41] Referring to this parallel in their situations, Pope told Caryll that he would "set before me that excellent example of that great man and great saint, Erasmus, who in the midst of calumny proceeded with all the calmness of innocence, the unrevenging spirit of primitive Christianity!"[42] In his protective loyalty toward Erasmus's reputation (and by implication to the values which he represented), Pope warned his Catholic critics to "suffer the mention of him to pass unregarded least I should be forced to do that for his reputation which I would never do for my own, I mean to vindicate so great a light of our Church from the malice of past times and the ignorance of the present."[43]

What particularly angered these critics in the passage from the *Essay* was not the praise of Erasmus in isolation, but the sharp contrast

---

39. Lines 66–67; Sherburn, *Correspondence*, 3:81.

40. Chester Chapin, "Alexander Pope: Erasmian Catholic," *Eighteenth-Century Studies* 6 (1973): 424.

41. Lines 693–94. For the objections by Catholics to this section of the poem, see Sherburn, *Correspondence*, 1:122–23, 127–28.

42. Sherburn, *Correspondence*, 1:118.

43. Ibid., 1:119.

that Pope drew between his virtues and the predominant character of the medieval clergy; the latter are held culpable for the ignorance and superstition during a gaping thousand-year chiasmus in European civilization between the fall of Rome in 476 and the revival of the arts under Pope Leo X (elected in 1513). During this period, Pope writes, "With Tyranny, then Superstition join'd, / As that the Body, this enslav'd the Mind; / Much was Believ'd, but little understood, / And to be dull was constru'd to be good; / A second Deluge Learning thus o'er-run, / And the Monks finish'd what the Goths begun."[44] Pope maintained this negative view of the medieval Catholic past consistently throughout his career, in passages from *To Mr. Addison* (lines 11–14) and *The Dunciad* (I.145–54, III.52, 83–122), as well as *An Essay on Criticism* (lines 440–45, 681–96). England was not exempt from the general tide of medieval superstition, as the description in Book III of *The Dunciad* made clear: "'Behold yon' Isle, by Palmers, Pilgrims trod, / Men bearded, bald, cowl'd, uncowl'd, shod, unshod, / Peel'd, patch'd, and pyebald, linsey-wolsey brothers, / Grave Mummers! sleeveless some, and shirtless others. / That once was Britain.'"[45] Pope's overriding antipathy to the Catholic Middle Ages derives from his place in the classical humanist tradition, to which Erasmus belonged and to which he saw the medieval church in general as opposed: for him the period was a "long Gothic night"[46] in which all the literary and cultural achievements of the Greco-Roman world were nearly extinguished.

When Pope moves forward to the two centuries of English history immediately preceding his own time, his historical judgments become more personal: the Catholic experience to which he extends his imaginative sympathies is no longer that of Erasmus, "oppressed and persecuted"[47] by zealots of his own faith, but the plight of the English Catholic community as a whole since the reign of Elizabeth, suffering

---

44. Lines 687–92.
45. Lines 113–17.
46. As he termed it in the "Prologue to *Sophonisba*," line 1.
47. Sherburn, *Correspondence*, 1:128. As Thomas Woodman has pointed out, the analogy between the poet persecuted for his devotion to truth and the Christian martyrs—including those English Catholics who had suffered for their faith over the previous two centuries—forms a recurring motif in Pope's poetry: see Woodman, "Pope: the Papist and the Poet," 228–32.

under the same legal persecutions that had impinged repeatedly upon Pope's life. The links between Pope's religion and his historical ideas here are not the unambiguously Jacobite ones that Dennis charged; but they do set apart his Catholic-inflected vision of the national past from that of his Protestant friends and colleagues in the Opposition to Walpole, with whom he is often too readily identified by scholars. These links also suggest a new approach to the contentious question of whether or not Pope maintained either an active allegiance to or passive sympathy for the Stuart cause, which has been vigorously debated over the last twenty-five years.[48] For just as Pope's steadfastness in the Catholic faith resulted less from an adherence to its doctrines and practices than from his deeply rooted loyalty to the community of English Catholics, his Jacobite allegiance is less an imaginative affinity for the pre-1688 Stuart monarchs themselves than one for the period in which they reigned, in contrast with what came before and after it.

The monarch whose reign immediately preceded those of the Stuarts was, of course, Elizabeth; but here, the major effect of Pope's religion on his historical vision is one of omission, as he avoids the glorification of her that was common among his friends and allies in the Opposition to Walpole. His few references to the Virgin Queen are noncommittal, apart from the convenient parallel with Anne in *Windsor-Forest*,[49] which he draws to glorify Anne rather than Elizabeth—after

---

48. See Howard Erskine-Hill, "Alexander Pope: The Political Poet in His Time," in *Modern Essays on Eighteenth-Century Literature*, ed. Leopold Damrosch, Jr. (New York: Oxford University Press, 1988), 123–40, and *Poetry of Opposition and Revolution: Dryden to Wordsworth* (Oxford: Clarendon Press, 1996), 57–108; Douglas Brooks-Davies, *Pope's Dunciad and the Queen of Night: A Study in Emotional Jacobitism* (Manchester: Manchester University Press, 1985); and Murray G. H. Pittock, *Poetry and Jacobite Politics in Eighteenth-Century Britain and Ireland* (Cambridge: Cambridge University Press, 1994), 107–19. For rebuttals of the Jacobite thesis, see Maynard Mack, *Alexander Pope: A Life* (New Haven: Yale University Press, 1985), 261–66; J. A. Downie, "1688: Pope and the Rhetoric of Jacobitism," in *Pope: New Contexts*, ed. David Fairer (New York: Harvester Wheatsheaf, 1990), 9–24; and Chester Chapin, "Pope and the Jacobites," *Eighteenth-Century Life* 10 (1986): 59–73.

49. "There Kings shall sue, and suppliant States be seen / Once more to bend before a British QUEEN" (lines 383–84). For Pope's neutral allusions to Elizabeth—or at least ones that stop well short of his friends' glorification of her—see *The Fourth Satire of Dr. John Donne*, line 41 and "Verses to be placed under the Picture of England's Arch-Poet," lines 3–4, 29–30.

all, it is she who, after the Act of Union (1707), became a *British* queen where Elizabeth had been merely an English one.[50] Moreover, much-discussed figures from Elizabeth's reign such as Drake, Raleigh, and her minister Lord Burghley are absent from Pope's poetry. By contrast, Pope's mentor and patron Viscount Bolingbroke, to whom he paid extravagant tribute in a whole cluster of statements that verge at times on idolatry,[51] turned to Elizabeth as his primary model for the benevolent constitutional monarch. Bolingbroke asserted in *The Idea of a Patriot King* that Elizabeth, inheriting a kingdom divided by religious strife, had "united the great body of the people in her and their common interest, she inflamed them with one national spirit, and, thus armed, she maintained tranquillity at home, and carried succour to her friends and terror to her enemies abroad."[52] In particular, as he explained in his *Remarks on the History of England*, by vigorously opposing King Philip II of Spain, she had "rendered all the projects of universal monarchy vain; and shook to the foundations the most exorbitant power which ever disturbed the peace, or threatened the liberties of Europe."[53] In addition to Bolingbroke, some of Elizabeth's foremost admirers were the Patriot Whigs, with a subset of whom—the so-called "Boy Patriots," including Lord Marchmont, William Pitt, George Lyttelton, Viscount Cornbury, and William Murray—Pope maintained close personal and political ties in the 1730s. He described them to Swift in 1736 as "a few chance-acquaintance, of young men, who look rather to the past age than the present, and therefore the future may have some hopes of them."[54] As with Bolingbroke, Elizabeth's aggressively Protestant

---

50. For an argument which lays much greater emphasis on Elizabeth's role in the poem, see Vincent Carretta, "Anne and Elizabeth: The Poet as Historian in *Windsor-Forest*," *Studies in English Literature, 1500–1900* 21 (1981): 425–37.

51. For Pope's praise of Bolingbroke, see *An Essay on Man* IV.373–98; *Epistle* I.i.1–2; *Epilogue to the Satires* II.138–39; and Spence, *Observations*, 1:119–21, 123–25, 127. On the relationship between the two men, see Hammond, *Pope and Bolingbroke*, passim.

52. Henry St. John, Viscount Bolingbroke, *Political Writings*, ed. David Armitage (Cambridge: Cambridge University Press, 1997), 272.

53. Bolingbroke, *Historical Writings*, ed. Isaac Kramnick (Chicago: University of Chicago Press, 1972), 242.

54. Sherburn, *Correspondence*, 4:51. On the relationship between Pope and the Patriots, see Christine Gerrard, *The Patriot Opposition to Walpole: Politics, Poetry, and National Myth, 1725–1742* (Oxford: Clarendon Press, 1994), 68–95.

foreign policy endeared her to the Patriots; for them, this bold stance contrasted with Walpole's humiliating passivity toward Catholic France and Spain.[55]

And here lay Pope's motive for passing over this period in his own works. He, unlike Bolingbroke and the Patriot Whigs, was a Catholic; he resented rather than admired the vigorous Protestantism for which Elizabeth was being lauded. She had served her faith at home as well as overseas, by initiating the statutory persecution of English Catholics that "set the pattern and formed the basis of English Catholic policy for the next two hundred years" after she succeeded her sister Mary (the last English Catholic monarch before James II) in 1558.[56] After her death Elizabeth was "invoked whenever the security of a Protestant succession was imperilled"; during the Popish Plot scare and the Exclusion Crisis of 1678–81, she served as a focus for anti-Catholic displays such as the burning of the Pope's effigy in front of her statue.[57] In the mid-eighteenth century, the penal laws that Elizabeth set in motion were still obstructing Pope and his coreligionists at every turn. On this count alone, the poet had good reason to abstain from the general chorus of praise. In doing so, he struck out independently to convey a view of the English past that grew out of intensely personal sympathies in the present.

As a consequence of these sympathies, the reigns of the seventeenth-century Stuart kings gained a luster in Pope's mind from the contrast between the prospects of English Catholics during this period and their condition immediately before and after it. Pope's distaste for Elizabeth, who preceded James I, is mirrored by his disdain for William of Orange, who expelled James II. In *Windsor-Forest* (1713), Queen Anne embodies the Stuart line restored, with the family name invoked as a good in itself: "Rich Industry sits smiling on the Plains, / And Peace and Plenty tell, a STUART reigns."[58] Pope's praise of Anne is poised against his covert attack in lines 43–84 on William III, veiled beneath the explicit target of another foreign conqueror who had dealt harshly with the Catholic

---

55. See Gerrard, *The Patriot Opposition to Walpole*, 105–6, 150–84.
56. Aden, *Pope's Once and Future Kings*, 4.
57. Gerrard, *The Patriot Opposition to Walpole*, 152.
58. Lines 41–42.

Church, William I, the "haughty Norman."[59] In a deleted couplet from an early version of the poem (later appended in a note to line 91), Pope appears to allude to the renewed enforcement of the penal laws which followed the Prince of Orange's arrival in Britain, alongside his forebodings about the actions of the Hanoverian sovereigns who would succeed Anne: "Oh may no more a foreign master's rage / With wrongs yet legal, curse a future age!"

Despite his hostility to their predecessor Elizabeth and their successors William and George I, Pope was by no means a fervent admirer of the Stuart monarchs themselves, on whose political and personal behavior he commented unfavorably many times. He did praise Anne, whom loyal Whigs as well as Jacobites could honor as the rightful queen; and he paid his respects to the royal martyr Charles I ("sacred Charles"[60]), reverence for whose memory "remained close to unanimous in signed and published pronouncements" throughout Pope's lifetime.[61] But his remarks on the more controversial of the earlier Stuarts often sound like those of the most zealous Whig. The criticisms of Charles II in *An Essay on Criticism* that Dennis seized on are echoed in Epistle II.i.139–54, where Pope claims that the deterioration of morals under Charles also had a pernicious effect on the arts: "No wonder then, when all was Love and Sport, / The willing Muses were debauch'd at Court."[62] James I is castigated just as severely in Book IV of *The Dunciad*, where the Goddess Dulness wistfully recalls his vanished "pedant Reign," and wishes for another king like him to "Give law to Words, or war with Words alone, / Senates and Courts with Greek and Latin rule, / And turn the Council to a Grammar School!"[63] The triumph of Dulness under James's leadership followed directly from the "Arbitrary Sway" which he practiced, and which is preserved in the doctrine of Dulness's priests: "'The RIGHT

---

59. Line 63. See J. R. Moore, "*Windsor-Forest* and William III," in *Essential Articles for the Study of Alexander Pope*, ed. Maynard Mack (London: Frank Cass, 1964), 232–36.

60. *Windsor-Forest*, line 319; cf. *Epistle* II.i.386, "the Martyr Charles."

61. George Watson, "The Augustan Civil War," *Review of English Studies* 36 (1985): 325. On another occasion, however, Pope repeated a story that showed Charles to be untrustworthy: see Spence, *Observations*, 1:243.

62. Lines 151–52.

63. Lines 175, 178–80.

DIVINE of Kings to govern wrong.'"[64] Pope's most categorical denunciations of the seventeenth-century Stuart kings occur within comments recorded by Joseph Spence, to whom he remarked in 1743 that "There was not any one honest minister in all their [the Stuarts'] reigns . . . except Lord Clarendon," before adding: "Yes, Lord Godolphin. He was a good man, though he had underhand dealings with the Pretender at first."[65] Eight years earlier, he had stated his feelings even more plainly in an offhand reference to "James the First, which was absolutely the worst reign we ever had—except perhaps that of James the Second."[66]

Given the cumulative force of these quotations from the whole length of Pope's career, Douglas Brooks-Davies is certainly right to single out Pope's "evident commitment to the Stuarts as an ideal while, except for Anne, rejecting almost all that they represented in terms of administrative inadequacy."[67] Pope's sympathy with his fellow Catholics across time leads him to broaden this commitment to the Stuarts as an imaginative ideal into a hearkening back to the period in which they reigned, as contrasted with what preceded and followed it. Pope glorified the pre-1688 past while he was simultaneously decrying the present, in his satires of the 1730s; before then he spoke of it in *Windsor-Forest* less glowingly, as a troubled time when Albion "saw her Sons with purple Deaths expire, / Her sacred Domes involv'd in rolling Fire, / A dreadful Series of Intestine Wars, / Inglorious Triumphs, and dishonest Scars."[68] While Anne still lived, Pope remembered the seventeenth century as punctuated by wars (the Civil War of 1642–51 and Monmouth's Rebellion of 1685), natural disasters (the Great Plague of 1665 and Great Fire of 1666), and the "Inglorious Triumph" of the Glorious Revolution. After her death and the arrival of the Hanoverians, he focused only on the last of these; and it was the event that had ended the century of rule by Stuart kings, a period which now gained retrospective appeal for a Catholic living under the reinvigorated penal laws of Pope's own day.

---

64. Lines 182, 188.
65. Spence, *Observations*, 1:243.
66. Ibid., 1:242.
67. Brooks-Davies, *Pope's Dunciad and the Queen of Night*, 140.
68. Lines 323–26.

For Charles I, Charles II, and James II, whatever their other flaws, had all harbored strong Catholic sympathies. Each was married to a Catholic queen, and the latter two themselves converted to Catholicism—James II before he ascended the throne, Charles II on his deathbed (though many Tories believed that Charles had been a secret Catholic since before the Restoration[69]). Charles I's efforts to relax the penal laws anticipated the Declarations of Indulgence proclaimed by each of his sons in 1672 and 1687–88, respectively. All three attempts to improve the lot of Catholics were foiled—the first two by Parliament and the third by the Glorious Revolution itself. Under subsequent monarchs the statutes would only be enhanced, and there would never again be a realistic prospect of reform in Pope's lifetime. For Pope, so resentful of these persecutions, the years between 1625 and 1688—with the exception of the Civil War and the Commonwealth interlude of 1649–60, which he deplored[70]—contrasted as a better past with his degraded present. These were not the idyllic "Golden Days"[71] that he had heralded for Britain in *Windsor-Forest* while Anne still reigned; but they did represent the last time when Pope and his coreligionists could nurture realistic hopes for emancipation.

Two passages from Pope's satires of the 1730s illustrate this habit of glancing back favorably to the period before 1688 in contrast with the plight of English Catholics beginning immediately after the Revolution and continuing into the eighteenth-century present. In both poems, the historical backwards glance is dependent upon the defining aspect of Pope's religious position discussed above: his personal sympathy with and loyalty to his fellow English Catholics, including his beloved parents. In the *Epistle to Dr. Arbuthnot* (1735), Pope's first 387 lines form a grand apologia for his poetic career, situating him within the world of contemporary literature and tracing his path to satire. In lines 380–81, Pope refers to his parents at the end of a sequence detailing all the offenses that he has patiently borne; among these, he claims to have "Let the

---

69. Daniel Szechi, *Jacobitism and Tory Politics, 1710–14* (Edinburgh: John Donald Publishers, 1984), 37.
70. For Pope's harsh view of Cromwell, see *An Essay on Man* IV.284; *Epistle to Cobham*, l. 147; and *Epilogue to the Satires* II.228 and fn.
71. Line 424.

Two Curls of Town and Court, abuse / His Father, Mother, Body, Soul, and Muse." But then in the next line he unexpectedly shifts to discussing his parents as a subject in their own right. Partly this shift serves to bolster Pope's claims for his purity of motive and action; by praising his father as a man of humble virtue, Pope can tacitly lay claim to the same qualities and refute his enemies' charges of malevolence. We have seen that Pope's refusal to abandon his faith, despite all the legal disadvantages that it entailed, emerged in part out of a loyalty to his parents and to the wider English Catholic community. Here the praise of his father's virtues includes the latter's own loyalty to the church, which provides a model for the son's conduct. Moreover, the manners and morals of Alexander Pope, Sr., belong not only to him as an individual but to a vanished era of the English past, for he stands as a lingering representative of old-fashioned virtue in the midst of present decline:

> Of gentle Blood (part shed in Honour's Cause,
> While yet in Britain Honour had Applause)
> Each Parent sprung—"What Fortune, pray?"—Their own,
> And better got than Bestia's from the Throne.
> Born to no Pride, inheriting no Strife,
> Nor marrying Discord in a Noble Wife,
> Stranger to Civil and Religious Rage,
> The good Man walk'd innoxious thro' his Age.
> No Courts he saw, no Suits would ever try,
> Nor dar'd an Oath, nor hazarded a Lye:
> Un-learn'd, he knew no Schoolman's subtle Art,
> No Language, but the Language of the Heart.
> By Nature honest, by Experience wise,
> Healthy by Temp'rance and by Exercise:
> His Life, tho' long, to sickness past unknown,
> His Death was instant, and without a groan.[72]

Just before this passage, Pope's footnote to line 381 goes out of its way to mention that "Mr. Pope died in 1717, aged 75; She [Mrs. Pope] in 1733, aged 93," thus establishing that they belonged to the generation

---

72. Lines 388–403.

immediately before 1688 (the year in which Pope was born). In addition, the first couplet of the passage points firmly, if obliquely and via the deceptive casualness of parentheses, to the pre-1688 Stuart past. The relatives of Pope's parents are said to have shed their blood "in Honour's Cause, / While yet in Britain Honour had Applause"; as Pope's footnote further explains, of his mother's three brothers, one "was kill'd, another died in the Service of King Charles." In other words, both perished while supporting the Royalist side in the Civil War—"Honour's Cause." The footnote and the couplet together covertly glorify the Stuart past as the time when "yet in Britain Honour had Applause" (a chivalric idiom common in Jacobite rhetoric). On the other side of the historical dichotomy, after the Revolution Pope's father refuses the strategy that some Catholics followed of insincere compliance with the Oaths of Allegiance and Supremacy ("Nor dar'd an Oath, nor hazarded a Lye"). His honesty and loyalty contrast with the unprincipled behavior of men like the Duke of Marlborough ("Bestia"), who reap huge profits from their machinations: Marlborough's defection to William had helped to deprive James II of the throne, and this line seems to allude to his benefiting from that act of treachery (elsewhere Pope wrote that a "Punishment" for the Whig poet Sir Richard Blackmore would be for "Marlb'rough [to] serve him like a Friend"[73]). Moreover, the commitment of Pope's father to ideals of natural honesty, wisdom, and temperance ("the Language of the Heart"), as opposed to the "Schoolman's subtle Art," echoes his son's distaste for the Catholic scholastic philosophy of the Middle Ages, along with all other forms of religious disputation;[74] the elder Pope's avoidance of "Civil and Religious Rage" also calls to mind his son's frequent condemnations of zealotry, intolerance, and persecution. The poet's concluding wish, "Oh grant me thus to live, and thus to die! / Who sprung from Kings shall know less joy than I,"[75] makes explicit the implied link between his values and those of his father, which are also those of the period before 1688. Pope's ethic of virtuous independence is anchored here, subtly but inescapably, in

---

73. "Verses to be placed under the Picture of England's Arch-Poet," lines 25, 32.
74. See, for example, *An Essay on Criticism*, lines 440–45, and Spence, *Observations*, 1:134–35.
75. Lines 404–5.

his imaginative loyalty to a specific period of national history—a loyalty which is itself shaped by his experiences as a Catholic living under the Protestant Hanoverian regime.

A similar cluster of ideas appears within *Epistle* II.ii (1737), where just as in *To Dr. Arbuthnot*, it takes the form of an admiring portrait of Pope's father and the values that he exemplified through steadfastness in his faith. And here as in the earlier poem, these values belong to the period before 1688, though Pope himself (following his father's example) continues to lay claim to them in the 1730s present. He also offers a glimpse of his childhood in the years immediately following William's victory and, with it, his fullest account of the injustice of the penal laws:

> Bred up at home, full early I begun
> To read in Greek, the Wrath of Peleus' Son.
> Besides, my Father taught me from a Lad,
> The better Art to know the good from bad:
> (And little sure imported to remove,
> To hunt for Truth in Maudlin's learned Grove.)
> But knottier Points we knew not half so well,
> Depriv'd us soon of our Paternal Cell;
> And certain Laws, by Suff'rers thought unjust,
> Deny'd all Posts of Profit or of Trust:
> Hopes after Hopes of pious Papists fail'd,
> While mighty WILLIAM's thundring Arm prevail'd.
> For Right Hereditary tax'd and fin'd,
> He stuck to Poverty with Peace of Mind;
> And me, the Muses help'd to undergo it;
> Convict a Papist He, and I a Poet.[76]

Pope brings this bit of personal history into the poem smoothly enough; he has been telling why he cannot write poetry now, and after relating a parable about a soldier in "ANNA's Wars" (lines 33–51) to explain his behavior, he delves into the details of his life. The passage describes how Pope turned adversity to his advantage by training himself to be

---

76. Lines 52–67.

a poet; it therefore occupies a crucial place within the self-defense that sets the poem going on its subject. And yet, while Pope prides himself on the achievements won against powerful obstacles, the evil of the change in 1688 still shines through. The break between better past (lines 52–57) and debased present (lines 58–67) occurs in the years following the Revolution.[77] Before it he passed an idyllic life at home receiving lessons in literature from books and lessons in morality from his father; after it he became aware of the restrictions that hedged him round as a Catholic, those "knottier Points" of religion and politics that brought so much suffering to those who "knew [them] not half so well" (however well they understood the principles of morality—"The better Art to know the good from bad"). The renewed persecutions were the direct consequence of the change from James to William: "Hopes after Hopes of pious Papists fail'd, / While mighty WILLIAM's thundring Arm prevail'd." John Butt speculates that this couplet refers to hopes nurtured by English Catholics that William, who came from a tolerant country, would relax the penal laws.[78] But this interpretation seems unlikely, given that William's arrival in England had been precipitated by the efforts of James II to improve the status of his coreligionists; Catholics would hardly have welcomed the man who came to oust James for his efforts on their behalf. Rather, the syntax of lines 62–63 implies that the Catholic hopes raised by James's efforts to extend toleration failed *because* of William's military triumph over James at the Battle of the Boyne in 1690.

Pope and his father are united within the passage in their experience of these events. The historical and the personal converge in Pope's description of his own status as an English Catholic, deprived by law of a university education ("Maudlin's learned Grove"), a home ("our Paternal Cell"), and the opportunity to enter the professions or hold

---

77. In lines 58–59 Pope is alluding either to his family's departure from Hammersmith to Binfield in 1700 or to its shift from Binfield to Chiswick in 1716, both of which were prompted by the penal laws; however, since intensified persecution of English Catholics followed both the Glorious Revolution and the failed Jacobite rebellion of 1715, these lines can be taken as referring to both periods simultaneously. On these moves, see Gabriner, "The Papist's House, the Papist's Horse," *passim.*

78. John Butt, ed., *The Twickenham Edition of the Poems of Alexander Pope*, 11 vols. (London: Methuen, 1938–68), 4:169 (note to line 62).

public office ("all Posts of Profit or of Trust"). He reacts to all these persecutions not by abandoning his faith or succumbing to despair, but by redirecting his energies into poetry, just as his father rests secure in the knowledge of his own moral integrity ("He stuck to Poverty with Peace of Mind"). If the father is found legally culpable as a Catholic ("Convict a Papist He"), the son is by the same grammatical construction destined to write ("and I a Poet"), "help'd to undergo" these hardships by the Muses. And though it is Pope's father here who "stuck to Poverty with Peace of Mind" when "For Right Hereditary tax'd and fin'd" (a phrase that explicitly identifies him as a Jacobite sympathizer), the couplet nevertheless echoes the poet's boast in *Satire* II.ii about his own uncomplaining response to the punitive taxation of Catholics: "Fortune not much of humbling me can boast; / Tho' double-tax'd, how little have I lost?"[79] This theme will continue throughout the remainder of *Epistle* II.ii, as Pope offers himself as the preeminent example of indifference to power, wealth, place, and all the other temptations to corruption that prevail in the present. What was conveyed in the autobiographical passage as past experience—the ability of Pope and his father to withstand persecution—is reformulated later in the poem as present wisdom and practice. Indeed, Pope's own practice of the equanimity that he preaches (and that he learned from his father) is what enables him to reflect back calmly here on the injustices he has suffered.

It was only in the last years of his life that Pope allowed himself to envision the possibility of an England in which religious differences would not matter; and ironically, when he did so, the impulse came out of despair rather than hope. In *One Thousand Seven Hundred and Forty* (written in the title year), Pope concludes with a desperate appeal to a figure whose characteristics match those that he would assign to Brutus, the legendary descendant of Aeneas and founder of the British people, in the outline for the blank-verse epic that he continued to plan up to the month before his death.[80] The nameless redeemer of Britain in *One Thousand Seven Hundred and Forty* will be "honest" and "wise," his title to the crown confirmed by his "public virtue," "Whatever his religion

---

79. Lines 151–52.

80. One of Pope's remarks to Spence about the ongoing *Brutus* project dates to April 1744: see Spence, *Observations*, 1:134.

or his blood"—like Bolingbroke's tract *The Idea of a Patriot King*, Pope's phrasing leaves room for either Frederick, Prince of Wales (whose liability in Jacobite eyes was his lineage), or the Pretender James Stuart (whose liability was his Catholic faith) to fill the role.[81] "Unministered, alone," he will "free at once the Senate and the Throne," while esteeming "the public love his best supply, / A [King]'s true glory his integrity"; under his rule, "Europe's just balance and our own may stand, / And one man's honesty redeem the land."[82] In the outline, Brutus too is ready to act alone, resolving "to go in a single ship, and reject all cowards" when his companions hesitate at the Pillars of Hercules; he seeks to "disperse tyranny and Error and spread truth and good Government" as well as "Love of Liberty," just as the redeemer in *One Thousand Seven Hundred and Forty* had been called on to "free at once the Senate and the Throne"; and Brutus's "purpose of Extending Benevolence" and his despising "the mean thought of making only themselves happy" also point back to the "public virtue" of the earlier hero.[83]

But amidst all these similarities, there is one crucial difference: Brutus lives so far back in the mists of time that the questions of religion and blood that Pope must raise even to dismiss them in *One Thousand Seven Hundred and Forty* are rendered irrelevant. Brutus is neither a Catholic nor a Protestant, neither a Stuart nor a Hanoverian, but transcends such categories as a simple monotheist: Pope told Spence that "the religion introduced by him is the belief in one God and the doctrines of morality," and the outline describes Brutus's aim of "introducing true Religion void of Superstition and false notions of the Gods" to the natives, who already possess "the Druids Doctrine tending to a nobler Religion, a better Moral suited to his Purposes."[84] Brutus serves as a model leader in part because his actions demonstrate how the religious questions that were dividing the country in Pope's day might have been a source of strength and unity rather than discord and oppres-

---

81. See Simon Varey, "Hanover, Stuart, and the *Patriot King*," *British Journal for Eighteenth-Century Studies* 6 (1983): 163–72.

82. Lines 86–98.

83. Friedrich Brie, "Popes *Brutus*," *Anglia* 63 (1939): 149–51 (where Pope's outline is reproduced).

84. Spence, *Observations*, 1:153; Brie, "Popes *Brutus*," 149–50.

sion. It is an idealistic vision, and an ahistorical one, entirely removed from the realities of eighteenth-century Britain. In it we can hear Pope's final, wistful longing for a time when the principles that defined his own faith—sympathy and moderation, tolerance and charity, all coexisting alongside a steadfast loyalty—could be shared by Protestants and Catholics alike, and reconcile all Englishmen to one another.

# More Light? Biblical Criticism and Enlightenment Attitudes

*Norman Vance*

Goethe's dying words—his request for *Mehr Licht*, more light in the darkened sickroom—were meant literally, but they were immediately given metaphorical significance.[1] What did they signify? Did they imply Olympian confidence that more intellectual light would keep flooding in—or frustration and despair at the lack of it? A similar ambiguity is reflected in the history of biblical criticism, an archetypal Enlightenment enterprise that somehow failed to obey the rules and deliver as hoped and failed to obey the rules, despite all the dry light shed upon it. When Jürgen Habermas responded to the award of the Adorno Prize in 1980, he famously described and defended Modernity (*die Moderne*) as an uncompleted project initiated by the Enlightenment.[2] After a further thirty years of Modernity, aspects of the project are still apparently incomplete. Has Enlightenment reason still more work to do on the Bible, after all this time, or was this reason largely misapplied in the first place?

Habermas's understanding of both Modernity and Enlightenment was influenced by the pioneer sociologist Max Weber. With Weber, it

---

1. See G. H. Lewes, *The Life and Works of Goethe* (1855), Everyman ed. (London: J. M. Dent, 1908), 576.
2. Jürgen Habermas, "Die Moderne—ein unvollendetes Projekt," trans. Seyla Ben-Habib as "Modernity versus Postmodernity," *New German Critique* 22 (Winter 1981): 3–14.

was an article of faith inherited from the Enlightenment that traditional religion—and by implication the associated belief in the authority of biblical narrative, particularly narratives of the miraculous—would simply fade away in a natural process of progressive disenchantment. This rather romantic way of putting it has its own history. Romantic poetry is at least partly predicated on a sense of loss articulated by imaginative identification and re-creation of that which has been lost. One of the functions of ancient myth is to testify to an elusive sense of the numinous, a world of legitimized fancy and the imagination, and Schiller's celebrated poem "The Gods of Greece" ("Die Götter Griechenlands," 1788) revisits and re-creates the imagined world of classical mythology when nature itself was regarded as instinct with divinity (*die engotterte natur*), only to regret that this numinous or enchanted world has now passed over into the domain of poetry.[3] Weber's reiterated view of secularization as the "disenchantment of the world" (*Entzauberung der Welt*)[4] follows Schiller in its elegiac nostalgia, while insisting that such disenchantment was bound to happen.

However, the process of disenchantment was, at best, unaccountably sluggish and erratic, particularly in relation to the Bible. Biblical miracle, called into question in the sixth chapter of Spinoza's *Tractatus Theologico-Politicus* (1670), has been more or less under sustained attack in Britain ever since David Hume included a skeptical "Essay upon Miracles" in his *Philosophical Essays Concerning Human Understanding* (1748). In the notorious fifteenth chapter of *Decline and Fall of the Roman Empire* (1776–89), Edward Gibbon dryly noted the frequent suspension of the laws of nature for the benefit of the church. A century later, the agnostic scientist T. H. Huxley was still fighting Hume's battles and Matthew Arnold was still trying to talk down the opposition by insisting in *Literature and Dogma* (1873) that miracles do not happen. Another century later, the biologist Richard Dawkins has again found

---

3. Friedrich Schiller, "Die Götter Griechenlands," in *Sämtliche Werke*, vol. I (Munich: Carl Hauser Verlag, 1958), 169–73.

4. Max Weber, The Protestant Ethic and the Spirit of Capitalism (1904–5), trans. Talcott Parsons (London: Routledge, 1992), 105; Max Weber, "Science as a Vocation" (1918), in *From Max Weber: Essays in Sociology*, ed. H. H. Gerth and C. Wright Mills (London: Routledge, 1940), 155.

it necessary to renew the attack on scripture in his controversial best seller *The God Delusion* (2006), harking back to Huxley and Hume and other Enlightenment figures such as Thomas Jefferson.

As far as the Bible was concerned, the Enlightenment had little real impact in Britain, at least not until the nineteenth century. While Spinoza's seventeenth-century critique of biblical miracle and his claim that scripture is unscientific in that it does not attempt to explain things by their secondary causes but presents things in a way that will appeal to the religious imagination had considerable influence on the development of German religious thought—particularly through Friedrich Schleiermacher's *Reden über die Religion* (1799, translated in 1893 as *Religion: Speeches to its Cultured Despisers*)—the *Tractatus* was not available in English translation until 1862 and attracted little attention in England until it was picked up by well-informed Victorian essayists such as G. H. Lewes and J. A. Froude.[5]

The maverick Irish rationalist John Toland was sympathetic to Spinoza's general theological outlook and is credited with inventing the term "pantheism" to describe it, but his own notoriety after the publication of the controversial *Christianity not Mysterious* (1696) did nothing to commend radical ideas about the scriptures. In Toland's later work, *Amyntor* (1699), he reviewed excluded or apocryphal writings relating to the New Testament period in a way that threatened to destabilize the official canon of scripture. Later still, his *Nazarenus* (1718) illustrated the unstable variousness of early Christianity and heretically suggested that institutional Christianity might have lost its way by selecting and following one particular, probably late tradition and ignoring and suppressing others. He left his readers with the uneasy impression that pious fraud and ignorant credulity were characteristic of the early church and that there might have been a degree of arbitrariness and special pleading in what was included in and excluded from

---

5. G. H. Lewes, "Spinoza: His life and Writings," *Westminster Review* 39 (May 1843): 372–407; J. A. Froude, "Spinoza," *Westminster Review* 64 (July 1855): 1–37; Matthew Arnold's "A Word More about Spinoza," *Macmillan Magazine* 9 (December 1863): 136–42, is a review of Robert Willis's pioneering English translation of the *Tractatus* (1862).

the scriptures. From that perspective, could anyone ever be certain that any of the canonical books of the New Testament were genuine?[6]

A different kind of destabilization of biblical authority arose from anxieties about the integrity of the biblical text itself, endlessly copied and preserved in numerous manuscripts that were, understandably, not all quite the same. John Mill (or Mills), Principal of St. Edmund Hall in Oxford, laboriously compared or reviewed more than one hundred manuscripts over a thirty-year period, and by 1707 he was able to report some 30,000 variants, mostly of a trivial nature. Mill himself was not dismayed by his findings, thinking that they would help to restore the purity of scripture. This view was shared by the great classical scholar Richard Bentley; however, others feared that these variations would encourage anti-Christian and Catholic sneers at Protestant reliance on an unreliable text. In his originally anonymous *Discourse of Free-Thinking* (1713) the Deist Anthony Collins, already fascinated by the problems of canonicity, ironically praised churchmen for "owning and laboring to prove the Text of the Scripture precarious" and found in this another convenient reason to discount the Bible altogether. He claimed it was a tricky book and the way it was used was tricky if not positively dishonest. In a later work, *Discourse of the Grounds and Reasons of the Christian Religion* (1724), Collins argued that the Christian appropriation of Old Testament messianic passages involved an allegorical rather than an obvious and literal reading of the Old Testament.[7] Another Deist, Matthew Tindal, critical of priestcraft and organized religion, argued that Christianity was a version of an age-old religion of nature, reason, and morality and tried in his book *Christianity as Old as the Creation* (1730) to separate religion as he understood it from the religious history conveyed in the biblical record, particularly the Old Testament.

---

6. Jonathan Sheehan, *The Enlightenment Bible* (Princeton: Princeton University Press, 2005), 39–43; David S. Katz, *God's Last Words: Reading the English Bible from the Reformation to Fundamentalism* (New Haven: Yale University Press 2004), 138–43.

7. Sheehan, 44; Collins is quoted in Katz, 188; Hans Frei, *The Eclipse of Biblical Narrative: A Study in Eighteenth and Nineteenth Century Hermeneutics* (New Haven: Yale University Press, 1974), 67–69.

Such ideas had little immediate impact in England, but they were soon taken up in the great German universities, coming back to the land of their birth only in the nineteenth century.[8] These ideas were discussed and developed alongside Lessing's publication in 1774 and 1777 of the anonymous "Wolfenbüttel fragments" (eventually identified as the work of Lessing's friend, the late H. S. Reimarus), with their skeptical reflections on miracles such as the crossing of the Red Sea (Exodus 14). Increasingly rigorous methods of addressing questions of authorship, composition, and source in classical texts were extended to the scriptures. While J. G. Eichhorn of Göttingen described this approach as "*die höhere Kritik*" in 1787, the equivalent English term, "the higher criticism," was not widely current until the 1880s.[9] Coleridge read Eichhorn in German, rather critically; Eichhorn had few other readers in England. David Strauss, later the biographer of Reimarus, drew on a century of mainly German rationalist scholarship and criticism in his controversially demythologizing *Leben Jesu* (1835–36), which George Eliot translated for English readers in 1846. Ernest Renan used Strauss (widely available in France in the positivist polymath Émile Littré's French translation of 1839–40) and his knowledge of Hebrew and the ancient world for his own equally controversial anti-miraculous *Vie de Jésus* (1863). These books, much discussed in England, were soon followed by the home-grown *Ecce Homo* (1866) by the historian J. R. Seeley, a discussion of the life and mission of Christ in humanistic, rather than theological or supernatural, terms. In 1874 an anonymous writer, eventually identified as W. R. Cassels, published the now long-forgotten *Supernatural Religion: An Inquiry into the Divine Revelation*, attacking the authenticity and supernatural claims of the New Testament, which sparked off lively and prolonged controversy.[10]

---

8. Thomas Albert Howard, *Protestant Theology and the Making of the Modern German University* (Oxford: Oxford University Press, 2006), 120.

9. J. G. Eichhorn, *Einleitung ins Alte Testament*, 2nd ed., vol. 1 (Leipzig: Weidmans Erben, 1787), vi. According to the *Oxford Dictionary of the Christian Church*, ed. F. L. Cross, revised 3rd ed., (Oxford: Oxford University Press, 2005), the currency of the term "higher criticism" in English derives from its use in William Robertson Smith's *The Old Testament in the Jewish Church* (1881).

10. Among the more effective scholarly responses to *Supernatural Religion* was a series of articles in the *Contemporary Review* by the leading New Testament scholar J. B. Lightfoot.

All these works provoked widespread hostility. They did not stand alone in the pillory of Victorian public opinion. *Essays and Reviews* (1860), which included critical discussion of traditional approaches to scripture, had seven contributors, mainly clergymen, who were condemned as the "Seven against Christ" (alluding to Aeschylus's *Seven against Thebes*), and legal proceedings for heresy were initiated against several of them. A similar outcry greeted Bishop Colenso of Natal's critical discussion of the historicity of the Pentateuch (1862–79), revisiting issues such as the miraculous Red Sea crossing, which had been raised in Germany almost a century before. There were prolonged attempts to deprive him of his bishopric. There were also noisy protests against the Revised Version, the scholarly new translation of the Bible based on a revised text, issued in 1881–85. Its departure from the long-familiar King James Version of 1611 caused considerable upset. There were accusations of anti-Trinitarian bias.[11] Among other revisions, it finally got rid of the notorious "Johannine comma," a theologically convenient and very late addition to Latin versions of 1 John 5:7 referring to three witnesses in heaven, the Father, the Word, and the Holy Ghost. This was not found in any early Greek manuscript, but it had been used as a proof-text for the orthodox doctrine of the Trinity. Erasmus had raised questions about it, Gibbon had sneered at it as an example of pious fraud, and Benjamin Jowett in *Essays and Reviews* had deplored its presence in the King James Version.[12]

*Essays and Reviews*, the Revised Version of the Bible, and Colenso's researches all drew on the well-established tradition of critical scholarship, and all provoked both popular outcry and clerical denunciation. This was not an isolated Victorian phenomenon or a last gasp of unreformed opinion—even a century later there were strangely similar outraged responses in Britain to the publication of the New English Bible version of the New Testament in 1961 (some of the old jokes about

---

11. William Morris, *The Revised and Arianized Version of the English New Testament: A Protest and Testimony* (London: Elliott Stock, 1881).

12. See Katz, 11–12; Edward Gibbon, *Decline and Fall of the Roman Empire* (1776–88), ed. David Womersley, vol. 2 (London: Allen Lane, 1994), 442–43, chap. 37; Benjamin Jowett, "On the Interpretation of Scripture," *Essays and Reviews* (1860), 7th ed. (London: Longman, 1861), 352.

the Revised Version were told again, such as the alleged claim that the King James Version should stand as it had been good enough for Jesus Christ and good enough for St. Paul). The uproar that greeted John Robinson's demythologizing *Honest to God* (1964) and the similar controversy attending the collection of essays edited by John Hick entitled *The Myth of God Incarnate* (1977) recalled the outrage generated by *Essays and Reviews*.

Is this continuing hostility to rationalist scholarship and critique in biblical matters simply another example of invincible ignorance, complacency, and self-delusion on the part of the still-unenlightened? Or does it support the claim advanced by Max Horkheimer and Theodor Adorno in *Dialectic of Enlightenment* (1947) that Enlightenment rationality, by its very nature, may be ultimately self-defeating—what begins as liberating reason too easily transforms itself into repressive orthodoxy that has to be resisted? Is the apparently undeluded Richard Dawkins in *The God Delusion* the self-appointed voice of a dogmatic postchristian orthodoxy? Or does biblical criticism still provoke resistance because of a postmodern retreat from brashly optimistic intellectualism and loss of confidence in progressive enlightenment as an aspect of the grand narrative of modernity? Or could it be that while there may be some truth in all these possibilities, the real problem is misplaced self-confidence on all sides and repeated misunderstanding, by both radical critics and conservative apologists, of the nature and function of the Bible?

It seems appropriate to start at the beginning, with the controversies associated with the Genesis creation narratives. The Bible began by placing man at the center of the created world, soon followed by the Fall and the expulsion from Eden. That great Enlightenment pioneer and philosopher of science, Francis Bacon, had seen the Fall as a challenge to man to recover his lost dominion over creation through arts and sciences, to use reason and nature instrumentally and strategically. Horkheimer and Adorno develop this reading for their own purposes, noting the ultimately reductive and coercive character of the specialized form of rational or scientific knowledge that identifies value as use-value. Knowledge as power becomes not just power over (aspects of) nature but power over those without that kind of knowledge. From a rationalist perspective, myth, including the Genesis creation stories, is usually regarded as not just pre-scientific but as wrong, as that which science attacks and dispels. But myth itself can be seen more positively as a way of putting things—as a different model for making narrative and imaginative sense of natural process and religious awareness that narrowly rationalist critique fails to recognize.

More or less reductive approaches to myth and to biblical narrative, particularly Old Testament narrative, identifying mere poetic legend and strategic fabling in what religious tradition had assumed (or was held to have assumed) was reliable history, are a central aspect of Enlightenment biblical criticism. The rhetoric of intellectual light being shed implies a gradual overcoming of prior darkness. In the "Preliminary Discourse" to the *Encyclopédie* (1751), Jean le Rond d'Alembert deplored what he saw as the silencing of reason under the theological despotism and prejudice of earlier ages, by implication including early modern England in the reign of Queen Elizabeth (1558–1603). He described the proto-enlightenment figure Francis Bacon (1561–1626) as "born in the depths of the most profound night" to work in the shadows preparing the light that would eventually illuminate the world.[13] This essentially linear model of Enlightenment as a process required an identifiable starting point, perhaps Bacon himself, and therefore could not easily accommodate the possibility of pre-Baconian enlightenment or rational understanding. If Bacon was born into deep darkness, it was hard to explain the illumination offered centuries before by Jewish rationalists such as Maimonides (1135–1204) or early church fathers such as Origen (ca.185–ca. 254) and Augustine (354–430), usually ignored or dismissed by Enlightenment thinkers, who had already moved beyond narrowly literal biblical interpretation in their writings on Genesis.

Nineteenth-century secularists and rationalists saw themselves as heirs of the Enlightenment. The type was sufficiently familiar for Flaubert to introduce the caricatured Voltairean chemist Monsieur Homais into *Madame Bovary* (1857). In England, Hume and Gibbon's writings were

---

13. Jean Le Rond D'Alembert, *Preliminary Discourse to the Encyclopedia of Diderot*, trans. Richard N. Schwab (Chicago: University of Chicago Press, 1995), 73–74.

eventually followed by a new generation of iconoclastic works such as G. W. Foote's *Biblical Romances* (1882) and the anonymous and skeptical *Plain Commentary on the First Gospel* by "an Agnostic" (1891). The cruder versions of secularist argument insisted that modern science, represented by geology, historical criticism, scientific cosmology, and evolutionary biology, now made it impossible to take Genesis and other books literally. This implied that owlish literalism had been more or less universal until the eighteenth century and was still widespread before Charles Lyell's *Principles of Geology* (1833), Strauss's *Life of Jesus* (1835–36), and Charles Darwin's *Origin of Species* (1859). But this picture of literal-mindedness and almost universal intellectual darkness was itself absurd, a convenient myth constructed for strategic reasons. The much-mocked biblical chronology associated with Archbishop Ussher, specifically his pre-geological opinion that the world was created in 4004 BC, was not an almost immemorial tradition, vested with the authority of the Bible itself and standing or falling with it, but a relatively recent conjecture, included in English Bibles only since 1701. It was less an example not so much of fallible biblical teaching as of reading the Bible the wrong way, a by-product of the Renaissance passion for precise knowledge and certainty even in areas where precision and certainty were not available and not important. It was easier for the late Old Testament period where nonbiblical chronologies and histories could be consulted, but the biblical evidence of chronology and passing time available for the early period, in the genealogies and accounts of patriarchal longevity in Genesis, was incidental and unreliable. There are discrepancies in the numbers between the Masoretic text of the Hebrew Bible and the Septuagint Greek translation that is based on an older version of the Hebrew text, so that in Genesis 11:12, for example, it is not clear whether Noah's grandson Arphaxad was 35 (Hebrew) or 135 (Greek) when he became the father of Salah (Hebrew)—or was it Cainan (Greek)?

Ussher represented the high point of a tradition of European Renaissance scholarship that included other landmarks such as J. J. Scaliger's *De Emendatio Temporis* (1583). There were many other Renaissance chronologists, but the mathematical certainty and precision they all sought eluded them. Estimates for the creation ranged from 4103 BC (Brian Walton) to 3928 BC (John Lightfoot), and before them Jewish teachers had fixed on 3760 BC, the date still used today as the basis of the Jewish calendar. "You will find it easier to make the wolf agree with the lamb than to make all chronologers agree about the age of the world," claimed the Heidelberg mathematician Jacobus Curio in 1557.[14] The lack of consensus indicated that on the available evidence no precise dating was possible, though this seems to have generated no traumatic anxieties at the time; the matter was apparently regarded as scientifically interesting rather than of any particular theological importance. It was not until much later that it became a reason or an excuse for belittling the Bible.

Precise dates and scientific detail were hardly the main point of the Creation story or other stories in the Bible, and this was recognized in ancient Jewish tradition. Detailed public discussion of the formalized six-day creation account and other problem passages, such as the mysterious vision of the chariot in the opening chapter of Ezekiel, was officially discouraged in the second-century Mishnah and again in the sixth-century Babylonian Talmud; much of the material was held to be an esoteric mystery, and it was felt that the literal sense of the details did not necessarily matter much. Jerome (ca. 342–420), one of the earliest and greatest of Christian biblical scholars, acknowledged and reported this without dismay.[15] In any case, details could be treated imaginatively when it suited. The Bible spoke of days, but what was a day? Rabbis quoted in the Talmud found it perfectly legitimate to recall the psalmist's claim that "a thousand years in thy sight are but as yesterday" (Psalm 90:4) and to deem the days of the creation account a vividly poetic way

---

14. For Lightfoot and other renaissance chronologists see C. A. Patrides, "Renaissance Estimates of the Year of Creation," *Huntington Library Quarterly* 26 (1963): 315–22; Jacobus Curio, *Chronologicarum Rerum Liber*, vol. II (Basle, 1557), is quoted in Philip C. Almond, *Adam and Eve in Seventeenth-century Thought* (Cambridge: Cambridge University Press, 1999), 83.

15. *Mishnah*, Hagigah 2.1; *Talmud* Hagigah 11b, invoked by Jerome, Letter 54 to Paulinus, on the study of scripture, in Migne, *Patrologia Latina* (PL) 22.547. References to the Mishnah are to the Herbert Danby translation (London: Oxford University Press, 1933); all references to the Talmud are to the English translation of the Babylonian Talmud, ed. Isidore Epstein, 18 vols. (London: Soncino Press, 1962).

of indicating periods of a thousand years.[16] Biblical numbers were often symbolic anyway, and large numbers such as a thousand are themselves frequently rhetorical rather than strictly mathematical in ancient and indeed modern texts.

Recognition that the Genesis creation account was useless as science and could not be taken literally did not need to wait for the Enlightenment: it had been noted by Galen, the great Greek physician of the second century of the Common Era. He had come across the book of Genesis, probably in Greek translation, and complained that by the standards of modern Greek science, Moses—traditionally credited with authorship of the first five books of the Bible—had not produced a philosophical or scientific account of the beginning of things when he described the creation of the world in six days. Everything was attributed directly to the creative word of God without any reference to the secondary causes through which things actually happen. Galen had anticipated Spinoza by many centuries, noticing what many skeptics apparently failed to notice: that the Genesis creation account was theological rather than scientific.[17]

If early modern chronologists were misguidedly trying to make scientific sense of biblical time, astronomers of the same period and later were trying to make sense of sun and moon and stars in the Bible. The wonderfully dramatic biblical story of the sun standing still over the earth at Gibeon, so that Israel would have extra daylight in which to defeat its enemies (Joshua 10:12–13), which had already taxed the ingenuity of Maimonides, presented similar challenges to the new Renaissance appetite for quasi-mathematical certainty and was still being debated by German critics such as G. L. Bauer at the end of the eighteenth century. How could such a thing happen? The astronomer Galileo, aware with Copernicus that it was the earth that moved round the sun rather than the other way round and eager to demonstrate that modern science did not undermine the integrity of scripture, published

---

16. Sanhedrin 97a; Rosh Hashanah 31a. All biblical quotations are from the 1611 King James Version unless otherwise indicated.

17. See R. Walzer, *Galen on Jews and Christians* (London: Oxford University Press, 1949) which prints, translates, and discusses the six references to Jewish or Christian ideas that have survived in Greek or Arabic texts of Galen.

a *Letter to the Grand Duchess Christina* (1615) in which he ingeniously interpreted the passage to make it accord with the new heliocentrism, only to get into trouble for even raising a matter that had not previously caused much anxiety or concern. Spinoza, unhappy about miracle and unhappy with convoluted exegesis of this kind, argued that the point of the passage was to tell sun-worshipping Gentiles that the sun was subject to the higher power of God; what must actually have happened was imagined and described as something quite different for religious reasons and in the light of preconceived ideas. Bauer suggested that this was an ancient poetic fragment taken over, and taken literally, by a later historical writer.[18] But poetic reading of scripture was not a dangerously new-fangled German idea or an Enlightenment rationalization of a scientifically impossible text—it was well established before Galileo and Copernicus. Dean Colet of St. Paul's (ca. 1466–1519) had written that the opening chapters of Genesis contained poetic rather than scientific truth.[19]

Biblical literalists and Enlightenment and Victorian skeptics and scoffers, not to mention modern critics such as Richard Dawkins, seem to have forgotten or have never known that people had long ago realized that the Bible was not—and was never meant to be—a scientific book. Early and respected Christian commentators, such as Origen in the third century and Gregory of Nyssa in the fourth, could be seen to have ranged well beyond the literal sense of scripture, particularly the terse formal austerity of the creation narrative in Genesis, to tease out or impose meaning, system, and coherence in the light of established teaching of the church and the Greek philosophy of their time. Origen in particular showed a frankness that would have got him into serious trouble in the Victorian church. Material preserved in the

---

18. Maimonides, *The Guide of the Perplexed*, trans. Shlomo Pines (Chicago: University of Chicago Press, 1963), part II, chap. 35; see T. M. Rudavsky, "Galileo and Spinoza: Heroes, Heretics and Hermeneutics," *Journal of the History of Ideas* 62 (October 2001): 611–31; Spinoza, *Tractatus Theologico-Politicus* [*A Theologico-Political Treatise*], trans. R. H. M. Elwes (1883) (New York: Dover, 1951), 93; for G. L. Bauer's *Hebräische Mythologie* (1802) see J. W. Rogerson, *Myth in Old Testament Interpretation* (Berlin: Walter de Gruyter, 1974), 8–9.

19. For Colet see J. K. S. Reid, *The Authority of Scripture: a Study of the Reformation and Pre-Reformation Understanding of the Bible* (London: Methuen, 1957), 24.

*Philocalia*, an early selection of his writings, reveals that he had noted commands in the Law of Moses that he felt were either unreasonable or, if taken literally, impossible. He had also identified what seemed to him obviously unhistorical elements in both Old and New Testament narratives, incidents that never happened though they were a figurative means of revealing certain mysteries. With considerable originality, and minimal scriptural warrant, he transformed the Genesis creation story into a lofty cosmic myth. He proposed a two-stage model of creation: first, a spiritual creation of a finite number of noetic beings or disembodied rational essences, co-eternal with God, simultaneously created through the divine Logos or Word before time, and then, after these of their own will had fallen away from God; a corporeal creation binding souls to bodies in the material world as we know it.[20]

Gregory, much influenced by Origen, was another who saw the Genesis creation account not as history but as storytelling, a way of placing doctrines before the faithful in the form of narrative. He complemented his brother Basil's extended meditations on the six-day work of creation by devoting a treatise specifically to the creation of man, claiming, again without specific scriptural authority, that for this last and summative work of creation God carefully prepared matter beforehand and incorporated the possibilities of earlier forms of life.[21]

Augustine, the great expositor of the scriptures, found it necessary to go beyond the literal sense—even in a commentary on the literal text of Genesis. What he meant by "literal" was "original" or "historical," what he assumed God must have meant by the words used. His exposition was theological rather than scientific and intended to make a sophisticated epistemological point about eternity and time. Influenced by Plato's view that time was created with the world, and alert to the epistemological gulf between divine (or angelic) and human consciousness, between eternity and time, Augustine suggested, like

---

20. Origen, *Philocalia* 1 "Of the Inspiration of the Divine Scripture," 16–20; *De Principiis* 1.8.1, 2.2, 2.6.3, 2.9, etc., in Migne, *Patrologia Graeca* (PG) 11.176, 186–87, 211, 225–33, discussed by J. N. D. Kelly, *Early Christian Doctrines*, 5th ed. (London: Continuum, 2006), 180–81.

21. Gregory of Nyssa, *Oratio Catechetica* 5, Migne PG 45.21–4; *De Opifico Hominis* 3.2, Migne PG 44.136.

Origen before him, that the entire work of creation was pre-temporal and simultaneous through the Eternal Word of God, with time, place, and historical sequence in the world as we know it following from that initial creative act. He argued ingeniously that the formal narrative division into six days, separating creation into distinct phases, represented a kind of translation into the human world of space and time, necessary to convey the wonder and multiplicity of the creation to time-bound believers.[22]

When Spinoza courted ostracism and won posthumous fame as a father of the Enlightenment by challenging literal readings of the Bible in his *Tractatus Theologico-Politicus* (1670), he felt he could ally himself with an already ancient tradition of Rabbinic scholarship. Although he sometimes sharply disagrees with Maimonides, he follows him in suggesting that prophets were endowed not so much with the literal power to see God, or special access to divine truth, as with particularly vivid and idiosyncratic religious imaginations, expressed in scripture in figurative language and forms of parable.[23] He cites a commentary on Deuteronomy by Aben Ezra, or Abraham Ibn Ezra, (ca. 1093–ca. 1164), Robert Browning's wise Rabbi Ben Ezra in *Dramatis Personae* (1864), which he claims hints at his own controversial assertion (following Hobbes and other bold spirits) that, despite the tradition to the contrary, Moses was not the author of the Pentateuch, which must have been written long after his death.[24] Spinoza's contemporaries were unconvinced and indignant.[25] Aben Ezra may have been less of a Spinozist than Spinoza claimed he was for tactical purposes, but he certainly anticipated Spinoza's rational humanistic outlook. His *Yesod Mora* (Foundation of Reverence) suggests that religious understand-

22. Augustine, *De Genesi ad Litteram*, 4.33, 34, Migne PL 34.317–9; Plato, *Timaeus*, 37d, e. There is a useful, if argumentative, discussion of Augustine on Genesis in Henry Woods, S. J., *Augustine and Evolution. A Study in the Saint's "De Genesi ad Litteram" and "De Trinitate"* (San Francisco: Universal Knowledge Foundation, 1924).

23. Maimonides, *Guide*, part 2, chap. 47; Spinoza, *Tractatus*, 24–42.

24. *Tractatus*, 120–21.

25. For example, see Jean Filleau de la Chaise, *An Excellent Discourse Proving the Divine Original and Authority of the Five Books of Moses*, trans. W[illiam] L[orimer], (London: T. Parkhurst, 1682). Discussed by Richard Popkin, "Spinoza and Bible Scholarship," in *The Cambridge Companion to Spinoza*, ed. Don Garrett (Cambridge: Cambridge University Press, 1996), 386–90.

ing or knowledge of God, the ultimate purpose of human existence, does not depend exclusively on study of the Torah but on innate human reason.[26] Both Jewish and Christian tradition took note of Maimonides and Aben Ezra, often grouped together as rationalist commentators.

It may now seem surprising that Spinoza's denial of the Mosaic authorship of the Pentateuch caused so much trouble, yet when the French Catholic scholar Richard Simon (1638–1712), otherwise critical of Spinoza, made a similar point in his *Histoire critique du Vieux Testament* (1678), he was expelled from his religious order. In his *Conjectures* (1854), Jean Astruc identified two different levels of tradition in the Pentateuch, suggesting that the text as we have it had been compiled from two earlier sources and anticipating the more elaborate and once widely-accepted four-document hypothesis of the German scholar Julius Wellhausen (1844–1918). This, too, provoked fierce criticism. The tradition of Moses as original author, though not directly claimed in scripture itself, linked the actual text with an authoritative religious figure who had been close to God and supported the conventional view of scripture as the directly inspired word of God. Attributing the text to an unidentified author or authors, or to an editorial process, rather than to Moses himself, seemed to weaken its authority.

Why was early awareness of biblical narrative as often poetic or figurative and man-made, religious, and imaginative rather than scientific or literal so strongly resisted and so easily forgotten? Why did rational and enlightened approaches come and go rather than cast a steady light? Part of the answer is that too much was expected of the Bible after the Reformation. The Council of Trent in 1546 assigned equal authority to the Bible and to the traditions of the Church. But Reformation revulsion from nonbiblical practices and teachings that had gradually crept into the church fuelled distrust of what was held to be corruptible ecclesiastical authority, sustained by traditions that, it was argued, were more human than divine. The removal of these traditions left only the Bible, and suggestions that it, too, was shaped or limited by human perception or agency were unwelcome. The Church of England formally accepted

---

26. For Ibn Ezra see Tzvi Langermann, "Abraham Ibn Ezra," *Stanford Encyclopedia of Philosophy*, ed. Edward N. Zalta (Fall 2008), http://plato.stanford.edu/archives/fall2008/entries/ibn-ezra/ (accessed July 12, 2010).

the supreme authority of the Bible in 1562 in the sixth of the Thirty-Nine Articles, "Of the Sufficiency of the Holy Scriptures for Salvation." The authority of Scripture, independent of the Church and its traditions, was reiterated, in more severely exclusive terms, in the fourth article of the *Westminster Confession of Faith* (1647), originally intended as the basis of the national religion and respected in Britain and America by conservative Presbyterians and nonconformists ever since:

> The authority of the holy Scripture, for which it ought to be believed and obeyed, dependeth not upon the testimony of any man or church, but wholly upon God (who is truth itself), the Author thereof; and therefore it is to be received because it is the Word of God.[27]

The meaning, or the meaning of the portions that mattered, was clear enough and there on the surface, so that "not only the learned but the unlearned, in a due course of ordinary means, may attain unto a sufficient understanding of them."[28] This was a reference to the sometimes extraordinary allegorical readings of scripture that had been developed by Origen and his successors, overelaborately systematized into four distinct levels of meaning by later commentators such as the fifth-century monk John Cassian.[29] There was a risk, not always avoided, of getting carried away and disregarding the literal or surface meaning altogether. The parable of the Good Samaritan (Luke 10:30–37) provides one example. It was, and is, a good story, and the meaning is clear enough, but in the hands of Augustine and others almost every detail was seized upon for possible allegorical significance. The luckless traveler who fell among thieves between Jerusalem and Jericho was the human race, being left half-dead (or half-alive, *semivivus* in the Latin of the Vulgate) indicated the imperfect spiritual state of sinful man, and the inn to which he was brought to be looked after was clearly the Church.[30]

---

27. Text from Philip Schaff, ed., *The Creeds of Christendom*, 6th ed., vol. 3 (1931; Grand Rapids, MI: Baker Books, 2007), 602, 604.

28. Ibid., 602, 604.

29. John Cassian, "De Spirituali Scientia," *Collationes* 14.8, Migne PL 49.963–64.

30. Augustine, *Quaestiones Evangelii* 2.19, Migne PL 35.1340.

It is easy to see why the reformers objected. John Calvin particularly reprehended the use of allegorical readings of often enigmatic scripture as a basis for disputed doctrines such as Transubstantiation or the practice of Confession.[31] But the pendulum swung too far in the opposite direction, discouraging figurative or poetic readings even of passages that clearly merited it and providing stimulus to skeptics and scoffers as well as to demythologizing scholarship. Pre-Enlightenment Europe had had at least the capacity for a commonsense approach to the scriptures. Sensitive poetic or symbolic reading preceded and challenged biblical literalism. For Origen, the Pauline claim that "the letter killeth but the spirit giveth life" (2 Corinthians 3:6) justified reading scripture for spiritual rather than just literal meaning.[32]

However, both the devout and the detractors alike became obsessed with the letter. T. H. Huxley amused himself by controversially poking holes in the story of the Gadarene swine (Luke 8), probing the precise geography and the morality of allowing a man's pigs to be drowned, but the spiritual or religious significance was overlooked.[33] The tension or disjunction between letter and spirit, written text and religious life, religious law and pastoral realities, is as old as scripture itself. A difficult passage in Jeremiah (8:8–9) seems to indicate prophetic impatience with the scribes, the custodians of the written tradition, and with a people who might have the written text of the law but still go astray:

> How do ye say, we are wise, and the law of the Lord is with us? Lo, certainly in vain made he it; the pen of the scribes is in vain [or, the false pen of the scribes has made it into a lie (Revised Standard Version)]. The wise men are ashamed, they are dismayed and taken: lo, they have rejected the word of the Lord; and what wisdom is in them?

---

31. John Calvin, *The Second Epistle of Paul the Apostle to the Corinthians* (1548), trans. T. A. Smail (Edinburgh: Oliver and Boyd, 1964), 43, commenting on 2 Cor. 3:6; *Institutes* 2.5.19; see also *Institutes of the Christian Religion*, ed. J. T. McNeill, trans. F. L. Battle, Library of Christian Classics, 2 vols. (Philadelphia: Westminster Press, 1960), 3.4.5; 4.17.22.

32. For discussions of "letter" and "spirit" see Origen, *De Principiis* 1.1.2 (Migne PG 11.122); *Contra Celsum* 7.20 (Migne PG 11.1449); Commentary on Matthew, 15.1, discussing Matthew 19:12 (Migne PG 13.1256).

33. T. H. Huxley, "Agnosticism," *Nineteenth Century* 25 (February 1889), 144–70, reprinted in *Essays upon Some Controverted Questions* (London: Macmillan, 1892).

The key contrast is between the written "law of the Lord" and the spoken, prophetic "word of the Lord" to which the scribes are deaf, foolishly deluded into thinking that possession of the written law on its own gives all necessary wisdom.[34] The protestant reaction against allegorical excesses and nonbiblical sources of authority in matters of belief and behavior encouraged an ahistorical sense of the Bible as an undifferentiated whole, as Law, what Matthew Arnold called "Hebraism" in *Culture and Anarchy* (1869). This often went with excessive biblical literalism and narrow prescriptive views of doctrine and conduct, particularly sexual conduct, which could seem very remote from the spirit of the gospel and the religious possibilities of mercy and love. In protest, Thomas Hardy used "the letter killeth," leaving the spirit out of it, as the epigraph for his last and angriest novel *Jude the Obscure* (1895), in which the institutional church is represented as self-absorbed, obsessed with dogma and detail, and seemingly impervious to human pain.

But would the spirit come through if the letter was challenged or disregarded? This was a recurring anxiety, found in its most extreme form in the alarmed responses to Matthew Tindal's Deistic *Christianity as Old as the Creation* (1730) which proposed a minimalist natural religion almost without content effectively bypassing the scriptures altogether. Religious conservatives, particularly in nineteenth-century Oxford, had always been disposed to blame German biblical critics for encouraging infidelity. It did not help that, despite pioneers such as Coleridge and Thomas Carlyle, the German language and German culture were still not widely studied in Britain. Distance lent disenchantment, distortion, and downright caricature to British views of German scholars and German critical scholarship. Secondhand accounts were often hostile and undiscriminating. J. W. Burgon, Dean of Chichester, who should have known better, claimed, preposterously, that the brief scholarly marginal notes in the Revised Version of the Bible, which owed much to German textual criticism and philology, had "unsettled the faith of millions."[35]

---

34. Discussed in John Bright, *Jeremiah* (The Anchor Bible) (Garden City, New York: Doubleday, 1965), 63–64.

35. [J. W. Burgon], "New Testament Revision: The New English Version," *Quarterly Review* 153 (January 1882): 2.

German scholars may not have been entirely blameless. The Enlightenment-inspired traditions and conventions of German biblical scholarship developed in an academic atmosphere of free enquiry, protected by a tradition of academic freedom but insulated from the pastoral life and the concerns of the churches and the people who actually read the Bible. This had obvious advantages: if such protection had been available in Britain, the clerical contributors to *Essays and Reviews* would have been safe from prosecution for heresy in the church courts, and the great Old Testament scholar William Robertson Smith would not have been dismissed from his teaching post in the Free Church College in Aberdeen in 1881 by the Free Church of Scotland. By being formally separated, both scholarship and the church suffered instead of learning from each other.[36] Churchmen came to distrust and resent biblical scholarship and rationalist critique, often imperfectly understood, as nothing to do with them or indeed positively injurious to faith, and this distrust spread from Germany to Britain and North America. Biblical scholars, addressing students and other scholars rather than church congregations, could be arrogant, tactless, and religiously insensitive about how they presented their findings, sometimes offering bold speculations to dazzle rather than to illuminate, and they could lose touch with the special character of their materials. The insights gained from the study of classical texts could be valuable when applied to the Bible, but no religious anxiety could possibly attach to possible transcription error or problems of source or textual evolution or questions of composition or coherence in Homer or Aeschylus. It was a different matter if the authority, integrity, and authorship of all or parts of the Bible seemed to be called in question.

This is not to say that the scriptures should have been protected from the critics or that the concerns or results of biblical criticism were invariably religiously unimportant. The critics could direct attention to what really mattered. Their attempts to get behind inconsistency, odd detail, obscure poetic idiom, and occasionally unintelligible and probably corrupt text, in both the Old and the New Testament, could help to identify or clarify the ultimate religious purpose of the writings.

---

36. Howard, *Protestant Theology*, 370.

Developing a sense of original historical and religious context for individual books or even portions of books, even if this could never be an exact science, could make it easier to learn more about the connections between history and religion as Bible writers understood them at different times. The growing awareness that the Pentateuch embodied different kinds of religious understanding from different stages of Jewish religious history was a reminder that the outward forms and formulations of religion are, and always have been, subject to change and development.

Other matters were interesting, rather than religiously significant, and had to do with the letter rather than the spirit. Questions of disputed authorship, first raised in connection with Moses and the Pentateuch, could turn out to be less important than they seemed when it was recalled that the concept of authorship was essentially modern: there was no real Hebrew equivalent for "author" and the nearest term, *sofer*, meant something like "account keeper" or "tally clerk," applied to numbers as well as narrative, the person who wrote things down for the record rather than an original creative artist. The text mattered more than the particular writer, whether in its allegedly original or its later, possibly edited, form. Spinoza had pointed out that

> The truth of a historical narrative, however assured, cannot give us the knowledge nor consequently the love of God, for love of God springs from knowledge of Him ... the truth of a historical narrative is very far from being a necessary requisite for our attaining to the highest good.[37]

There was accordingly little spiritual profit in detailed interrogation of the detail of biblical historical narrative. There was no need to be negative and destructive and make heavy weather of myth and miracle: all that was really needed was awareness that these represented ancient ways of conveying religious truth. But brash critical attributions of mythic or legendary elements could cause anxieties and misunderstandings, and stimulate equally brash and unsubtle secularist scoffing of the kind represented by G. W. Foote, who asked, "Is the resurrection of Jesus Christ

---

37. *Tractatus*, 61

a fact, or a legend that comes to us from the far-off ages of ignorance and credulity? Let the reader decide the question for himself."[38]

The dogmatic harshness of the extreme secularist position articulated by Foote and later freethinkers, and echoed at the end of the line by Richard Dawkins in the pride of his undeludedness, demonstrates the potential for tyranny in Enlightenment critique as applied to the scriptures, even if this may not have been exactly what Horkheimer and Adorno had in mind. It fails to address the emotional and pastoral inadequacy of merely reductionist approaches to the mythic that caused a distressed and "Strauss-sick" George Eliot, though no longer a conventional believer, to keep an engraving of Delaroche's *Christ* and a cast of Thorwaldsen's *Risen Christ* before her as she struggled to complete the enormous task of translating Strauss's harshly demythologizing *Leben Jesu*.[39]

George Steiner has drawn attention to the Jewish model of unending textual exploration and commentary on the scriptures—perhaps reflected in Kafka's baffled probing around abysses of meaning—not as an end in itself, but so it could issue in moral action and enlightened conduct in each succeeding age. He contrasts this with scholastic exegesis, which seeks a halt to the exegetical process and leads to the formulation of dogma, which can be regarded as "hermeneutic punctuation."[40] Biblical literalists, biblical critics, and skeptics are perhaps equally guilty here, breaking off from their reading too soon and delivering, at best, fragments of truth, overconfident that they have seen all the light there is. The post-Enlightenment challenge may be to keep on reading, open to the richness and complexity of meaning and to the rebirth of the reader in every generation rather than dogmatically assuming that either conservative literalism or various kinds of radical critique or hypothesis within or outside the church can ever have the last word.

---

38. G. W. Foote, *Bible Romances* (1882), 4th ed. (London: Pioneer Press for Secular Society, 1922), 224.

39. G. S. Haight, *George Eliot: A Biography* (Oxford: Clarendon Press, 1968), 58–59, quoting a letter of February 1846.

40. George Steiner, *Real Presences: Is There Anything in What We Say?* (London: Faber, 1989), 40–44.

C. H. Dodd, nonconformist churchman and biblical scholar, stressed the importance not of dogma but of religious experience in the Bible in his book *The Authority of Scripture* (1928), invoking the German scholar Rudolph Otto's influential discussion of the numinous, or the idea of the holy.[41] Otto, as the editor of Schleiermacher's *Reden* (1899), which was much influenced by Spinoza's emphasis on the knowledge and love of God, puts us in touch with a less familiar and less aggressive or iconoclastic version of Enlightenment tradition, focused on the experience and knowledge of God. This can be traced back through the ages to the Hebrew scriptures themselves and the psalmist's injunction "O taste and see that the Lord is good: blessed is the man that trusteth in him." Or, in the words of a popular seventeenth-century paraphrase:

> O make but trial of his love;
> Experience will decide
> How blest are they, and only they,
> Who in his truth confide.[42]

---

41. C. H. Dodd, *The Authority of the Bible* (London: Nisbet, 1928); Rudolph Otto, *The Idea of the Holy* (*Das Heilige*, 1917), trans. John W. Harvey, 2nd ed. (Oxford: Oxford University Press, 1950).

42. Psalm 34:8; Nahum Tate and Nicholas Brady, *A New Version of the Psalms of David* (1696).

# Jonathan Edwards's Metaphors of Sin in Indian Country

Joy A. J. Howard

The move to Indian country was an uncommon one for a preacher of Jonathan Edwards's status and age, but the seven years he lived in Stockbridge preaching to Mohawks, Mohicans, and colonial settlers proved to be some of the most fruitful of his career. Jonathan Edwards accepted the position in Stockbridge after his Northampton congregation voted to dismiss him in 1750 and, after visiting the mission town multiple times, he was officially installed as pastor in August of 1751.[1] Edwards valued Protestant mission imperatives, and although the pastorate was

---

1. The reasons for Jonathan Edwards's dismissal are not important to my argument; however, one of the most succinct explanations of his dismissal can be found in *The Sermons of Jonathan Edwards: A Reader*, eds. Wilson H. Kimnach, Kenneth P. Minkema, and Douglas A. Sweeney (New Haven: Yale University Press, 1999), pages xxxiii–xxxiv. For a fuller treatment of his dismissal, see Christopher Grasso, "Misrepresentations Corrected: Jonathan Edwards and the Regulation of Religious Discourse," in *Jonathan Edwards's Writing: Text, Context, Interpretation*, ed. Stephen Stein (Bloomington: Indiana University Press, 1996), 19–38; Kevin Sweeny's dissertation "'River Gods'; Patricia Tracy's *Jonathan Edwards, Pastor*"; David Hall's introduction to volume 12 of *The Works*, 1994; and Stephen J. Nichols, "Jonathan Edwards: His Life and Legacy," in *A God Entranced Vision of All Things: The Legacy of Jonathan Edwards*, ed. John Piper and Justin Taylor (Wheaton, IL: Good News Press, 2004). For a fuller explanation of how Edwards conceptualized the mission project to the Indians, see Gerald R. McDermott, "Missions and Native Americans," in *The Princeton Companion to Jonathan Edwards*, ed. Sang Hyun Lee (Princeton: Princeton University Press, 2005).

remote and he faced a significant language barrier between him and his new congregation, the move offered him the opportunity to be involved in important mission work as well as the opportunity to engage with political activity of the colony as it expanded. The Stockbridge Indian Mission was founded by the Society for the Propagation of the Gospel in New England—most often just called the New England Company. In 1724, the Housatonic Mohican Indians—eastern Algonquians—sold some of their land to the General Court and English settlers who arrived the following year. In 1736, the General Court changed course and created Stockbridge along the Housatonic River, which would be a town for both Christian Indians and for white colonists. It was an important military outpost for the French and Indian wars. The Mohicans had ties with western Indians in Ohio, and their alliance with the British was crucial to ongoing warfare with the French.[2] Stockbridge was on the very edge of settled British territory in a region where indigenous people interacted often with missionaries, soldiers, traders, settlers, and each other—a middle ground, to borrow Richard White's geographic and conceptual phrase.[3]

Edwards thrived in this middle ground, and many scholars have noted that he produced some of his most important philosophical works during this period.[4] *Original Sin* was in many ways the culmination of years of practical ministry and deep theological exploration. Its influence when it was published cannot be overstated; furthermore, its influence on Protestant theology continues today as is evidenced by its inclusion on the reading lists for first-year seminary students across the world. But when Edwards arrived in Stockbridge in 1751, the town was troubled. The English education for the Mohawk and Mohican children was faltering at best, and even more vexing was the so-called Christian "example" the

---

2. Ethnographers use the term *Mahican* for this particular group of Native Americans, but I am following Rachel Wheeler's lead and using *Mohican* because that is the name by which the tribe identifies itself today.

3. Richard White, *The Middle Ground: Indians, Empires, and Republics in the Great Lakes Region, 1650–1815* (New York: Cambridge University Press, 1991).

4. I.e., *Freedom of the Will* in 1754, *The Nature of True Virtue* in 1757, and *Original Sin* in 1758.

English settlers were failing to offer their Indian neighbors.[5] Much of Edwards's time was taken up advocating for the Indians and ensuring that other pastors—domestically and abroad—knew how land-hungry settlers threatened commonly held Christian mission goals. Edwards called Stockbridge "a place much exposed," referring to its location on the frontier during the French and Indian War (1755–1763).[6] Stockbridge was a place where some of his culturally insensitive and inaccurate assumptions were exposed to him. As the pastor of Mohawks and Mohicans, he apparently reconsidered one of his most basic metaphors—the sinner as a captive of savage cannibals—and I argue that this change may have been just as influenced by his congregation's interests as by his engagement with Enlightenment philosophy and logic. In this article, I analyze Jonathan Edwards's Indian sermons preached in Stockbridge and consider how his use of bodily metaphors for sin drops out of his theology after he settled in the town.

---

5. It must have been a relief for Edwards to get away from the conflicts that had driven him out of his pulpit in Northampton, but we are amiss to imagine Edwards's using Stockbridge as a quiet place to write. Rachel Wheeler and George Marsden have each presented strong arguments that contradict the previous wilderness-intellectual-retreat myth that Stockbridge Indian Mission had become. His years in Stockbridge were not without conflict. Edwards butted heads with many in his English congregation, and most of the conflict seems to have centered on Colonel Ephraim Williams. Williams felt that the Indian school was a good labor source, and Edwards wholeheartedly disagreed. Edwards was also appalled that Williams maneuvered to acquire increasing amounts of Indian land and that these transactions often included wine. By the time the New England Company sorted everything out, many of the Mohicans and most of the Mohawks had left the town and taken their children out of the school. This occurred fairly early in Edwards's tenure in Stockbridge. The boys' schoolhouse burned in February of 1753 and many Mohawks had left Stockbridge then, so there were not too many still at the mission later. For a fuller treatment of Edwards's disagreements with Colonel Williams, see Lion G. Miles, "The Red Man Dispossessed: The Williams Family and the Alienation of Indian Land in Stockbridge, Massachusetts, 1736–1818," *New England Quarterly* 67, no. 1 (1994): 46–76; James Axtell, "The Rise and Fall of the Stockbridge Indian Schools," *Massachusetts Review* 27 (1986): 367–78; and Philip F. Gura, *Jonathan Edwards: America's Evangelical* (New York: Hill and Wang, 2005), 65–186.

6. Jonathan Edwards, "To the Reverend John Erskine," in *Works of Jonathan Edwards Online*, vol. 16, *Letters and Personal Writings*, ed. George S. Claghorn (New Haven: Jonathan Edwards Center, Yale University, 2008), 665.

## The Social and Literary Contexts of the Indian Sermons

In my reading of Edwards's metaphors for sin, I address an ongoing debate about Jonathan Edwards's later works from this period in his life. His later texts—including the Indian sermons that I review here—are more philosophical than his earlier texts about evil and sin. They are decidedly heart based rather than based on particular sinful actions, and scholars disagree on the reasons for this change. Many, such as Avihu Zahai, Paul Helm, and Sang Lee, see Edwards responding to troubling Enlightenment ideas of human morality.[7] These scholars claim that this shift in his ontology is evidence of his genius and philosophical adeptness in responding to an Enlightenment culture where intellectuals found delight in inquiry and reason. What Leon Chai and others such as Paul Helm, Josh Moody, and David Laurence have brought to this debate recently is an understanding that Edwards developed his theology as a member of the Enlightenment; in other words, he was engaged as a member of a community.[8]

Leon Chai points out that one of the aspects of Locke that Edwards found appealing was the shakiness of human perception. The matter that concerned Edwards the most in *Religious Affections* was that the perception of divine spirit possession during ecstatic religious experience was not always true. He worried that people can so easily be fooled by the devil and that others can so easily fool themselves. False perception leads to unfulfilled salvation because the heart was not involved. "Perception," for John Locke, "is distinctly an act of the mind" which is

---

7. Avihu Zahai, "The Age of Enlightenment," in *The Cambridge Companion to Jonathan Edwards*, ed. Stephen J. Stein (New York: Cambridge University Press, 2007), 80–99; Paul Helm, "A Forensic Dilemma: John Locke and Jonathan Edwards on Personal Identity," in *Jonathan Edwards: Philosophical Theologian*, ed. Paul Helm and Oliver D. Crisp (Burlington, VT: Ashgate, 2003), 45–49; Sang Hyun Lee, *The Philosophical Theology of Jonathan Edwards* (Princeton: Princeton University Press, 2000).

8. Josh Moody, *Jonathan Edwards and the Enlightenment: Knowing the Presence of God* (Lanham, MD: University Press of America, 2005); and David Laurence, "Jonathan Edwards, John Locke, and the Canon of Experience," *Early American Literature* 15, no. 2 (Fall 1980): 107–23.

entirely what Edwards was concerned about.[9] "Edwards speaks merely of sensations," Chai writes of Edwards's reasoning in *Freedom of the Will*. "From these sensations, he goes on to say, we *infer* the existence of things external to ourselves. . . . Our sensations, then, convey nothing that by itself could produce the content of perception."[10] What happens to metaphor when all of the "things external"—the histories containing cultural tidbits that point toward the otherness of savages such as the Mohican and Mohawk peoples at Stockbridge—can no no longer be trusted because one's very sensations were corruptible? As Helm writes, "Locke was not used simply as a convenient peg on which to hang the coat of Calvinism," but rather the ideas that Edwards developed throughout his career in New England were very much a part of the Enlightenment milieu.[11] Indeed, I agree with this scholarship and I tend to also agree with Stephen H. Daniel's assessment when he asserts that part of Edwards's elusiveness lies in his very use of ontology, which is different than John Locke's. Commenting on this shift in his philosophy, Daniel writes,

> Of greater concern to Edwards though, is that in this fallen consciousness the mental is erroneously substituted for the spiritual. That substitution begins with the assumption that to be human necessarily means being an embodied individual. . . . However . . . by describing the Fall as the isolation of the self (defined as a body), Edwards shows how the interpretative confusion about his account of original sin itself relies on the fallen notion that sin is something that an individual self does, rather of what an individual self is.[12]

This critic notices that Edwards did not give examples of bodies *doing* evil things; he wrote about hearts that *were* evil. For Edwards our bodily

---

9. Leon Chai, *Jonathan Edwards and the Limits of Enlightenment Philosophy* (New York: Oxford University Press, 1998), 11.
10. Ibid., 109.
11. Paul Helm and Oliver Crisp, *Jonathan Edwards: Philosophical Theologian* (Burlington, VT: Ashgate, 2003), 45.
12. Stephen H. Daniel, *The Philosophy of Jonathan Edwards: A Study in Divine Semiotics* (Bloomington: Indiana University Press, 1994), 143.

existence is not "extrinsic relation of the individual."[13] It is the result of the Fall. The individual's sinfulness cannot stem from the body because physical experience depends entirely on perception.

Structuring his message in this manner not only makes sense from a philosophical perspective, it also makes sense when one considers Edwards's goals in Stockbridge. He was a smart theologian and, according to most, a good pastor in the mission. He wanted to articulate the gospel message in a way that did not push the Indians away. Preaching against sin that is no longer dependent on embodiment not only spoke more accurately to the Enlightenment ideas Edwards accepted, but also solved the problem of culturally complicated metaphors that risked failing with his Indian congregation. The Indians he preached to for seven years shaped the way in which he wrote about the fundamental condition of evil in the human heart, and considering that pastors today still use the texts he published while in Indian country, we begin to see that reading closely can reveal voice and power often assumed invisible or nonexistent.

To hear the voices of Indians that are silent in other readings of Edwards's sermons, my analysis also incorporates several important shifts in scholarship of early American Christianity in that conversion should not only be viewed as a weapon of oppression and of colonization, but also as a manner of cultural exchange. Faith is multifaceted, complex, and at times flexible to accommodate the hearts of indigenous believers as they struggled to understand what their new faith meant to them. In my approach to reading Jonathan Edwards's bodily metaphors of sin—before and then in Indian country—I am drawing on the recent scholarship surrounding the concept of "lived religion." Religion studies such as this and those exemplified by David D. Hall and Robert Orsi are defined by daily practices in many places, not only churches.[14] This approach examines "a study of how particular people, in particular places and times, live in, with, through, and against the religious idioms available to them in culture—*all* the idioms, including (often enough) those not explicitly their 'own.' . . . Religion comes into being in an

---

13. Ibid.
14. David D. Hall, ed., *Lived Religion in America: Toward a History of Practice* (Princeton: Princeton University Press, 1997).

ongoing, dynamic relationship with the realities of everyday life."[15] I am particularly interested in what Orsi says about idioms—those figures of speech or metaphors that help a discourse community make sense of their world and their place in it—because he suggests that those idioms are just as dynamic as practices and theologies.

Orsi continues by saying,

> Men and women do not merely inherit religious idioms, nor is religion a fixed dimension of one's being, the permanent attainment of a stable self. People appropriate religious idioms as they need them, in response to particular circumstances. All religious ideas and impulses are of the moment, invented, taken, borrowed, and improvised at the intersections of life.[16]

Douglas L. Winiarski and Richard W. Pointer each draw on Orsi and Hall's thesis to explore the faith of Native Americans and how their faith influenced the European colonists. Winiarski examines the lives of Indians after King Philip's War (1675-77) who were indeed both Native and Christian. Winiarski emphasizes that from the complex worldview of these Indian Christians, Christianity did not replace their Native identities, identities that in turn did not exclude a vibrant and viable faith within their own culture.[17] This sense of multiple threads that weave a coherent whole is important to studying the Indians involved in the Stockbridge mission. The Indians were already well versed in Christianity—both from the British and the French—and they participated in the mission as people with a faith. Pointer also highlights that those engaged in evangelism to native people were (and are) perhaps most aware that spiritual encounters were "fundamentally reciprocal and often mutually transformational."[18] Just as Dorinda Outram asserts that a definition of the Enlightenment is best constructed with threads of logic and morality coupled with threads of cross-cultural contact and

---

15. Robert Orsi, "Everyday Miracles: The Study of Lived Religion," in *Lived Religion in America*, 7.

16. Ibid., 8.

17. Douglas L. Winiarski, "Native American Popular Religion in New England's Old Colony, 1670-1770," *Religion and American Culture* 15, no. 2 (2005): 147-86.

18. Richard W. Pointer, *Encounters of the Spirit: Native Americans and European Colonial Religion* (Bloomington: Indiana University Press, 2007), 8.

conflict, scholarship of Edwards is best constructed using an approach that places him in Enlightenment company and in the Stockbridge mission community.[19]

This approach is complicated by a simple lack of details available about Edwards's Indian congregation and his interactions with them. We do not know details of the relationships he had with most of the Indians in Stockbridge, although it seems that they liked him. Edwards was frustratingly silent about individual Indians he knew well—preferring instead to write numerous letters that were more political in nature to secure much-needed funding for the mission, its teachers, and interpreters (all of which were chronically underfunded from Edwards's perspective). We do not know exactly how his friendships with Mohican and Mohawk leaders or with interpreters affected his daily life and thus his thinking about key theological issues with which he grappled. The details we do have point toward Edwards's heartbreak over how often the Indians at the mission were mistreated. Even before the Seven Years' War broke out, violence was too common in the Indian mission, and Edwards realized that the English settlers were often their own worst enemies. For example, in a letter to a friend in 1755 Edwards emphasized the numerous political injustices suffered by the Indians at the mission. "I have nothing very comfortable to write concerning my own success in this place," he laments. "The business of the Indian mission, since I have been here, has been attended with strange embarrassments." His primary concern was the violence against the Indians that continued to crop up despite his best efforts to quell it.[20] He says two English travelers killed one of the Stockbridge Indians "in the woods" and expresses his dismay at the fact that they "escaped without sentence of death."[21] To add insult to injury, two men dug up a newly buried Christian Indian's grave because an award had been offered for French Indian scalps. Even more disturbing to Edwards was the reaction of English settlers when French Canadian Indians attacked Stockbridge on a Sunday in between worship gatherings. The attacking Indians killed three English settlers

---

19. Dorinda Outram, "Cross-Cultural Encounters in the Enlightenment," in *The Enlightenment World*, ed. Martin Fitzpatrick (New York: Routledge, 2004), 551–65.
20. Jonathan Edwards, "To the Reverend John Erskine," 663.
21. Ibid.

in one family and then another man "coming into the town from some distant houses."[22] The settlers raised the alarm, and "multitudes" ended up acting "very foolishly towards our Indians on this occasion, suspecting them to be guilty . . . and threatening to kill them, and the like."[23] From his tone, Edwards found it confusing and annoying that the settlers did not apparently know how to tell "our Indians" from the French Indians who attacked in the first place. In his letters from Stockbridge, there follows a litany of incredibly unfortunate happenings as more English settlers moved west and the Indian community bore the weight of this violent undertaking.[24]

We lack an archive that reveals to us what practices Edwards might have gleaned from the Indian Christians in his congregation, and his own writings fail to offer the type of narrative we seek. I would therefore like to suggest that we read his Indian sermons in a way that helps us understand that, as Orsi writes, "Theologies are not made in a single venue only—in the streets or in the churches, at shrines or in people's living rooms."[25] Knowing that Edwards walked the streets of Stockbridge, shared meals, and worshipped with members of his Indian congregation, we can bring those Indians into the theology Edwards developed during this period of his life. I attempt to read his sermons as "necessary and mutually transforming exchanges between religious authorities and the broader communities of practitioners, by real men

---

22. Ibid.
23. Ibid.
24. Daniel P. Barr, *Unconquered: The Iroquois League at War in Colonial America* (Westport, CT: Praeger, 2006); and Fred Anderson, *A People's Army: Massachusetts Soldiers and Society in the Seven Years' War* (Chapel Hill: University of North Carolina Press, 1984). Stockbridge certainly was "a place much exposed" as Edwards said. The summer of 1755 brought what would later be called the Seven Years' War, or the French and Indian war. The key fort the English sought control over was roughly 150 miles north of Stockbridge on the border of what is now Vermont and New York. Both the English and the French claimed the Champlain Valley, and the French built the fort in 1731 to guard the lake. There were no other forts between Albany, New York—about 40 miles from Stockbridge—and Lake Champlain. The English were able to drive off the French and capture their supply lines although they did not capture the fort. Many Indian allies in this battle made their home in Stockbridge.
25. Robert Orsi, "Everyday Miracles," 9.

and women in situations and relationships they have made and that have made them."[26]

Rachel Wheeler has done a nice job opening up Jonathan Edwards's latter writings to the possibility of a discourse community that included the Stockbridge Indians. At first glance, the Indian sermons vividly use descriptions of nature and hunting in ways that earlier sermons do not. But the change is even more significant than that. These descriptions contained simpler rhetoric, which meant it was easier for his translators to work with his ideas. Wheeler's recent study of Moravian Indians and the Indians at Stockbridge in the seventeenth and eighteenth centuries illustrates what a dynamic community these particular Indians built. Leaders such as Hendrick Aupaumut came from Stockbridge. Aupaumut—a good friend of Mohegan minister Samson Occom—was born the year before Jonathan Edwards left the mission.[27] Rachel Wheeler suggests that Aupamut might even have been baptized by Edwards as a baby.[28] Throughout his life, Aupaumut corresponded with Edwards's son Timothy, and they seem to have enjoyed a close friendship. What Wheeler finds most compelling is Edwards's emphasis on the sinfulness of all people, regardless of race, country of origin, or gender. And while she is quick to point out that Edwards did not differ from other thinkers of his time, in that he thought that the Indians were heathen, he greatly differed in his explanation for it. Since all souls, as Edwards asserts in *Original Sin*, are equally sinful and degraded, the only advantage Europe has had over Africa and America is access to God over a longer period of time.[29]

Finally, in addition to the complex social context of the sermons, the structure of the Stockbridge Indian sermons themselves presents

---

26. Ibid.

27. Samson Occom eventually led Christian Indians from Stockbridge and other Praying Indian towns to form an intertribal Christian separatist movement, and these Indians moved to New Stockbridge after the American Revolution. See Joanna Brooks, "Samson Occom and the Poetics of Native Revival," in *American Lazarus: Religion and the Rise of African-American and Native American Literatures* (New York: Oxford University Press, 2003): 52–114.

28. Rachel Wheeler, "Hendrick Aupaumut: Christian-Mahican Prophet," *Journal of the Early Republic* 25, no. 2 (2005): 187–220.

29. Rachel Wheeler, "'Friends to Your Souls': Jonathan Edwards' Indian Pastorate and the Doctrine of Original Sin," *Church History* 72, no. 4 (2003): 736–65.

a challenge. The Indian sermon manuscripts—of which we have about 230—were previously assumed to be quickly revised and significantly shortened Northampton sermons, but Wheeler has illustrated that perhaps as many as 180 of the Indian sermons were new.[30] While Edwards did rework some material, the majority of the sermons were significantly original. Even in their creativity, the sermons were short and often exist only in outline form. Many appear to only be a list of topic sentences. The outline structure begs questions about Edwards's commitment to the mission. Did he indeed only preach for ten or fifteen minutes to the Mohawks and Mohicans on many Sundays? Surely, he needed to allow time for translation, but even with translation, many of the sermon outlines amount to ten minutes if read as written.[31] Preaching with an interpreter is cumbersome in many ways, but practically, it meant that his sermons would be shorter since the speaker would need to stop and wait for the interpreter to catch up with him.[32] No one that we know of took notes during the Stockbridge sermons, and it is difficult to imagine just what those sermons sounded like with Edwards's voice joined with at least two other translators and with other Indian

---

30. Rachel Wheeler, "Edwards as Missionary," in *The Cambridge Companion to Jonathan Edwards*, ed. Stephen J. Stein (New York: Cambridge University Press, 2007); and Wheeler, "'Friends to Your Souls.'"

31. Rachel Wheeler, "Jonathan Edwards: Missionary," in *Works Jonathan Edwards Online*, ed. George S. Claghorn (New Haven: Jonathan Edwards Center, Yale University, 2008), http://edwards.yale.edu/research/about-edwards/missionary. John Waumaumppequunaunt, a translator for the famous missionary David Brainerd, translated for the Mohicans while Rebecca Kellogg Ashley, a former Deerfield captive, translated for the Mohawks.

32. For more on how interpreters functioned in British territory among the English and Iroquois Six Nation people during colonial expansion, conflict, trade, and mission work, see Nancy Hagedorn, "Communications," in *American Eras: Early American Civilizations and Exploration to 1600*, ed. Gretchen Starr-LeBeau (Detroit: Gale Research, 1998), 77–101; Nancy Hagedorn, "Brokers of Understanding: Interpreters as Agents of Cultural Exchange in Colonial New York," *New York History* 76 (October 1995): 379–408; Nancy Hagedorn, "'A Friend To Go Between Them': The Interpreter as Cultural Broker During Anglo-Iroquois Councils, 1740–1770," *Ethnohistory* 35 (Winter 1988): 60–80. And her forthcoming manuscript from the University of Nebraska Press currently entitled *A Great Deal Depends Upon the Interpreters: Anglo-Iroquois Relations in the Colonial Northeast, 1664–1774*, is expected to be published in 2011.

leaders chiming in, since Mohawk and Mohican rhetorical traditions seem to have valued interactive listening.[33]

So while it is true that the Indian sermons are shorter, they do not lack literary value. Donald Weber writes that fragmentary sermons and sermon outlines reflected the "upheaval" of the Revolution and the Great Awakening.[34] Weber suggests that New Lighters used fragments because "fragments, then, were perhaps the only form [they] could trust in a time when traditional narrative could no longer mediate experience. . . . The Awakening, that is, demanded a new rhetorical mode to render a new experience, and fragments met the requirements of the ideology of new birth."[35] An outline form also lends itself to dialogue, especially the outlines that Edwards wrote for the Indians because they included so many rhetorical questions. Richard Bauman writes that this form of preaching offers a "high degree of control over the dynamic and direction of the interaction" while fostering a "collaborative" relationship as well.[36] Edwards's outlines fall within this framework, and although he's usually characterized as a preacher who relied heavily on notes and spoke in monotone, his outlines suggest that he might have been more like his fellow evangelists, at times preaching more extemporaneously.[37] The sermon outline as a literary form is readable in a way that is different from a published sermon that is more complete, but readable in its own right. It requires that we have a creative scholarly imagination to flesh out the rhetorical situation that included the Mohican and Mohawk Christians at Stockbridge since the sketch we have remaining in the archive is incomplete, as Weber has so nicely illustrated.

---

33. It is worth noting that many of his New York and Northampton sermons were only outlines. We have no indication in those sermons what Edwards added as he spoke, although we assume he did indeed add a significant amount of material and did not end after a ten-minute lesson.

34. Donald Weber, *Rhetoric and History in Revolutionary New England* (New York: Oxford University Press, 1988).

35. Ibid., 11, 27.

36. Richard Bauman, *Let Your Words Be Few: Symbolism of Speaking and Silence Among Seventeenth-Century Quakers* (New York: Cambridge University Press, 1983), 149.

37. Alan Heimert, *Religion and the American Mind: From the Great Awakening to the Revolution* (Cambridge: Harvard University Press, 1966), 230.

# Metaphors of the Sinner before Stockbridge: Captive, Sick Man, and Soldier

Before Stockbridge, Edwards's bodily metaphors for sinners fall into three roughly designated categories: the sinner as a slave or captive, the sinner as a sick man, and the sinner as a soldier of Satan. The figure of the captive in Edwards's sermons is especially dynamic because it relies on a grand narrative about captors and captives—something colonists faced every day—and often conflates the captive, the slave, and the servant into one hapless body in the example.[38] To be a captive to the devil or a servant to Christ draws upon well-established biblical metaphors, but Edwards's particular manner of fleshing out his tropes points to a seventeenth-century colonial notion of captivity and slavery.

In a sermon preached in New York early in Edwards's career, sin is a "tyrant," a slave owner who "commands" its slave or captive—the sinner—to do labor that does not give him any advantage at all.[39] Edwards asserts in the doctrine that if his congregation cannot see that they are in sin, it is because they are indeed in sin and are blind to it.[40] He emphasizes that the sinner should not only fear death, but should fear for his quality of life on earth:

> And there are multitudes of other ways whereby sin destroys the comfort, happiness and good things of this life. . . . There is never any advantage [that] accrues to men from any sin. They never are the happier for pride, malice, revenge, drunkenness, lasciviousness, swearing, cursing and damning: these things do

---

38. Edwards preached through several colonial wars and ongoing conflicts. When he was a young boy, Queen Anne's War between the French and English raged as far south as Florida and as far north as Nova Scotia. The raid on Deerfield, Massachusetts, occurred in 1704 as a part of this war. John Williams, the pastor who would later pen *The Redeemed Captive Returning to Zion* (1707), was Edwards's grandfather Stoddard's son-in-law and one of the more than one hundred settlers taken north. Williams's wife, Eunice, died soon after leaving Deerfield.

39. Jonathan Edwards, *Works of Jonathan Edwards Online*, vol. 10, *Sermons and Discourses, 1720–1723*, ed. William H. Kimnock (New Haven: Jonathan Edwards Center, Yale University, 2008), 337–51.

40. Ibid., 340–41.

a man no manner of good, neither in this world or the world to come.[41]

From here he works to clarify what kind of tyrannical master sin is. Edwards warns that "other masters have only the outward man in their service, can rule only their outward actions and have no dominion over their thoughts and wills, but sin enslaves the very soul."[42] Near the end of the sermon, he returns to the tyranny of sin by way of a cannibal example. He says,

> Consider how cruelly and tyrannically you are dealt with by sin. ... Thus cruelly are you dealt with by your master; the work he sets you about is to whet a knife whereby your own throat is to be cut, to sharpen and poison arrows that are to be thrust into your own hearts, to make a fire for yourself to be burnt in. For every sin a wicked man commits is a laying up wrath against the day of wrath, is a whetting the sword of vengeance, a poisoning the arrows of wrath that are to be whet in your own heart's blood, and a throwing fuel into hellfire. They do by you as I have heard they do in Guinea, where at their great feasts they eat men's flesh. They set the poor ignorant child who knows nothing of the matter, to make a fire, and while it stoops down to blow the fire, one comes behind and strikes off his head, and then he is roasted by that same fire that he kindled, and made a feast of, and the skull is made use of as a cup, out of which they make merry with their liquor. Just so Satan, who has a mind to make merry with you.[43]

This example from the 1720s is by far one of the most vivid, but it is hardly unique. In 1734, Edwards described the sinner as a potential captive of Satan in another sermon, this time to his Northampton church. "Be exhorted therefore earnestly to take heed," he preached, "lest you be led away and taken captive by Satan."[44] And again in 1747

---

41. Ibid., 342–43.
42. Ibid., 344.
43. Ibid., 348–49.
44. Jonathan Edwards, *Works of Jonathan Edwards Online*, vol. 19, *Sermons and Discourses, 1734–1738* (New Haven: Jonathan Edwards Center, Yale University, 2008), 129.

his sermon outline indicated that "being of sin" was like being taken captive by "barbarous Indians" and taken to Canada or captured by the French and made into slaves.[45]

In the passage quoted above, the cannibals ready to feast personify sin while the child represents the sinner who is captive. The cannibals here are sneaky. They slip behind the child on tiptoe and chop off his head. This is after they watch as "the poor ignorant child" makes them a fire over which his own body will roast. The cannibals wait until the flames need fanning and kill the child when he bends over to do so. The child's skull is fashioned into a communal cup from which the cannibals share some rum. The victim is a child, connoting not only innocence but also ignorance. People are small when compared with the devil and at risk, much like children captured in the wilderness without a mother or father to protect them from their enemies. Stories of cannibalism were robust and pervasive in Western thought to connote religious difference; later the stories connoted racial difference as well. Edwards meant the "us" to connote "Christians"—or, at the least, he meant to connote those aware of sin—and the "other" to be pagans, the heathens who were unaware of their sinfulness. And by the eighteenth century, stories of cannibals were more than stories of religious heathens; they were about what made a person human. More and more, it was about particular people of particular races and places.

Africans, Caribbean natives, and American Indians were all made into cannibals in the seventeenth and eighteenth century, and cannibalism took on shades of racism. Representation of cannibalism during this period was about race, inhumanness, and cultural inferiority. Europeans used stories of cannibalism to indicate the "otherness" of the indigenous people they met during colonization. The Spanish said the Indians in the West Indies were cannibals. Columbus told stories of cannibalism. Cotton Mather in *Decennium Luctuosum* spoke of the Indians who are cannibals and infant killers who are not unlike Quakers. Narratives of cannibalism articulate fears about the culture of another, as Colin Ramsey illustrates, and Jonathan Edwards was awash

---

45. Jonathan Edwards, *Works of Jonathan Edwards Online*, vol. 65, *Sermons, Series II, 1747* (New Haven: Jonathan Edwards Center, Yale University, 2008), 870; Proverb 10:24(b).

in this discourse.[46] John Norton's captivity narrative *The Redeemed Captive* was published just a few years before Jonathan Edwards moved to Indian country, and in it the Indians and the French are demonized via descriptions of cannibalism. "After some time the Indians seemed to be in a Russle," John Norton writes, "and presently rushed up into the Watch-Box, bro't down the dead Corpse, carried it out of the Fort, scalpt it, and cut off the Head and Arms: A young Frenchman took one of the Arms and Flay'd it, roasted the Flesh, and offere'd some of it . . . to eat."[47] It is not surprising then to presume that Edwards's congregation in New York would indeed have imagined Indians near them as the cannibals even as he said he was speaking of cannibals in Guinea. Wilson Kimnach in his article on how Edwards adeptly revised his sermons depending on his audience asserts that the cannibal metaphor worked because he wanted to stress "the black comedy of the paradoxically 'innocent' sinner's predicament."[48] The metaphor functioned well rhetorically for Edwards because they did cultural work that was quick and dirty and frightening.

The cannibal story in the New York sermon brought a subtext of otherness and wicked exoticism that connoted pure evil in the minds and hearts of the listeners. After all, what could be a worse sin than "roasting" and eating the flesh of a child? In a sense, the fears of cannibalism conflate fears of devil-possessed Indians in the wilderness of New England with the Caribbean- and African-based fears of black bodies eating their captives. The Indian body and the native body stood in for sin manifested on earth, and the captured victim at Satan's mercy stood in for sinners. The point is not whether Indians in New England were or were not cannibals: rather, the point is the way in which the texts work to conflate the bodies of the "other" into the body of sin and use that description to then lead a listener out of sinfulness and into salvation.

---

46. Colin Ramsey, "Cannibalism and Infant Killing: A System of Demonizing Motifs in Indian Captivity Narratives," *Clio* 24, no. 1 (1994): 55–68.3

47. John Norton, *The Redeemed Captive*, in *Narratives of Indian Captives*, vol. 6 (1748; repr., New York: Garland, 1978), 9–10.

48. Wilson H. Kimnach, "Jonathan Edwards' Sermon Mill," *Early American Literature* 10, no. 2 (1975): 171.

## Indian Sermons: Sin without a Body

When Edwards preached the Mohawk Treaty sermon in August of 1751, he spoke to the newly arrived contingent of Mohawks who were in the process of moving to Stockbridge for the first time as well as visiting Moravian Mohicans, Moravian missionaries, Stockbridge Mohicans, Stockbridge colonists, British army officials, and colonial representatives. The Indians knew Edwards; he sat on the board of trustees for the boarding school from 1743 to 1747, and the Northampton congregation financially supported the mission work during those years. The Mohawks arrived in Stockbridge to participate in treaty negotiations with the British, and there is little doubt that Edwards's presence helped move the talks along. The Indian commission desired that the Mohawks relocate to Stockbridge, and when the meetings adjourned later that week, about fifty chose to stay and others left with the promise to send their children to the school at the mission. Those that stayed joined the 250 Mohicans already settled.[49]

As Edwards preached to this large group, those in attendance heard his voice and the voice of his translators—one of whom was Rebecca Kellogg Ashley, the woman the Mohawks requested translate for them. The Indians knew Ashley because, arguably, she was one of them. She had lived most of her adult life in French Indian territory in a village called Kahnawake across the St. Lawrence from Montreal because she had been captured as a child in the infamous Deerfield, Massachusetts, raid in 1704. She married a Mohawk and had several children who lived in the north even though she had returned to British-controlled land. Her sister, Joanna, on the other hand, like the better-known Eunice Williams, chose to stay in the Mohawk community and never returned.

To the English community, Rebecca Kellogg Ashley was a redeemed captive—a survivor of a lengthy captivity who had remembered her roots, came back home to English colonial grounds, renounced Catholicism (as she must have to then work with Jonathan Edwards), and married an English settler. In later letters, Edwards depicted Rebecca Kellogg Ashley as integral to the mission success

---

49. Stephen J. Nichols, "Last of the Mohican Missionaries," 48.

among the Mohawks.[50] Edwards tells his colleagues how Rebecca Ashley's presence drew other Christian Mohawk leaders to the mission because they knew her. Gideon Hawley would later write that everyone agreed Rebecca Kellogg Ashley should be

> our interpreter and that Benjamin Ashley her husband should be employed and have a salary. This could not be avoided if we had his wife but he was a fanatick and on that account unfit to be employed in the mission. His wife was a very good sort of woman and an extraordinary interpreter in the Iroquois language.[51]

But, on the day Edwards preached during the Mohawk treaty talks, he had not worked with Ashley before and certainly had not yet formed the alliance they forged against those (including her older brother) who would prefer to use the Indian children as little more than slave laborers than spend the time and money educating them.[52] Not knowing her, he had not yet reevaluated his metaphors of sinfulness and therefore uses the captivity metaphor he had used before. This would be the first and last time he would do so in Indian country.

At the heart of the 1751 Mohawk Treaty sermon was a thesis that knowledge could only be accessed through scripture. The sermon can be divided into scripture, doctrine, and application, although they are not marked. "These honorable gentlemen treat in the name [of King George]," he begins by referring to the British colonial officials

---

50. Jonathan Edwards, "Letter to the Reverend Isaac Hollis. 1752," in *Works of Jonathan Edwards Online*, vol. 16, *Letters and Personal Writings*, ed. George S. Claghorn (New Haven: Jonathan Edwards Center, Yale University, 2008).

51. Gideon Hawley, "A Letter from Rev. Gideon Hawley of Marshpee Containing a Narrative of his Journey to Osohoghgwage. 1791," in *The Documentary History of the State of New-York*, ed. Christopher Morgan and Edmund B. O'Callaghan (New York: Weed, Parson, 1850), 1033–46.

52. Edwards, Ashley, and Hawley found themselves up against several influential town leaders, including the Williamses, the Dwights, and Captain Martin Kellogg, Rebecca's brother, who had control of the boarding school for boys before Hawley's arrival. As time progressed, it became clear that Captain Kellogg fundamentally disagreed with his sister and Edwards about the purpose of the school. Ashley disagreed with the management style of her brother, but rather than aligning herself with Edwards or her brother, she aligned herself with the Mohawks.

listening, "but I in the name of Jesus Christ."[53] He then establishes how God, through scripture, intervened into man's dark, evil ways and thoughts that resulted because of the Fall. "Some worshipped [the] sun and moon and stars, some worshipped images of gold and silver, brass and iron, wood and stone. Some worshipped serpents and other beasts. And some worshipped the devil, that used to come to 'em, and appear to 'em, and 'em believe that he was the true God."[54] The doctrine—the teaching part of the sermon—establishes that either one has scripture, can read it, and chooses not to, or one has the scripture but cannot read it. Positioning his new mission as the anti-French mission, he says that unlike the French, he wants the Indians to learn to read and do so quickly. He wants to "open the Bible to the Indians."[55]

The end of the sermon begins with the rhetorical turn of enough is enough: "But you have been neglected long enough," he says speaking to this group of Indians who were contemplating whether a move to Stockbridge is in their best interests.[56] Edwards had tremendous hope for the mission he had just joined: "'Tis now high time that some more

53. This sixteenth century notion of "treat" was not generally used this way in Edwards's day: *treat*, v. "The action or an act of treating, or discussing terms; parley, negotiation; agreement; treaty" (*OED*).

54. Jonathan Edwards, "Mohawk Treaty Sermon," in *The Sermons of Jonathan Edwards: A Reader*, ed. Wilson H. Kimnach, Kenneth P. Minkema, and Douglas A. Sweeney (New Haven: Yale University Press, 1999).

55. Ibid., 107. Edwards's choice of phrase, "open the Bible," is worth noting, as Lisa Gordis illustrates in *Opening Scripture: Bible Reading and Interpretive Authority in Puritan New England* (Chicago: University of Chicago Press, 2003). The phrase indicates both a physical sense of opening up the book that is the Bible and the underlying belief that the Holy Spirit could help a believer make sense of a text that might be difficult to understand. With this one phrase, Edwards is extending his beliefs of English Christians quite dramatically to include the Indians at the treaty. And just as Gordis asserts about John Eliot, this extension is not one to be taken lightly. Although literacy was an important part of New England Puritan culture, it was almost always tied to one's ability to read scripture (Gordis, 98–105). Edwards preaches decades after Eliot, but he is still highly invested in most of the same theological concerns as his predecessors. He expands the need for literacy beyond the Bible, however, and this is interesting. He carefully admits the sins of many English and Dutch, and so learning to read English is a skill that has a practical imperative as well as a theological one. "For as long as they keep you in ignorance," he says in this section, "'tis more easy to cheat you in trading with you." He wants the Indians to learn to read so they can have a more even hand in trading.

56. The most often quoted phrase in Edwards's Indian sermons appears in this section: "We are no better than you in no respect."

effectual care should be taken that you may be really brought into the clear light." He concludes, "When you are dead, your eyes will be open. Then this world will look little to you, and you shall know that religion is infinitely the greatest concern." He warns them that the devil tries to blind the eyes of men, and if he succeeds, then mankind will live eternally in hell after death.

In conclusion, he offers what must have been intended as a striking metaphor of sinfulness: a child captured by feared enemies. He is kept alive by his captors, but only because they want to eat him. The child represents a person trapped by the devil, completely unaware that the food he eats is making him more desirable to his captors. The cannibals represent the devil working to keep people in the dark about the conditions of their souls so they do not change or try to escape.

> 'Tis because men are blind that they are not more concerned for the good of their souls and the souls of their poor children. 'Tis because they are blind that they go in drunkenness and spend away their lives in wickedness. The devil blinds men's eyes and tries to his utmost to keep 'em in the dark, that he may destroy them. I have read of some nations, that when they take children captives in war, they keep them well for a while and feed them with the best till they are fat, and then kill them and eat them. So the devil does by wicked men. Now, therefore, look well about you and consider what is best for yourselves and your children.[57]

How did the metaphor—the poor sinner captive by flesh-hungry natives—work in Indian country? Imagining the hundreds of Indian faces watching Edwards and his translators speak on this important August day complicates the connotations that were easily accessible to Edwards just weeks prior. How should the sinner's body be imagined? Did Rebecca Kellogg Ashley feel that her captors—one of whom she married and raised children with—were accurate stand-ins for the devil seeking to destroy the sinner? How should the bodies of the captors who eat the sinner's flesh be sketched out? Indians were usually figured

---

57. Jonathan Edwards, "The Mohawk Treaty Sermon," 105–10.

as the captors, but this audience would have known that they were also the captives.

Most likely many in the audience recognized the crudely drawn metaphor for what Edwards intended it to be, but more likely is a scenario where captivity and danger was too real to be used in a sermon in this way. More likely it was a discourse community that knew all too well that in colonial cannibal stories, they were the cannibals, not the innocent child captured. The signification is not clear any longer; thus, the function of the metaphor fails at its purpose: to draw the sinner's soul into experiencing grace with a savior. Some of this is speculative, of course, since we do not know what happened between Edwards and his new congregation members after this sermon or after any other sermon. We cannot know for sure why Edwards dropped the metaphor of the sinner captured by native cannibals from his sermons, but we can look to his later sermons as evidence of how his new rhetorical situation pressed him to preach in ways that were more culturally sensitive and more complicated philosophically.

For example, Edwards starts his conclusion of "All Mankind of all Nations" in much the same way he did above; he emphasizes how blind a person is to his own sin, but he does not flesh out the example with a story of captivity and cannibalism. We do not have an exact date for "All Mankind," but it is a Stockbridge Indian sermon and most likely an early one.[58] "They who don't see how wicked they be and how they deserve to perish can't come with their hearts to Christ," Edwards says. What he does not do is extend the metaphor to make the blind sinner food for a cannibalistic devil as he did before. Those who are "headed for destruction" are "beasts" and "are heathen," but the sinners are not embodied in any real way. In another early Indian sermon entitled "Heaven's Dragnet," Edwards imagines those who are sinners and those who are saved as fish. However, the sinners' bodies and actions are not imagined to be any worse than those of the saved. Edwards says,

---

58. Jonathan Edwards, "All Mankind of All Nations," in *The Blessing of God: Previously Unpublished Sermons of Jonathan Edwards*, ed. Michael McMullen (Nashville: B&H Academic, 2003), 225–30.

When a fisherman casts a net into the sea, what he aims at is only good fish that are good for food. He don't desire to catch any but good fish, but yet the net will gather every sort, good and bad. So none ought to come into the Christian church but good men: but because ministers can't know men's hearts, every sort will come in, good and bad. As there will be some bad fish in the net, so there will be some bad men in the kingdom of Christ. The fishermen, when their net was full, drew the fish out of the sea. The fish, after they were in the net, were but a short time in the sea: they were soon drawn to the shore. So the professors of religion will be but a short time in this world: they will soon be taken away out of this world into the other world. While the fish were in the net in the sea, it could not be seen what the fish were, whether good or bad; but when they were drawn to shore, then it could be seen plainly what they were and the bad could easily be distinguished from the good. So, while professors of the Christian religion are in this world, often-time we can't certainly say what they be, whether good or bad men; but men are taken out of the world, and when this world comes to an end, then it will be seen.[59]

Sin in this metaphor of fishing becomes more philosophically complex than sin embodied by a native cannibal. The sinful fish caught up in the net of the church—before the moment of judgment before God on the shore—were not less colorful, worse swimmers, or cannibalistic piranhas as imagined by Edwards. They looked and acted like everyone else even though their hearts were sinful. There is nothing external to indicate how the story will end for a specific fish, and in this way sin became much more about the condition of one's heart rather than the state of the body.

Before Indian country, Edwards used the fish metaphor to explain that some bad fish end up in the net (meaning the church) regardless of the best intentions of the fisherman (in this instance, meaning the

---

59. Jonathan Edwards, *Works of Jonathan Edwards Online*, vol. 25, *Sermons and Discourses, 1743–1758* (New Haven: Jonathan Edwards Center, Yale University, 2009), 576–82.

preacher). He writes: "The fisherman did not desire to catch any bad fish in his net for any good that the bad fish will do or receive there, or because any of his purposes as a fisherman are answered by them, but because 'tis unavoidable." In the Indian sermon, he has added a nuanced argument about the reason the fisherman could not help but catch both bad and good fish. It was not just that it was "unavoidable"; it was because sinfulness was not so easily characterized.

It could be said that Edwards adapted how he talked about sin because he attempted to become culturally sensitive to a new discourse community. To a certain extent it is true that he changed some of his cultural and linguistic codes, as Rachel Wheeler has noted. Edwards made use of more nature metaphors such as rivers and trees and mentioned hunting on the Sabbath as an activity he'd prefer the Indians to curtail. It is also true that he did not radically change his opinions of Indians being closer to evil than Europeans, as Gerald R. McDermott has illustrated, but regarding Edwards's fish metaphor, the subtle change in the way Edwards preached about sin is significant.[60] As I have suggested, then, it is useful to return to Stephen Daniel's commentary on how disconnecting the body from the concept of sin allows Edwards to engage Enlightenment problems of untrustworthy perception and sensation. Before living in Indian country, Edwards could reduce Indian cannibals to a role in his articulation of evil. An Indian could represent the idea of sin by capturing a sinner who was not even aware he was about to become lunch. But after living in Indian country, Edwards seems to suggest that it is difficult to tell who is sinful and who is not and therefore it is useless to represent sin in such broad strokes as a cannibal or the cultural other. In his fish metaphor, he preaches that "it could not be seen what the fish were, whether good or bad." The fisherman, who represents Jesus in the tale, is the only one who can tell who is truly good—a Christian—and who is bad when the net is pulled to shore and the fish spill out in front of him. If what Hall and Orsi assert about religion being an "ongoing, dynamic relationship" is true, it makes sense that Edwards's metaphors would have been affected by

---

60. Gerald R. McDermott, "Jonathan Edwards and American Indians: The Devil Sucks Their Blood," *The New England Quarterly* 72, no. 4 (1999): 539–57.

Edwards's relationships. My point here—that the presence of Mohican and Mohawk Christians at the Stockbridge mission shifted the way Edwards metaphorically figured the sinning body—not only frames Edwards's seven years in Indian country more wholly, it also speaks to the larger issue of reimagining the world of Native Christianity in the colonial world as being part of the same intellectual and spiritual sphere as other Enlightenment projects.

# Holy Land Travel and the Representation of Prayer in the Enlightenment

*Michael Rotenberg-Schwartz*

> Religious practice in the Land of the Bible tends to encourage exclusivity and discrimination rather than love and magnanimity. There is no place like the Holy Land to make one cynical about religion.
> —Raja Shehadeh, *Palestinian Walks*[1]

Something about publicized supplication embarrasses critical readers, especially of the Enlightenment, who, since Samuel Johnson, have been trained to doubt if not the sincerity at least the efficacy of rhetoricized prayer. Milton was "nothing satisfied" with the preliminary eight stanzas of his unfinished lyric "The Passion," for example, and printing it anyway has been cause enough for his critics to remain so.[2] For one, the closest Milton gets to the scene of

---

1. Raja Shehadeh, *Palestinian Walks: Forays into a Vanishing Landscape* (New York: Scribner, 2007), 140.

2. Milton's postscript to the poem reads: "This subject the Author finding to be above the yeers he had, when he wrote it, and nothing satisfy'd with what was begun, left it unfinisht." John Milton, *The Riverside Milton*, ed. Roy Flannagan (Boston: Houghton Mifflin Company, 1998), 52. Roy Flanagan's headnote to the poem informs readers that "The Passion" is "generally rated as Milton's worst English poem" and includes John Shawcross's condemnation of it as "inept and overreaching" as well as Philip Gallagher's assessment that it lacks "divine inspiration" (50). All subsequent references to the poem are to this edition and line numbers are cited parenthetically within the text.

the crucifixion is Jesus's tomb *after* the resurrection; he finds the "sad Sepulchral rock / That *was* the Casket of Heav'ns richest store" (43–44; emphasis added). More at issue is his use of metaphysical conceit. In the last stanza, the poet imagines he might from a mountaintop hear so many echoes of his infectious weeping that he'll think "(for grief is easily beguild)" he had impregnated a cloud with a race of mourners (54). Thomas Corns has shown the congruity of such imagery with contemporary Laudian commemoration poetry,[3] but for Barbara Lewalski such "extravagant" images fail because Milton's "Protestant imagination was not stirred by the Passion."[4] Similarly, Roy Flanagan conjectures that the verse seems forced because "Milton's heart is not in this poem," the death of Christ being "a distasteful subject to Protestants of Milton's era, who would have associated the Crucifixion with Roman Catholic iconography." Aptly describing this take on the Protestant imagination as an oversimplification, Noam Reisner counters that the Passion "clearly did stir Milton's Protestant imagination, otherwise he would not have attempted this poem to begin with."[5] Rather than assume it limited by an overly generalized Protestant episteme, Reisner treats the poem as a failure of Milton's own making, identifying in its rhetoric a reluctance in Milton to stifle his prophetic ambition and let himself be moved to a loss of emotional and verbal control. Unlike in the "Nativity Ode," where the poet succeeds by positioning himself in an intermediary role between angels and humans, in "The Passion" Milton's insistence on self-reference makes him "unable to create the sacramental space necessary" for the meditation to work.[6]

About "The Passion," Johnson has little to say, save that Milton's overfondness for his early verse implies a lack of respect for his readers' discrimination. But the problem of self-preoccupation noticed by Reisner comes up in the "Life of Waller," where Johnson defines four kinds of pious meditation—faith, thanksgiving, repentance, and

---

3. Thomas Corns, "'On the Morning of Christ's Nativity,' 'Upon the Circumcision' and 'The Passion,'" in *A Companion to Milton*, ed. Thomas N. Corns (Oxford, UK, and Malden, MA: Blackwell Publishers, 2003), 217–19.

4. Barbara Lewalski, *The Life of John Milton* (Oxford: Blackwell, 2000), 38.

5. Noam Reisner, "The Prophet's Conundrum: Poetic Soaring in Milton's 'Nativity Ode' and 'The Passion,'" *Philological Quarterly* 83, no. 4 (Fall 2004): 383.

6. Ibid. 385.

supplication—in physical terms, implying that genuine prayer involves a loss of voice. Faith cannot be dressed or "invested" with decoration; thanksgiving is "to be felt rather than expressed"; repentance, or "trembling" before God the judge, admits no time for pointed expression; supplication can "only cry" for mercy. If the immediacy of devotion involves being humbled before an infinite, omnipotent creator, a poetic reflection that articulates individual experience must be problematic.[7] Thus, "of sentiments purely religious, it will be found that the most simple expression is the most sublime." Even when written simply, pious poetry may aid memory and please the ear, but will teach nothing of Christian truth, which is "too simple for eloquence, too sacred for fiction, and too majestick for ornament." And so, Johnson concludes, to amplify religion in verse is like trying "to magnify, by a concave mirror, the sidereal hemisphere," to dilate upon the vastness of God by artificially, mechanically limiting it.[8]

Remarkably, Johnson's doubt of mediation particularly in prayer but even in science anticipates Jonathan Sheehan's suggestion that, even after defining the Enlightenment as a constellation of media in and

---

7. Before God's awful presence, the self is too occupied to be self-occupied. In the "Life of Young," written by Croft for Johnson, Young's poem the "Last Day" is said to disappoint because "the thought of the Last Day makes every man more than poetical, by spreading over his mind a general obscurity of sacred horror, that oppresses distinction, and disdains expression." Samuel Johnson, *The Lives of the Most Eminent English Poets; with Critical Observations on their Works*, vol. 4, ed. Roger Lonsdale (Oxford: Clarendon Press, 2006), 164.

8. Samuel Johnson, *The Lives of the Most Eminent English Poets; with Critical Observations on their Works*, vol. 2, ed. Roger Lonsdale (Oxford: Clarendon Press, 2006), 53–54. On Johnson's attitude to religious verse, see Lonsdale's notes to paragraphs 135–41, 282–84. See also, David R. Anderson, "Johnson and the Problem of Religious Verse," *Age of Johnson* 4 (1991): 41–57. For a provocative association of Satan's with Johnson's feeling that gratitude and worship were better felt than expressed, for "when expressed it exposes the dirty secret of worship . . . to recognize divine worship for what it is makes it appear almost as a kind of idolatry," see Andrew Barnaby, "Cringing before the Lord: Milton's Satan, Samuel Johnson and the Anxiety of Worship," in *The Sacred and Profane in English Renaissance Literature*, ed. Mary A. Papazian (Newark: University of Delaware Press, 2008), 329. For a summary of Johnson's conception of faith and its place in his theology, see Gregory Scholtz, "Sola Fide? Samuel Johnson and the Augustinian Doctrine of Salvation," *Philological Quarterly* 72, no. 2 (Spring 1993): 185–213; and, on Johnson's fideism, David Venturo, *Johnson the Poet: The Poetic Career of Samuel Johnson* (Newark: University of Delaware Press, 1999), 104–34.

through which new religious cultures and practices could be formed, still "certain religious domains might be, by and large, external to these media: private devotion, prayers, certain liturgical elements, church law, and so on."[9] Beyond expression and proof, moments of spiritual piety paradoxically are written out of definitions of religion and enlightenment. In at least one kind of writing, however, prayer manifests in discursive passages precisely where writers face the challenge of stating their beliefs in a space where multiple Christianities exist and might possibly be said to exert an influence on them: namely, narratives of travel to the Holy Land (particularly, the Church of the Holy Sepulchre; the Latin and Greek chapels at Calvary, and the chapels of the sepulcher itself, within it), too-often considered from a purely secular viewpoint by scholars. Attending to the way these narratives make time for and even enable faithful devotion by conceiving of piety and curiosity as potentially simultaneous and mutually beneficial impulses, I hope not only to illuminate the expressive failure of Milton's "Passion"—the publication of which marks a lingering desire to see and pray by at least giving voice to what it would but cannot—but also to locate a place for prayer and pious devotion in the Enlightenment, a period during which writers seem reticent when dealing with spiritual piety. Religion having been reified as a discrete object of study by nineteenth-century predecessors, philosophers such as Derrida and Žižek see the modern secular age sharply dividing spirituality and curiosity, the sacred and the secular, even the ineffable and the recordable, to dismiss faith but yet, because it is defined by this rejection, demand faith in others.[10] Scholars

---

9. Jonathan Sheehan, "Enlightenment, Religion, and the Enigma of Secularization: A Review Essay," *American Historical Review* 108, no. 4 (October 2003): 1076. Sheehan calls the representation of these new religious forms secularization. Defining secularization as differentiation, C. John Sommerville, "Secular Society/Religious Population: Our Tacit Rules for Using the Term 'Secularization,'" *Journal for the Scientific Study of Religion* 37, no. 2 (June 1998): 249–53, recognizes that its "structures are secular, but the population itself may be religious" (251).

10. I borrow this formulation of Modernist secularism from two unpublished talks by David Sherman: "Faith, Second-Hand: Modernism and the God of the Other," presented at the annual conference of the Northeast Modern Language Association in Boston, February 27, 2009; and "Overheard Music: Crisis Management in Modern Faith," a plenary lecture presented at the Brandeis University Graduate Student Conference, October 9, 2009.

should understand the Enlightenment, however, as constituted by what was still a struggle to discover whether religious phenomena could be represented as personal experiences.

The Holy Land pertains to "The Passion," of course, because in the sixth stanza an angel suddenly transports the poet's spirit to a mountain from which he envisages Jerusalem drowned in blood and sits "in pensive trance, and anguish, and ecstatic fit" (42). In the following stanza, the poet imagines catching sight of the Holy Sepulchre:

> Mine eye hath found that sad Sepulchral rock
> That was the Casket of Heav'ns richest store,
> And here though grief my feeble hands up-lock,
> Yet on the softened Quarry would I score
> My plaining vers as lively as before;
> For sure so well instructed are my tears,
> That they would fitly fall in order'd Characters. (43–49)

If the poet were at the tomb itself, he imagines, though grief would move him to prayer (not poetry, just as Johnson would have it), his tears nevertheless would carve words onto Jesus's tomb itself. Even so, his tears being "instructed" to "fitly fall" makes their pious language seem less individual than quasi-Providential. Moreover, they would fulfill again and ironically Johnson's demand for silence; unlike "On the Morning of Christ's Nativity," which is comprised mainly of "The Hymn," here Milton does not know or will not say what he "would" cry and moves on.[11] Before wishing this rhetorical silence signaled divine qualities more than the poet's gestures, then, which conclusion might only reproduce satirical attacks of the age on users of high-church liturgy (for example, Samuel Butler's characterization of a Catholic as one who "Says his Prayers often, but never prays, and worships the Cross more than *Christ*"), it is worth comparing its speculative representation of a meditative experience with that of actual seventeenth-century travelers

---

11. Merrit Hughes compares Milton's to Crashaw's use of the conceit in "Upon the Death of a Gentleman," John Milton, *Paradise Regained, The Minor Poems, and Samson Agonistes*, ed. Merrit Y. Hughes (New York: Odyssey Press, 1937), 176, footnote to lines 48–49.

who write about being at the Church of the Holy Sepulchre.[12] For it is at this time, as Thomas Noonan has shown, that travelers supplement litanies of places, relics, and ceremonies with portrayals of their own interiority, especially the struggle to convey the intimate emotional experiences of pilgrimage.[13]

Though Reisner speaks of sacramental space, he says nothing of these lines or to what they may be referring, but in its Holy Land setting Thomas Warton detected a specific source, George Sandys's *A Relation of a Journey* (1615):

> [Milton] seems to have been struck with reading Sandys's description of the Holy Sepulchre at Jerusalem; and to have catched sympathetically Sandys's sudden impulse to break forth into a devout song at the aweful and inspiring spectacle. 'It is a frozen zeal that will not be warmed with the sight thereof. And, oh that I could retain the effects that it wrought, with an unfainting perseverance! Who then did dedicate this hymn to my Redeemer, &c.[14]

Warton's belief that Sandys's "sudden" impulse could be withstood, retained with "unfainting perseverance," and then spread (like the contagion in the final stanza of "The Passion") to Milton not only reflects a difference of opinion with Johnson on the power of the minor lyric to convey enthusiastic feelings but also reveals an awareness that by reading a narrative of travel one might experience the Holy Land vicariously and, at least sometimes, spiritually.[15] Sandys's verses themselves, which Warton does not quote, are not said to be an influence, just the idea of wanting to "retain the effects" of the "aweful and inspiring

---

12. Samuel Butler, *Characters*, ed. Charles W. Daves (Cleveland and London: Case Western University Press, 1970), 103.

13. F. Thomas Noonan, *The Road to Jerusalem: Pilgrimage and Travel in the Age of Discovery* (Philadelphia: University of Pennsylvania Press, 2007), 241.

14. John Milton, *Poems upon Several Occasions, English, Italian, and Latin, with Translations, by John Milton . . . With Notes Critical and Explanatory, and other Illustrations, by Thomas Warton* (London, 1785), 289.

15. His headnote welcomes this comparison, defending the ode in general from "a great critic" who doubted in the "Life of Milton" whether short compositions could attain sublimity. Of the ode's potential, Warton writes, "We have the proof before us." Ibid., 286.

spectacle."[16] But Sandys's did include them in his narrative,[17] contradicting a commonplace in early modern studies that English Holy Land travel in this era was thoroughly secular in goal and design.[18]

Seventeenth- and eighteenth-century English travelers to the Holy Land[19] have not generally been treated as pilgrims but as enlightened skeptics and proto-Orientalists in whose writing religion manifests itself

---

16. The poem reads:
> Saviour of mankind, Man, Emanuel:
> Who sinless died for sin, who vanquisht hell:
> The first-fruits of the grave: whose life did give
> Light to our darkness; in whose death we live:
> O strengthen thou my faith, correct my will,
> That mine may thine obey: protect me still,
> So that the latter death may not devour
> My soul seal'd with thy seal. So in the hour
> When thou, whose body sanctifi'd this Tombe,
> Unjustly judg'd, a glorious Judge shalt come
> To judge the world with justice; by that sign
> I may be known, and entertain'd for thine.

George Sandys, *A Relation of a Iourney begun Anno Domini 1610* (London, 1615), 167. Acceptance of the poem as pious verse is evinced in Richard Cattermole's inclusion of it among Sandys's Psalm translations in *Sacred Poems of the Seventeenth Century*, ed. Richard Cattermole (London, 1836). Whereas Milton inscribes his words on the sepulchre, Sandys describes his soul as being imprinted with the seal of a God. Sandys's poem addresses the Son, the savior who was human and "God among us"; Milton's addresses potential muses and the poet's grief.

17. He is one of two English writers in the seventeenth and eighteenth centuries to include a meditative lyric in his narrative of travel to the Holy Land. Aaron Hill, who was moved to moral versifying at the Tomb of Kings and printed them in *The Present State of Aethiopia, Egypt, Palestine, and the Whole Ottoman Empire* (London, 1709), is the second (283).

18. Exceptions to this are Noonan's *Road*, which focuses mainly on European travelers but argues throughout that Protestant travelers such as Leonhard Rauwolf (1581) and Jonas Korte (1741) belong to a pilgrimage tradition; and Daniel J. Vitkus, "Trafficking with the Turk: English Travelers in the Ottoman Empire During the Early Seventeenth Century," in *Travel Knowledge: European "Discoveries" in the Early Modern Period*, ed. Ivo Kamps and Jyotsna G. Singh (New York: Palgrave, 2001), which emphasizes the iconoclasm of "anti-pilgrims" but acknowledges their occasional piety. Sensing a complexity of motives in William Lithgow's Travels, Clifford Bosworth nonetheless casts the religious element as a throwback; see, Clifford Edmund Bosworth, *An Intrepid Scot: William Lithgow of Lanark's Travels in the Ottoman Lands, North Africa and Central Europe, 1609–21* (Aldershot, UK, and Burlington, VT: Ashgate, 2006), 11.

19. Or Palestine; or the Ottoman sanjaks of Jerusalem, Gaza, Nablus and Lajjun, within the vilayet of Damascus. On use of the name "Palestine" in this period, see Haim

merely in Protestant chauvinism (remarks against Roman Catholics, members of the Eastern churches, Muslims, and occasionally Jews) and antiquarian exertions to map a Biblical rather than contemporary landscape.[20] In "English Travel Books about the Arab Near East in the Eighteenth Century," for example, Mohamad Ali Hachicho divides near eastern travel into three distinct classes—devout, commercial, and learned—and says that the "chain of pilgrims who had no other interest or motive but to behold the heritage of Jesus Christ" ended in 1506 with Sir Richard Guilford.[21] Likewise, implying that Western European travelers were motivated exclusively by their interest in history, ancient remains, geography, and current affairs, Nathan Schur includes "Holy Places" in his taxonomy of thirty thematic topics to be found in itineraries of the Holy Land but says nothing about religious devotion.[22] There is justification for this. One reason typically offered for the sixteenth-century decline in pilgrimage is the taking of Jerusalem by the Ottoman Empire in 1517, as well as the siege of Vienna twelve years after that.

---

Gerber, "'Palestine' and Other Territorial Concepts in the 17th Century," *International Journal of Middle East Studies* 30, no. 4 (November, 1998): 563–72.

20. Of course Catholics also represent their Holy Land experiences in diverse ways. For two, see John Mocquet, *Travels and Voyages into Africa, Asia, and America, the East and West-Indies; Syria, Jerusalem, and the Holy-Land* (London, 1696), in which Mocquet seems fulfilled by his self-proclaimed religious voyage (312); and Jean de Thevenot, *The Travels of Monsieur de Thevenot into the Levant* (London, 1687), in which the author enjoys seeing Christians of all sects celebrate Easter on the same day, but emphasizes the difficulty of enjoying a spiritual experience amid a throng of other pilgrims (191–92). See also Thevenot's trip to the Jordan, where "I received the Sacrament, but it was very incommodious" (193); like Sandys, Thevenot was moved at the Holy Sepulchre: "This place inspires great Devotion even into the most undevout; as I found by my self" (187).

21. Mohamad Ali Hachicho, *English Travel Books about the Arab Near East in the Eighteenth Century, Die Welt des Islams* 9, no. 1 (1964), 18. Richard Torkington, a Catholic priest who traveled to the Holy Land in 1517, is not mentioned, but William Lily and Andrew Boorde are said to have traveled as pilgrims though they "still had other major interests" (19). In David Falconar, *A Journey from Joppa to Jerusalem in May*, 1751 (London, 1753), the author once calls his trek to Jerusalem a *"bunyaning it on,"* but like most statements in the narrative, with irreverence and sarcasm (11). Bunyan's *Pilgrim's Progress*, of course, allegorizes a spiritual as a physical journey, and anyway uses vernacular imagery to describe biblical sites.

22. Nathan Schur, "Itineraries by Pilgrims and Travelers as Source Material for the History of Palestine in the Ottoman Period," in *Palestine in the Late Ottoman Period: Political, Social and Economic Transformation*, ed. David Kushner (Jerusalem: Yad Izhak Ben-Zvi Press, 1986).

Another, of course, is the advent of Protestantism, which attacked the attribution of holiness to particular sites as well as the link between pilgrimage and the abuse of indulgences.[23] While the transfer of relics throughout Europe over the centuries shifted focus away from the one real to many virtual Jerusalems, in the fifteenth century, the Devotio Moderna, Thomas à Kempis's *Imitation of Christ* most famously, "eased" access to a heavenly Jerusalem by conceiving of it as an inward journey (albeit through the sacraments of baptism and communion). In a meditation on the Holy Sepulchre, Kempis writes that the site's having been once holy means little now:

> Truly this *sepulcher* was then *holy ground*. . . . Persons indeed since have visited this place, some out of curiosity, and many out of superstition. But what did Christ leave the *power* or *merit* of his death in his *sepulchre*? Must persons, to be buried *with him* or partake of his *death*, undertake long pilgrimages from the end of the earth? No, I need not go there for this; or if I did, I should not find it there. For my Lord Christ has vouchsafed

---

23. Some early church fathers themselves, Jerome and Gregory of Nyssa, for example, who both made pilgrimage to Jerusalem, felt ambivalently about the status of Palestine. Whatever holiness it possessed would not necessarily rub off on visitors; plus, there was no reason to suppose one place holier than another. What matters, Jerome wrote to Paulinus of Nola, is not to have been at Jerusalem but to have lived a good life while there: "The true worshippers worship the Father neither at Jerusalem nor on mount Gerizim. . . . Therefore the spots which witnessed the crucifixion and the resurrection profit those only who bear their several crosses. . . . Access to the courts of heaven is as easy from Britain as it is from Jerusalem." St. Jerome, "Epistle LVIII," in *Jerome: Letters and Select Works*, trans. W. H. Fremantle, vol. 6 of *A Select Library of the Nicene and Post-Nicene Fathers of the Christian Church*, ed. Philip Schaff and Henry Wace (New York: Christian Literature Company, 1893), 120. Gregory went further, stating that one ought to prevent others from undertaking the journey. Of his own experience, Gregory denied being changed: "We confessed that the Christ Who was manifested is very God, as much before as after our sojourn at Jerusalem. . . . We derived thus much of profit from our traveling thither, namely that we came to know by being able to compare them, that our own places are far holier than those abroad." Moreover, he argued that when one holds on to wicked thoughts, "even if thou wast on Golgotha, even if thou wast on the Mount of Olives, even if thou stoodest on the memorial-rock of the Resurrection, thou wilt be as far away from receiving Christ into thyself, as one who has not even begun to confess Him." Gregory of Nyssa, "On Pilgrimages," in *Select Writings and Letters of Gregory, Bishop of Nyssa*, trans. by William Moore and Henry Austin Wilson, vol. 5 of *A Select Library*, ed. Schaff and Wace, 382–83.

to convey this by another channel, and ordained that we should be buried together with him by another means, even in his own appointed sacrament of *baptism*. Faith indeed, without a bodily pilgrimage, will carry and place thee near the *sepulchre*, to lament.[24]

It is not far from here to the general Protestant view that considered Palestine "holy" only nominally.[25] If any space could be holy, it was only in the sense of setting it apart from common use and appropriating it to God. "For that is the meaning of the word *holy*," Hobbes writes in Chapter 45 of *Leviathan*, "which implies no new quality in the place or image, but only a new relation by appropriation to God." Stronger claims than that, however, would be tantamount to paganism: "But to worship God as inanimating or inhabiting such image or place—that is to say, an infinite substance in a finite place—is idolatry. For such finite gods are but idols of the brain, nothing real, and are commonly called in the Scripture by the names of *vanity*, and *lies*, and *nothing*."[26] One looking for meditative space, in other words, might just as well seek it at home—and this could be true for Catholics too.[27]

---

24. Thomas à Kempis, *Meditations, with Prayers, on the Life and Living-kindnesses of Our Lord and Saviour, Jesus Christ*, trans. Henry Lee (London, 1760), 278–89. A meditation "On the glory of the heavenly Jerusalem" for August 7, 1759 in *Considerations upon Christian Truths and Christian Duties Digested into Meditations for Every Day in the Year. Part II. For the last six Months* ends with reference to Kempis (76).

25. The Royalist Thomas Fuller satirically defended himself against religious reformers who might complain about his inclusion of the term in a mere listing of the names by which the geographical region has been known: "But fear makes me refrain from using this word, lest whilest I call the Land holy, this Age count me superstitious." Thomas Fuller, *A Pisgah-Sight of Palestine and the Confines Thereof* (London, 1662), 3.

26. Thomas Hobbes, *Leviathan with Selected Variants from the Latin edition of 1668*, ed. Edwin Curley (Indianapolis: Hackett, 1994), 446. In fact, Hobbes conflates distinctions early Christians would have made between their sites, which were holy by virtue of saintly human deeds, and pagan shrines, said to be holy from indwelling spirits; see, Sabine MacCormack, "Loca Sancta: The Organization of Sacred Topography in Late Antiquity," in *The Blessings of Pilgrimage*, ed. Robert Ousterhout (Urbana and Chicago: University of Illinois Press, 1990), 18–19.

27. Fénelon writes that the stations of the cross are ordinarily performed in churches but might be performed anywhere ("nor, indeed, is there any Place, but is fit to perform this holy Devotion in, whether the Church, the Closet, the Field, or the Garden; every Place is proper to remember and reflect on the *Passion* of our Blessed Saviour"), at any time ("all Times are fit, and no Time amiss for this so holy an Exercise," though some

That said, even at the beginning of the nineteenth century, the holiness in the geographical epithet could be said to apply because of Christianity's continuing influence in the world. Although he vociferates against superstitious beliefs, Edward Daniel Clarke (1801) nonetheless justifies his preference for the name "Holy Land" (over "Palestine" and "Syria") by explaining in a preface that "so long as the blessings of Religion diffuse their consolitary balm of hope, and peace, and gladness, this land may be accounted holy."[28] Nabil Matar has argued that by using biblical place names, English writers "signified the unchangeableness of the land since its conquest by Joshua," and Gerald MacLean has described this as an irresistible impulse, writing of William Biddulph (1600) that he "could not help imagining himself performing within the timeless present of scriptural history," but Clarke offers one instance in which this is not exactly the case.[29] The land was not holy in essence but by virtue of its past, which was a living presence—though not, Clarke laments, in Palestine itself: "The pure Gospel of Christ, everywhere the herald of civilization and science, is almost as little known in the Holy Land as in Caliphornia or New Holland."[30] This is not to deny that Clarke sees the continuation of a savage past in the present; in a passage on the slaughter by Vespasian of tribes in the northern Galilee region,

---

times are better than others, like Lent and Easter week), and advises that fathers and mothers "would do well to read one every Day, publickly in their Houshold Prayers." François Fénelon, *The Christian Pilgrimage: or a Companion for the Holy Season of Lent*, trans. Jane Barker (London, 1718), 2–3.

28. Edward Daniel Clarke, *Travels in Various Countries of Europe, Asia, and Africa . . . Part the Second. Greece, Egypt, and the Holy Land. Section the First* (New York: Whiting and Watson, 1813), ix.

29. Nabil Matar, *Turks, Moors, and Englishmen in the Age of Discovery* (New York: Columbia University Press, 2000), 132; Gerald MacLean, *The Rise of Oriental Travel: English Visitors to the Ottoman Empire, 1580–1720* (New York: Palgrave MacMillan, 2004), 102–3. Oddly, Matar and MacLean seem unaware that, if ahistorical, this way of envisaging the land bears a resemblance to the ancient pilgrim practice of forming a living icon in the landscape. On living icons, see Gary Vikan, "Pilgrims in Magi's Clothing: The Impact of Mimesis on Early Byzantine Pilgrimage Art," in *The Blessings of Pilgrimage*, ed. Robert Ousterhout (Urbana and Chicago: University of Illinois Press, 1990), 101.

30. Clarke, *Travels*, 224. A comparable passage in Richard Pococke, *A Description of the East, and Some other Countries*, vol. 2, part 1 (London, 1745), one of the exemplary "academic" travel accounts of the eighteenth century, implies that there is something worth venerating at Holy Land sites (40). Clarke later complains that while missionaries are sent around the world, ignorance is allowed to propagate itself in the Holy Land (238).

he characterizes the present inhabitants as basically the same, "unable . . . to sustain a life of peace, and exhibiting, eighteen hundred years ago, the same state of society which now characterizes the inhabitants of that country."[31] But considering the land and its inhabitants under a heavenly curse, as so many do, involves seeing with a kind of historical lens, and a Christian one at that.[32]

That English travelers were not likely to be pilgrims in a programmatic way (many bought relics, for example, thereby supporting an institution of pilgrimage) need not mean they were always stubbornly unmoved by their experiences—after all, the idea that life itself was a symbolic pilgrimage recurs in writing throughout the period. Moreover, even the most enlightened traveler might come home with the Holy Land ever in his eyes.[33] Yet MacLean emphasizes that even when travelers at the turn of the sixteenth century like Biddulph and Fynes Moryson (1597) saw with biblical eyes, they each felt a duty to "remain steadfast, unchanged by his experience" in the land, and so were careful always to make distinctions "between what he himself was doing, traveling as a representative of the Church of England, and being a pilgrim intent on visiting sacred sites in hopes that doing so would guarantee his personal salvation."[34] Here they see a biblical land but with the sensibility of ecclesiastical politicians.[35] Later travelers like Henry Maundrell (1697) were "more skeptical," beginning the trend "for drawing careful

---

31. Clark, *Travels*, 290–91.

32. As many of the seventeenth-century Holy Land narratives were collected in *Purchas his Pilgrimes*, James P. Helfer's comment that Purchas "conceived of travel in the spiritual terms of pilgrimage" should encourage readers to think more flexibly even about collections of disparate travel narratives; see "The Explorer or the Pilgrim? Modern Critical Opinion and the Editorial Methods of Richard Hakluyt and Samuel Purchas," *Studies in Philology* 94, no. 2 (Spring 1997): 160–86.

33. An eighteenth-century biography of Richard Pococke includes a story that, "'When travelling through Scotland (where he preached several times to crouded congregations), he stopped at Dingwal, and said he was much struck and pleased with its appearance; for the situation of it brought Jerusalem to his rememberance, and he pointed out the hill which resembled Calvary.' The same similitude was observed by him in regard to Dartmouth." *A New and General Biographical Dictionary*, vol. 12 (London, 1784), 713–14.

34. MacLean, *Rise*, 52 and 101.

35. Among the Maronites, MacLean notes, Biddulph felt sufficient distance from Protestant/Catholic politics to admire their use of vernacular liturgy and think it an object lesson for Protestant reform (ibid., 81).

plans and taking exact measurements of ancient sites in an attempt to extend knowledge of the ancient world by means of scientific method," and so must have been spiritually unmoved.[36] Matar's description of biblical tourism similarly treats it as a dry antiquarian exercise: "The approach to the land was as methodical as a paint-by-numbers exercise. ... he had specific locations to see that he subsequently 'checked off.' ... The human interaction that he must have had, the smells and sounds of inner Jerusalem, did not matter since the city was biblical but not contemporary, archeological not experiential."[37] In reality, Maundrell and others were inconsistently skeptical and sometimes responded to the ambiguities they discovered in the scriptural landscape by contriving explanations that renewed faith in the biblical text.[38] The land was indeed a challenge, Maundrell wrote, but only to those lacking religious confidence: "But it is certain that any man, who is not a little biass'd to infidelity before, may see, as he passes along, arguments enough to support his faith against such scruples."[39] Even Eitan Bar-Yosef, whose book on "vernacular Orientalism" qualifies Edward Said's claim

---

36. MacCormack, "Loca Sancta," 29, offers a similar formulation.

37. Nabil Matar, "Two Journeys to Seventeenth-Century Palestine," *Journal of Palestine Studies* 29, no. 4 (Autumn 2000): 46.

38. That even early pilgrims could feel skeptical may be seen in St. Silvia's remark on the Dead Sea site of the pillar of Lot's wife: "We certainly saw the place, but we saw no pillar; I cannot deceive you about this matter." St. Silvia of Aquitania, *The Pilgrimage of S. Silvia of Aquitania to the Holy Places* (Circa 385 A.D.), trans. John H. Bernard, in vol. 1 of *The Library of the Palestine Pilgrims' Text Society* (London, 1896), 28. One person's skepticism is another's dubiety. Thus, in his preface Clarke describes nearly all his predecessors—even those some today consider enlightened—as too believing: "Those who have formed their notions of the Holy Land ... from the observations of Adrichomius, Sandys, Doubdan, Maundrell ... or even from the writings of Pococke ... will find their prejudices frequently assailed in the following pages." Clarke, *Travels*, x. His chosen model is Rauwulf, upon whose piety Noonan remarks.

39. To a certain degree, even later travelers demonstrate trust in traditional attributions, at least for certain sites. See, for example, Shaw, *Travels*, 334–35 and Clarke, *Travels*, 280–82. For a contemporary instance of this, see John Wilkinson, "Jewish Holy Places and the Origins of Christian Pilgrimage," in *The Blessings of Pilgrimage*, ed. Robert Ousterhout (Urbana and Chicago: University of Illinois Press, 1990), 51. Skeptics who challenge their guides might have seen in the claims of contending sites the existence of contending traditions; for a fascinating instance of which, see Elchanan Reiner, "From Joshua to Jesus: The Transformation of a Biblical Story to a Local Myth," in *Sharing the Sacred: Religious Contacts and Conflicts in the Holy Land*, ed. Arieh Kofsky and Guy G. Stroumsa (Jerusalem: Yad Izhak Ben Zvi, 1998).

that Orientalism was a "secularized" practice by demonstrating the influence of the Bible on nineteenth-century English encounters with Palestine, states that "curiosity rather than piety" led seventeenth-century Englishmen to Jerusalem, where "their Protestant skepticism often fed into a sober tone, anticipating some characteristics of the higher biblical criticism.... Commerce, too, was an incentive."[40] In his rush to equate Protestantism with the broader epistemological and metaphysical claims of the Enlightenment, Bar-Yosef forgets that travel can be motivated by both piety and curiosity, and that Protestant piety may in fact consist in both simultaneously. In so doing he accepts a false dichotomy, travel as either curious or pious, premised by Said in his explanation of why Orientalist learning intruded upon private musing and allowed it expression only in aesthetic terms:

> Every pilgrim sees things his own way, but there are limits to what a pilgrimage can be for, to what shape and form it can take, to what truths it reveals. All pilgrimages to the Orient passed through, or had to pass through, the Biblical lands; most of them in fact were attempts either to relive or to liberate from the large, incredibly fecund Orient some portion of Judeo-Christian/Greco-Roman actuality. For these pilgrims the Orientalized Orient, the Orient of Orientalist scholars, was a gauntlet to be run, just as the bible, the Crusades, Islam, Napoleon, and Alexander were redoubtable predecessors to be reckoned with. Not only does a learned Orient inhibit the pilgrim's musings and private fantasies; its very antecedence places barriers between the contemporary traveler and his writing, unless, as was the case with Nerval and Flaubert in their use of Lane, Orientalist work is severed from the library and caught in the aesthetic project.[41]

If there are limits to pilgrimage, Said leaves them undescribed. And in fact, there are compelling reasons to avoid marking them. Victor and Edith Turner's classic conception of pilgrimage as a social process

---

40. Eitan Bar-Yosef, *The Holy Land in English Culture 1799–1917: Palestine and the Question of Orientalism* (Oxford: Clarendon Press, 2005).

41. Edward W. Said, *Orientalism* (New York: Vintage Books, 1978), 168.

wherein individuals leave behind their worldly differences and enter a spiritual *communitas* has been complicated by anthropologists who now recognize not only social but psychological conflict within pilgrimage communities.[42] In other words, to assume a monolithic pilgrimage activity is to efface the distinctions inherent within pilgrimage culture. Moreover, historians such as Jaś Elsner and Ian Rutherford articulate why there is good reason to consider pilgrimage an evolving concept:

> some object "that a pilgrim is one who must *believe in full* before embarking on a sacred journey." . . . Yet belief is a term notoriously redefined by Christianity, and the notion of *full* belief is ever harder to explain or substantiate historically, except in Christian theological terms. Another line of attack has been to argue that "pilgrimage implies a journey by a devotee in pursuance of a primarily religious objective"—which is so purist a formulation of pilgrimage as to disqualify not only Pausanias but most other pilgrims. . . . It is extremely difficult, perhaps impossible to determine the boundaries between pilgrimage proper (if there is such a thing) and other kinds of travel such as tourism. Indeed, one might say that for the religiously minded (or for those with a tendency to become so) any kind of journey has the potential to become a pilgrimage.[43]

A more flexible notion of travel is needed for understanding seventeenth- and eighteenth-century English travelers as well, who, surprisingly, have been taken at their word as to the motives for their peregrinations.

---

42. Eade and Sallnow see pilgrimage as a realm of competing discourses: "Pilgrimage is above all an arena for competing religious and secular discourses, for both the official co-optation and the now-official recovery of religious meanings, for conflict between orthodoxies, sects, and confessional groups, for drives towards consensus and communitas, and for counter-movements towards separateness and division." John Eade and Michael J. Sallnow, *Contesting the Sacred: The Anthropology of Christian Pilgrimage* (1991), 2. On the experience of "sibling rivalry" at pilgrimage sites, see Yoram Bilu, "The Inner Limits of Communitas: A Covert Dimension of Pilgrimage Experience," *Ethos* 16, no. 3 (September 1988): 302–25.

43. Jaś Elsner and Ian Rutherford, "Introduction," in *Pilgrimage in Graeco-Roman and Early Christianity: Seeing the Gods*, ed. Jaś Elsner and Ian Rutherford (Oxford: Oxford University Press, 2005), 4–5.

Certainly, writers often distinguish devotional from "curious" travel. There were political reasons for doing so. For example, Biddulph's excuse of his visit to Jerusalem as the product of an accidental circumstance (that is, plague in Aleppo) may be true—"nor moued as Pilgrims with any superstitious deuotion to see Relikes, or worship such places as they account holy; but as Trauellers and Merchants, occasioned by Dearth and sicknesse, pestilence and famine in the City where we soiourne"— but serves as an anticipatory defense of his religious beliefs from the kind of attack he, ironically, levels at Henry Timberlake (1601), who was coerced into participating in some Catholic rituals with his Franciscan hosts.[44] Whatever their actual feelings, the need to sound anti-Catholic limits how writers portray themselves. Such excuses, therefore, are worth probing. For instance, Sandys reports that the Father Guardian asked if he and his companions had come for "devotion or curiosity," and that they "contented our selves with an historical Relation."[45] That he was asked should remind readers that categorization of motives was also imposed from the outside.[46] What Henry Maundrell writes about his trek to the Jordan River, that he did so "in order to satisfy that curiosity and devotion, which brought us thither," moreover suggests that even

---

44. William Biddulph, *The Travels of Foure English Men and a Preacher* (London, 1612), 74.

45. Sandys, *A Relation*, 163. A century later, Hill describes the consequences of answering either way: "It is a Question, always ask'd, if you design your *Visit* to those *Holy Places*, from a Motive of *Religious Zeal*, or *Common Curiosity*; If from the *first*, they pester you with *Beads*, and other superstitious *Tokens of* Devotion, which direct the strict Injunction of repeating two, four, six, eight, ten or twenty *Pater Nosters*, at such and such *more* Sacred, or *less* Holy Places; but if you assure them, that the *latter Motive* tempted you to Travel thither, they are complaisantly *passive* in the matter, and accompany you about from *Place to Place*, without observing your *Deportment* in them" (280).

46. Of approximately 344 British travelers who visited Jerusalem between the years 1561 and 1695 and were signed into the Franciscan registry—19 as hailing from Scotland, 1 from Ireland, 106 from London, and 37 from areas outside of London—15 were deemed by the Franciscan custodians of Jerusalem to be Catholic, 13 heretic, and 216 alienated from Catholicism. Fifteen were said to have refused confession. These numbers are based on tallies I made from *Navis Peregrinorum: Ein Pilgerverzeichnis aus Jerusalem von 1561 bis 1695*, ed. Bertrand Zimolong, vol. 12–14 of *Palästina-Hefte des Deutschen Vereins vom Heiligen Lande* (Köln: Verlag J. P. Bachem, 1938). Aaron Hill writes of seeing this registry, but must have taken only a cursory count or simply misremembered the result, and in any case correctly attests to its limited reliability (280).

if distinct, curiosity and devotion might be of a piece.[47] Similarly, when Moryson blames his journey on envious wanderlust ("And first I thinke good to professe that by my iourny to this City, I had no thought to expiate any least sinne of mine; much lesse did I hope to merit any grace from God; but when I had once begun to visite forraigne parts, I was so stirred up by emulation and curiosity, as I did neuer behold any without a kind of sweete enuy, who in this kind had dared more then my selfe. Thus affected, I thought no place more worthy to be viewed in the whole world, then this City"), he adds, "confesses" actually, that the places affected him: "yet I confesse that (through the grace of God) the very places struck me with a religious hurrour [sic], and filled my mind prepared to deuotion, with holy motions."[48] Such admissions are reason enough not to employ rigid categories, but, unlike with those referring to "curiosity," scholars react to such statements skeptically.

The particular challenge here involves reconciling curiosity with religious experience. In a nuanced study of the topic, Barbara Benedict maintains their opposition when differentiating her sense of curiosity from Stephen Greenblatt's concept of the marvelous: "Pious, passive, and aesthetic, wonder, like awe, reveres the novelty it encounters. Early modern curiosity, however, seeks to explain it. . . . curiosity arrogates the power to determine value and subordinates the observer as object. It is irreligious and proactive."[49] This seems unexceptional.

---

47. Henry Maundrell, *A Journey from Aleppo to Jerusalem at Easter A.D. 1697* (Oxford, 1703), 81. See also the essay appended to a later edition of Timberlake's narrative, where it says that "even until this day, [the Church of the Holy Sepulchre] is much resorted to, both by pilgrims from all parts of the Romish church, and by divers gentlemen of the reformed churches; partly for curiosity and partly for the antiquity of the place." *Memorable Remarks upon the Ancient and Modern State of the Jewish Nation* (Bolton, 1786), 54. This construction makes it into eighteenth-century books on the Bible as well, such as Nicholas Fontaine, *The History of the Old and New Testament, Extracted out of Sacred Scripture and Writings of the Fathers*, 4th ed. (London, 1711): "To this *City of Jerusalem* there is a great resort of *People*, as well of *Protestants as Papists*, tho' for sundry ends, that is, as well for Devotion as Curiosity" (139).

48. Fynes Moryson, *An Itinerary Written by Fynes Moryson Gent* (London, 1617), 217.

49. Barbara M. Benedict, *Curiosity: A Cultural History of Early Modern Inquiry* (Chicago: Chicago University Press, 2001), 5. Marjorie Swann recognizes a diminishing ability of the curious to stir wonder; for her, a thirst for wonders existed in the period because "once a 'marvellous' item became familiar and widely disseminated, it lost the strangeness, the radical quality of difference necessary to excite wonder in European

After all, Samuel Butler defined the superstitious man as one whose religion "is too full of Curiosities to be sound and useful, and is fitter for a Hypocrite than a Saint; for Curiosities are only for Show, and no Use at all."[50] Moreover, Johnson's analogy of ornamental language and the telescope also suggests that seeing has little to do with faith. For Johnson, just as seeing is not believing, pure faith means the repression of curiosity. Thus he insists in the "Life of Cowley" that it is profane to amplify sacred history, which "has been always read with submissive reverence, and an imagination over-awed and controlled," and on the veracity of which one should always trust with "such humble confidence, as suppresses curiosity."[51]

The problem, however, was not curiosity as such, which was only natural, but its abuse by priests.[52] Thus Aaron Hill (1703) worries that the curiosity of travelers is abused by dissembling Franciscans, who "accompany the Strangers *up and down, within* the City and *without*, and shew them every Place, worth observation, which they constantly perform with *admirable Artifice*, appearing wond'rous Civil, and exciting those, they guide, to think their *Curiosity a Meritorious Zeal*, in hopes thereby, that others may at their return to their respective Countries, be induc'd to undertake a Journey *thither*, and by that means swell the *Perquisites* of their Dependance to additional Abundance."[53] But to Sandys, a self-proclaimed curious traveler, the "sight" of the sepulcher could and did melt all but the coldest of spirits. And even in *The History of Rasselas*, Johnson has Imlac tell the prince that, like many religious acts, pilgrimage "may be reasonable or superstitious, according to the principles upon which it is performed." Truth may be found anywhere if sought for honestly, and travel might dissipate the

viewers." Marjorie Swann, *Curiosities and Texts: The Culture of Collecting in Early Modern England* (Philadelphia: University of Pennsylvania Press, 2001), 25.

50. Butler, *Characters*, 227.

51. Samuel Johnson, *The Lives of the Most Eminent English Poets; with Critical Observations on Their Works*, vol. I, ed. Roger Lonsdale (Oxford: Clarendon Press, 2006), 223. One hears a similar idea in Thomas à Kempis, *Thomas à Kempis . . . His Four Books of the Imitation of Christ* (London, 1722), 373–74.

52. See John Richardson, *The Great Folly, Superstition, and Idolatry, of Pilgrimages in Ireland* (Dublin, 1727), 10.

53. Aaron Hill, "Of the Present State of the Holy-Land" in *The Present State of the Ottoman Empire in All Its Branches* (London, 1709), 280.

mind, Imlac continues, but why deny that people might be altered by experiencing a place when such happens commonly:

> since men go every day to view the fields where great actions have been performed, and return with stronger impressions of the event, curiosity of the same kind may naturally dispose us to view that country whence our religion had its beginning; and I believe no man surveys those awful scenes without some confirmation of holy resolutions. That the Supreme Being may be more easily propitiated in one place than in another, is the dream of idle superstition; but that some places may operate upon our own minds in an uncommon manner, is an opinion which hourly experience will justify. He who supposes that his vices may be more successfully combated in Palestine, will, perhaps, find himself mistaken, yet he may go thither without folly: he who thinks they will be more freely pardoned, dishonours at once his reason and religion.

The main problem here is not curiosity but setting off with proper expectations. Certain effects will never occur, but curious travel may operate on the mind in "an uncommon manner."[54]

As much may be evinced by comparing travelers' responses to the cleft in Calvary, said to be formed at the earthquake which struck the moment of Jesus's death (Matthew 27:51–53), and thus part of the site from which Milton notoriously turns away. There is no unanimity here, some believing the miracle, others that the rock was split by an earthquake, but not one coeval with the crucifixion; still others that there never was an earthquake and that the crack may be attributed to human activity. Laurence Aldersey's (1581) description seems plainly descriptive ("the rent also of the mountaine is there to be seene in the creuis, wherein a man may put his arme") until one reconsiders the

---

54. Interestingly, Rasselas's reply that Imlac is using "European distinctions" suggests an awareness that the tidy oppositions Imlac here depends upon, while nominally securing a place for legitimate pilgrimage, nevertheless perpetuate the idea that pilgrimage is an either/or affair when it comes to being motivated by piety or curiosity. Samuel Johnson, *Rasselas and Other Tales*, ed. Gwin J. Kolb, vol. 16 of *The Yale Edition of the Works of Samuel Johnson* (New Haven: Yale University Press, 1990), 48. Also see Kolb's note 6.

latter clause.[55] Did he insert his arm into the cleft? And if so, out of what kind of curiosity? Calling the rock a "thing worth observation," Timberlake recognizes on it the signs of human labor ("for it is slit like as it had been cleft with Wedges and Beetles").[56] Biddulph defines the cleft as such: "And neere unto the Sepulchre there is a great stone clouen with hammers and set one peece a foot from another: and this say they is the [word] of the Temple which rent in sunder at the time of Christs suffering, which is most ridiculous."[57] William Lithgow (1611) even suggests the scriptural text has been misinterpreted and that "it was not a rock, but the temple, that did rent in two from the bottom to the top, wherein these silly soul-sunk friars are merely blinded, understanding no more than lying traditions."[58] Unlike these, Sandys, at other sites dubious but in the Church of the Holy Sepulchre open to reverie, remarks, "He is void of sense, that sees, believes, and is not then confounded with his passion. . . . The in-sides do testifie that Art had no hand therein; each side to other being answerably rugged, and there were un-accessible to the Work-man."[59] Most striking is how many of the later travelers believe at least part of the story. So Maundrell writes that while no evidence exists "that this rent was made by the Earthquake, that happen'd at our Lords Passion," still it is obvious "that it is a natural, and genuine breach, and not counterfeited by any Art, the sence and reason of every one that sees it may convince him, for the sides of it fit like two Tallys to each other, and yet it runs in such intricate windings as could not well be counterfeited by Art, nor arriv'd

---

55. Laurence Aldersey, "The first voyage or iourney, made by Master *Laurence Aldersey*, Marchant of London, to the Cities of Ierusalem, and Tripoli, &c. In the yeere 1581" in *The Principal Navigations, Voyages, Traffiques and Discoveries of the English Nation*, vol. 2, ed. Richard Hakluyt (London, 1599), 153.

56. He adds, "Nor is the rent small, but so great in some places, that a man might easily hide himself in it." Henry Timberlake, "A strange and true Account of the Travels of Two English Pilgrims some years since, and what admirable Accidents befell them in their Journey to Jerusalem, Grand Cairo, Alexandria, &c." in *Two Journeys to Jerusalem . . . Collected by R.B.* [Nathaniel Crouch] (London, 1685, 46).

57. Biddulph, *Travels*, 112.

58. William Lithgow, *Travels and Voyages, through Europe, Asia, and Africa, for Nineteen Years*. 11th ed. (Edinburgh, 1770), 252.

59. Sandys, *A Relation*, 164.

at by any Instruments."[60] Likewise Aaron Hill: "*Art* could have no hand in the *prodigious Rent*."[61] Finally, while discussing the miraculous rock at Merivah, even Thomas Shaw, a natural historian and member of the Royal Society who toured the Holy Land in 1738, expresses faith in Calvary: "It likewise may be further observed, that Art or Chance could by no means be concerned in the Contrivance. For every Circumstance points out to us a Miracle, and, in the same Manner with the Rent in the Rock of Mount *Calvary at Jerusalem*, never fails to produce a religious Surprize in all who see it."[62]

Doubting Thomas was also Thomas the Believer. So too, for some, even if not for Johnson, scientific curiosity might enable faith. This is a point Robert Fleming makes in a footnote on the cleft rock in his *Christology*:

> *A worthy Gentleman, that travelled through* Canaan *told me, that an ingenious Person his Fellow-Traveller, who was a Deist, used to make merry with all the Stories that the Romish Priests entertain'd them with, as to the Sacred Places and Reliques they went to see; and particularly when they first shew'd him the Clefts in the Rock of Mount* Calvary, *which is now included within the Great Dome that was built over it, by Constantine the Great. But when he came to examine the Clefts more narrowly and critically, he told his Fellow-Travellers, that now he began to be a Christian. For, said he, I have been long a Student of Nature, and the Mathematicks, and I am sure these Clefts and Rents in this Rock were never made by a natural or ordinary Earthquake. For, by such a Concussion the Rock must have split, according to the Veins, and where it was weakest in the Adhesion of the Parts. For thus, said he, I have observ'd it to have been done in other Rocks, when separated or broken after an Earthquake: And Reason tells me it must always be so. But it is quite otherwise here: For the Rock is split quite a-thwart, and cross the Veins, in a most strange and preternatural, or supernatural manner. This therefore I can easily*

---

60. Maundrell, *A Journey*, 72–73.
61. Hill, 287.
62. Shaw, *Travels*, 353.

*and plainly see to be the Effect of a real Miracle, which neither Nature nor Art could have ever effected. And therefore, said he, I thank God that I came hither, to see this standing Monument of a miraculous Power, by which God gives Evidence, to this Day, to the Divinity of Christ.*[63]

I have not discovered this story in anyone's published travel narrative, and it is conceivably made up to serve Fleming's didactic purposes. This would only emphasize the point, however, that the tools of enlightenment could be seen to enable revelatory experience. Indeed, even for Byzantine pilgrims seeing and touching sometimes meant believing, as Gary Vikan shows when discussing two ampullae that depict the story of Doubting Thomas, "to remind the pilgrim of the Gospel account of Thomas's incredulity, and specifically of the fact that he was rebuked by Christ for his lapse of faith—a faith which was restored only after Thomas had seen and touched the wounds of Christ. Of course, seeing and touching were basic to the pilgrim's experience."[64] This observation even illuminates Quaker missionary George Robinson's trip (at the age of eighteen or so) to Jerusalem in 1658, in which refusing to sightsee negatively affirms that others awaited or hoped for spiritual effects from the physical vision of holy sites. Framed as a prophetic journey overseen by God, Robinson's narrative consists of spiritual trials rather than tourism, in which Robinson, once threatened with death or conversion in a mosque, insistently refuses to be named a pilgrim despite several times being detained from Jerusalem by the Franciscan friars who feared he would prophesy in Jerusalem (an act that would stir trouble not only for him but possibly the entire Christian community): "I said, at the present I had no business to visit [the holy sites], and in their manner I should not visit them at all (that is to say, worship

---

63. Robert Fleming, *Christology: A Discourse Concerning Christ: Considered I in himself, and III in relation to his subjects and their Duty to Him*, vol. 2 (London, 1705), 97–98. See a reference to this passage in Philip Doddridge, *The Family Expositor: or a Paraphrase and Version of the New Testament*, vol. 2 (Edinburgh, 1772), 555.

64. Gary Vikan, *Byzantine Pilgrimage Art* (Washington, DC: Dumbarton Oaks, 1982), 25.

them)."[65] He had undergone the arduous journey from England to the Holy Land not to see but to refuse sight as well as to espouse a spiritual vision to the gentiles. The fulfillment of (and conclusion to) his brief narrative therefore occurs the moment he is able to deliver a message to the qadi of Jerusalem:

> [He] asked me the ground of my coming to *Jerusalem*? I answered him, The Lord God of Heaven and Earth had appeared unto me, and commanded me to come thither, and in obedience unto him I was come; and further, in the power of the Lord I declared the great and tender love of God in visiting them, and his great and compassionate mercies that he would gather them in this the Day of his gatherings. And this was that which lay upon me from the Lord to declare unto them, whether they would hear or forbear.
> And thus, my dear Friends, I cleared my Conscience.[66]

Although Robinson himself was unaware of it, his was an ironic ending, for the man to whom he delivered his message and thereby cleared his conscience was not the Ottoman judge of Jerusalem but a Christian friar in disguise.

Predicated on not seeing, Robinson's journey, in fact, failed because he could not see. Though it might seem likewise to diminish sight, a passage in John Sanderson's travels (1601) differently indicates its importance. Because he traveled with Jews outside of Jerusalem and was hosted by the Greek Orthodox within it, Sanderson was initially barred by the Franciscans from entering the Church of the Holy Sepulchre. When later invited to see the church, he allowed himself proudly to refuse entry, but only because he was afforded an indirect way of seeing what he desired. He would not enter, he writes, for having already

> to my content seene enough when the dores weare opened for me, and alike out of the Patriarkes house, which joyneth to the

---

65. George Robinson, "An Additional Account of George Robinson's: Shewing his Call to go to Jerusalem; and how God in his Journey thither was present with, and did preserve him from the Hands of those who sought to take his Life, &c." in *A brief history of the voyage of Katharine Evans and Sarah Cheevers, to the island of Malta* (London, 1663), 291.

66. Ibid., 292.

church, in whose pocession the whole steeple and half the tarras is . . . wheare ar three great grates of iron open, servinge to geve light into the church . . . at which I did see as much as yf I had stoad in the church, and drewe with my penn the forme of the inside and alike the outside. More lower, in a rome at a windowe out of the Patriarkes house I stoad and drewe the forme of that which is erected right over the sepulcre.[67]

Sanderson's dislike of Catholicism did not turn him away from the Holy Sepulchre altogether. Not before one but two windows, he stands "as if" inside, looking long enough to make sketches.

Yet early modern scholars consistently read the probative gestures of travelers as skeptically or empirically charged.[68] Like MacLean, Joan Taylor dilates upon the growing trend for drawing detailed plans. In her speculative account of Timberlake's voyage, Taylor starkly contrasts the impulses to measure and pray: "As always, Timberlake was remarkably unimpressed in terms of personal piety, and was moved with wonder at things other pilgrims tended to pass over. . . . Timberlake loved measuring things. He was one of the most intrepid measurers ever to visit Jerusalem. While other pilgrims spent their hours in prayer and contemplation, Timberlake was busily beavering around counting his steps and making compass-readings."[69] This overlooks not only the medieval and Renaissance architectural traditions of transferring the measurements of the Churches of the Nativity and Holy Sepulchre to

---

67. John Sanderson, *The Travels of John Sanderson in the Levant 1584–1602*, ed. Sir William Foster (London: Hakluyt Society, 1931), 108–9.

68. The impulse to measure accurately could differ from the actual methods used, as Clarke's reliance on sailors to estimate the dimensions of the Sea of Galilee shows; see Clarke, *Travels*, 259. Perhaps more significantly, William Wittman, *Travels in Turkey, Asia-Minor, Syria, and Across the Desert into Egypt During the Years 1799, 1800, and 1801. In Company with the Turkish Army, and the British Military Mission* (London, 1803), hints that, at least by the end of the eighteenth century, the Franciscan priests willingly enabled such practices. Dubious at his host's account of fruits and vegetables grown near the Dead Sea, Wittman was not only assured by the father superior "that he had sent several of these oranges to Europe as a curiosity," but upon his departure weeks later was given "a present of fruits and of curious plants collected near the Dead Sea, accompanied by two bottles of the water taken from that sea, the taste of which was peculiarly saline and pungent" (172, 188).

69. Taylor, *The Englishman, the Moor*, 167.

European sites (enabled by such exact measurers as Bourchard of Mount Zion), but also the use of measurement in meditative and predictive (as in chronologies and almanacs) practices.[70] One obvious explanation for Timberlake's activity is that he wished to help his readers envisage the place for themselves, as he writes before describing the geographical situation of Jerusalem:

> Now how the Country about *Jerusalem* lyeth, for your more easy and perfect understanding, I will familiarly compare their several places, with some of our native English Towns and Villages, according to such true estimation as I have made of them. Imagine I begin with *London*, I mean much upon the point of distance. The City of *Bethlehem* . . . is from *Jerusalem* as *Wansworth* is from *London*. . . . The plain of *Mamre* is from *Jerusalem*, as *Guilford* is from *London*. . . . *Beersheba* is from *Jerusalem*, as *Alton* is from *London*.

Likewise, the intention of Christianius Adrichomius, whose *Briefe Description of Jerusalem* sets out to "rightly dispose the places of Christ his Passion, and represent every thing which he suffered in every place, even as if they were now done before our eyes, and so represented, that I might explain it with plainness and brevity," is to fuse the perceptual experience of the Passion with daily devotion, here made an issue, as in Milton's poem, of representation.[71] Thus he offers a step by step tour of the Via Dolorosa—there are 26 steps (35 feet) between Pilate's house and where the cross was placed on Jesus; 80 steps northwest (200 feet) from the latter to where Jesus fell the first time; 60 steps and 3 feet (153 feet) onward to where Mary and John met Jesus; etc., to a grand total of "a thousand three hundred and seven steps; or by another account, three thousand two hundred sixty and eight foot" from Pilate's house to

---

70. On the former, see Robert Ousterhout, "Loca Sancta and the Architectural Response to Pilgrimage," in *The Blessings of Pilgrimage*, ed. Robert Ousterhout (Urbana and Chicago: University of Illinois Press, 1990); and Robert Ousterhout, "Flexible Geography and Transportable Topography," in *The Real and Ideal Jerusalem in Jewish, Christian and Islamic Art*, ed. Bianca Kühnel, *Jewish Art* 23–24 (1997–1998): 393–404.

71. Christianius Adrichomius, *A Briefe Description of Jerusalem and of the Suburbs thereof, as It Flourished in The Time of Christ*, trans. Thomas Tymme (York, 1666), 145–46. The same applies to Fénelon's imaginative paces in his *Christian Pilgrimage*.

Golgotha—so that "every Christian man, in all places, even in the doors of his house, or walking oftentimes in his garden, or being in a journey, or in the Temple, either lying in his bed, may by the imagination of his minde conceive the like way, and with godly affection of the heart, may meditate upon the passion of Christ."[72] Just as measurement conduces to manifold experiences, skepticism has wide meaning as a practical exercise. At Jesus's tomb, for example, Biddulph "made no doubt" of the location's authenticity, then interrogated his guide as to whether any of the original structure remained and seemed indifferent when given a negative reply: "it gaue me content that I had seene the selfe same place where the Sepulchre of our blessed Sauiour was; as I in heart did then, and doe still perswade my selfe it is."[73] Like curiosity, skepticism does not preclude and may sometimes intermingle with belief. Thus, identifying seventeenth and eighteenth century English travelers as curious and skeptical should only encourage interrogation of their representations of prayer.

Representations of prayer or spiritual experience may not abound in British travel narratives to the Near East,[74] but it is well to remember that a traveler to anywhere might be expected to pray regularly, as James Howell reminds the reader of his *Instructions and Directions for Forrein Travell*: "At his first coming to any Citie hee should repaire to the chiefe Church to offer up his sacrifice of thanks, that he is safely

---

72. Ibid., 63–64.
73. Biddulph, *Travels*, 107–8.
74. The chaplain of the "last" English pilgrim, Richard Guildford (who became ill upon reaching Jaffa and died just days after reaching Jerusalem), reports that in the Church of the Holy Sepulchre "euery man yaue hym selfe to prayer and contemplacion, bysely vysynge the holy places aforesayde after theyr deuocyon durynge the hole nyght, and erly in the mornynge all we that were prestes sayd masse, some at Caluery, some at our Ladyes chapel, and some at ye holy Sepulchre after our deuocyon"; and on the third and final night, he writes, "[we] used our self in euery thing in suche fourme and maner as we dyd the nyghte before . . . with the more zele and deuocion bycause we rekenyd it for the laste tyme that we shuld se them in all our lyues." Richard Guildford, *The Pilgrimage of Sir Richard Guylforde to the Holy Land, A.D. 1506*, ed. Henry Ellis (Camden Society, 1851), 27 and 41. The first passage is copied nearly verbatim in Richard Torkington's travel narrative, which generally plagiarizes from Guildford; see, *Ye Oldest Diarie of Englysshe Travell: Being the Hitherto Unpublished Narrative of the Pilgrimage of Sir Richard Torkington to Jerusalem in 1517*, ed. W. J. Loftie (London: Field and Tuer, 1884), 45.

arrived thither."[75] Besides the exceptional practices of others, praying at a church in the Holy Land might go without saying (after describing Catholic ceremonies during Easter week, for example, Sandys notes that "those ceremonies that are not locall, I willingly omit") and helps explain the matter-of-fact, passing quality of references to personal devotion that occasionally appear in writers' accounts.[76] On the Mount of Olives, Sanderson notes not only where his Greek Orthodox guide prayed—"My Greeke Priest shewed a great devotion at [the tomb of Mary] (so did hee at the place where our Saviour sweat water and bloud, and at the ascension place on top of Mount Olivet.)"—but, once parenthetically, where he did too:

> then to the place where Saint Steven was stoned; (the Greekes say our Saviour had made him an Arch-deacon) so to Jesami where Christ was in a bloudy sweat (here I prayed) and likewise I saw the place where the Apostles slept; then to the place where hee taught his disciples the Pater noster . . . and where he stood when hee wept over Jerusalem, and the place where hee was betrayed by that reprobate servant Judas. . . . Then to Orostoelo, the place of Christs ascension, which is on the very top of this Mount Olivet, a stone yet remaining wherein is the print of a foot: all those Christians hold assuredly, that it is the signe of our Saviours foot, most formall and proportionably it is to bee perceived, but worne much by the touching and kissing of Christians: here I prayed and hope my Saviour beheld mee.[77]

---

75. James Howell, *Instructions and Directions for Forrein Travell* (London, 1650), 17. In fact, Howell recommends prayer in the closet as a remedy for homesickness (23). Believing it "very requisit" a person "should be well grounded & settled in his *Religion*, the *beginning* and *basis* of wisdom, & somwhat vers'd in the Controversies 'twixt us & other Churches," before departing, Howell assumes his traveler, "an University Man," will have "suck'd the pure milk of tru Religion, and Orthodoxall truth" and so will be "rather confirmed, than shaken in the tenets of his *Faith*" (9). Such a one will return from "the very midst of the *Roman See*, (or *Geneva lake* either) and shoot the most dangerous *Gulphs* thereof," not only untainted but "confirmed in his zeal to his owne *Religion*" (11).

76. Sandys, *A Relation*, 170.

77. "The Pilgrimage of Iohn Sanderson from Constantinople, to the Holy Land, and so to Triply in Syria, Begunne the Fourteenth Day of May, 1601 Ended the Fourteenth of August," in *Purchas His Pilgrimes . . . the Second Part* (London, 1625), 1632. The Hakluyt Society reprint does not place "heare I prayed" in parenthesis; see John Sanderson, *The*

One wonders but can never know why, of all the places listed, Sanderson chose or was moved to pray at the Garden of Gethsemane and the Church of Ascension. From his expression of "hope" one can tell, however, that he would like at least to represent his prayers as sincere.

Yet when moments like this have not been overlooked, they have been critically dismissed precisely on the grounds of disingenuousness. Thus, on Biddulph's statement that upon gaining sight of Jerusalem he and his fellow travelers began singing psalms ("beholding the prospect of the City, we were somewhat cheered and reuiued, and solaced our selues with singing of Psalmes until we came neere unto the City"), MacLean opts for sarcasm: "he and his companions might very well have been mistaken for enthusiastic pilgrims racking up points that would get them into heaven. . . . Despite the devotional nature of his approach, Biddulph's trip to Jerusalem was not so much a spiritual odyssey as an exciting and often uncomfortable adventure."[78] Why MacLean claims that Biddulph's experience is merely a self-serving performance is unclear, but Timberlake, who arrived to Jerusalem just days before Biddulph, attests to a similar experience: "departing in the morning, being our Lady day in Lent, and 9 of the clock beforenoon, I saw the City of *Jerusalem*, when kneeling down, and saying the Lords Prayer, I gave God most hearty Thanks, for conducting me thither, to behold so holy a place with my eyes, whereof I had read so often before. Coming within a furlong of the gates, I with my Companion Mr. *John Burrel*, went singing and praising God, till we came to the West Gate of the City."[79] Admittedly, in 1581 Laurence Aldersey refers to this as a programmed ritual (many first-time visitors to Israel still kiss the ground upon first touching ground): "Being come within sight of *Ierusalem*, the maner is to kneele downe, and giue God thankes, that it hath pleased him to bring us to that holy place where he himselfe had beene."[80] But William Lithgow's moment of arrival to Jerusalem embellishes the scene:

---

*Travels of John Sanderson in the Levant 1584–1602*, ed. Sir William Foster (London: Hakluyt Society, 1931), 104.
    78. Biddulph, *Travels*, 97; MacLean, *Rise*, 102.
    79. Timberlake, "Strange and True," 24–25.
    80. Aldersey, "The first voyage," 152.

At last we beheld the prospect of Jerusalem, which was not only a contentment to my weary body, but also, being ravished with a kind of unwonted rejoicing, the tears gushed from my eyes for too much joy. In this time the Armenians began to sing, in their own fashion, psalms to praise the Lord; and I also sung the 103d psalm all the way, till we arrived near the walls of the city, where we ceased from our singing for fear of the Turks.[81]

As in Sanderson, one might notice the rather neutral description of Eastern practitioners. More significantly, here Lithgow virtually participates in prayer with the Armenians; like them, he sings from the book of Psalms.[82] As numerous passages in his narrative show, Lithgow professes prejudiced, provincial, and skeptical attitudes; nonetheless, at Jesus's tomb he again speaks of a shared Christian experience: "within the entry of the second door, we saw the place where Christ our Messias was buried; and prostrating ourselves in great humility, every man, according to his religion, offered up his prayers to God."[83] If Lithgow's sentimental tears, like Milton's incessant ones, seem off-putting, this may be due to Johnsonian discomfort with devotional writing. Not the idea of praying but when and how to express prayer is the concern here, especially as a matter of post-Reformation politics.[84] This may explain

---

81. Lithgow, *Travels*, 222.
82. Unlike MacLean with Biddulph, Bosworth trusts Lithgow here (Bosworth, *An Intrepid Scot*, 79). In the sixteenth century, John Locke records an incident where the independent, spontaneous prayer of pilgrims who had just reached the Holy Land stirred trouble, not fellow-feeling: "Then the pilgrimes after supper, in salutation of the holy lande, sang to the prayse of God, *Te Deum laudamus*, with *Magnificat*, and *Benedictus*, but in the shippe was a Frier of *Santo Francisco*, who for anger because he was not called and warned, would not sing with vs, so that he stood so much vpon his dignitie, that he forgot his simplicitie, and neglected his deuotion to the holy land for that time, saying that first they ought to haue called him yer they did beginne, because he was a Fryer, and had beene there, and knewe the orders." John Locke, "The Voyage of Mr. Iohn Locke to Ierusalem," in *The Principal Navigations, Voyages, Traffiques and Discoveries of the English Nation*, vol. 2, ed. Richard Hakluyt (London, 1599), 106.
83. Lithgow, *Travels*, 249–50.
84. In his account, Biddulph castigates Timberlake for participating in Roman Catholic services when in Jerusalem, though Timberlake, having been arrested by Ottoman authorities for insisting on identifying himself as English (rather than French or

why George Ballard could only think to describe a manuscript of Margery Kempe (whose weeping annoyed her fellow pilgrims and lasted for the rest of her life), in which is shared a vision of Jesus informing her not only that "thinking, weeping, and high contemplation is the best life in earth" but that "as oftentimes as thou sayest or thinkest: *Worshipped be all the holy places in Jerusalem, where Christ suffered bitter pain and passion in*: thou shalt have the same pardon as if thou were there with thy bodily presence, both to thyself and to all those that thou wilt give to" as "written in the style of our modern quietists and quakers, concerning the internal love of God, perfection, &c."[85] With proof lacking either way, it may have seemed safer not to include much by way of prayer at all. On Easter, Henry Maundrell thus laconically writes: "This day being our Easter, we did not go abroad to visit any places, the time requiring an employment of another nature."[86]

Seventeenth- and eighteenth-century English travelers were variously occupied, and of those activities prayer might be one. Religion colors the experience of travelers, not in the same but different ways. Said is thus only partially right when he argues that religion returned in Orientalist writing as naturalized supernaturalism. Like so many others, for example, Clarke's first encounter with Jerusalem moved him and many, though not all, of his fellow travelers to Johnsonian silence:

> Suddenly the sight burst upon us all. How shall I describe it? The effect produced was that of total silence throughout the whole company. Many of the party, by an immediate impulse, took off their hats, as if entering a church, without being sensible of so doing. The Greeks and Catholics shed torrents of tears; and presently, beginning to cross themselves, with unfeigned devotion, asked if they might be permitted to take off the

---

Catholic), was only released on the condition he do so. At the place of Mary's annunciation, Timberlake relates an instance of resistance to Catholic prayer (Timberlake, "Strange and True," 34).

85. George Ballard, *Memoirs of British Ladies, Who Have Been Celebrated for Their Writings or Skill in the Learned Languages, Arts and Sciences* (London, 1775), 6.

86. Maundrell, *A Journey*, 96.

covering from their feet, and proceed, barefooted, to the Holy Sepulchre.[87]

As important as his initial uncertainty of expression (*how* to describe the experience is an issue) is Clarke's assertion that many acted on "impulse" and without "being sensible" of their actions, much like Milton's "well-instructed" tears.

More than once Clarke announces his disbelief in the authenticity of sites, and he heaps scorn on Helena, Constantine's mother, for removing every trace of Jesus's era, even if to build monuments in God's honor: "Had the Sea of Tiberias been capable of annihilation by her means, it would have been dessicated, paved, covered with churches and altars, or converted into monasteries and markets of indulgences, until no feature of the original remained: and this by way of rendering it more particularly holy."[88] This pique indicates a desire to see and believe—if not holy at least archaeological links to the Christian past. Crucially, his disappointment was not always an obstacle to devotion. With all his "skeptical feelings thus awakened," Clarke confesses, his visit to the holy sepulcher still provoked a sympathetic response out of him and his companions:

> when we entered into the *Sanctum Sanctorum*, and beheld, by the light of lamps, there continually burning, the venerable figure of an aged monk, with streaming eyes, and a long white beard, pointing to the place "*where the body of our Lord was*," and calling upon us "to kneel and experience pardon for our sins." . . . we knelt, and participated in the feelings of more credulous pilgrims. Captain Culverhouse, in whose mind the ideas of religion and of patriotism were inseparable, with firmer emotion, drew from its scabbard the sword he had so often yielded in the defence of his country, and placed it upon the tomb.[89]

---

87. Ibid., 286.
88. Ibid., 244.
89. Ibid., 297–98.

Before rationality stepped in, faith and even sympathy with non-Anglican practitioners could make themselves known. Visitors like Culverhouse often not only rubbed objects over but left marks on holy sites including the Holy Sepulchre. Laurence Aldersey saw such graffiti on his visit to Jerusalem in 1581, about which he recorded this negative response: "the outside of the sepulchre is very foule, by meanes that euery man scrapes his name and marke vpon it, and is ill kept."[90] William Lithgow had himself tattooed there in 1612. Paris O'Donnell has read his gesture, as well as the graffiti of other seventeenth-century English travelers at sites like the Holy Sepulchre, not as devout but defiant: "the act of writing at the holy place ... come in these narratives to reveal travellers' assumptions of an alternative, minority identity, and to express defiance and resistance towards the devotional practice of pilgrimage."[91] But because it is true that their acts were complex, it is also a simplification to say they defy and resist the devotion of pilgrimage as though said devotion did not itself admit any complexity. Participating not in the acts but the feelings of other pilgrims, all the while remaining distant enough to recognize something different about Culverhouse, for whom religion and patriotism are said to be one, Clarke shows that just as there is no one British response to the Holy Land, so too representations of individual acts in the Church of the Holy Sepulchre often connote simultaneous experiences.

---

90. Aldersey, "The first voyage," 153. Egeria, a fourth century pilgrim, records that one pilgrim even took a bite out of the True Cross during a Good Friday mass.

91. Paris O'Donnell, "Souvenir-Taking and Souvenir-Leaving: Pilgrims' Remembrances in Late-Medieval and Early-Modern Travel to the Holy Land." *Trinity College Dublin Journal of Postgraduate Research* 5 (2005): 85.

# Theological Enlightenments and Ridiculous Theologies: Contradistinction in English Polemical Theology

David Manning

> When I praise what I believe, and laugh at what you believe, how do you think we are to judge, or what are we to do? . . . with God himself, not men, now inwardly strengthening and illumining our mind.
>
> —(St. Augustine, *Against the Fundamental Epistle of Manicheaus*)[1]

In 1730 high-churchman Richard Grey (1696–1771) delivered a sermon at St. Mary's Church, Leicester, in which he revelled in England's "Enlighten'd Age . . . where the Gospel shines forth in its utmost purity," unfettered "from those Corruptions and Superstitions, which so much disguise and dishonour it in other places."[2] Grey went on to use this representation of the epistemological superiority

---

This essay has its origins in a paper delivered to the 2008 NACBS at Cincinnati. I would like to thank all those who provided feedback on that paper. I am also most grateful to Gareth Atkins for his comments on an earlier draft of this essay.

1. Quoted in John Calvin, *Institutes of the Christian Religion*, bk. 1, chap. 7, par. 3. For a full translation of the original text, see: http://www.newadvent.org/fathers/1405.htm.

2. Richard Grey, *The Perpetuity of Christ's Church. A Sermon Preach'd at St. Mary's Leicester, August 20th, 1730* . . . (Oxford, 1730), 10.

of England's established faith to lament the status of an apparently belligerent minority who would not or could not discern the truth of the Church of England. Such claims had long been part of the Church's Reformation mantra against heretics in general and Roman Catholics in particular. Peter Lake has suggested that, "near the centre of the antipopish impulse [there was] an ideal of 'enlightenment', as the light of the gospel was shone on [the] errors, illusions and lies of popery."[3] It may be posited that the discourse of Reformation significantly revived an idea and language of spiritual enlightenment. Indeed, the Reformation motto that emanated from Geneva was *post tenebras lux*.[4] According to John Calvin, "'No one can receive anything except what is given him from above'" (John 3: 27): it was "a special illumination" when "the Lord through his Spirit gives understanding."[5] Subsequently, many orthodox Protestants believed that "God did not only lighten that *Luminare magnum*, his holy Scripture, but lightened also *luminare minus*, a less light, the light of reason; by help of arts and sciences."[6] In this context enlightenment became both a theological claim about truth and a rhetorical strategy that described the acquisition of that truth via the powerful metaphor of light. As truth was to falsehood, so light was to darkness; and such contradistinction was part of the polemical theology of the age. The discourse of enlightenment was fundamental to the construction of binary positions that fuelled the battles between orthodox Protestantism and Catholicism and among competing manifestations of Protestantism.[7]

---

3. Peter Lake, "Anti-Puritanism: The Structure of a Prejudice," in *Religious Politics in Post-Reformation England: Essays in Honour of Nicholas Tyacke*, ed. Kenneth Fincham and Peter Lake (Woodbridge, UK: Boydell Press, 2006), 82–83.

4. Theodore Beza, *A Briefe and Pithie Summe of the Christian Faith Made in Forme of a Confession . . . Translated out of French by R. F.* (London, 1565), title page. I wish to thank John Coffey for bringing this phrase to my attention.

5. Calvin, *Institutes*, bk. 2, chap. 2, par. 20. See also bk. 1, chap. 16–17.

6. W[illiam] Gearing, *The Arraignment of Pride, or, Pride Set Forth, with Causes, Kinds, and Several Branches of It . . .* (London, 1660), 144.

7. In this essay the notion of orthodox Protestantism is derived from Ian Green's definition, that is to say the broad category of ideas which were informed by conformist and non-conformist clerical opinion (as opposed to lay spiritualism or rationalism). See Ian Green, *Print and Protestantism in Early Modern England* (Oxford: Oxford University Press, 2000), 553–66.

While there is nothing particularly novel about acknowledging the way in which some contemporary Protestants described the imparting or receiving of spiritual knowledge via metaphorical references to light, this point has invariably been overlooked in the relevant historiography.[8] (In this essay, established historiographical labels will be placed in quotation marks so as to differentiate them from references to the contemporary discourse of enlightenment). Scholarship on "the Christian Enlightenment" has been largely preoccupied with progressive modes of irenicism and rational criticism. Helena Rosenblatt, among others, has pressed the view that "Enlightened Christians, wherever they were from, shared a commitment to a few central ideas and values," whereby an irenic "reasonableness" promoted a simpler, more moderate and more tolerant religion.[9] It has long been argued that "Enlightenment goals—like criticism, sensibility or faith in progress—throve in England *within* piety"; but John Pocock has stated that the discourse of enlightenment "was a polemic against the orthodox theology of Christ's divinity, against the Trinity and the Incarnation, the Council of Nicea, the Athanasian Creed . . . the Gospel according to St. John and the doctrine of the Word made Flesh."[10] Consequently, C. D. A. Leighton has had cause to consider contemporary non-jurors such as Charles Leslie (1650–1722) in the context of a "Counter-Enlightenment" culture that placed doctrine, history, and morality before human rationalism.[11] Furthermore, Brian Young has argued that the mystical

---

8. J. C. D. Clark makes reference to enlightenment as the imparting of spiritual knowledge, but does not significantly develop the point; see J. C. D. Clark, *English Society 1660–1832* (Cambridge: Cambridge University Press, 2000), 9.

9. Helena Rosenblatt, "The Christian Enlightenment," in *Enlightenment, Reawakening and Revolution 1660–1815*, ed. Stewart J. Brown and Timothy Tackett (Cambridge: Cambridge University Press, 2006), 284.

10. Roy Porter, "The Enlightenment in England," in *The Enlightenment in National Context*, ed. Roy Porter and Mikuláš Teich (Cambridge: Cambridge University Press, 1981), 6; J. G. A. Pocock, "Within the Margins: The Definitions of Orthodoxy," in *The Margins of Orthodoxy: Heterodox Writing and Cultural Response, 1660–1750*, ed. Roger D. Lund (Cambridge: Cambridge University Press, 1995), 50. See also Knud Haakonssen, ed., *Enlightenment and Religion: Rational Dissent in Eighteenth-Century Britain* (Cambridge: Cambridge University Press, 1996); Mark Goldie, "Alexander Geddes at the Limits of the Catholic Enlightenment," *Historical Journal* 53, no. 1 (2010): 61–86.

11. C. D. A. Leighton, "The Non-Jurors and their History," *Journal of Religious History* 29, no. 3 (2005): 241–57.

critique of rational theology by the likes of William Law (1686–1761) and John Wesley (1703–1791) gave expression to a heterodox "Counter-Enlightenment."[12] Despite Pocock's welcome acknowledgment that "'Enlightenment' is a word or signifier, and not a single or unifiable phenomenon which it constantly signifies," it is somewhat unfortunate that, due to an enduring focus on the role of human reason in the interpretation of enlightenment as phenomenon, scholars have yet to give due consideration to either the claims of contemporary orthodox Protestants or the rhetoric of enlightenment in the Christian tradition.[13] Consequently, the history of Richard Grey's "Enlighten'd Age" has yet to be fully acknowledged, let alone understood.

The historiography has also tended to view irreverent irony as the boisterous younger sibling of antidogmatic, rational theology.[14] In particular, the anticlerical rhetoric of eighteenth-century wits such as Anthony Ashley Cooper (1671–1713), third earl of Shaftesbury, mobilized ridicule as a distinct strategy of engagement. Modern theorists have identified Shaftesbury as an exponent of a type of ridicule that was new to the time and based upon the conviction that the object of humor was the incongruous.[15] This idea drew inspiration from aesthetics and was used to advance epistemological claims. Congruities were seen as objective evidence of truth and sincerity, while incongruities were believed to be proof of falsehood and insincerity. So, for example, a witty remark about an intemperate clergyman that produced laughter would not only provide due merriment, it would also expose and condemn intemperate clergy as unworthy impostors. Conversely, an attempt to ridicule an honest, well-mannered clergyman would fail

---

12. B. W. Young, *Religion and Enlightenment in Eighteenth-Century England* (Oxford: Clarendon Press, 1998), 120–21.

13. J. G. A. Pocock, "History and Enlightenment: A View of Their History," *Modern Intellectual History* 5, no. 1 (2008): 83.

14. For example, see John Redwood, *Reason, Ridicule, and Religion: The Age of Enlightenment in England, 1660–1750* (London: Thames & Hudson, 1976); James A. Herrick, *The Radical Rhetoric of the English Deists: The Discourse of Skepticism, 1680–1750* (Columbia: University of South Carolina Press, 1997); Isabel Rivers, *Reason, Grace, and Sentiment: A Study of the Language of Religion and Ethics in England, 1660–1780* (Cambridge: Cambridge University Press, 2000), 2:31–49.

15. Michael Billig, *Laughing and Ridicule: Towards a Social Critique of Humour* (London: Sage, 2005), 68–70, 74–77.

to produce laughter because these virtues were seen as being harmonious with the true character of a clergyman. Such a strategy seemed to rely upon audiences and the wit sharing the same assumptions about the harmony and discord between certain ideas and actions. Nevertheless, the ridicule of incongruity was purported to be a rationally applied rhetorical tool that could be used to expose corrupt epistemological hoodwinkers, whether they were Church of England priests, religious enthusiasts, pseudo-philosophers, or whoever: for "without Wit and Humour, Reason can hardly have its Proof or be distinguish'd."[16]

It would, however, be erroneous to suggest that all contemporary ridicule of religion was of this type. For example, in a celebrated sermon at Salters' Hall in 1734, the Presbyterian minister Joshua Bayes (bap. 1671, d. 1746) drew attention to what he perceived to be the Roman Catholic folly of using Latin in holy worship by using the following biblical analogy: "The apostle [St. Paul] represents their [the Corinthians] using an unknown tongue in their religious assemblies, as what had a tendency to *expose* them in their worship to . . . contempt and ridicule . . . and so confirm them in their infidelity."[17] Here ridicule was represented as a response to self-evident error: truth was advanced by exposing mere verisimilitude as ridiculous. Scripture provided a precedent for when such ridicule was legitimate and necessary: for "thou, O Lord, shalt laugh at them; thou shalt have all the heathen in derision" (Psalm 59:8). Unlike the ridicule of incongruity, this model of ridicule was initially concerned with the desire of an agent to assert their superiority over another and, hence, it was commonly conceived within the discourse of orthodoxy.[18] Moreover, this type of ridicule had dominated the discourse of mockery ever since Aristotle had suggested

---

16. [Anthony Ashley Cooper], *Sensus Communis: An Essay on the Freedom of Wit and Humour. In a Letter to a Friend* (London, 1709), 22. See also Alfred Owen Aldridge, "Shaftesbury and the Test of Truth," *Publications of the Modern Language Association* 60 (1945): 129–56.

17. Joshua Bayes, *The Church of Rome's Doctrine and Practise with Relation to the Worship of God in an Unknown Tongue Examined in a Sermon Preached at Salters-Hall March 6, 1734–35* (London, 1735), 20.

18. Notwithstanding this distinction, there was a degree of overlap between the two types of ridicule that ought to be acknowledged, even if it cannot be expounded upon here.

that the object of comedy was the inferior.[19] The most notable exponent of so-called superiority theory in the seventeenth century was Thomas Hobbes (1588–1679). Hobbes stated that "men laugh at *Jests*, . . . some *absurdity* of *another* . . . the Passion of Laughter is nothing else but *sudden glory* arising from sudden *conception* of some *eminency* in our selves, by comparison with the *infirmity* of others."[20] This type of ridicule was a polemical expression of self-identified superiority which also sought to undermine the position of any challengers to that superiority. To a greater or lesser extent, the effectiveness of this strategy relied upon perceptions of orthodoxy that had been shaped by preexisting intellectual and sociopolitical paradigms. Nonetheless, in Reformation contexts, a diverse range of religious groups sought to make theological truth claims by rendering other theologies ridiculous. In other words, the discourse of ridicule was also part of the rough and tumble of polemical contradistinction.

This essay seeks to explore the orthodox Protestant history of two characteristic features of "the Enlightenment"; namely, the phenomenon of enlightenment qua enlightenment and the ridicule of dogmatic theology. This will be achieved by focusing on the issue of polemical contradistinction. The power of contradistinction was its perceived ability to shape and defend orthodoxy by representing the division of all people into two groups, for true believers were defined via characteristics that were contrary and opposite to those of nonbelievers, and vice versa. It will be demonstrated that, in seventeenth- and early eighteenth-century England, the discourses of theological enlightenments and ridiculous theologies were crucial to the construction of binary positions such as those between orthodox Protestants and Catholics, and between

---

19. Aristotle, *Poetics*, 1449a32–36. See also Adam Fox, "Libels and Popular Ridicule in Jacobean England," *Past and Present* 145 (1994), 47–83; Edward Berry, "Laughing at 'Others,'" in *The Cambridge Companion to Shakespearean Comedy*, ed. Alexander Leggatt (Cambridge: Cambridge University Press, 2002), 123–38; Billig, *Laughing and Ridicule*, 37–56.

20. Thomas Hobbes, *Humane Nature: Or, the Fundamental Elements of Policy. Being a Discovery of the Faculties Acts and Passions of the Soul of Man* . . . 2nd ed. (London, 1650), 102–3. See also Quentin Skinner, "Hobbes and the Classical Theory of Laughter," in *Leviathan after 350 Years*, ed. Tom Sorell and Luc Foisneau (Oxford: Clarendon Press, 2004), 139–66.

orthodox Protestants and other manifestations of Protestantism. Yet, as Peter Lake has pointed out, the notion that certain ideas and opinions were "constructed" marks the beginning of an argument and not the end.[21] So this essay is also designed to stimulate new debates by fundamentally challenging the current historiography of "the Christian Enlightenment." It will be argued that orthodox Protestants confidently utilized the rhetoric of enlightenment and ridicule to perpetuate the vital polemic of contradistinction that had been inaugurated by the Reformation; yet their monopoly over these linguistic signifiers of orthodoxy was gradually rendered ineffective by the direct and indirect effects of theological pluralism. This emphasis on discourse will not only revive a hitherto overlooked set of convictions among orthodox Protestants but also question the historiographical application of the term *enlightenment*. The remainder of this essay will be divided into two parts. The first part will consider the nature of the discourse of enlightenment as a form of polemical contradistinction; the second part will consider the nature of the discourse of ridicule as an expression of superiority, but will also include a short case study of the ridicule of Christ's miracles by the notorious clergyman Thomas Woolston.

# I

If theological enlightenment was represented as an ideal of divine communication, then one might reasonably suspect the initial actions of conversion and baptism to be significant. Peter Marshall has noted that "light from heaven had of course been central to the archetype of Christian conversion narratives [since] Paul's experience on the Damascus road," so it was perhaps inevitable that the "metaphor of enlightenment was a recurrent one in evangelical sources" relating to conversion.[22] Furthermore, the Church of England divine John Tillotson (1630–1694) had claimed that the state of being "*enlightened*" was

---

21. Lake, "Anti-Puritanism," 87–90.
22. Peter Marshall, "Evangelical Conversion in the Reign of Henry VIII," in *The Beginnings of English Protestantism*, ed. Peter Marshall and Alec Ryrie (Cambridge: Cambridge University Press, 2002), 24.

reached by being "solemnly admitted into the church by baptism" and that among primitive Christians, "those who were baptized were called, . . . enlightened persons."[23] However, Pauline theology went much further by representing spiritual enlightenment as a divine process: "the Father of glory, may give unto you the spirit of wisdom and revelation in the knowledge of him: the eyes of your understanding being enlightened; that ye may know what is the hope of his calling . . . For ye were sometimes darkness, but now are ye light in the Lord: walk as children of light" (Eph. 1:17–18; Eph. 5:8). Following this trajectory it may be argued that the language of light and enlightenment formed an allegory through which the spiritual process of becoming aware of God's truth was both understood and explained. This not only helped orthodox Protestants grasp the central tenets of their faith, it also afforded them a rhetorical device to assert and defend that truth against their enemies.

The orthodox allegory of light appears to have woven together two interrelated representations of enlightenment. The first laid emphasis on the relationship between God and believers. According to John Calvin, "God illumines the minds of his own with the spirit of discernment . . . now no abyss is here; rather, a way in which we ought to walk in safety, and a lamp to guide our feet, the light of life, and the school of sure and clear truth."[24] Thus, it was understood that "The Word, without the Spirit's enlightenment, Is as good Seede sowne on vntilled ground."[25] All good Calvinists were instructed by their ministers to "Submit your selves to the good word of the Lord, and not only be willing and content to be thus enlightened, but labour for it, that thou maiest prevent the Judgements deserved by the same."[26] The allegory of light was, however, never far from various ideas of covenant theology and was no more owned by Calvinism than by any other Reformed ideology. The

---

23. John Tillotson, *The Works of the Most Reverend Dr. John Tillotson* (London, 1748), 7:181.

24. Calvin, *Institutes*, bk. 1, chap. 17, par. 2.

25. Robert Aylett, *The Song of Songs, which Was Salomons Metaphrased in English Heroiks by Way of Dialogue* . . . (London, 1621), 83.

26. Thomas Hooker, *The Soules Preparation for Christ. Or, a Treatise of Contrition Wherein Is Discovered How God Breaks the Heart and Wounds the Soule, in Conversion of a Sinner to Himself* (London, 1632), 57.

highly influential Arminian theologian Richard Allestee (1622–1681) concluded his *Causes of the Decay of Christian Piety* (1667) as follows:

> *let us humbly and earnestly invoke the Father of lights, to* illuminate *all those whom the God of this world hath* blinded, *that after he hath sent into the world the* Image *of his own eternal brightness; caused the* Sun of Righteousness *so long to shine upon us, it may not serve only to involve us in that most* dreadful condemnation, *which awaits those who love* darkness *more than* light; *but that answering the purpose of our* holy calling, *walking as* Children of light.[27]

This Anglican appropriation of the allegory of light would have been hotly contested by Quakers, whose whole theology was based upon the principle of the Light Within. For the Quaker leader William Penn (1644–1718), the theological "*Necessity* of an *Inward Principle*, to Enlighten our Minds" was borne out of the belief that "*GOD is Light*, and that GOD is in CHRIST, and that CHRIST by his Light *Lighteth every Man that cometh into the World*; and dwelleth with them that obey him in his Inward and Spiritual Manifestation."[28] However, the allegory of light was so pervasive within Pauline theology that it was also used to explicate the doctrine of "false apostles" (2 Cor. 11:13–15). Consequently, anti-Quakers like Charles Leslie were able call upon scripture to describe Quakerism as nothing but "Satan transform'd into an angel of light."[29]

Biblical metaphors of light and dark, and the corresponding states of enlightenment and nonenlightenment, were readily appropriated and reappropriated by different Christians, primarily because such language was seen as crucial to providing legitimate truth claims about spiritual knowledge. Further study is certainly required to advance a historical interpretation of the threefold relationship between hermeneutic,

---

27. Richard Allestree, *The Causes of the Decay of Christian Piety, or, an Impartial Survey of the Ruines of Christian Religion, Undermin'd by Unchristian Practice* . . . (London, 1667), 438.

28. W. P. [William Penn], *Truth Further Clear'd from Mistakes Being Two Chapters out of the Book Entituled, Primitive Christianity Reviv'd* . . . (London, 1698), 32, 34.

29. Charles Leslie, *The Snake in the Grass: Or; Satan Transform'd into an Angel of Light* (London, 1696).

rhetoric, and confessional politics with respect to the allegory of light.[30] That being said, there is value in C. S. Lewis's idea that allegory was fundamental to the representation of immaterial subjects; and Jonathan Charteris-Black has recently reminded scholars that "*light* and *dark* are prototype metaphors of Christianity."[31] Hence, it is hardly surprising to see metaphors of light and dark represented as ciphers of orthodoxy and heterodoxy, respectively. The degree to which theorists such as Charteris-Black now recognize the power of the conceptual metaphor of "spiritual knowledge is light" should provoke a revaluation of the history of enlightenment. Through the Reformed theology of John Calvin, orthodox Protestantism seemed to reaffirm the Augustinian principle that "we ourselves are not that light which enlighteneth every Man that cometh into the world; but we are enlightened by thee: as who having been sometime in darkness, may now be light in thee" (Eph. 5:8).[32] Historical accounts, which represent enlightenment as monopolized by those who believed in the primacy of human reason, do not give adequate consideration to the idea and language of enlightenment present in biblical and doctrinal theology.

For contemporary orthodox Protestants, theological enlightenment was largely conceived under the rubric of God's omniscience, and it was arguably an expression of the doctrine of "right reason." The twofold principle that human knowledge of God and His creation was

---

30. Starting points include Brian Vickers, "The Royal Society and English Prose Style: A Reassessment," in *Rhetoric and the Pursuit of Truth: Language Change in the Seventeenth and Eighteenth Centuries*, ed. Brian Vickers and Nancy S. Struever (Los Angeles: William Andrews Clark Memorial Library), 3–76; Veronica Kelly, "'Embody'd Dark': The Simulation of Allegory in The Dunciad," in *Enlightening Allegory: Theory, Practice, and Contexts of Allegory in the Late Seventeenth and Eighteenth Centuries*, ed. Kevin L. Cope (New York: AMS Press, 1993), 351–72; Mark Knights, *Representation and Misrepresentation in Later Stuart Britain: Partisanship and Political Culture* (Oxford: Oxford University Press, 2005), 9–10, 207–381; John Pendergast, *Religion, Allegory, and Literacy in Early Modern England, 1560–1640: The Control of the Word* (Aldershot, UK: Ashgate, 2006), 119–32.

31. C. S. Lewis, *The Allegory of Love: A Study in Medieval Tradition* (London: Oxford University Press, 1938), 44; Jonathan Charteris-Black, *Corpus Approaches to Critical Metaphor Analysis* (Houndmills, UK: Palgrave Macmillan, 2004), 185. For an extended discussion of metaphorical descriptions of God, see Sallie McFague, *Metaphorical Theology: Models of God in Religious Language* (London: SCM Press, 1983).

32. Augustine, *Confessions*, bk. 9, chap. 4. See also Augustine, *The City of God against the Pagans*, bk. 8, chap. 7.

dependent upon and inferior to divine knowledge created the necessity for the theological enlightenment of humankind: for "hath not God made foolish the wisdom of the world?" (1 Cor. 1:20). Representations of human reasoning that were seen as conforming to this principle, and its associated soteriology, were afforded the label of "right reason," which in turn became another manifestation of the rhetoric of contradistinction that set supposed orthodoxy against various erroneous beliefs. With regards to scripture, it was decreed that "Before you read a Chapter in the Bible, beg God to enlighten your Minds, and to work upon your Wills, that you may cheerfully do what he requires of you in his Word, and to bestow spiritual Wisdom upon you, that you may understand what you read."[33] Revelatory knowledge, however, had to be grasped in the moment and the signs of providence had to be accurately interpreted. To such ends, John Tillotson made the following impassioned plea:

> O LORD GOD of truth, I humbly beseech thee to enlighten my mind by thy holy spirit, that I may discern the true way to eternal salvation: and to free me from all prejudice and passion, from every corrupt affection and interest that may either blind or seduce me in my search after it. Make me impartial in my inquiry after truth, and ready whenever it is discovered to me to receive it in the love of it, to obey it from the heart, and to practise it in my life.[34]

The notion of "right reason" was crucial to the representation of the Christian virtuoso who would stand as vanguard against all the supposed ills of the unilateral application and elevation of human reason in the field of natural philosophy. It was believed that "The Holy Ghost will enlighten the Minds, and give Courage and Resolution to the Hearts of good Men" against the dangers of "*Pagan* Philosophy," which encouraged "Man to make himself completely happy, without the Help of any other" and perversely give "him the Precedence" over

---

33. Anthony Horneck, *Several Sermons upon the Fifth of St. Matthew; Being Part of Christ's Sermon on the Mount*, 2nd ed. (London, 1706), 1:18.

34. Tillotson, *Works*, 12:248.

God.[35] In opposition to Lockean attempts to unhinge epistemology from orthodox theology, the natural philosopher Robert Boyle (1627–1691) championed their continued integration. "Right reason," he argued, "may be looked upon as a catholic principle, of which philosophy is but an application," for the "heavenly light" of revelation provided the human intellect with "such benefits as the air does in a clear day from the beams of the sun, by which it is both enlightened and expanded."[36]

The works of Tillotson and Boyle were regularly republished, read, and used throughout the eighteenth century, and their influence on the evolution of orthodox Protestantism should not be underestimated.[37] Tillotson was a vehement Anglican apologist, notwithstanding his low-church sympathies, and in this context it would be perhaps misleading to stress particular aspects of his anti-Calvinism over and above his commitment to a relatively orthodox conception of "right reason." Boyle's theology has hitherto received only limited attention. Yet through his friendship with the Calvinist theologian Thomas Barlow (1609–1691), as well as the long-term significance of the *Discourse of Things above Reason* (1681) and his posthumously endowed lecture series, Boyle's theological legacy may be viewed as an eager desire to persist with orthodox, albeit modified, principles.[38] While several early eighteenth-century Boyle Lecturers proved to be anything but orthodox, the lectures themselves became a perennial performance against the supposed evil of hyperrationalism.

The second representation of enlightenment followed from the first and emphasized the relationship between enlightened and unenlightened people. The former were represented, implicitly and explicitly, as righteous, good, humble, in the light, and able to see, while the latter

35. John Moore, *Of the Truth and Excellency of the Gospel. A Sermon Preach'd before the Society for the Propagation of Foreign Parts, at their Anniversary Meeting, in the Parish-Church of St. Mary-le-Bow, on Friday the 20th of February, 1712/11* (London, 1713), 35.

36. Robert Boyle, *The Works of Robert Boyle* (London, 1772), 6:713–14. See also Lotte Mulligan, "Robert Boyle, 'Right Reason,' and the Meaning of Metaphor," *Journal of the History of Ideas* 55, no. 2 (1994): 235–57.

37. For Tillotson, see Rosemary Dixon, "The Publishing of John Tillotson's Collected Works, 1695–1757," *Library* 8, no. 2 (2007): 154–81.

38. Jan W. Wojcik, "The Theological Context of Boyle's Things above Reason," in *Robert Boyle Reconsidered*, ed. Michael Hunter (Cambridge: Cambridge University Press, 1994), 139–55.

were depicted as unrighteous, evil, full of pride, in the dark, and, hence, blind to both the truth and their error. Ethical and metaphorical polarities were superimposed upon one another, not only to stress mutual exclusivity but to provide the necessary description to allow for polemical contradistinction among competing Christian groups. Once again the Reformed theology of John Calvin was crucial: "No one should now hesitate to confess that he is able to understand God's mysteries only in so far as he is illumined by God's grace. He who attributes any more understanding to himself is all the more blind because he does not recognize his own blindness."[39] John Tillotson's view on this theme was no less certain: "As the spirit of GOD is said *to enlighten the understandings* of men, and *to open their hearts that they may believe*: so the devil is said *to blind the minds of them that believe not*" and "*this is the condemnation, that light is come into the world, and men loved darkness rather than light, because their deeds were evil*" (John 3:19).[40] In the inaugural Boyle Lecture series of 1692, Richard Bentley (1662–1742) attacked those who denied the potency of divine reason, stating that "unless it please God by extraordinary methods *to help their unbelief, and enlighten the eyes of their understanding*; they will carry their Atheism with them to the Pit; and the flames of Hell only must convince them of their Error."[41] To complete this foray into the discourse of theological enlightenments, it is worth delving into the polemical application of such language to gain a sense of how it was used to set Protestants against Catholics, and orthodox Protestants against lay rationalizing Protestants.

The polemical war between Protestants and Catholics was bitter and enduring; however, despite valuable studies on religious prejudice and stereotyping, more work still needs to be done to analyze the rhetorical processes of contradistinction which allowed each side to construct and affirm ideological positions which were superimposed upon the fundamental binary of true and false.[42] While it is axiomatic

---

39. Calvin, *Institutes*, bk. 2, chap. 2 par. 21.

40. Tillotson, *Works*, 12:62–63, 72.

41. Richard Bentley, *The Folly and Unreasonableness of Atheism Demonstrated from the Advantage of a Religious Life . . . in Eight Sermons Preached at the Lecture Founded by the Honourable Robert Boyle . . . in the First Year, MDXCII*, 4th ed. (London, 1699), 14.

42. To date, the best studies include Peter Lake, "Antipopery: The Structure of Prejudice," in *Conflict in Early Stuart England: Studies in Religion and Politics, 1603–1642*,

that different types of Protestants shared a conviction that "In contradistinction from the *Roman Schism* and *Corruptions* we are *Protestants*," historians have yet to appreciate fully the cultural affinity between discourse of this kind and a contemporary sense of Protestantism vis-à-vis Catholicism.[43]

John Foxe's *Book of Martyrs* was rarely out of print during the seventeenth and eighteenth century, and it informed readers how "The church [had been] enlightened by the martyrdom of saints."[44] In particular, the text was able to reappropriate the Catholic representation of fire for heretics and turn the burning Hugh Latimer (1485–1555) into a personification of theological enlightenment: "Mr. Latimer said, Be of good comfort, Mr. Ridley, and play the man, we shall this day light such a candle by God's grace in England, as I trust shall never be put out."[45] Placing Latimer's execution within the context of the allegory of light significantly embellished the notion of martyrdom and facilitated the representation of Protestant enlightenment in contradistinction to the apparent blindness and evil of Latimer's executioners. In a pointed jibe against the Roman Catholic Church, John Tillotson asked, "if the great design of the Son of GOD was to enlighten the world with the knowledge of divine truth, what shall we think of those, who make it their great endeavour to stifle and suppress this light . . . ?"[46] Yet within the pages of Foxe's *Book of Martyrs* it was also acknowledged that Roman Catholics had believed that "at the very beginning of [Queen Mary's] reign, a new light, as it were, of God's religion seemed to us

---

ed. Richard Cust and Ann Hughes (London: Longman, 1989), 72–106; Colin Haydon, *Anti-Catholicism in Eighteenth-Century England, c. 1714–80: A Political and Social Study* (Manchester, UK: Manchester University Press, 1993); Alexandra Walsham, *Charitable Hatred: Tolerance and Intolerance in England, 1500–1700* (Manchester, UK: Manchester University Press, 2006).

43. Richard Baxter, *Sacrilegious Desertion of the Holy Ministery Rebuked . . .* (London, 1672), 7. For an example of innovative research in this area, see Hilary Larkin, "The Measure of Englishness in the Early-Modern Era" (PhD dissertation, University of Cambridge, 2008), 157–219.

44. John Foxe, *The Book of Martyrs: Containing an Account of the Sufferings and Death of the Protestants in the Reign of Queen Mary the First . . .* (London, 1732), 488.

45. Ibid.

46. Tillotson, *Works*, 12:115.

for to spring and rise."[47] Catholic polemists probed Tillotson's claims by asking "Whether God by any Miracle, or any thing like a Miracle, gave testimony of the Truth of the Reformation? If God did not, how will the Doctor convince me that this is not *ignis fatuus*, a false Light, and a real *Egyptian* Darkness."[48] Nevertheless, the Reformation had endowed the Church of England with significant power to prescribe orthodoxy and, particularly after the so-called Toleration Act of 1689, nonconformists may have been more inclined to voice a mutual hatred of Roman Catholicism, if only to try to promote their orthodox credentials.

In an Anglican anti-Catholic tract of 1706 it was noted that "The *Papists* are taught to believe as their Church believes, without weighing or considering why they do so . . . They are kept as much as 'tis possible in the dark."[49] Set against the backdrop of the 1715 Jacobite uprising, one commentator narrated the "history of the rise and progress of the Reformation of the Church here in England, from Popish Darkness and Superstition."[50] Posthumous reprints of Nathaniel Bacon's pseudo-history of the demise of Francis Spira (d. 1548), the quintessential Protestant apostate turned damned Roman Catholic, were used to represent God's vengeance upon those blasphemous souls who sinned "against Light and Knowledge."[51] Throughout the 1730s and beyond, anti-papal tirades continued to employ the idea and language of enlightenment to affirm orthodox Protestantism. Daniel Defoe (1660–1731) used the device of a dialogue between a father and his daughter to posit that "the Introduction of [Popish] Error is always clandestine; the Nature of the Thing requires it; 'tis a Work of Darkness; People would not receive

---

47. Foxe, *The Book of Martyrs*, 104.

48. [Anon.], *A Vindication of the Roman Catholicks from the Foul Aspersions Thrown upon Them by John Tillotson in a Sermon Preached by Him in November, 1687* (London,1688), unpaginated [10].

49. Lewis Atterbury, *An Answer to a Popish Book, Intituled, A True and Modest Account of the Chief Points of Controversie, between the Roman Catholicks and the Protestants . . .* (London, 1706), 4.

50. Daniel Disney, *A Compendious History of the Rise and Progress of the Reformation of the Church here in England, from Popish Darkness and Superstition* (London, 1715).

51. Nathaniel Bacon, *A Relation of the Fearful Estate of Francis Spira, after Turn'd Apostate from the Protestant Church to Popery. Also the Miserable Lives, and Woeful Deaths, of Mr. John Child . . .* (London, 1734), unpaginated note to the reader [12], signed off "B. H." See also Calvin, *Institutes*, bk. 3, chap. 3, par. 22.

such Things in the Light . . . , indeed, 'tis not likely they should bring such Things openly in the Face of Authority, and of Truth."[52] Theological enlightenment brought forth the possibility to discern truth from error, banishing both Reformation paranoia and the carping criticisms of Roman Catholics: "If the Scriptures then can rejoice the Heart, enlighten the Eyes, and make us clean . . . *Thou, through thy Commandments, hast made me wiser than mine Enemies.*"[53] In one form or another, eighteenth-century orthodox appeals to theological enlightenment were very much self-styled vindications of the English Reformation.

Within the Protestant tradition, however, proponents of orthodoxy faced two significant challenges from within their own ranks. Misunderstanding and polemical contrivance led to all manner of theological positions being represented as either manifestations of "enthusiasm" or "Deism." The three-way intellectual war—among radical spiritualism, orthodox Protestantism, and lay rationalizing Protestantism—for the right to define the relationship between theology and epistemology inevitably involved polemical battles over the nature of enlightenment. Putting aside the topic of radical spiritualism, some historiographical attention has been given to the rise of what Steve Shapin has called "epistemological decorum" among rationalists. However, this has been to the detriment of understanding the continued appeal to the orthodox doctrine of "right reason."[54] Despite innovative philosophical discourses, many contemporary Protestants held fast to a theological criterion of truth which was guided by questions such as, "Dost thou desire to be enlighten'd by God[?]"[55] The orthodox conceptualization of enlightenment continued to provide an intellectual underpinning to the soteriological necessity of repentance, bolstering the notion that human

52. [Daniel Defoe], *A Family Instructor; Containing, a Brief and Clear Defence of the Christian Religion in General, against the Errors of the Atheists, Jews, Deists & Sceptics: And of the Protestant Religion in Particular, against the Superstitions of the Church of Rome*, 10th ed. (London, 1732), 146.

53. Benjamin Andrewes Atkinson, *The Holy Scriptures a Perfect Rule, and Popish Objections Answered. A Sermon Preached on . . . Jan. 26, 1734–5 in St. Thomas Apostle, London* (London, 1735), 16.

54. Steven Shapin, *A Social History of Truth: Civility and Science in Seventeenth-Century England* (Chicago: Chicago University Press, 1994), 193–242.

55. James Ellesby, *The Sick Christian's Companion: Consisting of Prayers, Meditations, and Directions . . .* (London, 1729), 87.

beings were inferior to the Almighty and dependent upon Him. Here, claims that imply "reason" and "revelation" were somehow antithetical are somewhat inaccurate; the battle was between two paradigms: one placed God as the continued provider of truth and human knowledge; the other did not. From the position of the former, the advocates of the latter were to be pitied and feared for having "only the Guidance of unenlightened Reason."[56]

John Tillotson had led a major battle against Socinianism in his sermons at St. Lawrence Jewry during the winter of 1679–80. This epistemological tussle was also, in part, a fight for key linguistic signifiers: was human reason enabled by "natural light" or "divine light"? Tillotson acknowledged the potential value of "natural light," but used the discussion to expose its failings and limitations, ironically elevating "the great *Masters of Reason*" before dismissing them as unable to comprehend that "the *God of Truth* lead us into Truth, and enlighten the Minds of those who are in Error, *and give* them *Repentance to the acknowledgement of the Truth.*"[57] A similar strategy appears to have been pursued a generation later by the likes of Henry Felton (1679–1740) in his 1728–29 Lady Moyer's Lectures, which had been endowed a decade before to combat the rise of "Christian deism" emanating from Oxbridge.[58] On a more straightforward tack, Boyle Lecturers such as Lilly Butler (fl. 1696–1716) continued to reiterate their conviction that "we cannot think it beyond the Power of an Almighty Being, the Maker of Heaven and Earth, in Ways unknown to us, to enlighten the Minds, and to improve the Understandings of Men."[59] For clergymen such as Charles Leslie, the historical reality of Christ's divinity was of "a light shining

---

56. Nicolas Brady, *Several Sermons, Chiefly upon Practical Subjects* (London 1730), 1:82.

57. John [Tillotson], *Sermons concerning the Divinity and Incarnation of Our Blessed Saviour: Preached in the Church of St. Lawrence Jewry . . .*, 3rd ed. (London, 1702), 66–67, 103.

58. Henry Felton, *The Christian Faith Asserted against Deists, Arians, and Socinians in Eight Sermons Preach't at the Lay Moyer's Lecture in the Cathedral Church of St. Paul 1728, 1729 . . .* (Oxford, 1732); Scott Mandelbrote, "Eighteenth-Century Reactions to Newton's Anti-Trinitarianism," in *Newton and Newtonianism: New Studies*, ed. James E. Force and Sarah Hutton (Dordrecht, Neth.: Kluwer Academic, 2004), 93–112.

59. Lilly Butler, *A Discourse, Proving, that the Faith and Practice of True Christians, Are No Just Matter of Shame or Reproach. Being Eight Sermons Preached at the Cathedral*

in a dark place, until the Day dawn, and the Day-star arise in your Hearts. Which God grant," and hence all who challenged the doctrine of the Trinity were unenlightened.[60] Once such a view was contextualized by the Old Testament prophecy that warned, "Woe unto them that call evil good, and good evil; that put darkness for light, and light for darkness" (Isa. 5:20), fiery clergymen such as Brampton Gurdon (c. 1672–1741), the Boyle Lecturer of 1721–22, were able to expound the evil nexus between the unbelief of hyperrationalists and practical sins.[61] In contrast to such extreme anxiety, the high-church apologist Francis Atterbury (1663–1732) drew upon a historical analogy of the birth of Christianity: "Then did the Glorious Light of the Gospel shine forth, and dazzle the Eyes even of those who were thought to see best and farthest. . . . The Doctrine of the Cross shewed itself bare-faced to all the Wits and Sages of both *Rome* and *Athens*; and defied their Doubts and their Reasonings."[62] The inference was that the ideas of unorthodox philosophers had once before acquiesced to the light of God's truth, and it was inevitable that this would happen again.

Once understood in the context of metaphor and allegory, the discourse of enlightenment becomes notable for its rhetorical significance and its ideological insignificance. Theological enlightenments were rhetorical constructs that facilitated polemical contradistinction in order to nurture and defend orthodoxy. Orthodox Protestants sought to crystallize the ideal of Reformation via appeals to the discourse of enlightenment, which in turn led to explicit and implicit representations of supposed heretics as unenlightened. This strategy utilized the power of language to give theological and epistemological meaning to one of Christ's most uncompromising decrees, that those that were not with

---

*Church of St. Paul in the Year 1709, at the Lecture Founded by the Honourable Robert Boyle* (London, 1711), 201.

60. [Charles Leslie], *A Short and Easie Method with the Deists, wherein the Certainty of the Christian Religion Is Demonstrated by Infallible Proof from Four Rules . . .* , 7th ed. (London, 1727), 32.

61. Brampton Gurdon, *The Pretended Difficulties in Natural or Reveal'd Religion No Excuse for Infidelity, Sixteen Sermons Preach'd in the Church of St. Mary-le-Bow, London; in the Years 1721 and 1722: at the Lecture Founded by the Honourable Robert Boyle* (London, 1723), 295–327.

62. Francis Atterbury, *The Church of England Man's Compendium. Consisting of Five Essays . . .* (London, 1733), 61.

Him were against Him (see Matt. 12:30). Furthermore, the history of the metaphor of light as truth negates claims of the ideological and chronological exceptionalism of one particular "Enlightenment" or set of "Enlightenments," made by Jonathan Israel and John Pocock respectively.[63] Modern scholars should be more circumspect when using the biased descriptive term *enlightenment* to categorize ideas and phenomena; not to do so risks perpetuating the polemical act of contradistinction inaugurated by the historical agents under investigation.

## II

If the discourse of enlightenment was part of a positive strategy in the war for truth, then ridicule, as an expression of superiority, was arguably a complementary, negative discourse that emphasized the idea and language of nonenlightenment. This type of ridicule (hereafter the only sort to be referred to, unless explicitly stated) provided a means by which falsehood could be described and, hence, more clearly delineated in contradistinction to truth. Ridicule was a function of culture, facilitating the affirmation of certain beliefs through a renunciation of others. Nowhere was this more apparent than in popular manifestations of antipopery.

The Roman Catholic sacrament of the Eucharist was a perpetual source of mirth among Protestants who were only too willing to mock the apparent inadequacies and absurdities of their mortal enemy. One epigram to an anti-Catholic pamphlet of 1617 read as follows:

> A Curate old within the Town of Bresse,
> Did an a time to Masse himself address:
> He was an honest man esteem'd of all,
> But yet a great mishap did him befall,

---

63. Jonathan Israel, *Enlightenment Contested: Philosophy, Modernity, and the Emancipation of Man 1670–1752* (Oxford: Oxford University Press, 2006); Pocock, "History and Enlightenment," 83–96.

For's sight being bad, and also in hast,
I'th Alter clothes he wrapt his God of paste . . .[64]

Here the depiction of a poor sighted, unenlightened curate was used to construct a jest about how Roman Catholic worship was actually directed at a false God of human creation. Rather than pursue the charge of idolatry, however, the text sought to undermine Catholicism as an ideology by emphasizing the ridiculousness of worshiping divinity through the fabrication of the Mass. Over two generations later, vitriolic broadsides were still pressing similar themes:

The poor man is brought under,
A wond'rous blind ridiculous Story,
By Masses and by Purgatory,
Heav'n, Earth, and Hell they plunder.[65]

Authoritative polemists such as the Church of England clergyman Gilbert Burnet (1643–1715) were never too far behind and always ready to stick the proverbial boot in: "The Church of *Rome* enjoys those that live in its Communion to pray to their fellow creatures . . . to Heroes and Saints (of whom they feign so many ridiculous Stories)."[66] After the Exclusion Crisis, it seemed necessary to ward off Catholic recalcitrance by reminding would-be apostates that "It would make a man amazed to see what ridiculous things our Ancestors believed in the dark times of Popery here in *England*."[67]

---

64. N. S., *Merry Iests, concerning Popes, Monkes, and Friers whereby Is Discouered Their Abuses and Errors . . . Written First in Italian by N. S. and thence Translated into French by G. I. and Now out of French into English, by R. W.* [Rowland Willet] (London, 1617), 137.

65. [Anon.], *Rome's Hunting-Match for III Kingdoms; England, Scotland and Ireland: Plainly Shewing All the Plots and Contrivances of the Papists against the Protestants . . .* (London, 1680), broadside.

66. Gilbert Burnet, *The Protestant's Companion, or, an Impartial Survey and Comparison of the Protestant Religion as by Law Established, with the Main Doctrines of Popery wherein Is shewn that Popery Is Contrary to Scripture, Primitive Fathers and Councils* (London, 1685), 7.

67. E. B., "Preface," in Thomas Crenius [i.e., Thomas Theodorus Crusius], *The Origine of Atheism in the Popish and Protestant Churches shew'n by Dorotheus Sicurus, 1648; Made into English . . . (1684)*, unpaginated [ii]. For vital context, see Mark Goldie, "Roger L'Estrange's Observator and the Exorcism of the Plot," in *Roger L'Estrange and the Making*

Stock anti-Catholic sermons denouncing papal corruptions and unbiblical practices were commonplace through the early eighteenth century, and many sermons took the opportunity to enforce theological claims by employing ridicule as a polemical strategy of contradistinction. In 1713, the Protestant convert William Aylmer (d. 1733) delivered a showcase sermon in front of the Bishop of Oxford in which he condemned the idea that the words *"this is my Body"* should be taken as a literal description of the Eucharist as "Absurd, Ridiculous and Impossible."[68] Based upon St. Peter's prophecy on "false apostles" (2 Pet. 2:1), this sermon was evidently more meaningful to contemporaries than a superficial reading of such seemingly banal slurs might suggest. To explicitly identify a ridiculous theology was perhaps as much a part of the process of ridicule as formulating a joke. Such an assertion enforced epistemological superiority and aided the practice of correctly identifying the fundamental distinctions between fake religion and true religion, despite the former's attempts at trickery and illusion. This process was undoubtedly contextualized within a long established Reformation culture of hate that demonized Catholics and assumed that opposition to popery was *"ipso facto* godly."[69] This latter point was the very rationale behind the continued recourse to ridicule as a polemical strategy of contradistinction: "If Scripture be true, many . . . [Roman Catholic] Doctrines must be false; great part of her Worship must be idolatrous; many of her practices absurd and superstitious."[70]

However, when it came to representing wayward ideologies within the Protestant tradition, orthodox Protestants tended to adopt an alternative way of applying the rhetoric of ridicule. Scripture related how "A scorner seeketh wisdom, and *findeth it* not" (Prov. 14:6) and in one of

---

*of Restoration Culture*, ed. Anne Dunan-Page and Beth Lynch (Aldershot, UK: Ashgate, 2008), 67–88.

68. William Aylmer, *A Recantation-Sermon against the Errors of Popery, Particularly Transubstantiation. Preach'd at St. Martin's in Oxford, Sept. 20th, 1713* . . . (Oxford, 1713), 15.

69. Anthony Milton, *Catholic and Reformed: The Roman and Protestant Churches in English Protestant Thought, 1600–1640* (Cambridge: Cambridge University Press, 1995), 36.

70. George Smyth, *The Church of Rome's Claim of Authority and Infallibility Examined. In a Sermon Preached at Salters-Hall January 30th, 1734* (London, 1735), 34.

his Boyle Lectures for the year 1700, the clergyman Offspring Blackall (bap. 1655, d. 1716) decreed that "to *ridicule* our holy *Religion*" was to "Boast" of one's "unbelief."[71] This principle was readily inverted by polemists eager to expose their theological enemies as so blasphemously wicked that they would ridicule God Himself. In other words, supposed heretics and infidels were sometimes represented as so full of pride and so blind to the truth that they deluded themselves into thinking that their ideology was superior to orthodoxy. The very act of obstinately pursuing an alternative theology was, therefore, represented as ridiculing God. Such a perception was most strikingly invoked during debates against Socinianism and Quakerism.

Orthodox polemic against Socinianism reached fever pitch during the Trinitarian controversy of the late seventeenth and early eighteenth century.[72] Responding to the supposed Socinianism of the Oxford don Arthur Bury (1624–1713), one tirade by the theologian William Nicholls (1664–1712) caught the prevailing mood: "I have hardly patience to answer this abominable Blasphemy; to see a foolish Philosopher thus horridly to affront his Creator, and in this witless Buffoonery to ridicule the infinite satisfaction of his blessed Redeemer; because he cannot make it agree with a system of Physicks."[73] While many like-minded diatribes were stricken with confusion and malice, there was a palpable fear that Socinianism "ridiculed without any Learning or Common Sense, the Athanasian *Creed, and the Doctrines of the Trinity and Incarnation.*"[74] Archbishop Tillotson and the bishop of Worcester Edward Stillingfleet (1635–1699) made clear that Socinianism "not only Disputed, but most Blasphemously Ridiculed the

---

71. Offspring Blackall, *The Sufficiency of the Scripture Revelation, as to the Proof of It. Part 1. A Sermon Preach'd in the Cathedral-Church of St. Paul, March the 4th 1699/1700. Being the Third for the Year 1700, of the Lecture Founded by the Honourable Robert Boyle* (London, 1707), 127.

72. For further details, see David Manning, "Blasphemy in England, c. 1660–1730," (PhD dissertation, University of Cambridge, 2009), 197–234.

73. William Nicholls, *An Answer to an Heretical Book called the Naked Gospel*... (London, 1691), 29.

74. William Sherlock, *An Apology for Writing against Socinians, in Defence of the Doctrines of the Holy Trinity and Incarnation*... (London, 1693), 2.

Doctrine of the *B. Trinity*."[75] Like many orthodox controversialists, Charles Leslie was convinced of an unholy alliance between Socinianism and Quakerism. Such a view may initially seem unfathomable since the former emphasized Christ's humanity, while the latter stressed His divinity. However, the offence of non-Trinitarianism lay not merely in its description of the Godhead, but also in its theological implications. Staunch anti-Quakers were convinced that Quakerism "Runs on Blaspheming, and (with the *Socinians*) *Ridiculing* the Doctrine of *Satisfaction* by *Jesus Christ*, whom he Denies to be *God-Man* or the *Saviour of the World*."[76] It was assumed that Quakers believed in "not only Another *Faith, but another Christ*" and, consequently, "They *Reject* our *Christ*, and *Ridicule* Him!"[77] The doctrine of the light within was censured, among other reasons, for its capacity "to ridicule (though not wittily. . . . ) the whole of the Gospel Ordinances, by turning them into a thing . . . [called] *Essence*."[78] In 1709, Francis Bugg (1640–1727), the former Quaker turned vicious Anglican polemist, likened Quakers to the archetypal renegade "Julian the Apostate" on account that they "Ridicule our Blessed Saviour" by calling him "a Dead Christ . . . an Idol-God, and other Names of Contempt."[79] In short, orthodox apologists believed that Socinianism and Quakerism were united through the act of ridiculing the Holy Trinity.

Here, then, there was a tendency among orthodox apologists to represent ridicule as a quintessential sin. The notion that the object of ridicule was the inferior was hypothetically inverted so as to construct a twofold interpretation of the rhetoric of ridicule. First, heterodox agents

---

75. John Tillotson and Edward Stillingfleet, *A Seasonable Vindication of the B. Trinity. Being an Answer to This Question, Why Do You Believe the Doctrine of the Trinity?* (London, 1697), unpaginated preface [iii].

76. [Charles Leslie], *A Defence of a Book Intituled, the Snake in the Grass. In Reply to Several Answers Put out to It by George Whitehead, Joseph Wyeth &c.* (London, 1700), 181.

77. [Charles Leslie], *The Present State of Quakerism in England. Wherein Is Shew'd, that the Greatest Part of the Quakers in England Are So Far Converted, as to be Convinced. Upon Occasion of the Relapse of Sam. Crisp to Quakerism . . .* (London, 1701), 2.

78. Benjamin Keach, *The Breach Repaired in God's Worship: Or Singing of Psalms, Hymns, and Spiritual Songs, Proved to Be an Holy Ordinance of Jesus Christ . . .* (London, 1691), 123.

79. Francis Bugg, *Quakerism Anatomized and Finally Dissected: Shewing, from Plain Fact, That a Rigid Quaker Is a Cruel Persecutor . . .* (London, 1709), 428.

were represented as the employers of ridicule while denying them the epistemological superiority traditionally attributed to such an action. It was then hoped that the blasphemous perversity of ridiculing the Almighty would expose their ultimate folly. To what extent the aims and consequences of such a stratagem were ever actually considered at the time is unclear, but it may be postulated that one underlying ambition was to craft an effective polemic of contradistinction. A propensity to use ever more elaborate means to try to strip many sophisticated truth claims of legitimacy and label them as contrary and opposite to orthodox perceptions of truth via the rhetoric of ridicule was a continued feature of orthodox Protestantism at least until the early eighteenth century. Yet such a ploy arguably had a destabilizing effect on the very paradigmatic presuppositions that the rhetoric of ridicule was designed to confirm; consequently the validity and efficacy of ridicule to orthodoxy was put under immense strain. For example, one commentator lamented that "[the Quakers'] Presumptuous and ridiculously confident Assertions, doth oft excite the Reader to laughter, who should rather be weeping over the manifest Effrontry done to the holy and precious Truths of God."[80] The problem was it was far from clear how orthodox Protestants would effectively keep a monopoly over the language of ridicule. The historical and historiographical significance of this destabilization in linguistic authority and structure can be explored through a reevaluation of Thomas Woolston's ridicule of Christ's miracles.

After many years of unassuming and diligent patristic scholarship, the Church of England clergyman and onetime Fellow of Sidney Sussex College, Cambridge, Thomas Woolston (bap. 1668, d. 1733) unleashed a rambunctiously polemical tour de force in the form of the *Discourses on the Miracles of Our Saviour* (6 vols., 1727–29).[81] The central thesis of the *Discourses* was that "the literal history of many of the miracles of

---

80. John Brown, *Quakerism the Path-Way to Paganisme, or, A Vieu of the Quakers Religion Being an Examination of the Theses and Apologie of Robert Barclay* . . . (Edinburgh, 1678), unpaginated epistle to the reader [iv].

81. The following section is derived from a comprehensive reinterpretation of the nature and reception of the *Discourses* in Manning, 283–329, which is due to appear in revised form as "'Radical Orthodoxy': Reinterpreting Thomas Woolston's Theology," in *The Church of England as "Primitive Christianity Restored"? Claims to Orthodoxy from the 1580s to the 1730s*, ed. David Manning (Farnham, UK: Ashgate, forthcoming). This work

Jesus as recorded by the Evangelists, does imply absurditys, improbabilities, and incredibilitys, consequently they, either in whole or in part, were never wrought."[82] Woolston dismissed the scriptural narration of Christ's resurrection as a "Sham-Miracle" that was the most "self evident Imposture that ever was put upon the World."[83] He then scolded contemporary clergy as "incredulous" and even mocked the "Evangelical Story of *Jesus's* Apparitions after his Death" as reminiscent of "*Robinson Cruso* filling his Pockets with Biskets, when he had had neither Coat, Wast-coat nor Breeches on."[84] By mocking Christ's miracles for their supposed verisimilitude, the Discourses were, unsurprisingly, berated for their blasphemous ridicule. The text provoked over fifty withering replies and, in 1729, Woolston was successfully prosecuted by the Attorney General for publishing "the most Blasphemous Book that ever was Publish'd in any Age whatsoever."[85] With his infamy secured, Woolston died in prison in 1733.

The dominant historiographical view is that Thomas Woolston was a deistical wit, a lesser-known champion of "the Radical Enlightenment."[86] M. F. Suaraz has suggested that by "routinely marshalling ridicule instead of reason," Woolston proved himself to be the rhetorical heir to the third carl of Shaftesbury.[87] The substance of the *Discourses* has been widely interpreted as merely a foil for the execution

---

will supersede the most accurate study on Woolston to date: William H. Trapnell, *Thomas Woolston: Madman and Deist?* (Bristol, UK: Thoemmes, 1994).

82. Thomas Woolston, *A Discourse on the Miracles of Our Saviour, in View of the Present Controversy between Infidels and Apostates* (London, 1727), 4.

83. Thomas Woolston, *A Sixth Discourse on the Miracles of Our Saviour, in View of the Present Controversy between Infidels and Apostates* (London, 1729), 27.

84. Ibid., 30–1.

85. [Thomas Woolston], *The Tryal of Thomas Woolston . . .* (London, 1729), 2.

86. For example, see John Leland, *A View of the Principle Deistical Writers that Have Appeared in England in the Last and Present Century . . .* (London, 1754), 126–43; J. C. D. Clark, *English Society 1660–1832* (Cambridge: Cambridge University Press 2000), 331–32, 348; Jonathan I. Israel, *Radical Enlightenment: Philosophy and the Making of Modernity 1650–1750* (Oxford: Oxford University Press, 2001), 471–72; Wayne Hudson, *Enlightenment and Modernity: The English Deists and Reform* (London: Pickering & Chatto, 2009), 49–72.

87. M. F. Suarez, "The Mock Biblical: A Study in English Satire from the Popish Plot Trials to the Pretender Crisis (1678–1747)" (DPhil dissertation, University of Oxford, 1999), 264.

of an irreverent rhetoric that used ridicule as a specific method to assail the very fundamentals of Christianity. Roger Lund, among others, has argued that it was the rhetoric of the *Discourses* that was blasphemous, being a subversive attack on "decorum."[88] Despite few explicit references to theory, it would appear that most scholars have assumed Woolston to be an exponent of the ridicule of incongruity. Yet it may be argued that a scholarly preoccupation with the contemporary battle between ironic subterfuge and "epistemological decorum" has led to Woolston's ridicule being incorrectly categorized. A comprehensive reassessment of Woolston's theology must rest with another study; however, beyond the scandalizing nature of Woolston's claims, a case can be made for understanding Woolston's ridicule as an expression of superiority. The following reevaluation of the typology of Woolston's ridicule not only exposes the current historiography to be flawed but also provides a further dimension to the historical understanding of ridicule as a form of polemical contradistinction.

The *Discourses* were the culmination of work that had begun with *The Old Apology for the Truth of the Christian Religion against the Jews and Gentiles Revived* (1705). The latter was a piece of considerable patristic scholarship that, as one subsequent critic of the *Discourses* conceded, treated the miracles of Christ with "decency."[89] *The Old Apology* offered a painstaking examination of the relationship between the Emperor Tiberius, Pontius Pilate, and Christ. Marshalling evidence from the work of St. Barnabas, St. Clement, Origen, St. Cyprian, Tertullian, Dionysius of Alexandria, and Eusebuis, among others, Woolston became convinced that Moses's influence over Pharaoh was prophetic of the relationship between Christ and Tiberius and that, consequently, Pilate was aware of Christ's divinity. *The Old Apology* accepted the role

---

88. Roger D. Lund, "Irony as Subversion: Thomas Woolston and the Crime of Wit," in *The Margins of Orthodoxy: Heterodox Writing and Cultural Response, 1660–1750*, ed. Roger D. Lund (Cambridge: Cambridge University Press, 1995), 170–94; Laura M. Stevens, "Civility and Scepticism in the Woolston-Sherlock Debate Over Miracles," *Eighteenth Century Life* 21, no. 3 (1997), 57–70.

89. Richard Smalbroke, *A Vindication of the Miracles of Our Blessed Saviour; in which Mr. Woolston's Discourses on Them Are Particularly Examin'd, His Pretended Authorities of the Fathers against Truth of Their Literal Sense Are Set in a Just Light, and His Objections in Point of Reason Are Answer'd* (1727–31), 2:ii.

of miracles in demonstrating the divinity of Christ, but like the works of many early Fathers, and those of Origen (185–232) in particular, it was coy about the suggestion that they provided whole or unique proof.[90] Woolston sensed that proof by miracles could be easily undermined by the enemies of Christianity, particularly atheists, deists, Jews, and those apostates who had become overly reliant upon reason and biased against primitive Christianity.[91]

William Trapnell has observed how Woolston's work became polemical only after it became apparent that contemporary clergy were not convinced by, or willing to engage with, his scholarship.[92] In a marked change to his previous publications, Woolston's *A Free-Gift to the Clergy* (1722) berated "all *Ministers of the Letter*" for sailing too close to the wind of apostasy. The urgency of Woolston's campaign was intensified when the philosopher Anthony Collins (1676–1729) penned *A Discourse of the Grounds and Reasons of the Christian Religion* (1724), which argued that the Old Testament prophesied a temporal, not a spiritual, messiah and that Jesus did not completely or uniquely fulfil such prophecies. Woolston responded with *The Moderator between an Infidel and an Apostate* (1725), which adopted a high-risk strategy of arguing that proof by prophecy was the only alternative to the untenable position of believing that the truth of Christianity could be proved by Christ's miracles. In the introduction to the first *Discourse*, Woolston laid bare his modus operandi as follows:

> I believe this Controversy will end in the absolute Demonstration of Jesus's *Messiahship* from Prophecy, which is the only way to prove him to be the *Messiah* . . . the Proof of *Jesus's Messiahship* should be by an Allegorical Interpretation, . . . the very same Way, that all the Fathers of the Church have gone.[93]

---

90. Thomas Woolston, *The Old Apology for the Truth of the Christian Religion against the Jews and the Gentiles Revived* . . . (Cambridge, 1705), 289–90; Anton Friedrichsen, *The Problem of Miracle in Primitive Christianity*, trans. Roy A. Harrisville and John S. Hanson (Minneapolis, MI: Augsburg, 1972).
91. Woolston, *Old Apology*, 366, 368, 370.
92. Trapnell, *Thomas Woolston*, 89–92.
93. Woolston, *Discourse*, 2.

It may therefore be argued that the *Discourses* should be primarily contextualized within what R. M. Burns has called "the great debate on miracles": a contemporary series of sceptical and apologetic enquiries into miracles vis-à-vis Christianity.[94] In this context it is difficult to argue that Woolston's methodological claims were somehow a cover for the execution of the witty ridicule of incongruity.

Indeed, Woolston explicitly stated that "I shall not confine myself only to Reason, but also to the Fathers . . . in the first Ages . . . [For they are] very great Scholars, and the most Orthodox Divines. Whatever they concurrently assert, I firmly believe."[95] Thus, Woolston's willingness to give primacy to patristic theology—rather than integrate it with a contemporary notion of rational theology—seemingly set him far apart from other sceptical writers and made people question the genuineness of his aims and arguments. It may be argued that this disillusioned Anglican sought to establish a radical form of Christian apology which aimed to replace the contemporary orthodox proof of Christianity with an alternative and more convincing proof based upon the criterion of prophecy. The issue then was the imposition of an extreme form of polemical contradistinction, whereby the literal interpretation of Christ's miracles were rendered ridiculous in order to make way for proof by prophecy to be accepted as the new orthodoxy. In other words, Woolston sought to appropriate the rhetoric of ridicule to force orthodox Protestants to reaffirm their principles through new criteria and evidence.

Even after his trial, Woolston continued to claim that he was "no *Infidel*, but a Believer of Christianity, notwithstanding . . . [the] *Discourses*."[96] Scholars have consistently dismissed this claim because Woolston's treatment of Christ's miracles appears so patently irreligious.

---

94. R. M. Burns, *The Great Debate on Miracles from Joseph Glanvill to David Hume* (Lewisburg, PA: Bucknell University Press, 1981); Hans J. Hillerbrand, "The Historicity of Miracles: The Early Eighteenth-Century Debate among Woolston, Annet, Sherlock, and West," *Studies in Religion* 3 (1973–74): 132–51; Peter Harrison, "Prophecy, Early Modern Apologetics, and Hume's Argument against Miracles," *Journal of the History of Ideas* 60 (1999): 241–56.

95. Woolston, *Discourse*, 4, 5.

96. Thomas Woolston, *Mr Woolston's Defence of His Discourse on the Miracles of Our Saviour, against the Bishops of St. David's and London* . . . (London, 1729), 14.

On first inspection, this is difficult to refute. Woolston combined a relentless questioning of the scriptural description of Christ's miracles with contemptuous irreverence, seemingly designed to cause maximum offence and consternation. In referring to Jesus casting devils out of a man into a herd of swine (Mark 5:1–20; Luke 8:26–40), Woolston had commented, "There are many circumstances in the Story literally consider'd, that would induce us to call the Truth of the Whole into Question.... [For example] The Jews are forbidden to eat Swine's Flesh; what then should they do with Swine [?]" Woolston interwove many other similar doubts with the shocking claim that "*Workers of Inequity, and even some Artists amongst the Jews*" had performed similar acts of "Exorcism" and as such they were "no Proof" of Christ's 'Divine Authority.'" To emphasize this point, he concluded, "if any *Exorcist* in this Age and Nation had pretended to expel the Devil out of one possess'd, and permitted him to enter into a Flock of Sheep, the people would have said, that he had bewitch'd both; and our Laws and Judges ... would have made him swing for it."[97] This example, perhaps more than any other, has been used by scholars as evidence that Woolston was a wit in the Shaftesburian mould.

Yet the concern that supposed miracles could be replicated by magicians or evildoers was an established trope as old as Christianity itself. With specific reference to Christ casting devils out of a man into a herd of swine, the ancient Greek philosopher Celsus (fl. 175–180), whom Origen had been compelled to refute, mischievously asked, "Are those miracles done through sorcery and wicked daemons, while no miracle at all is accomplished by the divine and blessed nature of God [the Father]?"[98] He then went on to claim that St. Matthew supported such a view, when the scriptures stated that "there shall arise false Christs, and false prophets, and shall shew great signs and wonders; insomuch that, if it *were* possible, they shall deceive the very elect" (Matt. 24:24).[99] Celsus's critique of other miracles were particularly carping: "Let us imagine what a Jew—let alone a philosopher—might put to Jesus: Is it not true, good sir, that you fabricated the story of your birth from a

---

97. Woolston, *Discourse*, 31–32, 31, 33–34.
98. Origen, *Contra Celsum*, bk. 2, par. 51.
99. Ibid., bk. 2, par. 50.

virgin . . . [for] she was pregnant by a Roman soldier named Panthera she was driven away by her husband—the carpenter—and convicted of adultery?"[100] In a similar fashion, he dismissed "those tricks about which your disciples boast: those cures and resurrections, or feeding the crowds with a few loaves . . . Monstrous tales, to be sure."[101] Such assertions were hardly based upon incongruity theory or, for that matter, any recourse to deistical wit. Celsus combined relentless and commonsensical questioning with targeted derisory jibes designed to expose the inherent absurdity of the position under scrutiny. It was, in part, in reaction to such questioning of Christ's miracles that Origen had developed his allegorical exegesis, which minimized the significance of the historicity of New Testament miracles, which in turn led to a highly internalized, spiritual theology.

There is little evidence to suggest that Woolston denied the divinity of Christ; however, while Woolston made a distinction between Christ's divinity and His ability to perform miracles, the vast majority of his contemporaries did not. It was Woolston's clear belief that the divinity of Christ could be unanswerably proved only by the fulfilment of Old Testament prophecy, in accordance with Origenist principles, because relying on proof by Christ's miracles could be easily and legitimately questioned. It may therefore be argued that the *Discourses* sought to utilize ridicule in an attempt to demonstrate that proof by miracles was inherently flawed. To this end, it may be further argued that in a final attempt to convince contemporaries of the fundamental inadequacies of proof by miracles, Woolston adopted Celsus's most uncompromising ridicule. The nature and tone of Woolston's scepticism bear the clear hallmarks of Celsus. Moreover, Woolston was particularly candid about the typology and purpose of his ridicule. In the first *Discourse* he stated, "I ridicule the Nonsense and Absurditys of *Jesus's* Miracles according to the Letter," concluding in the fourth *Discourse* that "So absurd is the Letter of this Story, that for the Honour of Jesus, and Credibility of his

---

100. Celsus, *On the True Doctrine: A Discourse against the Christians*, trans. R. Joseph Hoffmann (New York: Oxford University Press, 1987), 57.

101. Ibid.

Gospel, it is absolutely necessary to turn it into Allegory."[102] In the sixth Discourse Woolston stated clearly,

> I think Ridicule should here take Place of sober Reasoning, as the more proper and effectual means to cure Men of their foolish Faith and absurd Notions . . . And there never was a Polemical Divine, that, if he had an opportunity and Advantage over the Weakness of his Adversary, did not take such a ludicrous and merry Course with him.[103]

In declaring that his ridicule was not a rational but a polemical enterprise, expressly for the purpose of shocking his contemporaries into accepting what he believed to be self-evident truths about the flawed nature of proof by miracles, Woolston's ridicule was evidently an expression of superiority.

The *Discourses* ruptured the limits of understanding and toleration. Identifying such a breach in the context of Woolston's superior ridicule demonstrates how the discourse of ridicule could implode as a viable polemic of contradistinction, for in this case the agent employing the ridicule was unable to convince his audience of the absurdity of the subject being ridiculed. This discord was evidence of a fundamental disagreement about the nature of orthodoxy. Woolston's vision of how to go about proving the truth of Christianity was simply not shared by the vast majority of Protestants. However, the Woolston affair might be viewed as symptomatic of the destabilization of the paradigmatic underpinnings of ridicule which had been caused by the overly complex and risky polemic of earlier generations of Protestants. The notion that superior ridicule was a valid and effective means of affirming orthodox Protestantism had been undermined to the point that it could be reappropriated by usurpers such as Woolston, who were ready to try and establish a new orthodoxy. Moreover, orthodox Protestants had arguably made themselves hostage to fortune by previously representing the ridicule of God as the quintessential sin, for when Woolston

---

102. Woolston, *Discourse*, 65; Thomas Woolston, *A Fourth Discourse on the Miracles of Our Saviour, in View of the present Controversy between Infidels and Apostates* (London, 1728), 63.

103. Woolston, *Sixth Discourse*, 50.

actually did ridicule Christ's miracles, orthodox Protestants could see nothing but the most terrible blasphemy.

The historiography has consistently misinterpreted Woolston's rhetoric by assuming too much and unintentionally giving primacy to the views of Woolston's critics through an assessment of contexts that were relatively marginal. It is somewhat difficult to suggest that the *Discourses* constituted an exemplary form of Shaftesburian wit, and it is doubtful that Woolston can be convincingly seen as a proponent of "the Radical Enlightenment." In using superior ridicule, the *Discourses* were an outrageous attempt to use an orthodox rhetoric of contradistinction against orthodoxy.

## III

Orthodox Protestants of the seventeenth and early eighteenth century were significantly involved in espousing the virtue of their enlightenment. For them, the shining beacon of Hugh Latimer shone through time to guide the faithful in solidarity against a range of foes, from Roman Catholics to Socinians. It was through Reformation that orthodox Protestantism had gained a monopoly over some of the key linguistic signifiers of orthodoxy. Considering the attempt to maintain that monopoly provides a fascinating insight into both contemporary Protestantism and the abstract processes by which an ideology becomes culturally manifest. The orthodox rhetoric of enlightenment and ridicule were powerful components in the polemical art of contradistinction which fostered belief in a Protestant view of truth through a linguistic affirmation of the supposed brutal reality that all of humankind was divided into two camps. The case of Thomas Woolston demonstrates how both the rhetoric of this strategy became ineffective amid the confusion and anxiety created by theological and exegetical pluralism. Yet it would be historically disingenuous for modern scholars to label subsequent appeals to irenicism or the primacy of human reason as evidence of a definitive enlightenment.

On the evidence of this essay, the phenomenology of enlightenment cannot be divorced from its rhetoric. On this basis, the history of "the

Christian Enlightenment" requires rewriting to account for the divisive rhetoric of polemical contradistinction; yet this would complicate the now established distinctions between "Enlightenment" and "Counter-Enlightenment" histories. Perhaps the time has come for a wholesale reassessment of the historiographical validity of such labels?

# "Chastisements of a Heavenly Father": The Meaning of the London Earthquakes of 1750

## Christopher Smyth

When two earthquakes struck London early in 1750, terror and fury broke forth just as suddenly as the shaking of the earth. Clergymen, newspaper writers, and concerned laymen poured forth angry diatribes on the sins that brought England to the brink of ruin. Scores of sermons flowed off the presses, condemning the instinctive panic of the populace even as they added to it. Hundreds fled the city, certain it was about to be swallowed up. For a month, the religious meaning of the shocks swamped all other discussions, as Englishmen confronted the seemingly obvious fact that God was angry with them.

England's consternation—produced by two rather mild earthquakes—may seem surprising. It sits uneasily with the more usual eighteenth-century celebration of the harmony of the natural world and of the pleasant and reasonable sociability that fostered such attitudes. But yet almost everyone at that time interpreted the earthquakes as a sign of divine displeasure at the conduct of the nation. That alone makes the reaction to the earthquakes worthy of study. So how were such divergent perceptions reconciled?

Englishmen in the eighteenth century believed that the natural order reflected the moral order. But they were less certain about exactly how it did so. "Enlightened" attitudes saw a rejection of portents, astrology, and the monitory power of the marvelous, even as these attitudes persisted among the less self-consciously sophisticated.[1] Instead, educated observers preferred to extol the regularity and bounty of the ordinary course of the natural world, pointing to it as evidence of the wisdom and goodness of the Creator.

Yet such rhapsodies could hardly be applied to earthquakes. Events that threatened utter ruin in a minute could never be pleasant and nor were they even regular. Charles Wesley preached in 1750 on the unnerving power of the events: "For a Man to feel the Earth, which hangeth upon nothing (but as some vast Ball in the Midst of a thin yielding Air) totter under him, must fill him with secret Fright and Confusion . . . For where can we think to escape Danger, if the most solid Thing in all the World shakes?"[2] Even though the two tremors felt in London in 1750 in fact did little physical damage, that in no way undermined the alarming religious import.

Earthquakes were frequent and devastating in the eighteenth century in areas from Lima to Bengal, and Jamaica to Calabria—one estimate puts the death toll from earthquakes at 130,000 in Europe alone between the years 1693 and 1783.[3] Prompted in part by such disasters, study of seismic activity proliferated across Europe, with philosophers making repeated attempts to classify and theorize earthquakes.[4] As to the moral and religious meaning of earthquakes in this period, scholarly attention tends to focus on the great Lisbon earthquake of 1755 and the extent to which this challenged providential views across Europe.[5]

---

1. See for instance Lorraine Daston and Katharine Park, *Wonders and the Order of Nature, 1150–1750* (New York: Zone Books, 1998); Patrick Curry, *Prophecy and Power: Astrology in Early Modern England* (Cambridge, UK: Polity, 1989).

2. Charles Wesley, *The Cause and Cure of Earthquakes: A Sermon Preach'd from Psalm xlvi. 8* (London, 1750), 15.

3. Stephen Tobriner, "Safety and Reconstruction of Noto after the Sicilian Earthquake of 1693—the Eighteenth-Century Context," in *Dreadful Visitations: Confronting Natural Catastrophe in the Age of Enlightenment*, ed. Alessa Johns (New York and London: Routledge, 1999), 51.

4. J. G. Taylor, "Eighteenth Century Earthquake Theories: A Case History Investigation into the Character of the Study of the Earth in the Enlightenment" (PhD diss., University of Oklahoma, 1975).

5. See for instance Theodore Braun and John Radner, ed., *The Lisbon Earthquake of 1755: Representation and Reaction* (Oxford, UK: Voltaire Foundation, 2005).

Yet this article concentrates on Britain, using a detailed examination of the two tremors in 1750 to argue against the common assumption that scientists' and researchers' refinement of natural explanations killed off English views of earthquakes as punishments. In fact, natural causes were well integrated with religious explanations, an understanding that persisted long past Lisbon.[6]

Indeed, the eighteenth-century British perception of earthquakes was surprisingly coherent, both with the more familiar exulting of regularity and with traditional understanding of the phenomena. If regularity and orderliness were generally taken as an argument for God's presence and benevolence, disorder could not count as an argument against these attributes. Nearly everyone who discussed earthquakes in the eighteenth century started by mentioning a caring, all-wise and all-knowing Creator, increasingly seen as exercising immediate control over nature. Examples of disorder such as earthquakes could not then be mistakes, since an omnipotent God does not err. They must therefore be deliberate acts of deity, and since that deity was a benevolent one, they must be designed for some good purpose.

In London of 1750, that purpose was generally believed to be, as one pamphleteer put it, "the chastisements of a heavenly Father."[7] This article examines how the response to the earthquakes unfolded across two months, over seventy pamphlets and numerous periodicals, and shows that the predominant discourse was one of sin and repentance (though this was not without its critics). I argue that there was a clear evolution of ideas about natural causes, particularly when compared to the previous earthquake felt in London in 1692, yet that this altered ideas on the moral end very little.

This points to the second reason the earthquakes are worthy of study: anthropologists have long looked on "disasters" as an important tool for understanding the underlying structures of social life and

---

6. Christopher Smyth, "Perceptions of Extraordinary Natural Events in England, 1692–1783" (PhD diss., University of Cambridge, 2007), 137–94.

7. Anon., *An Address to the Journeymen of the City of London; and to Servants in General: Occasioned by the Bishop of London's Letter concerning the Late Earthquakes* (London, 1750), 8.

thought.[8] In eighteenth-century terms, perceptions of the natural order can give an insight into how contemporaries saw the moral order. In 1750, the way in which an animated, often emotional, discourse about the earthquakes was integrated with ideas about social change, providence, and the nation provides a fascinating snapshot of a society more anguished and conflicted than it might outwardly like to appear.

## I. Surprise and Speculation

Just before half past twelve on the afternoon of February 8, 1750, the inhabitants of London felt a sudden tremor. The shock was strong enough to be "felt all over the Cities of London and Westminster, and parts adjacent," and was noticeable even as far as Hertford and Gravesend. The actual damage caused was not great—several chimneys fell and a "very old crazy building" in Southwark collapsed.[9] Nevertheless, the consternation of the inhabitants was considerable. The lawyers in Westminster Hall were reported to be greatly alarmed, believing they would be "buried in the ruins of that ancient building." The Duke of Newcastle and the Prince of Wales felt their residences move, while ordinary citizens were "struck with so great a Pannick, that they left their Houses; and ran into the Streets, believing their Houses were falling."[10]

The shock immediately became the talk of the town. According to one pamphleteer who wrote little more than a week after the earthquake, the event "attracted universal notice, and bec[a]me, not the

---

8. See for instance Kenneth Hewitt, "The Idea of Calamity in a Technocratic Age," in *Interpretations of Calamity from the Viewpoint of Human Ecology*, ed. Kenneth Hewitt (Boston: Allen & Unwin, 1983); Susanna Hoffman and Anthony Oliver-Smith, ed., *Catastrophe and Culture: The Anthropology of Disaster* (Santa Fe: School of American Research Press, 2002). The field however leaves even basic concepts uncertain. See varying definitions in Enrico Quarantelli, ed., *What Is a Disaster? Perspectives on the Question* (London and New York: Routledge, 1998).

9. *London Evening Post*, February 8–10, 1750; Anon., *An Appendix to the Reverend Mr. John Shower's Practical Reflections on the Earthquakes* (London, 1750), 15.

10. Anon., *Appendix to Shower's Reflections*, 15; *Northampton Mercury*, February 19, 1750.

common only, but almost the single Topick of Discourse."[11] The periodical press quickly seized on this unusual phenomenon. Many papers provided philosophical accounts of the earthquake and its possible causes. These accounts, while admitting the earthquake was terrible, discuss it generally as a curiosity. The *Bath Journal*, for instance, hoped its account would "not be unentertaining to [its] readers."[12] There was much debate as to what the causes of the quake were. The most common framework of interpretation, essentially unchanged since Pliny, was that large subterranean caverns were filled with water, air, or fire, and the vigorous motion of one of these elements caused the earth to shake. "With respect to the causes of these dreadful Phenomena, naturalists are greatly divided," wrote one correspondent in the *Gentleman's Magazine*, "but it is to be supposed as the basis of each hypothesis that the earth is full of subterraneous caverns."[13]

However, this hypothesis was not shared by all theorists, and arguments became increasingly heated after the second shock. There was also a significant body of opinion that held that the shocks were not in fact earthquakes at all, but were caused by explosions in the atmosphere, which became known as airquakes.[14] This theory on the cause of tremors was first introduced by John Flamsteed in a letter dated 1693, which was published for the first time in 1750 and backed by the Reverend Stephen Hales FRS.[15]

---

11. Anon., *A Dissertation upon Earthquakes, Their Causes and Consequences* (London, 1750). *The London Evening Post* carried an advertisement for this publication in its edition of February 17–20.

12. *Bath Journal*, February 19, 1750.

13. *Gentleman's Magazine*, February 1750, 89. See also Taylor, "Eighteenth Century Earthquake Theories."

14. See for instance *Bath Journal*, March 26, 1750.

15. John Flamsteed, *A Letter concerning Earthquakes, Written in the Year 1693* (London, 1750); Stephen Hales, *Some Considerations on the Causes of Earthquakes* (London, 1750). The debate became quite heated. See Anon., *The Theory and History of Earthquakes* (London, 1750), particularly p. 22; and Anon., *An Account of Explosions in the Atmosphere, or Airquakes* (London, 1750), particularly p. 58. On how this debate could become a controversy over the role of active principles, and therefore of God, in natural philosophy, see Simon Schaffer, "Natural Philosophy and Public Spectacle in the Eighteenth Century," *History of Science* 21 (1983): 1–43.

As well as discussion of possible causes of earthquakes, periodicals and pamphlets provided detailed accounts of past quakes in Britain and overseas, including those in Oxford in 1683, Sicily in 1693, Messina in 1718, and Leghorn in 1742.[16] In this form, such accounts not only provided a basis for philosophical speculation but also became polite entertainment, suitable for the discerning reader, and "not unworthy of the public Curiosity," as the chronicler of Leghorn described his work.[17]

## II. Sinning and Sermonizing

Stimulating curiosity was not the only thing the earthquakes were good for. Although the periodical coverage of the first shock focused almost exclusively on natural causes, this was noted and criticized by a pamphlet published soon after. The anonymous author targeted the *London Evening Post*, lamenting that instead of religious instruction, "we have seen a dry, cold, formal account of the natural causes of earthquakes, the author of which seems to account for it wholly by second causes, without the least regard to the great Creator and Judge of the World." Although this message eventually became popular enough for the work to go through five editions, in February 1750 it was a marginal voice.[18] This was to change after the second shock.

Most inhabitants of London were still in their beds when another earthquake hit around 5:30 a.m. on March 8, but they did not remain there for long. "The shock was so great in some parts, that the people ran from their houses and beds almost naked," according to some reports. This shock was generally considered much more violent than

---

16. Anon., *A Genuine Account of Earthquakes, Especially That at Oxford, in the Year 1695* (London, 1750); *Gentleman's Magazine* (April 1750), 166; S. Horton, *An Account of the Earthquakes Which Happened at Leghorn in Italy, Between the 5th and 16th of January, 1742* (London, 1750). This kind of account can be seen as a successor of the early modern description of wonders, where the careful, detailed observations of all the circumstances surrounding an unusual event remained, but portentous implications were removed; see Lorraine Daston, "Marvellous Facts and Miraculous Evidence in Early Modern Europe," *Critical Inquiry* 18 (1991): 93–124.

17. Horton, *Account of the Earthquakes Which Happened at Leghorn*, 4.

18. Anon., *A Serious and Affectionate Address to the Cities of London and Westminster; Occasioned by the Late Earthquake* (London, 1750), 14.

that of the previous month, and "in St James's park and all the open places, the ground moved very perceptibly." In addition to more collapsing chimneys, china collections in St. James and Piccadilly were smashed by the convulsion.[19] It wasn't just the rudely awoken and the teacup collectors who were thrown into consternation, however. The greater strength of this second quake and its eerie timing, coming as it did exactly four weeks after the first shock, caused general alarm and began a month of frenzied sermonizing, thunderous evangelizing, anguished repentance, and outright panic.

The religious interpretation of the earthquakes was led by Thomas Sherlock, Bishop of London. He swiftly penned a letter to the clergy and the people of London and Westminster, which was rushed into print by March 17 and comprised a ringing denunciation of the manifold sins of the nation.[20] He began by condemning "the wickedness and corruption that abound," and declared, "It is every Man's Duty, and it is mine to tell you, to give Attention to all the Warnings which God in his Mercy affords to a sinful People; such warning we have had by two great Shocks of an Earthquake, a Warning which seems to have been immediately and especially directed to these great Cities."[21] Sherlock then proceeded to enumerate the sins of which the nation, and the capital in particular, was guilty. The main targets of his ire were those diversions that drew people away from true religion. As he succinctly put it, the people "fly from the Church and crowd to the Playhouse."[22] Sherlock's state of appalled disgust is evident: "While I was writing this, I cast my Eye upon a News-paper of the Day, and counted no less than fifteen Advertisements for Plays, Operas, Musick, and Dancing, for Meetings at Gardens, for Cock-Fighting, Prize-Fighting, &c."[23] There was only one way out of this morass of decadence and that was repentance. Everyone had a part to play in this general reformation through personal repentance and being a good example to those under their care. As Sherlock

---

19. *Universal Magazine* (March 1750), 137; *Northampton Mercury*, 12 March 1750.
20. Thomas Sherlock, *A Letter from the Lord Bishop of London to the Clergy and People of London and Westminster, on Occasion of the Late Earthquakes* (London, 1750). Its publication was announced in the March 15–17 edition of the *London Evening Post*.
21. Sherlock, *Letter from the Bishop of London*, 3–4.
22. Ibid., 8–9, 11.
23. Ibid., 12.

summarizes, "In a word, let every Man, whatever his Status is, do his Part towards averting the Judgments of God."[24]

The reaction to the letter was overwhelming. It was reprinted at the beginning of April, and over the course of the year, seventeen different editions appeared in London, Cirencester, York, Waterford, Dublin, Williamsburg, Boston, and Glasgow. Subscriptions were raised to distribute the letter to the poor, and bulk orders lowered the price of the pamphlet from the original threepence to three shillings for one hundred copies, "that every Person may have it."[25] According to Horace Walpole, "Ten thousand were sold in two days; and fifty thousand have been subscribed for since the first two editions."[26] Its letters or extracts were also printed in several newspapers, and the periodicals generally esteemed it "excellent."[27]

The clergy, dissenting ministers, and concerned laymen were not slow to heed the bishop's call. There followed an outpouring of tracts bemoaning England's plight and predicting bloodcurdling calamities if repentance were not forthcoming. It is easy to imagine congregations being whipped into frenzies by sermons like that of the Methodist Samuel Hull, whose description of the March earthquake was particularly petrifying: "The Houses reeled with the furious stroke, and slumbering Mortals awoke in Terrors. Before the Sun had undrawn the Curtains of Night, the Day dawned in Horror."[28] Charles Wesley preached with a similar flourish: "When the Earth opens of a sudden, and becomes the Grave of whole Families, streets and Cities, and effects in less Time than you are able to tell the Story of it." The Port Royal earthquake of 1692, which destroyed the main

---

24. Ibid., 16–22.

25. Ibid.

26. Horace Walpole to Horace Mann, April 2, 1750, *The Yale Edition of Horace Walpole's Correspondence*, ed. W. S. Lewis, 48 vols. (London and Oxford: Yale University Press, 1937–1985), 133.

27. *Bath Journal*, April 9, 1750; *Cambridge Journal*, March 31, 1750; *Gentleman's Magazine*, March 1750, 123; *London Magazine*, March 1750, 139; *Universal Magazine*, March 1750, 138.

28. Samuel Hull, *The Fluctuating Condition of Human Life, and the Absolute Necessity of a Preparation for the Eternal World, Consider'd* (London, 1750), 6–27.

port of Jamaica and served as the basis of Wesley's description, was portrayed in graphic detail.[29]

The horror of such punishments was matched by the sins that produced them. And England, it seemed, was quite astonishingly sinful. "No one can deny," asserted the Sussex clergyman John Bristed, "whether sin is not notorious and triumphant amongst us." An anonymous London writer went even further, referring to the "Present Prevalency of Vice and Corruption, the Degeneracy and Depravity of Manners, and the almost total Neglect of Religion," while a Northampton clergyman lamented that national sins were of "so deep a dye" that newspapers seldom appeared without a "black catalogue of the most shocking indulgences and the most abominable crimes."[30]

All manner of such sins were mentioned in the welter of admonitory pamphlets following the earthquakes, ranging from sodomy to drunkenness, but the dominant theme was the neglect of religion. Too many, complained one clergyman, "make religion the last Thing they advance to."[31] We will see below how some writers complained of fashionable mockery of religion, but actual hostility to religion was a much less common complaint than simple disregard. Most people, as was held by almost all pamphleteers, had forsaken Christianity for diversion, and immoral diversion at that. "The licentiousness of Plays and Masquerades" came in for particular criticism, with

---

29. Wesley, *Cause and Cure of Earthquakes*, 14, 7–9. His description is taken from Heath, *A Full Account of the Late Dreadful Earthquake at Port Royal in Jamaica* (London, 1692), 2.

30. John Bristed, *The Two Late Shocks of an Earth-quake Admonitions to Repentance, a Sermon Preached at the Parish-church of St. Michael, in Lewes, Sussex, on Sunday, March 18, 1749* (London, 50), 3; "Citizen of London," *A Letter from a Citizen of London to His Fellow Citizens, and through Them, to the People of England in General, Occasioned by the Late Earthquakes* (London, 1750), 1; Clergyman of the Church of England, *The Late Uncommon and Terrible Shocks of Our Earth Considered as Alarming and Awakening Calls to a National Repentance* (Northampton, 1750), 8.

31. Clergyman of the Church of England, *A Vindication of the Bishop of London's Letter, Occasioned by the Late Earthquake* (London, 1750), 24–25; see also Zachary Grey, *A Chronological and Historical Account of the Most Memorable Earthquakes That Have Happened in the World* (Cambridge, 1750), 8.

theaters and ballrooms condemned as "places of sensual delight."[32] One pamphleteer branded masquerade balls as devil's universities, "to which the Nobility of H-ll send their children to complete their Education." Another was so incensed that he threatened vigilante violence against those attending a ball advertised at Ranelagh Gardens.[33] Of particular concern to many of these pamphleteers was that such diversions often took place on the Sabbath day, compounding impiety with impiety, deafening the sinner with calls to repentance—he could never learn true virtue if he spent his Sundays in the ale house rather than the house of God.[34]

The overriding sin, then, the vice that united all the others, was a love of pleasure. "Luxury, Pride, and the immodest Love of Pleasure are the leading capital Sins of our Day," as one itinerant preacher put it. Bishop Secker condemned a "madness for pleasure, from the highest to the lowest," while the Presbyterian William Crookshank branded men "Lovers of Pleasure, more than Lovers of God" (2 Timothy 3:4). This was both a consequence and a cause of what Sherlock described as "the almost infinite Places of Diversion in and about this Town." Almost all the religiously oriented pamphlets followed him in condemnation of "this eager resort to places of public Entertainment," this "extravagant Fondness for the Diversions that so much abound

---

32. Anon, *A Supplement to the Bishop of London's Letter to the Clergy and People of London and Westminster, on Occasion of the Late Earthquakes* (London, 1750), 10; Theophilus Lobb, *Sacred Declarations; Or, a Letter to the Inhabitants of London, Westminster, and All Other Parts of Great Britain* (London, 1750), 21.

33. Anon., *The Military Prophet's Apology; Or, Probable Reasons for Deferring the Earthquake* (London, 1750), 10; Anon., *Jubilee Masquerade Balls, at Ranelagh Gardens, a Bad Return for the Merciful Deliverance from the Late Earthquakes* (London, 1750), 7, 9, 19–21. The ball went off without major incident; *Newcastle Courant*, April 28–May 5, 1750.

34. Anon., *An Address to the Journeymen of the City of London; and to Servants in General: Occasioned by the Bishop of London's Letter concerning the Late Earthquakes* (London, 1750), 3; George Wightwick, *The Design, and Proper Effect of Temporal Judgements Considered. A Sermon on Occasion of the Late Earthquakes* (London, 1750), 31; James Cox, *God's Mercies Slighted and Neglected, a Challenge to His Justice* (London, 1750), 12. See also Philip Doddridge, *The Guilt and Doom of Capernaum, Seriously Recommended to the Consideration of the Inhabitants of London* (London, 1750), viii; Lobb, *Sacred Declarations*, 24.

in this Land of Levity."[35] Many blamed the aristocracy for setting a bad example in this respect.[36]

The perception of England as a land of levity cannot be dismissed simply as the inevitable hyperbole of preachers trying to hold an audience. It is clearly the reaction to a society where the variety and availability of leisure pursuits was visibly increasing. Historians have explained the proliferation of such pursuits as the result of an economy increasingly driven by domestic consumer demand. The result was a growth and commercialization of theater and the proliferation of venues for entertainment, most notably the opening of Vauxhall Pleasure Gardens in 1728 and Ranelagh Gardens in 1742.[37] Observers in 1750 were well aware of this process; the condemnation of it as sin and its linkage to the earthquakes represents an attempt to understand this novel change in society in traditional terms. Criticism of this thirst for pleasure fused ideas of temptation and sin with those of luxury and corruption. Immoral entertainments were both offences against God and debasements of oneself.[38]

---

35. John Milner, *The Duty of God's People under Apprehensions of Publick Judgments* (London, 1750), 28; Thomas Secker, "Sermon Preached in the Parish Church of St James Westminster, March 11, 1750, on Occasion of the Earthquakes," in *The Works of Thomas Secker LLD, Late Lord Archbishop of Canterbury*, 6 vols. (London, 1825), V: 154–76; William Crookshank, *The Causes and Effects, the Designs and Emprovement, of Earthquakes Considered* (London, 1750), 19; Sherlock, *Letter From the Bishop of London*, 12; Doddridge, *Guilt and Doom*, ix; Anon., *Address to the Journeymen*, 10.

36. Anon., *A Seasonable Memento to the Author of the Supplement to the Bishop of London's Letter, on Occasion of the Late Earthquakes* (London, 1750), 2. This vulgar imitation of aristocratic habits was also stressed by William Agate, *A Persuasive to Repentance; Or, God's Judgement, a Warning to a Sinful Nation* (London, 1750), 16; Milner, Duty of God's People, 29. See also "A Citizen of London," *A Serious Expostulation with the Right Reverend the Lord Bishop of London on His Letter to the Clergy and People of London and Westminster* (London, 1750), 27; "A Citizen of London," *A Letter to the Lord Bishop of London, on Occasion of His Lordship's Late Letter to the Clergy and People of the Cities of London and Westminster* (London, 1750); "A Citizen of London." *A Letter from a Citizen of London to His Fellow Citizens.*

37. See Neil McKendrick, John Brewer, and J. H. Plumb, *The Birth of a Consumer Society: The Commercialization of Eighteenth-Century England* (London: Europa, 1982); John Brewer and Roy Porter, *Consumption and the World of Goods* (London: Routledge, 1994); John Brewer, *The Pleasures of the Imagination: English Culture in the Eighteenth Century* (London: HarperCollins, 1997).

38. See John Sekora, *Luxury: The Concept in Western Thought, Eden to Smollett* (Baltimore, MD: Johns Hopkins University Press, 1977); Christopher Berry, *The Idea of Luxury: A Conceptual and Historical Investigation* (Cambridge, UK: Cambridge Univer-

In light of this, the dominant interpretation of the earthquakes was one of divine displeasure. And if the earthquakes were not destructive enough to count as a punishment for sin, they were undoubtedly a warning that such punishment would be forthcoming if repentance was not. The vast majority of pamphleteers (approximately forty-six out of the fifty-three that took a position on the matter) followed the Bishop of London's declaration that the quakes were "Warnings which God in his Mercy affords to a sinful People." To take just four examples, Anglican John Milner's sermon began by stating that "this is a day for serious reflection," because "God has manifested some tokens of displeasure." Presbyterian William Crookshank stated categorically, "Earthquakes are designed to be the Tokens of God's Displeasure against Sin and Sinners." The Wesleys wrote a hymn imploring the acceptance of "God of glorious majesty / Whose judgments are abroad." And the *Gentleman's Magazine* published an essay entitled "The Light in which We Are Taught by the Word of God to Consider Earthquakes," arguing that they were evidently methods "by which God punishes a rebellious and wicked People."[39]

---

sity Press, 1994); Maxine Berg and Elizabeth Eger, ed., *Luxury in the Eighteenth Century: Debates, Desires and Delectable Goods* (Basingstoke: Palgrave Macmllian, 2003). Bob Harris, *Politics and the Nation: Britain in the Mid-Eighteenth Century* (Oxford: Oxford University Press, 2002), 290–94, notes that both the earthquakes and new entertainments contributed to a heightened concern over morals of the midcentury, but Harris does not capture how it was these very entertainments that made the moral panic over the earthquakes so severe.

39. Milner, *Duty of God's People*, 1; Crookshank, *Causes and Effects*, 15; John and Charles Wesley, *Hymns Occasioned by the Earthquake, March 8, 1750* (London, 1750), 4; *Gentleman's Magazine*, April 1750, 169.

## III. Natural Causes and Moral Causes

None of this necessarily involved the denial that earthquakes had natural causes. The emphasis given to the role of natural causes varied significantly, from keen interest to outright scorn, but no pamphleteer explicitly made such a denial.[40] The conceptual role of physical causes was held to be the same by almost all authors. Nature was God's tool, and therefore natural causes were the means by which He effected His purposes. "I cannot conceive how the Operation of these natural Causes is inconsistent with a religious Acknowledgement of God in such Events," wrote a nonconformist divine eager to accept the role of such causes, for "the Operations of the Laws of Nature, are in truth nothing but the Operation of God by those laws."[41] Others made very similar arguments: "Nature in God's Hands is the Same Thing as Art in ours," wrote one clergyman. "No doubt there are natural causes of these Appearances," admitted a dissenting minister, "but what is Nature, but a God-governed Machine?"[42] As many put it, God uses natural causes as his "instruments."[43]

This did not imply a physical or even mystical sense in which sin caused earthquakes; nature was passive, lifeless matter, and only through God's original creation and His continual sustenance could anything at all happen in the physical world.[44] Thus there was no direct

---

40. I have found only one outright denial of natural causes and that came as a reader's submission to a provincial paper. Northampton Mercury, April 23, 1750.

41. Samuel Chandler, *The Scripture Account of the Cause and Intention of Earthquakes* (London, 1750), 6–7; see also Secker, "Sermon," 160.

42. "Clergyman," *Late Uncommon and Terrible Shocks*, 25; John Allen, *The Nature and Danger of Despising Repeated Reproofs, Considered* (London, 1750), 13. See also Crookshank, *Causes and Effects*, 10; Doddridge, *Guilt and Doom*, vi.

43. John Mason, *The Right Improvement of Alarming Providences. A Sermon Preached at Cheshunt in Hertfordshire, March 18th, 1749–50* (London, 1750), 18; Thomas Newman, *The Sin and Shame of Disregarding Alarming Providences* (London, 1750), 7; Anon., *The Sacred Philosophy of Earthquakes; Or, the City-Monitor* (London, 1750), 8.

44. This view had been of prime ideological importance in the seventeenth century, and a nuanced debate over the powers of matter continued during the eighteenth century. But with the fading of the freethinking threat in the midcentury, the issue had lost some of its urgency and divisiveness. The emergence of Joseph Priestley revived the controversy— see John Yolton, *Thinking Matter: Materialism in Eighteenth-Century Britain* (Oxford, UK: Blackwell, 1984), 114–24.

correspondence between human disorder and physical disorder. But the two were intimately connected through the will of God, who desired moral order and had the natural order under his control to achieve it. The phenomena of nature "are formed to answer the most important and benevolent Purposes, in the moral as well as the natural world."[45] It was in this sense that a pamphleteer could advise readers "to guard against all natural Evils, by that never successless Method, the avoidance of those that are moral."[46]

This meant that natural causes were necessarily subservient to religious ends. This is what G. S. Rousseau, one of the few scholars to have studied the earthquakes, fails to understand when he makes assertions like "most men gave equal weight" to religious and natural causes.[47] Men could not give equal weight because at the time religious causes were entirely dependent on natural causes. As one clergyman put it, "What are natural causes but the Rules and Methods by which God governs the natural World and makes it subservient to his purposes relating to the moral World?"[48] God made and maintained the world for moral purposes, and it was therefore evident that any events in this world, human or purely physical, must have some moral import. This was not seen as problematical for a law-based universe.[49] As John Allen declared: "Bring in thy Account, Philosophy! but know thy Place!"[50]

---

45. *Ipswich Journal*, March 31, 1750.
46. Anon., *Verses on the Late Earth Quakes: Address'd to Great Britain* (London, 1750), 2.
47. G. S. Rousseau, "The London Earthquakes of 1750," *Cahiers d'Histoire Mondiale* 11 (1968): 436–51. More recent scholarly interest has been similarly superficial, focusing largely on the religious reaction, rather than an analysis of it. Robert Ingram, "'The Trembling Earth God's Herald': Earthquakes, Religion and Public Life in Britain During the 1750s," in *The Lisbon Earthquake of 1755*, ed. Braun and Radner, 115.
48. Bristed, *The Two Late Shocks of an Earth-quake*, 4.
49. Some authors did discuss how God might have framed those laws. "Citizen," *Letter from a Citizen of London*, 4. Milner, *Duty of God's People*, 7. For the distinction between this kind of divine involvement and outright miracles, see William Warburton, *Julian; Or, a Discourse concerning the Earthquake and Fiery Eruption, Which Defeated That Emperor's Attempt to Rebuild the Temple at Jerusalem* (London, 1750), 241–43. For more discussion, see Smyth, "Perceptions of Extraordinary Natural Events," 161–69.
50. Allen, *The Nature and Danger of Despising Repeated Reproofs*, 13.

God's use of nature as punishment has a long history. This aim had seemed equally evident in 1692—and indeed in 1580.[51] Yet the terms in which this punishment was perceived had changed significantly. From 1692 through 1693, those who wrote about the earthquakes in London, Sicily, and Jamaica were much more ambivalent about the role of natural causes. Some denied them completely. For instance, Presbyterian minister Thomas Doolittle tentatively judged that "this Earthquake was from the immediate Hand of God." An anonymous account agreed that "it would seem that this Earthquake carried along with it some more than ordinary Marks of an immediate Stroke of Heaven." Robert Fleming, also a Presbyterian, surveyed the extent of the earthquake, which had been felt across northern Europe, and concluded that it was "not possible that in the ordinary course of nature the Influence of any subterranean Fires or Vapours should have so immediate a Conjunction with Places so vastly remote." Another pamphleteer thought the wide extent suggested that the earthquake was "mixt" or, in other words, that it "hath a natural cause, but extraordinarily, as it were increased by God, and in some sort enlarged beyond the Power of Nature."[52] Some of these writers seem to allow that the earthquake might equally have been natural or supernatural, and judge one way or another from the particular circumstances.

Yet by 1750, natural causes were generally assumed to operate even before any investigation of particulars. This can be seen as a result of the changing religious sensibility mentioned above. Thomas Doolittle declared in 1693 that "the glory of God is obscured, if where he acts immediately, and in an extraordinary manner, and that altogether divine, we enquire after second causes, which in such events are none."[53]

---

51. For reaction to the England earthquake of 1580, see Alexandra Walsham, *Providence in Early Modern England* (Oxford: Oxford University Press, 1999), 130–35.

52. Thomas Doolittle, *Earthquakes Explained and Practically Improved: Occasioned by the Late Earthquake on Sept. 8. 1692* (London, 1693), sig.A3v; Anon., *An Account of the Late Terrible Earthquake in Sicily; With Most of Its Particulars. Done from the Italian Copy Printed at Rome* (London, 1693), 6; Robert Fleming, *A Discourse of Earthquakes; as They Are Supernatural and Premonitory Signs to a Nation* (London, 1693), 17; "J. D. R., French Minister," *Observations Uupon Three Earthquakes Its Natural Causes, Kinds, and Manifold Effects and Presages* (London, 1694), 6.

53. Doolittle, *Earthquakes Explained*, 33.

From 1692 to 1693, it seemed fitting for great events to be attributed to God's supernatural power, but by 1750 this was no longer acceptable. Principally this was because, as I have suggested elsewhere, more emphasis on natural theology meant more emphasis on contrivance. It also seems likely that social pressures were again at work. The growing prestige of natural philosophy meant that to deny its claims was to cast doubt on one's intellectual credentials.[54] It is no coincidence that the most emphatic denials of natural causes in 1692 came from the populist pamphleteer Nathaniel Crouch, who declared that "it is very apparent that many [earthquakes] have been supernatural and caused by the immediate Hand of God," and dismissed natural explanations as "only the guesses of short-sighted men."[55] By 1750, it was those who denied any role for natural causes who seemed shortsighted.

When natural philosophers published about the 1750 earthquakes, they gave weight to both natural causes and religious ends. Two members of the Royal Society published pamphlets on the earthquakes: Stephen Hales and William Stukeley. They offered very different accounts of the causes of earthquakes. Hales argued that they were in fact "airquakes," caused by the build up of a sulphurous cloud, which, remaining undispersed on a windless day, eventually exploded with a force great enough to rock the earth. Stukeley, however, turned to a more modish explanation: "In an age when electricity has been so much our entertainment and our amazement . . . is it to be wondered at, that hither we most turn our thoughts, for the solution of the prodigious appearance of an earthquake?"[56]

Despite this divergence of opinion on natural causes, the two authors, both clergymen, were united on religious interpretation. Hales

---

54. English philosophy could also be contrasted with popish superstition—see for instance Horace Mann's comment that no one in Florence would have dared attribute natural causes because "the inquisition and priestly craft oblige them to pocket up all these judgments and miracles as may best serve their turn." Mann to Walpole, June 26, 1750, *Correspondence*, XX, 158.

55. [Nathaniel Crouch], *The General History of Earthquakes Being an Account of the Most Remarkable and Tremendous Earthquakes That Have Happened in Divers Parts of the World* (London, 1694), 7, 161.

56. Hales, *Considerations on the Causes of Earthquakes*, 17; William Stukeley, *The Philosophy of Earthquakes, Natural and Religious* (London, 1750), 18–20.

begins his pamphlet by defending the study of the natural aspect of earthquakes: "I must first obviate an objection of some serious well-meaning People, who are apt to be offended at any Attempt to give a natural Account of Earthquakes . . . but it ought to be consider that the ordinary course of Nature is as much carried on by the Divine Agency, as the extraordinary and miraculous Events." He then argues against the contrary view, saying, "On the other Hand, there are some who make light of Earthquakes because they are capable of being accounted for by natural Causes. But the Hand of God is not to be overlooked in these Things, under whose Government all natural Agents act." Clearly, authorities of the time gave weight to both natural and religious causes, but again, it was not equal weight.

In a sermon published with his Royal Society paper, Stukeley went further "to show how vain, and unmeaning, are all our philosophical inquiries, when destitute of their true view, to lead us into the more engaging paths of religion. . . . It certainly becomes a Christian philosopher, whilst he is investigating material causes, to look, and regard the moral use of them." As far as earthquakes are concerned, Stukeley is unhesitant. Of all natural phenomena, there are "none so proper to threaten, or to execute vengeance upon a guilty people."[57]

This attitude toward natural causes was shared by many writers who were not explicitly writing about physical processes. About half of the religious or moralizing pamphlets acknowledged a full role for natural causes, with, of course, the caveat that they were subordinate to the religious end.

Others were more skeptical about the role of natural causes, and some were outright scornful. Of the moralizing sermons, fifteen ignored the physical aspects of earthquakes altogether, while eleven mentioned them only to dismiss their relevance. The Bishop of London was foremost among these:

> Thoughtless or hardened sinners may be deaf to these calls; and little Philosophers, who see a little, but very little into natural Causes, may think they see enough to account for what

---

57. Hales, *Considerations on the Causes of Earthquakes*, 5–6; Stukeley, *Philosophy of Earthquakes*, 3–34.

happens, without calling in the Aid or Assistance of a special Providence; not considering, that God who made all Things, never put anything out of his own Power, but has all Nature under his Command to serve his Purposes in the moral Government of the World. But be their Imaginations to themselves, the Subject is too serious for trifling.[58]

The operation of nature was not denied by the bishop (though the ability of philosophers to discover it was doubted), but it was deemed a petty matter.

For some, such discussion was of no use at all. It is probably fair to say that these writers were predominantly Tories or high Churchmen, like Thomas Sherlock, though it is doubtful how far this identification can be pushed. Presbyterian Thomas Newman was one of the most passionate of railers against the "prattle" about natural causes, lamenting that "if we are but able to point to some visible cause (and when may we not do it) how generally doth it swallow up all sense of the invisible director and disposer! . . . If we do but consider the natural causes of events, we seem to be told they cannot hurt us."[59] It is not physical but moral lessons that should be drawn from the earthquakes.

Other notable troubles could be fitted into the same framework. Among those usually mentioned are the Jacobite rebellion, the Spanish War, and the ongoing cattle murrain. All were taken to be natural events that were also signs of God's displeasure. The chronic cattle disease was particularly often mentioned as "a memorial not to forget that He is yet angry."[60] To the modern eye, rebellion, war, earthquakes, and sick

---

58. Sherlock, *Letter from the Bishop of London*, 5.

59. Newman, *Sin and Shame*, 11. See also Anon., *Supplement to the Bishop of London's Letter*, 5.

60. Cox, *God's Mercies Slighted and Neglected*, 14. See also Crookshank, *Causes and Effects*, 1; Agate, *Persuasive to Repentance*, 9; Chandler, *Scripture Account*, 39; "Citizen," *Letter from a Citizen of London*, 3; Clergyman, *The Late Uncommon and Terrible Shocks*, 24; Grey, *A Chronological and Historical Account*, ix; Lobb, *Sacred Declaration, Continued in a Second Letter* (London, 1750), 37; Mason, *Right Improvement of Alarming Providences*, 20; Milner, *Duty of God's People*, 26. See also James Burton, *The Warning: A Religious and Divine Poem upon the Contageous Distemper amongst the Horned Cattle of this Kingdom: Also Touching the Late Rebellion, Earthquakes, and Ominous Signs and Wonders in the Heavens* (York, 1752), 10.

cows are quite distinct phenomena. Yet to observers in 1750, they were united in being examples of destructive disorder. This was contrary to the general course of the world, "the Regularity and Order of all Things" continually eulogized by eighteenth-century writers—the earthquake moralizers not excepted. Whether it was the "beauty, usefulness, order and grandeur" of the stars, or the "almost unbounded, but regular Luxuriousness" of plants, all this had been established by a benevolent God.[61]

This benevolence dictated that natural harm does not visit without reason. John Allen considered that the wise could plainly see the ease, abundance, and good order of the "settled course of nature," and "so any threatening Deviations from that Course are, in their Estimation, solemn Warnings to a guilty World."[62] Such reminders might have been terrible, but they were nonetheless evidence of God's goodness, for he had refrained from immediate destruction. By offering a warning, God was demonstrating his mercy.[63] His slowness to anger was demonstrated by the several methods He had used to try to reform the nation: the war, rebellion, murrain, "and now he has sent us an Earthquake; and shews us by the Course of his Providence, both that he is displeased at us, and yet reluctant to proceed to Severity."[64] It was natural, therefore, when disorders occurred, to seek out the transgressions that had roused God to send them. When such disorder is as alarming and potentially devastating as an earthquake, it is no wonder that such vigor and emotion was put into identifying and extirpating the nation's sins.

---

61. Bristed, *The Two Late Shocks of an Earth-quake*, 7; Newman, *Sin and Shame*, 6; Roger Pickering, *An Address to Those Who Have Either Retired, or Intend to Leave the Town, under the Imaginary Apprehension of the Approaching Shock of Another Earthquake* (London, 1750), 11.

62. Allen, *The Nature and Danger of Despising Repeated Reproofs*, 5.

63. Anon., *Genuine Account*, 24.

64. Anon., *Sacred Philosophy of Earthquakes*, 29; Agate, *Persuasive to Repentance*, 3. See also Bristed, *The Two Late Shocks of an Earth-quake*, 17. Some also theorized that earthquakes served a natural as well as a moral good by for instance releasing vapors necessary to plant life, "thus the Divine Being makes the greatest Evils the greatest blessings"; Anon., *The Theory and History of Earthquakes*, 13. Making the same point in a different way, another writer argued that volcanoes were in fact beneficial because they vented sulphur that would otherwise have caused an earthquake. Anon., *Particular Account*, 9.

This represents a subtle but significant change from 1692 through 1693. In 1750, disorders only seemed related to divine displeasure if they were both harmful and major. In the earlier period, however, earthquakes could be linked to all kinds of strange happenings under the category of "portents." They were often aligned with other events seemingly outside the ordinary course of nature, such as the comet of 1680. As one divine put it, "We would not be affected with what appeared over our heads. And now behold! We are call'd to take notice of what is felt under our feet." Crouch went even further in this, linking historical earthquakes to a whole variety of prodigies like multiple suns and rains of milk and corn.[65] This reflected a traditional view of natural operations very clearly expressed by Walter Cross. He distinguished between events that were purely natural, those that were purely divine (miracles), and those that stood between the two prodigies. Earthquakes, he declared, were "the Prince of Prodigies" because they were both portents and punishments in their own right. As one divine expressed the same idea, earthquakes were "not only Calamities themselves, but are the undoubted Emblems and Ensigns of other approaching Calamities to a nation." The independent minister Thomas Beverley agreed, declaring that "God hath generally usher'd in any great Changes he hath made in the World by such Signs and Wonders in Heaven, and shakings of the Earth beneath."[66]

This perception is no longer evident in 1750. Earthquakes could still be punishments or warnings because they were destructive, but they were no longer portents simply because they were unusual. Natural and moral order were no longer directly related in the way expressed by Crouch, or by Beverley, who declared "this is a shaking time, and God is not shaking all Nations" and linked earthquakes with conflict and revolution. The same applies to John Evelyn, who believed the earthquakes

---

65. Fleming, *A Discourse of Earthquakes*, 12; "Reverend Divine," *A Practical Discourse on the Late Earthquakes* (London, 1692), 22; Crouch, *General History of Earthquakes*, 69, 61, 34.

66. Walter Cross, *The Summ of Two Sermons on the Witnesses, and the Earthquake That Accompanies Their Resurrection. Occasion'd From a Late Earthquake, Sept. 8* (London, 1692), 22–27; "Reverend Divine," *A Practical Discourse on the Late Earthquakes*, 15; Thomas Beverley, *Evangelical Repentance Unto Salvation Not to Be Repented of, Upon 2 Cor. 7. 10* (London, 1693), 142.

would be "portentous of some extraordinary Revolutions."[67] God's absolute control over the universe eliminated the praeternatural, and unusual but harmless events were coming to be aligned with natural theological wonder rather than ominous terror.

## IV. Fashion and Religion

When the moralizers complained that their message was not being heeded, most blamed pleasurable distraction. But some also discerned a worrying fashion of scoffing at religion. Historians have regarded the 1750s as a low point for deism. After withering under an onslaught of rigorous orthodox attacks, the publication of deist tracts dried up after around 1740, and their influence went into decline.[68] However, if philosophical infidelity was not a significant threat to Christianity in 1750, fashionable infidelity certainly was. Many complained of wits using natural philosophy as an excuse to ignore religion. Even a provincial newspaper could complain of "the trifling Temper which appears in too many, even in Men of Sense and Wit; who, because they are able, in some degree, to account philosophically for these Appearances, imagine, that they have no relation to Religion, nor are any Indications of Divine Displeasure."[69] At the root of this, however, was not the work of the philosophers themselves but the uses to which it was put by "Moutebank Philosophers." The Whig divine William Warburton also stressed that when he criticized "the mathematicians," he meant the "Demonstrators of others inventions," not the "inventors and geniuses amongst them, whom I honour."[70] Satirical sketches of such figures can be found in

---

67. Beverley, *Evangelical Repentance*, sig.A2v, 137–38; Crouch, *General History of Earthquakes*, 140; *The Diary of John Evelyn*, Feb 19, 1693, ed. E. S. de Beer, 6 vols. (Oxford, UK: Clarendon Press, 2000), V 133.

68. See J. C. D. Clark, *English Society, 1660–1832* (Cambridge, UK: Cambridge University Press, 2000), 360–61.

69. *Ipswich Journal*, March 31, 1750.

70. Anon., *Sacred Philosophy of Earthquakes*, 13; *Bath Journal*, April 23, 1750; William Warburton to Richard Hurd, February 24, 1750; *Letters from a Late Eminent Prelate to One of His Friends* (London, 1809), 31.

contemporary periodicals. A young man is presented commenting on the Bishop of London's letter:

> I've read that excellent letter, as you call it, and think it's well enough to frighten poor ignorant old women and children, and keep up that superstitious dread of judgment, which makes people so easily priest-ridden. But for my part I have studied natural philosophy, and know the natural causes of these sorts of things; and whether caus'd by nitrous particles in the earth or explosions in the air, I know there was no miracle in't, and 'twas only the voice of nature, not (as the parsons would persuade us) the voice of God.

This young man, it is stated, had spent the winter in London, where clearly he had been exposed to the seductions of fashionable irreligious influences. His female companions are shown as less intellectually minded but equally misguided. One had not felt the earthquake, for she had been "sound asleep, having sat up the night before at brag." Another is most excited by the prospect of holding an earthquake-themed party.[71]

That such conversations were described as "fashionable dialogues" is crucial, for the root of the neglect of religion was not philosophy but fashion. Scorn and, more commonly, disregard for religion were constantly linked, not without reason, to the latest trends in dissolute high society and the world of leisure. Agate lamented how so many seemed resolved to ignore judgments and "to stifle all sense of them, by noisy Mirth, awry Pleasure, gay Diversion, Business, or Amusement."[72] Satirical accounts reinforce the picture.[73]

These are what stood in the way of the repentance and reformation urged by all but two of the pamphlets. The Church of England published a form of prayers "for the benefit of the Publick," allowing them to express this sentiment effectively: "O Lord God, uncontroulable in thy

---

71. *Newcastle Courant*, March 31–April 7, 1750; *The Student; Or, The Oxford and Cambridge Monthly Miscellany* (March 31, 1750), 96.

72. Agate, *Persuasive to Repentance*, 12.

73. Anon., *A Letter of Congratulation and Advice from the Devil, to the Inhabitants of Great Britain* (London, 1750); L. H., *A Narrative of What Passed at Bath, Upon Account of the Late Earthquake* (London, 1750), 3, 10. The *Bath Journal* gives no indication that the earthquake was in fact felt in the town.

Power and terrible in thy Judgments . . . engrave in our Hearts so deep a Sense of our own Sins, and the many and horrid Impieties of these great Cities, that we may, by true Repentance and humble Contritions of Heart, turn away thy wrathful Indignation from us."[74] Anguished calls for a national awakening run through these pamphlets.[75]

The severest contempt was reserved for those who responded to the earthquakes by fleeing the capital rather than making their peace with God. The greatest exodus from London came as a result of the predictions of an ex-soldier, John Mitchell, who came to be known as the "crazy lifeguard man" after his former regiment and his current state of mind. He publicly proclaimed his belief that a third, cataclysmic quake would strike London in April, either four weeks after the second, on April 5, or a month after, on April 8. Many believed him. A writer in the *London Magazine* said, "It is almost impossible to conceive the consternation, with which many credulous people were seized upon such a silly prognostication." One newspaper reported in early April that "the several Roads leading from London into the Country were never known to be more thronged than they were yesterday" as crowds stampeded out of the city. Walpole estimated that "within these three days, 730 coaches have been counted passing Hyde Park Corner."[76] With this evacuation underway, Charles Wesley thought that "London looked like a sacked city." But though he criticized the flight, he was not willing to disdain the panic entirely, for as he candidly admitted, "the late earthquake has found me work." On the night of April 4, he

---

74. Church of England, *By the Bishop of London, a Form of Prayers for the Use of Private Families. On Occasion of the Late Earthquakes, and Other Judgments of God upon This Nation* (London, 1750), 3.

75. Anon., *An Affectionate Letter, Address'd to the Clergy, and All Orders of Men; But in Particular to the Deists* (London, 1750), 3; *London Evening Post*, March 8–10, 1750; Burton, *The Warning*, 9; John and Charles Wesley, *Hymns Occasioned by the Earthquake*, 4.

76. *London Magazine*, April 1750, 186; Walpole to Mann, April 4, 1750; *Correspondence*, XX 136–37. Several hundred people were apparently provoked into leaving "upon the Report of a Hen's having laid an Egg whereon was inscribed in capital letters, BEWARE THE THIRD SHOCK!" *Bath Journal*, April 9, 1750. This seemingly odd report is obviously linked to the popular tradition of "comet eggs" giving omens of prodigies to come. See Sara Schechner Genuth, *Comets, Popular Culture and the Birth of Modern Cosmology* (Princeton: Princeton University Press, 1997), 120.

recorded that "fear filled our chapel, occasioned by a prophecy of the Earthquake's return this night. I preached my written sermon, with great effect, and gave out several suitable hymns. It was a glorious night for the disciples of Jesus."[77] The atmosphere of the time can be vividly sampled in a contemporary engraving of the flight from London in all its flustered foolishness (see Figure 1).

**Figure 1**

*The Military Prophet; or, A Flight from Providence* © British Library Board (Cup.21.g.37/38).

## V. Providence and Nation

Providence remained, then, the dominant explanatory concept into which the earthquakes were fitted, even if the mechanics of it had changed. Fleeing was seen as a foolish mistrust of this providence.[78]

---

77. *The Journal of the Rev. Charles Wesley*, April 4–5, 1750, ed. Thomas Jackson, 2 vols. (London, 1849), II 69.

78. Anon., *Affectionate Letter*, 28.

This providential interpretation of earthquakes had the sanction of both scripture and reason; the Bible is replete with examples of natural calamities being used by God as a punishment, of which the fate of Sodom is the best known. Perhaps most chilling for Londoners was that in August 1749 the dissenting minister Philip Doddridge had preached a detailed sermon on the fate of Capernaum, mentioned in Matthew 11:23–24. This was a rich and prosperous city, flushed with the bounty of God, given clear evidence of its religious duty by the miracles Jesus performed there. Yet the city did not repent and remained mired in luxury, enjoying its "exquisite Food, rich wines . . . Concerts of Music and other theatrical Events." Jesus decreed that the city "would go down to the depths" for impenitence greater than that of Sodom. From this Doddridge infers a terrible fate for the inhabitants: "Their Doom then shall be more terrible, than that which they [Sodom] suffered from the sulphurous Rain, the Earthquake, and the Pit, into which many of them no doubt went down alive." Doddridge saw a modern parallel to this flourishing city, neglecting all the advantages of religion for the gratifications of the flesh: "Is there no City that rises to our Thoughts, far superior to Capernaum in its Wealth and Magnificence, and in some respects more than equal to it in its Guilt? Oh LONDON, LONDON!" When that city was hit by an earthquake only five months later, it is not surprising that consternation ran high. Doddridge quickly published his sermon, clearly in a highly agitated state. "I have transcribed it with Tears and Trembling," he wrote in the preface.[79] With such dreadful vengeance apparently so imminent, national reformation could not be more urgent.

The national character of the judgment and repentance was vital. Again, ideas of providence explain why. The idea that God inflicted temporal punishments on individuals for their sins was no longer altogether respectable, associated as it now was with ignorance and superstition. Warburton described it as "bigotry" to "convert every unusual appearance of natural evil into a punishment." Joseph Addison devoted one essay in the *Spectator* to ridiculing this view.[80] Addison's targets

---

79. Doddridge, *Guilt and Doom*, passim.
80. Warburton, *Julian*, 259; *The Spectator*, ed. Donald Bond, 5 vols. (Oxford, UK: Clarendon Press, 1987), IV: 211–13.

are historians like Herodotus and Plutarch, but the reader might be forgiven for thinking of the Bishop of London. The crucial difference, however, was that the bishop was speaking of national judgments. As one defender of the bishop pointed out, "His Lordship is not addressing to Individuals, nor pointing out Particular Persons, but enumerating the Spring, Growth and Progression of National Vice."[81] Addison had felt that bad fortune was "a very strong argument for a State of Retribution hereafter"; individuals could be judged in the afterlife—nations, however, could not. "For though there be no Necessity for God's rewarding or punishing particular Persons, for their Vertues or Vices in this World," wrote William Agate, "yet as a Nation or Body of Men, we must be punished or rewarded here, or not at all." Judgments thus fall on nations "because nations as such no where exist but in this world, and can never be punished as nations at all, unless they are punished here."[82] Clearly this implies a conception of nations as entities distinct from the individuals who comprise them. These entities are religious entities, communities ordained by Providence for the fulfilment of God's ends in the world. If they failed in these ends, they were liable to temporal punishments, and of these, "earthquakes may be counted the most Dreadful and Tremendous."[83]

There is a clear sense in these pamphlets that England was just such a providentially blessed community—a chosen nation failing to live up to its godly task. The benefits bestowed by Providence on this "Queen of Isles" were many. It was "happy beyond Description . . . favoured with Blessings and Privileges beyond any Nation under the Sun."[84] The Church's official prayers specified some of these blessings: "O Lord, who in former Times hast redeemed the People of this Nation from temporal and spiritual Tyranny, and bestowed on us the Blessings of civil Freedom

---

81. "Clergyman of the Church of England," *A Vindication of the Bishop of London's Letters*, 28.

82. Agate, *Persuasive to Repentance*, 7; Wightwick, *The Design, and Proper Effect of Temporal Judgements Considered*, 7. See also Bristed, *The Two Late Shocks of an Earthquake*, 4; Cox, *God's Mercies Slighted and Neglected*, 7, 10.

83. "R. B.," *The General History of Earthquakes* (London, 1734).

84. Benjamin Stillingfleet, *Some Thoughts Occasioned by the Late Earthquakes. A Poem* (London, 1750), 9; Anon., *Appendix to Shower's Reflections*, 19.

and the glorious Liberty of the Gospel."[85] One pamphleteer believed that God had placed His plan to spread His kingdom around the world "under the Direction of a certain Nation, or People, which Providence has ordained to exist and flourish at the Times here pointed out for that Purpose." He was not thinking of France.[86] Linda Colley has argued that such views provided a foundation for a sense of British national identity. Military and economic success, she says, gave weight to claims of divine favor.[87] But in 1750 we see clearly the nation's fear that they had squandered those blessings. Instead of turning them to the glory of God, they had sunk into licentiousness. A "foreign observer" described how shocked he was that England, "the Seat of Liberty," should engage in such debased entertainments.[88] It was no wonder that God was angry. "But," wrote Sherlock, "let us not despair. There is still one remedy left." That remedy was national repentance. "What but national Repentance," asked Wesley, "can prevent national Destruction?"[89] Indeed, so great a change was needed that some said it amounted to a national reformation. Precisely because the Protestant sense of being a chosen people was so important for national identity, the need to live up to godly standards became urgent.[90]

To observers in 1750, it was not only reasonable but also obvious that the earthquakes were warnings. "Signs they are that explain themselves," wrote Thomas Newman, "that require no prophet to reveal them; addressed to our common understanding; speaking to our senses, and distinguishing enough to declare an approaching, incensed God."[91] "It is impossible without wilful Blindness," wrote another clergyman, "to

85. Church of England, *By the Bishop of London, a Form of Prayers for the Use of Private Families*, 8.
86. John Loudon, *The Scheme of Divine Providence upon Which the Christian Religion Is Founded, Set Forth in an Essay on the Prophetic Writings of the Old and New Testament* (London, 1750), 13.
87. Linda Colley, *Britons: Forging the Nation* (London: Pimlico, 1994), 11–54.
88. "Foreigner," *An Epistle to the Bishop of London; Occasion'd by His Lordship's Letter to the Clergy and Inhabitants of London and Westminster, On the Subject of the Two Late Earthquakes* (London, 1750), 25–31.
89. Wesley, *Cause and Cure of Earthquakes*, 18.
90. Sherlock, *Letter from the Bishop of London*, 15–17; Cox, *God's Mercies Slighted and Neglected*, 16; Anon., *Appendix to Shower's Reflections*, 26.
91. Newman, *Sin and Shame*, 21.

deny sins to be the moral cause of such tragical Events."[92] It is striking how different this interpretation of calamity is to that of Thomas Sprat in the previous century. He had seen claims to divine intervention as the mark of fractious sectarians, promoting natural explanations as a damper on such enthusiasm. The natural philosopher "cannot be suddenly inclin'd, to pass censure on mens eternal condition, from any *Temporal Judgments* that may befall them."

Of course, this is exactly what natural philosophers did in 1750. The change is striking, but it is hardly the result of a radically different view of God. It is, though, the result of a very different view of the state of religion. In 1667, the Church of England's situation was highly precarious. The sects of the day had not given up their ambition of replacing the Church with their own versions of ecclesiastical organization. Any means of claiming supernatural authority were therefore denied them.[93] By 1750, the Church had established a far more secure domination of religious life. The well-established dissenting sects did not wish to replace it as a national church. Nor even did they disagree on the reading of nature—there is no division of religious allegiance among the pamphleteers. When the Bishop of London presumed to interpret the secrets of heaven, no sect offered a challenge to him. Though dissenting ministers published roughly as many pamphlets as Church of England clergy, they all followed the line laid out by the bishop.[94]

The reaction to the earthquakes has clearly shown the Church's leadership of opinion, particularly in a time of stress when people revert to their most fundamental beliefs. Portraits were presented of people rushing back to church after a long absence. Even ostensible opponents of the church revealed their true colors—for instance, in the satirical picture of "Mr Query, who has been a perfect atheist many years, discovered all the symptoms of horror and despair" after the earthquakes and was seen running to the nearest church to pray. He then said he had

---

92. "Clergyman of the Church of England," *Vindication of the Bishop of London's Letter, Occasioned by the Late Earthquakes*, 9.

93. Thomas Sprat, *The History of the Royal-Society of London For the Improving of Natural Knowledge* (London, 1667), 358–64.

94. For a comparison of the Restoration period with the mid-eighteenth century, see Clark, *English Society*, 43–66, 99.

always really believed, "but I denied my Opinion sir, because you know it has of late been unfashionable."[95]

But the effect did not last. As April turned to May, it was often lamented that people were drifting back to their old ways. The alarm "sent them to their devotion for a few days," but soon they calmed down "and were as wicked and profane as before." The panic did not have the desirable lasting effects: "People lived afterwards, as they had done before, every one struggling to forget, rather than improve the Idea of what might happen." Some even made light of the whole thing by holding parties known as "earthquakes."[96]

## VI. Dissent and Demystification

There were a few dissenting voices, however. One anonymous pamphleteer specifically praised Sprat for not stoking "superstitious Fears" among the people over the plague and fire. Yet, like Sprat, the author did not see that the natural, nonpunitive character of the events made sin any less repugnant or repentance any less necessary.[97] Another pamphleteer, claiming to be a Quaker, upbraided the bishop for taking the quakes as judgment and presuming to know the intentions of God—but his main aim was to blame the failings of the clergy for the nation's crimes.[98]

There were opponents of the framework of sin and repentance. They were not many, and seem to have expressed themselves principally in private. Horace Walpole's worldweary correspondence with Horace Mann provides the clearest surviving example. Walpole made wry allusion to the prodigy tradition when he noted that the two shocks

---

95. *Newcastle Courant*, May 5–12, 1750; *The Student*, April 30, 1750.

96. Anon., *Appendix to Shower's Reflections*, 5; L. H., *Narrative of What Passed at Bath*, i; Anon., *A Supplement to the Bishop of London's Letter; Or, A Serious Address*, 4.

97. "Citizen of London," *Serious Expostulation*, 6–17. The only other author to take such a view was Anon., *An Account of Explosions in the Atmosphere*, 64. See also Sprat, *History of the Royal Society*, 363–64.

98. [Joseph Besse], *Modest Remarks upon the Bishop of London's Letter Concerning the Late Earthquakes. By One of the People Called Quakers* (London, 1750), 6–18. The work ran into seven editions and several attacks on it were published.

were "lowering the prices of wonderful commodities . . . you must not be surprised if by next post you hear of a burning mountain sprung up in Smithfield." But he soon became horrified by the "ridiculous panic," which he presented as an example of the unscrupulous clergy taking advantage of the naturally weak and credulous. "You will not wonder so much at our earthquakes, as at the effect they have had. All the women in town have taken them up upon the foot of judgments, and the clergy, who have had no windfalls of a long season, have driven horse and foot into this opinion. . . . There has been a shower of sermons and exhortations." Walpole was appalled at the behavior of Sherlock, whom he had considered more sensible, commenting on his letter, "you never read so impudent, so absurd a piece!" David Hume likewise commented slyly to a medical friend, "I think the parsons have lately used the physicians very ill, for, in all the common terrors of mankind, you used both to come in for a share of the profit; but in this new fear of earthquakes they have left you out entirely and have pretended alone to give prescriptions to the multitude."[99] Their reactions stemmed not from any natural understanding of earthquakes but from their skepticism of the clergy. Yet both recognized that the religious interpretation dominated public discourse and made their complaints only to friends.

Two such attacks did appear in print (though, significantly, both were anonymous). One was by the veteran anticlerical writer Thomas Gordon. Styling himself "a layman," Gordon offered *A Letter of Consolation and Counsel to the Good People of England*. In it he argued that if the people had an understanding of natural causes, this knowledge could be used to demystify events like earthquakes. Only the unscrupulous would do otherwise: "We are not to seek for, or suppose supernatural causes, where natural ones are obvious and certain; the latter will satisfy the reasonable mind, and supernatural causes are only sought and urged by visionaries, dealers in judgments, and sharpers in theology." The Bishop of London was just such a sharper; he was compared to those Spanish explorers who used their knowledge of an approaching eclipse to claim control over nature and thus frighten the

---

99. Walpole to Mann, April 11, 1750; Walpole to Mann, April 2, 1750; *Horace Walpole's Correspondence*, XX 130–33; David Hume to John Clephane, April 1750, *The Letters of David Hume*, ed. J. Y. T. Greig, 2 vols. (Oxford, UK: Clarendon Press, 1932), I: 141.

natives into obeying them. To Gordon, natural causes were much more suitable than moral ones for explaining what had happened. Of course, the moralists would have argued—indeed, they argued repeatedly—that the operation of natural causes made no difference to presence of judgments. Whatever logical coherence this had, it was not the point. Natural causes gave Gordon an alternative framework by which events could be explained, one over which the clergy did not have control. The availability of natural explanations denied the clergy a monopoly of interpretation over nature, which would otherwise allow them to "govern mankind without a sword," and Gordon praised natural philosophers for freeing mankind from this tyranny.[100]

Not only did it liberate men from the clergy, but blind nature seemed much more fitting to Gordon than divine purpose. As he noted pointedly, "The two late shocks were not more felt at Ranelagh and White's than in the Abbey." It did not seem fair to him that all should be punished for the sins of some, or that some sinners should be punished while others were not. This "would imply not only no equal providence, but no providence at all"—and this did not accord with Gordon's own view of God. Gordon's argument was, in essence, identical to Sprat's. But Sprat would never have intended it to have been used in this subversive way, against the established church rather than against dangerous sectaries. Both Sprat and Gordon employed the argument because it served their political and religious ends at their time of writing. The change in circumstances between those two times meant that the argument in 1750 could serve a position totally opposed to that which it had served in the 1660s.

This position, we have seen, was anticlericalism. The author of a second pamphlet opposing the framework of sin and repentance remained anonymous, but his position was made clear by his description of "the ignorant spiritual Quack" who "would have us all think ourselves sick, that we may be always under his Direction, and following his Prescription." The author styled himself "a little philosopher," after Sherlock's scornful put-down of those who sought natural causes.

---

100. Thomas Gordon, "A Letter of Consolation and Counsel to the Good People of England, Especially of London and Westminster, Occasion'd by the Late Earthquakes," in *The Pillars of Priestcraft Shaken*, ed. Richard Barron, 2 vols. (London, 1752), I: 27–313.

Like Gordon, he used these causes against the clergy: "He that cannot account for whatever happens in Nature, without having recourse to the Displeasure of the Almighty, or to supernatural Power, or to warping the Power of Nature, I will venture to pronounce him not so much as a little Philosopher."

The "little philosopher" used the separation of God and nature to dispense with a providential deity altogether. Even more robustly than Gordon, the author rejected the notion that the nation was groaning with sin. He noted with mocking glee that "since the Bishop has published his Letter, we have had small shocks of Earthquakes in some Places in the Country . . . are not those Country Places also, where Earthquakes are felt, greater sinners than here there were no such Shocks?" Clearly this was ridiculous. These quakes were purely natural, and so therefore were those in London. This being the case, "fasting with praying and mourning to prevent an Earthquake is full as stupid, as the same would be to prevent an eclipse."[101] But the little philosopher, as his advocacy of the legalization of prostitution served to underline, was a consciously marginal voice. His aim was to shock because he knew he could not persuade.

## VII. Conclusion

For such small tremors to become the source of such great disturbances, to spark what has been described by G. S. Rousseau as "one of the most memorable catastrophes in English history," shows that something was perceived to be deeply wrong.[102] Wrong not so much in the constitution of nature but in English society. On one level this was the product of a natural theology-inspired metaphysics whereby order and felicity were the natural state of God's universe. Sudden, unexpected, and threatening disorder had therefore to be seen as a divine warning, the fitting response to which was to seek out and extirpate the sins that had made

---

101. "Little Philosopher," *An Epistle to the Admirers of the Lord Bishop of London's Letter, Shewing the Harmony of His Doctrines, concerning Deity and His Providential Laws; the Honour He Has Done the King and Kingdom, and the Purity of His Religious Principles* (London, 1750), 10–57.

102. Rousseau, "The London Earthquakes of 1750," 436.

it necessary. On a deeper level, the perception grew from a society that was stable and prosperous but that despite this—or more likely, because of this—had grown debauched. The element of truth in this perception is derived from the growing popularity and availability of leisure activities in the eighteenth century. This preoccupation with entertainment was the greatest threat to religion and society in the mid-eighteenth century—the religious order was losing people not to secular enlightenment but to secular entertainment.

The dominant perception of a stable and corrupt society is perhaps the reason why millenarian interpretations were so uncommon. Those like William Whiston, who appeared to be dabbling in fevered prophetical speculations, became targets for satirists. William Warburton summed up the situation unkindly when he remarked, "The greatest mischief the earthquakes have hitherto done is only widening the crack in old Will Whiston's noddle."[103] To most, it did not feel like the end of the world, just an ignominious chapter in its history.

The natural status of earthquakes seemed clearer in 1750 than it had in 1692. Few would deny the existence of physical causes by the mid-eighteenth century, even if some were still ambivalent about the usefulness of such knowledge. Not only were earthquakes now clearly natural, but they were also nonprodigious; they could still be seen as punishments because they were destructive, but they were not warnings simply because they were unusual. But if the religious framework had changed, the panic that followed the earthquakes demonstrated that the clergy still had a firm hold on intellectual life. In times of danger, people turned to their religion and, while dissenters featured prominently in the debate, their interpretation followed the lead set by the Bishop of London. Many may have been superstitious or heedless, but this did not constitute a philosophical challenge to clerical hegemony, for all that it offered a practical challenge. Freethinkers used natural causes to rebut religious explanations, but theirs was a self-consciously marginal stance.

---

103. *General Advertiser*, March 14, 1750; Paul Whitehead, *A Full and True Account of the Dreadful and Melancholly Earthquake* (London, 1750), 6; Warburton to Hurd, April 5, 1750; *Letters from a Late Eminent Prelate*, 34.

For the vast majority, God remained not only involved but even immanent. He had given England the great blessings of his bountiful universe, but he had been spurned in favor of corrupt entertainments. Only His great mercy had so far prevented the unleashing of His terrible wrath. But His mercy could not be infinite, and only reformation could ultimately save the nation. The urgency of repentance was self-evident: London must imitate Ninevah, or it would share the fate of Capernaum.

# Porn, Popery, Mahometanism, and the Rise of the Novel: Responses to the London Earthquakes of 1750

*Samara Anne Cahill*

In February and March of 1750, two earthquakes hit London, provoking panic in the population and generating a great deal of providentialist rhetoric from religious authorities and self-proclaimed prophets alike. Public figures used the earthquakes as didactic opportunities to structure domestic identity and national security along gridlines of reason, faith, and national guilt. Such representations indicate not only that religious identity and faith remained important to Britons throughout the eighteenth century but also that, although Britons used Christian belief to structure their national identity, they were by no means convinced of the superiority of actual Christian behavior compared to that of other religious groups. The complexity of English attitudes toward religious "others" could complicate the understanding of—among other power relations—the imbrications of missionary activity, colonialism, and the novel that Edward Said and other postcolonialist theorists have described.[1]

---

1. Regarding the self-representation of imperialist powers, Said argues, "The dominant society comes to depend uncritically on natives and their territories perceived as in need of *la mission civilisatrice*." Edward W. Said, *Culture and Imperialism* (New York: Vintage Books, 1993), xix. All subsequent references are to this edition and will be cited parenthetically within the text. Empire's cultural hegemony is reinforced by a network of practices, from missionary activity to literary production. For Said, "the novel, as a cultural artefact

The continuing appeal of the rhetoric of earthquake jeremiads (which posited earthquakes as divine warnings to a sinful populace) during the seventeenth century and into the mid-eighteenth century suggests that modern historiography of the "Enlightenment" has exaggerated the influence of secularism in the eighteenth-century English public sphere. Such an exaggeration has important implications for the relationship between British national identity, colonialism, and the "rise" of the English novel.[2] An analysis of responses to the 1750 London earthquakes, the rhetoric of seventeenth-century earthquake jeremiads, and the providentialism of Samuel Richardson's novels, particularly *Pamela* (1740) and *Clarissa* (1747–48), indicates that all three sets of texts base their narrative impact on the contention that security (national or personal) is dependent on the recognition of temporal instability. This instability, in turn, underscores the preeminence of divine authority as the ultimate arbiter of temporal identity. National morality is therefore the bedrock of national security; religious fidelity

---

of bourgeois society, and imperialism are unthinkable without each other" (*Culture and Imperialism* 71). Homi Bhabha, considering Joseph Conrad's *Heart of Darkness* and V. S. Naipaul's *The Return of Eva Peron*, describes them as "texts of the civilizing mission" that "suggest the triumph of the colonialist moment in early English Evangelism and modern English literature." *The Location of Culture* (London: Routledge Classics, 2007), 149. And Gayatri Spivak, in analyzing Charlotte Brontë's decision to conclude *Jane Eyre* with the "tangent narrative" of the missionary St. John Rivers, notes that "a travesty of the categorical imperative can justify the imperialist project by producing the following formula: make the heathen into a human so that he can be treated as an end in himself." "Three Women's Texts and a Critique of Imperialism," *Critical Inquiry* 12, no. 1 (1985): 248. In other words, while all three theorists seem to acknowledge the possibility of sincere evangelism, they also see that this can "participate in one of the most artful technologies of colonial power" (Bhabha 151)—the notion that colonization equates to civilization.

2. I use the phrase "rise" advisedly. I agree with major challenges to Ian Watt's classic account of the development of the novel in *The Rise of the Novel* (1957)—that it is teleological (John Richetti), Anglocentric (Margaret Doody), and phallocentric (Jane Spencer). Nevertheless, I cautiously concur with Brean Hammond and Shaun Regan in finding the concept of a "rise" to be a useful way of describing the development of the genre of popular literature of eighteenth-century England that we now categorize as the "novel." See Brean Hammond and Shaun Regan, *Making the Novel: Fiction and Society in Britain, 1660–1789* (Basingstoke: Palgrave Macmillan, 2006), 18–28, especially p. 25. See also John Richetti, *Popular Fiction before Richardson: Narrative Patterns, 1700–1739* (1969; repr., Oxford: Clarendon Press, 1992); Margaret Anne Doody, *The True Story of the Novel* (New Brunswick, NJ: Rutgers University Press, 1996); and Jane Spencer, *The Rise of the Woman Novelist: From Aphra Behn to Jane Austen* (Oxford: Blackwell, 1986).

is the keystone to national salvation. Thus hostility to non-Anglicans (including Muslims, Roman Catholics, atheists, and others) derived not from a sense of complacent superiority, but from the conviction that a morally frail nation must either reform or collapse under divine wrath.

The structures of feeling within which people of faith make sense of their world depend on taking seriously concepts like heaven, hell, death, judgment, immortality, and the existence of God. That the referents of these concepts were assumed really to exist is evident in responses to the 1750 earthquakes and in Samuel Richardson's popular novels. His works' didactic moralism can seem extreme, artificial, and complacent to many modern readers when they do not discern Richardson's dark scatological vision (more akin to Jonathan Swift's than, I think, has so far been acknowledged). Recognition of the continued power of these structures of feeling in the mid-eighteenth century—indicated by the rise of the novel and the continuing influence of the jeremiads—calls for a revised historiography of the Enlightenment, one that complicates representing the era as the triumphant secularization of reason.

Gertrude Himmelfarb has pointed out the importance of distinguishing between the pro-religion British and American Enlightenments, which, she argues, saw no necessary divorce between reason and religion, and the French Enlightenment of the *philosophes*. As Himmelfarb sees it, the "driving force of the British Enlightenment was not reason but the 'social virtues' or 'social affections.' . . . For the British moral philosophers . . . religion was an ally, not an enemy."[3] Similarly, Robert Ingram notes of British reactions to the 1755 Lisbon earthquake, "providence was the most common explanation of causation in the period. Like Voltaire, most of the British were horrified by what happened in Lisbon in November 1755, but unlike him they seem to have found a reasonable explanation for this natural evil in traditional Christian theology."[4] Himmelfarb and Ingram join J. C. D. Clark in

---

3. Gertrude Himmelfarb, *The Roads to Modernity: The British, French, and American Enlightenments* (New York: Vintage Books, 2005), 19.

4. Robert Ingram, "'The Trembling Earth Is God's Herald': Earthquakes, Religion and Public Life in Britain during the 1750s," in *The Lisbon Earthquakes of 1755: Representations and Reactions, Studies in Voltaire and the Eighteenth Century*, ed. Theodore D. Braun and John B. Radner (2005; repr., Oxford: Voltaire Foundation, 2008), 115.

questioning the teleological, Whiggish version of "enlightened" progress that casts religion and reason as antithetical in the eighteenth century.

Clark has argued that "Cartesianism may have proposed a Godless, mechanical universe, with matter as inert, atoms colliding like billiard balls to create secondary qualities, but by the late 1660s this model had aroused English fears that the French doctrine would exclude Providence."[5] New philosophies could be as tainted with French associations as Roman Catholicism and political absolutism were following Louis XIV's revocation of the Edict of Nantes (1685). Furthermore, as Clark points out, "the limitations of the natural sciences at this stage of their development were as evident as their achievements."[6] A rational marriage between providentialist explanations of disaster (seeing God as the first cause and natural events as the second cause) and scientific explanations was normative, and this marriage is particularly evident in earthquake jeremiads from the late-seventeenth century through the mid-eighteenth century.[7] In other words, it made sense that England's national security, identity, and integrity rested on its Anglican faith and the recognition of temporal power's dependence on divine authority. Such a framework explains the perennial appeal of providentialist narratives evident in earthquake jeremiads and in the popular prose works that came to be grouped under the category of the "novel."

The continuing appeal of providentialist narratives, which necessarily rely on an eternal rather than a solely temporal perspective on human activity, sits uneasily with postcolonial accounts of the rise of the novel. Edward Said (relying on Ian Watt's canonical but much-challenged theory of the novel's rise) has said that the novel was

> inaugurated in England by *Robinson Crusoe*, a work whose protagonist is the founder of a new world, which he rules and

---

5. J. C. D. Clark, "Providence, Predestination and Progress: Or, Did the Enlightenment Fail?" *Albion: A Quarterly Journal Concerned with British Studies* 35, no. 4 (Winter 2003): 567.

6. Ibid., 566.

7. See, for instance, Maxine Van de Wetering, "Moralizing in Puritan Natural Science: Mysteriousness in Earthquake Sermons," *Journal of the History of Ideas* 43, no. 3 (July–September 1982), 417–38; and Robert Webster, "The Lisbon Earthquake: John and Charles Wesley Reconsidered," in *The Lisbon Earthquakes*, 118.

> reclaims for Christianity and England.... Fielding, Richardson, Smollett, and Sterne do not connect their narratives so directly to the act of accumulating riches and territories abroad.... These novelists do, however, situate their work in and derive it from a carefully surveyed territorial greater Britain, and that *is* related to what Defoe so presciently began. Yet [in accounts of the novel's development] ... the imperial perspective has been neglected. (*Culture and Imperialism* 70)

I concur with Said that the "imperial perspective" yields a great insight into the nature of the novel genre and its imbrications with social authority. But I suggest—based on the evidence of popular providential literature and its representations of British national identity—that it is a mistake to perceive English consciousness about religio-political others (territories or individuals) as a continuous, unvaried, and monolithic phenomenon. Said, Homi Bhabha, and Gayatri Spivak have, to be sure, laid out sophisticated arguments about the complexity of empire rather than treating it as a monolithic phenomenon; but, given Said's own timeline of the intertwined institutionalization of the novel and the British empire, the popularity of providential narratives in the mid-eighteenth century calls for further analysis of this intertwining. According to Said,

> By the time of World War One the British empire had become unquestionably dominant, the result of a process that had started in the late sixteenth century.... By the 1840s the English novel had achieved eminence as *the* aesthetic form and as a major intellectual voice, so to speak, in English society. (*Culture and Imperialism* 71–72)

But responses to the 1750 earthquakes and the association of providential narratives in sermons and novels with images of territorial instability indicate that Britons had an agonistic relationship to their national identity and did not, on the eve of full-fledged British imperialism, perceive themselves as temporally secure or morally exemplary. Such a conclusion has implications for any analysis of the "imperial perspective" of the novel or of the dynamics between British institutionalism (including the colonial apparatus of such practices as missionary activity, education, and the writing of novels) and England's overseas territories. Given Said's theory of the imperialist underpinning of the "rise" of the novel (as he takes it from Watt), and Brean Hammond's and Shaun Regan's more recent description of on the development of the novel as a response to specific market conditions after 1660, a consideration of the intersection of the jeremiads and Richardson's novels—contemporaneous genres of popular providential literature—would enrich current readings of fictionalized imperial consciousness and the representation of religio-political "others."

The connection among English national security, providentialist narratives and rhetoric, and the jeremiad and novel means that, on the eve of the heyday of British imperialism, hostile depictions of religious others by English writers and clergymen were not the result of a comfortable sense of intrinsic superiority to other cultural groups. Rather, they derived from the conviction that doom for unrepentant and unfaithful Christians was imminent and assured.

✶

Several accounts by Londoners of different Protestant persuasions afford to the modern scholar a suggestive, if not holistic, snapshot of contemporary reactions to the earthquakes. The first quake rocked London in the afternoon of February 8, 1750, with the second following almost exactly a month later in the early morning hours of March 8. Bluestocking correspondents Elizabeth Carter and Catherine Talbot exchanged letters lamenting the religious hysteria of the London populace; Charles Wesley, cofounder of Methodism, swiftly published a sermon and a two-part poem series; and Thomas Sherlock, Bishop of London, delivered a ringing sermon denouncing Londoners for their profligate ways—including vices such as lewdness, drunkenness, and failures of proper religious behavior—and identifying the earthquakes as warnings of God's impending punishment.[8] The contrasting

---

8. Catherine Talbot and Elizabeth Carter, *A Series of Letters between Mrs. Elizabeth Carter and Miss Catherine Talbot from the Year 1741 to 1770: To Which Are Added Letters from Mrs. Carter to Mrs. [Elizabeth] Vesey between the Years 1767 and 1787*, vol. 1 (London: F. C. & J. Rivington, 1808); Charles Wesley, "The Cause and Cure of Earthquakes," *A*

accounts of the earthquakes show the variety of positions that could be held regarding the intersection of national identity and Christian belief. The thematic content and rhetorical approach of popular literature of the mid-eighteenth century—including sermons, hymns, and novels—indicates that the Enlightenment in England was far from being a secular affair.

In "A Letter from the lord Bishop of London, to the Clergy and People of London and Westminster; On Occasion of the Late Earthquakes," Bishop Sherlock attributes the earthquakes to England's national sins of forsaking Protestant piety for pornography, popery, and infidelity that even a "Mahometan" nation would abhor. He rails against the "Lewdness and Debauchery that prevail amongst the lowest People," concluding that a "City without Religion can never be a safe Place to dwell in."[9] He identifies pornography (specifically John Cleland's erotic novel *Memoirs of a Woman of Pleasure*, an overtly sexualized response to *Pamela*) as the epitome of the general vice.[10] He asks,

> Have not all the Abominations of the publick Stews been opened to View by lewd Pictures exposed to Sale at Noon-day? Have not Histories or Romances of the vilest Prostitutes been published, intended merely to display the most execrable

---

*Sermon Preach'd from Psalm xlvi.8* (London, 1750); Charles Wesley, *Hymns Occasioned by the Earthquake, March 8, 1750. Part 1* (London, 1750); Charles Wesley, *Hymns Occasioned by the Earthquake, March 8, 1750. Part II* (London, 1750); Thomas Sherlock, *A Letter from Lord Bishop of London to the Clergy and People of London and Westminster; On Occasion of the Late Earthquakes* (London: Vertue and Goadby, 1750).

9. *A Letter from Lord Bishop*, 7. All subsequent citations are to this edition and are cited parenthetically within the text.

10. According to Peter Sabor—editor of the unexpurgated Oxford World's Classics edition of *Memoirs of a Woman of Pleasure*, otherwise known as *Fanny Hill*—Sherlock "blamed [*Fanny Hill*] for the two London earthquakes of February and March 1750, denouncing 'this vile Book, which is an open insult upon Religion and good manners, and a reproach to the Honour of the Government, and the Law of the Country'" (x). See note 8: the quote is from Sherlock's letter to the Duke of Newcastle dated March 15, 1750. Peter Sabor, "Introduction," in *Memoirs of a Woman of Pleasure*, unexpurgated text (Oxford: Oxford University Press, 2008), vii–xxvi. *Memoirs* can be seen as a sexually explicit response to *Pamela*. Both novels, narrated in the epistolary mode by Fanny and Pamela themselves, respectively, present the unexpected economic and social elevation of attractive teenage girls: Fanny through the sex trade, Pamela through the withholding of premarital sex.

Scenes of Lewdness ... What was the Encouragement for Men to dare giving such an Affront not only to the common Sense, but to the common Law of the Country? Was it not the quick Sale these Pictures and these Books had? (8)

The corruption at the heart of the nation is indicated by the populace's desire for pornography, an affront to common sense as well as to national laws. The result is that the English "fly from the Church and crowd to the Playhouse" (8), and Sherlock sternly queries what "Idea" such behavior must "give to all the Churches abroad, of the Manner in which *Lent* is kept in this Protestant Country?" (9). In Sherlock's view, the annual forty days of fasting, repentance, and alms-giving before Easter Sunday were nothing more than a carnival ground of "*Plays, Operas, Musick*, and *Dancing* ... Meetings at *Gardens* ... *Cock-fighting, Prize-fighting*, &c" (9) for Londoners in 1750.

Just as Sherlock believed the vice to be a national epidemic, he also viewed the moral vulnerability it created as a national threat, a weakening that could prove amenable to the incursions of foreign powers. Specifically, Sherlock points out "the great Increase of Popery in this Kingdom," explaining that when

Men have lost all Principles of Religion, and are lost to all Sense of Morality, they are prepared to receive any Superstition ... such Persons not able to digest the wholesome Food of Repentance, by which their spiritual Condition might be gradually mended, greedily swallow the high Cordial of Absolution, which like other Cordials gives some present Ease, but works no Cure. (10)

He concludes that the logical outcome of England's behavior "gives a great Advantage to the Emissaries of *Rome*" (10). Laxity in national morality threatens the very Protestant fabric of England, rendering those who do take religion seriously vulnerable to the blandishments of Roman Catholicism and its uncompromising insistence on the preeminent authority of the Pope in Rome. Catholicism was a religious and a political threat; a failure of Protestant piety was, for Sherlock, a failure of national security. Indeed, pornography and atheism together led to "Proofs of such Malice against the Gospel and the Holy Author of it, as would not be born even in a *Mahometan* Country" (6). England is "even the Mart for Infidelity" (6), and this failure of Christian piety leaves the next generation unfurnished with "Principles of Honour and Virtue" (13) and the nation as a whole vulnerable, in Sherlock's view, to the specious—and politically dangerous—appeal of a hostile foreign religious authority.

Sherlock, as a member of the Anglican religious establishment, was participating in a historical tradition of invoking the figure of the "Mahometan" when domestic troubles threatened the Anglican hierarchy. Nabil Matar, one of the most influential scholars of Anglo-Ottoman relations, observes in English representations of the Ottomans (and of Islam in general) that allusions to "Islam, 'Alcoran,' 'Mahometans' and 'Turks' began to appear in treatises and polemics with noticeable frequency as soon as the Civil Wars loomed in England and Scotland. Indeed . . . in seventeenth-century England, attention to Islam was proportionate to the religious anxiety in society."[11] Moreover, Islam and "Mahometan" societies were represented, according to Linda Darling, as the "negative ideal" and held up as precisely the extreme form of religio-political despotism that England ought to avoid.[12] Frequently, negative representations of Islam or Islamic "others" were grouped with denigrating references to Christian non-Anglicans, especially Roman Catholic "papists"—a much nearer and more insidious kind of domestic threat. If the Ottoman Empire had posed a threat to the geographical and religious integrity of Europe from the fourteenth to the late-seventeenth century, Roman Catholicism and the specter of the Stuarts and Jacobites posed a threat specifically to the English.

Only a few years before the earthquakes the "young Pretender" Charles Edward Stuart had staged an ill-fated invasion of England through Scotland that had resulted in the massacre of the Scottish Highlanders. Responses to the 1750 earthquakes compared the public reaction during the natural disaster to that prompted by the military

---

11. Nabil Matar, *Islam in Britain, 1558–1685* (Cambridge: Cambridge University Press, 1998), 103.

12. See Linda Darling, "Ottoman Politics through British Eyes: Paul Rycaut's *The Present State of the Ottoman Empire*," *Journal of World History* 5, no. 1 (1994): 92.

invasion. Charles Wesley believed God had averted a possible future earthquake just as "he stopt the Invaders in the Midst of our Land, and turn'd them back again, and destroy'd them."[13] And Talbot likewise reflects upon the public reaction to the earthquake: "There is something frightful in such a general panic. Once (when the rebels were expected) this spirit of cowardice, had not a gracious Providence interposed, must have been very fatal to this town."[14] If Islam was the religio-political negative extreme, Roman Catholicism was the threat in the backyard. To Sherlock, England's growing immorality left the back door wide open. It is this instability—the doubt raised about England's national integrity on the geographic, political, religious, and moral fronts—around which Sherlock's anxiety centered.

His sermon also fits squarely in the genre of the earthquake jeremiads that proliferated after the 1692 earthquakes in England, Sicily, and Jamaica. According to several of the jeremiads published in England and Scotland, earthquakes indicated failures of the English populace to rely on God's government. The earthquakes need not directly affect England to be considered a warning for, as John Shower argued, "*The Punishment of* One *People, or Person, should be a Warning unto* All. *The Greek word for* Punishment, *doth signify* Example."[15] He further remarks that some Britons expect a period of peace and stability to follow King William's "Conduct and Victorious Arms," but he concludes soberly "*How little Ground we have to expect this without* Reformation, *I leave to the Consideration of all who seriously believe God's Government of the World, and know what he hath done to other Nations, and People.*"[16] For Shower, temporal victory and military power will be short-lived if God is displeased with England's lack of faithfulness.

13. *The Cause and Cure of Earthquakes*, 20. All subsequent citations are to this edition and are cited parenthetically within the text.

14. Catherine Talbot to Elizabeth Carter, April 5, 1750, *A Series of Letters.*

15. John Shower, *Practical Reflections on the Late Earthquakes in Jamaica, England, Sicily, Malta, &c. Anno 1692. With a Particular, Historical Account of Those, and Divers Other Earthquakes.* (London: John Salusbury at the Rising Sun in Cornhill, and Abraham Chandler at the Chirurgion's Arms in Aldersgate-street, 1693), x. The italics are in the original. I have modernized all instances of the long *s*. My thanks to Nanyang Technological University for the Start-Up Grant that enabled me to access the seventeenth-century texts using the database *Early English Books Online.*

16. Ibid., viii.

Similarly, Thomas Doolittle situates the 1692 earthquake in a providential framework that encompasses the past generation of English history:

> Plague, Fire, and Earthquakes are amongst the most terrible Judgments, whereby the great and holy God doth manifest his sore displeasure against a sinful People . . . *These three* have befallen *London*. The *first* in the GREAT DYING Year, 1665. the *second* in the GREAT BURNING Year 1666. And the *last* in the GREAT TREMBLING present Year 1692.[17]

The providential framework demarcates and compresses history in a distinctive narrative: England is sinful and is being punished according to the three great judgments; whether a disaster occurs one year after or twenty-seven years after another is less important than that they conform to biblical precedents. Shower, Doolittle, and the writers of other jeremiads saw the earthquakes as a warning from God that England should be mindful of divine government if temporal government was to remain stable. One anonymous Scottish minister pointedly described the failures of temporal religious authority in terms of a non-Christian perspective:

> Let the *Mofttes* of Barbary, and *Musslemen* of Turky be limned with our silly Clergy, and their Paganism and Civility shall overreach, their Cristianity. . . . Our Clergy being these 30 Years, like the Woodcoks of *Denmark*, long nibs, fat bellies little brains, and so delight to be. Wittily replyed the Indian King to the Spaniard, he would rather dwell in Hell, as live him in Heaven with such company. . . . We cry out against, *Cain, Judas, Julian, Sodom and Gommorah*! Alas they are but glasses to see our hearts.[18]

---

17. Thomas Doolittle, *Earthquakes Explained and Practically Improved: Occasioned By the late Earthquake on Sept. 8. 1692. In LONDON, Many Other Parts in England, and beyond the Sea. By Thomas Doolittle M. A. Jamaica's Miseries Shew London's Mercies. Both Compared* (London: Printed for John Salusbury at the Rising Sun over against the Royal Exchange in Cornhill, 1693), A2r–A2v.

18. *Gods Voice to Christendom, or, Alarum to Europe: By the Remarkable Earthquakes with the Several Kinds Thereof. . . . By a Minister of CHRIST* (Edinburgh: repr. 1693), 16;

The minister's religious hostility is directed not at non-Christians but at the community of Christian clergy, missionaries, and conquistadores. He may consider members of non-Christian religions to be pagans, but he also considers them civil and witty in contrast to the Christian clergy who are lazy, stupid, and complacent. His contemporary Christians in England and Scotland are equated with the worst offenders in the Hebrew Testament and the Christian gospels; the earthquake should be considered, as his title declares, an "Alarum to *Europe*."

As these passages suggest, by 1750 a tradition of English responses to domestic and foreign earthquakes was well established. While some accounts of foreign earthquakes saw them as punishments of particular foreign populations, many saw earthquakes as general marks of God's displeasure: even foreign disasters ought to call English sinners to repentance.

Charles Wesley responded to the 1750 earthquakes with several texts: the sermon based on Psalm 46 and *Hymns occasioned by the Earthquake* (1750) in two parts, which he later reworked in response to the devastating 1755 Lisbon earthquake described by Voltaire in *Candide* (1759). Wesley structured his response to the earthquakes by contrasting the repentant and faithful chosen people with the unresponsive, unrepentant sinners within the English populace. In contrast to atheists and would-be scientists, Wesley declares that, according to Scripture as well as reason, "Earthquakes are GOD's strange Works of Judgment, the proper Effect and Punishment of Sin" (*Sermon* 6). He puts no faith in the power or endurance of temporal institutions or in individual efforts to flee. Escaping to the countryside will not save sinners from divine wrath, for when earthquakes strike "there is no Time to flee, or Method to escape, or Possibility to resist . . . no Sanctuary or Refuge remains . . . People, without Distinction, in the midst of Health, and Peace, and Business, are buried in a common Ruin, and pass all together into the eternal World" (*Sermon* 14–15). The swiftness with which an earthquake destroys "without Distinction" should, Wesley suggests, provoke a prompt repentance in those who truly believe in God's saving authority.

---

original spelling.

Throughout his sermon, Wesley emphasizes—in line with much seventeenth- and eighteenth-century providentialist rhetoric—the suddenness with which a perfectly quotidian reality can be traumatically disrupted. "Reality" as it has been known can evaporate instantaneously, and this means that the predictive power of "reality," and any calculation of probable outcomes based on it, cannot be relied upon. Karen B. Westerfield Tucker notes the likelihood that Wesley's "knowledge of Scripture, particularly his reading of the apocalyptic texts, inspired him to link the earthquakes with the second coming of Christ, thus giving the hymns a millennial tone."[19] Sometimes the anomalous is the reality. Wesley emphasizes that all of England, its entire population, is under the threat of divine wrath: "For is not this the Nation to be visited?" he asks. "What but national Repentance can prevent national Destruction" (*Sermon* 18).

Because it is faith in the risen Lord that will enable individuals to cry out for Christ's protection when the nation is consumed, anti-Trinitarians become the locus of Wesley's anxiety. In arguably his most specific reference to a particular group of sinners, Wesley addresses God, imploring him to "confound the misbelieving pride / Of those that impiously divide / Thy dearest Son and Thee, / Who will not Him thine Equal own, / But madly threaten to dethrone / The Filial Deity."[20] He categorizes anti-Trinitarians as "the men who infidels condemn, / Nor ever knew themselves the same, / Mere infidels in *heart*."[21] Like Sherlock, Wesley uses Muslims as the negative ideal—the religious group beyond the pale of English national identity. But it is the figure of the anti-Trinitarian, not the Muslim, which arouses his wrath: Islamic doctrine, in Wesley's view, is simply mistaken; anti-Trinitarian belief is willfully impious. In this distinction he coincided with the Scottish minister by explicitly contrasting the integrity of foreign religious groups with the failures of Christian clergy. Writers of seventeenth- and

---

19. Karen B. Westerfield Tucker, "'On the Occasion': Charles Wesley's Hymns on the London Earthquakes of 1750," *Methodist History* 42, no. 4 (July 2004): 217. I am grateful to the archivists of the General Council of Archival History—particularly Michelle Merkel-Brunskill, Assistant Editor of *Methodist History*—for providing me with this article.

20. *Hymns Occasioned by the Earthquake*, Hymn 5, stanza 5.

21. Ibid., stanza 6. Original italics.

eighteenth-century jeremiads were painfully aware that an intelligent non-European would be justified in scoffing at the current practices of so-called Christian piety.

After the first earthquake, and even more so after the second, self-styled prophets as well as clergymen indulged in doomsday predictions to which the populace responded with what amounted to hysteria. Londoners fled to the countryside en masse; multitudes camped out or swarmed the streets praying for deliverance; and many listened to Bishop Sherlock's sermon. Elizabeth Carter and Catherine Talbot saw the earthquakes in providential terms but did not project the sin onto a religio-political scapegoat. Like Sherlock they located the populace's reaction in superstition and wrong-thinking; in line with both Sherlock and Wesley, they saw it as a call to repentance and took it as an occasion to discuss what they considered to be the right kind of religious belief.

On April 3 Talbot wrote to Carter from London concerning the predictions made by a particular "poor madman" who had gained much public attention by claiming another earthquake would destroy London and Westminster on April 5.[22] She admits, "To hear them hawked about this morning almost chilled me; there was something horrid in it, though the only real horror belonging to it, is the pain it must give to weak low-spirited people."[23] Talbot was also aware of the public response to Sherlock's sermon and felt that it was "grievous to think of the scenes of distress, among good, though weak people, which last night was witness to," noting that all "Sunday they were crying about, *The Bishop of London's prayer* . . . The King and Prince have done all they could to check this wildness of fear."[24] In contrast to Sherlock, Talbot portrays the national hysteria not as a salutary movement to moral reform but as a disruption of, indeed a threat to, orderly government.

Talbot, who was basically a foster daughter to Sherlock's fellow clergyman Bishop Thomas Secker and a member of his household ("messages came hither to enquire where my Lord preached, and whether there were not to be prayers in the church at eleven," she noted

---

22. See Talbot to Carter, April 3, 1750, *A Series of Letters*, note 1.
23. Ibid., main text.
24. Talbot to Carter, April 5, 1750, *A Series of Letters*.

to Carter on April 5), saw the irrationality of the public response as an impediment to true piety. "I hope it has now spent itself," she exclaims,

> What grief to think that minds so susceptible of strong impressions, should have been thus affected, by such a foolish cause, that they must be ashamed of it, and perhaps of all serious and right impressions along with it! So from the vilest credulity, we shall I fear see them running into an utter disregard of every thing they ought to reverence and believe.[25]

For Talbot it is softness of mind—the failure to exercise personal rationality—that lies at the root of both immorality *and* religious hysteria. Carter responded with equal grief and bemusement at the state of national morality, particularly as embodied by Londoners who fled the capital, lamenting,

> What an amazing quantity of credulity is there in the world! A bottle conjuror, a madman, any thing but the true and rational objects of belief, are sure to be swallowed without the least examination. No doubt there are a great many of the runaways that deserve great compassion; ignorance and weak spirits are pitiable cases, but that those who have no such excuses should imagine it was in the power of any mortal to fix a day for the destruction of a city by an earthquake, seems strangely unaccountable, but from such principles as one is grieved to think on.[26]

Talbot and Carter lamented the frailty that would lead their fellow Christians to respond irrationally to imminent destruction rather than to use solid Christian faith to meet an adversity that could not, in any case, be accurately predicted.

But Talbot and Carter did see the earthquakes as a divine message, a wake-up call if not, as yet, a damnation. In this they were in agreement with Sherlock and Wesley. The difference resided in how each observer allocated national guilt: Talbot and Carter attributed the nation's frailty

---

25. Ibid.
26. Carter to Talbot, April 28, 1750, *A Series of Letters*.

to its fitful, insufficiently rational faith. Wesley envisioned a moral rejuvenation as necessary, the earthquake being a call to God's chosen people to forsake the world and seek refuge in the wounds of the risen Christ.[27] Sherlock saw the contemporary national proclivity for pornography as being little more than a summons for the papists to disseminate a foreign influence antithetical to the religion and laws for which he believed England stood. All of these writers—Sherlock as the Bishop of London, Wesley as an influential preacher of a populist Christian movement, Talbot as the foster daughter of Bishop Secker (later Archbishop of Canterbury)—had privileged vantage points from which to evaluate England's national religious identity. All likewise shared a belief in what George Starr has called the "subtractive" interpretation of earthquakes, the view that "disasters reveal something about the essential nature of human beings, by showing what is left when all the familiar customs and institutions of civilizations are taken away."[28] The "reality" beneath civilization, according to Sherlock, Wesley, Carter, Talbot, and the seventeenth-century jeremiads—that the temporal world is subordinate to the eternal one—is also crucial to the narrative force of Samuel Richardson's *Pamela*.

The first of Richardson's novels is particularly important in considerations of the "rise" of the novel because of the controversy it provoked, effectively dividing the literary public sphere between Pamelists and anti-Pamelists, the latter including Eliza Haywood (*Anti-Pamela; or, Feign'd Innocence Detected*, 1741) and Henry Fielding (*An Apology for the Life of Mrs. Shamela Andrews*, 1741). As Hammond and Regan point out, "*Shamela* soon became only one single shot, if the most effective, in a controversial battle between writers dubbed 'Pamelists' and 'anti-Pamelists,' the effect of which was to push imaginative fiction onto a higher plane of explicit theorization."[29]

★

---

27. See Westerfield Tucker's careful account of the unifying imagery of Wesley's sermon and poems in "'On the Occasion,'" especially pp. 211–18.

28. G. A. Starr, "Defoe and Disasters," in *Dreadful Visitations: Confronting Natural Catastrophe in the Age of Enlightenment*, ed. Alessa Johns (New York: Routledge, 1999), 32.

29. *Making the Novel*, 27.

*Religion in the Age of Enlightenment*  293

It would, perhaps, be fitting for Aaron Hill—friend of novelist Samuel Richardson, and an ardent defender of Richardson's popular and controversial novel *Pamela*—to have died "in the very minute of the earthquake" on February 8, 1750.[30] *Pamela*'s narrative is reliant upon precisely the confrontation with eternity underscored by the reality of death.

Richardson's servant girl heroine invests in an eternal perspective, which she imagines to be the point of view of a perfect, divine arbiter who judges individual immortal souls, determines earthly life's meaning, and reprioritizes temporal values within an absolute framework. Her consequent worldview enables her to resist her master's sexual advances, refuting the assumption that a servant girl cannot value her own free will. Pamela's fortitude convinces her would-be seducer, Mr. B., of her merit and the two eventually marry, causing surprise and distress among his aristocratic neighbors and relatives. In the fraught confrontation between the headstrong siblings Lady Davers and Mr. B. after the marriage, the personal identity of the heroine is debated using the vocabulary and imagery of the struggle between pagan and Judeo-Christian religious authorities.

Lady Davers accuses Mr. B. of being "worse than an Idolater," of having "made a graven Image" of his lowborn wife while he, "*Jeroboam* like, would have every body else bow down before [his] Calf!"[31] Shifting religious imagery, she imagines her brother as already dead, as having

---

30. Thomas Davies, *Memoirs of the Life of David Garrick, Esq: Interspersed with Characters and Anecdotes of His Theatrical Contemporaries. The Whole Forming a History of the Stage, which Includes A Period of Thirty-Six Years. From the Last London Edition.* Vol. 1 (Boston: Wells and Lilly, 1818), 118. Davies, however, states that the earthquake was February 5, not February 8. Christine Gerrard, in her recent biography of Hill, notes that there are conflicting accounts of the date of Hill's death but that Richardson was present. See Christine Gerrard, *The Muses' Projector, 1685–1750* (Oxford: Oxford University Press, 2003), 247.

31. Samuel Richardson, *Pamela; or, Virtue Rewarded*, ed. Thomas Keymer and Alice Wakely (Oxford: Oxford University Press, 2008), 423. (All subsequent citations are to this edition and will be cited parenthetically within the text.) In contrast, Pamela had likened her imprisonment in Mr. B.'s Lincolnshire house to that of the Jews during the Babylonian captivity in her paraphrase of Psalm 137 (317). As Ingram points out, earthquake jeremiads often cast the English as the biblical Israelites—the chosen people who had wandered far from God but who could hope for mercy after a timely repentance. He observes that by "encouraging the British to think of themselves as God's chosen people,

allied his aristocratic breeding to the dirt from which all mortal life arises and to which it ultimately returns. But Lady Davers unconsciously undermines her own argument: in thinking that she will injure her brother's snobbery by implying that in marrying a servant girl he has found his natural level, she ignores the leveling effect of death. For her, an indiscriminate allusion to the Christian funeral rite—"*Ashes to Ashes, and Dirt to Dirt!*" (424)—is an accurate description of the social suicide of marrying down, of classing oneself with the dirt of the street by disrupting the social hierarchy. But Mr. B., instructed by the arguments Pamela had used to resist his ignoble advances, reminds his sister that she is deploying the language of an eternal, not a temporal, perspective:

> Ay ... Lady Davers, and there we must all end at last; you with all your Pride, and I with my plentiful Fortune, must come to it; and then where will be your Distinction? Let me tell you, except you and I both mend our Manners ... this amiable Girl, whom your Vanity and Folly so much despises, will out-soar us both, infinitely out-soar us; and He that judges best, will give the Preference where due, without Regard to Birth or Fortune. (424)

Richardson's novels, like his heroines, can best be appreciated if the heroines' insistence on legitimating their identities through their relation to eternal, divine authority is taken seriously—not in order to indulge feeble sentimental piety or lachrymose death-bed scenes, but to recognize the heroines' agency in rejecting one system of authority in favor of another. Pamela goes so far as to compare her experience to that of the Virgin Mary, quoting the Magnificat in telling Mr. B., "*My Soul doth magnify the Lord*; for *he hath regarded the low Estate of his Handmaiden,— and exalted one of low Degree*" (311). In line with the earthquake jeremiads, she proclaims that God, not temporal authority, ultimately confers glory. Pamela meditates, during Mr. B.'s absence to visit a seriously ill friend,

> There is no living in this World, without too many Occasions for Concern, even in the most prosperous State. And it is fit

---

as latter-day Israelites, providentialism also served to forge a sense of national solidarity and identity in the face of a foreign enemy" (113).

it should be so; or else, poor Wretches as we are! we should look no further, but be like sensual Travellers on a Journey homeward, who, meeting with good Entertainment at some Inn on the Way, put up their Rest there, and never think of pursuing their Journey to their proper Home. (377–78)

The sentiment, and even the wording, of Pamela's meditation are close to those of the seventeenth-century jeremiads, indicating the continuing force of such rhetoric in popular literature a half century later.[32] Without a continual mindfulness to the instability of temporal status, one endangers one's position in the eternal afterlife. Richardson's central characters are therefore travelers, aliens, and sojourners; their identities are determined in the narrative by which "home" they choose as their final destination. The construction of identity in terms of the boundary between life and death, the subordination of the temporal to the eternal perspective, is widely recognized as crucial to the narrative framework of *Clarissa*.[33] But it is no less crucial to the construction of identity in *Pamela*.

Pamela herself uses the eternal perspective of personal identity to reject the reasoning of Lady Davers's haughty letter, in which the aristocrat demands that her brother not marry a servant girl. Having read the insulting document, Pamela concludes,

---

32. Indeed, the Scottish minister includes a verse meditation in his pamphlet that admonishes the reader regarding the temporal world:
*A place of travel not a place of stay,*
*Such well devoted Pilgrims count their way.*
*Rouze then thy thoughts think what it is,*
*To be partakers of Eternal bliss.*
*For when the dry land God did make appear,*
*Was not that man should think his Heaven here.* (*Gods Voice*, 13; original italics).

33. See particularly the chapter "Holy and Unholy Dying: The Death-bed Theme in Clarissa" in Margaret Doody, *A Natural Passion: A Study of the Novels of Samuel Richardson* (Oxford: Clarendon Press, 1974), 151–87. As Thomas Keymer also notes, "Richardson's practice is as reminiscent of the seventeenth-century divine as of the eighteenth-century sentimentalist: rather than foster a Rousseauvian festival of tears he played, quite dispassionately, on the sensibilities of his readers, and forced them to look death in the eye." Thomas Keymer, *Richardson's* Clarissa *and the Eighteenth-Century Reader* (Cambridge: Cambridge University Press, 2004), 203.

> One may see how poor People are despised by the Proud and the Rich; and yet we were all on a foot originally: And many of these Gentle-folks, that brag of their ancient Blood . . . never think what a short Stage Life is; and that, with all their Vanity, a Time is coming, when they shall be obliged to submit to be on a Level with us . . . Besides, do they not know, that the richest of Princes, and the poorest of Beggars, are to have one great and tremendous Judge, at the last Day; who will not distinguish between them, according to their Qualities in Life? (258)

Lady Davers is justifiably threatened by Pamela. The servant girl destabilizes the class hierarchy of mid-eighteenth-century England because she refuses to see its values as indicative of her actual worth; she insists on subordinating the sociotemporal hierarchy to the radical moral meritocracy she hopes for in eternity.[34] All human individuals, male or female, wealthy or impoverished, are on the same level in relation to the "tremendous Judge" of the "last Day."

Moreover, Pamela's evaluation of wealth and class is a trenchant foreshadowing of the moral squalor of Clarissa's grasping family, the Harlowes, and indicates a continuing fascination on Richardson's part with the leveling effect of death and time. Tellingly, Pamela remarks of the transience of earthly plenty, "How do these Gentry know, that . . . one hundred Years hence or two, some of those now despised upstart Families, may not revel in their Estates, while their Descendants may be reduced to the other's Dunghils?[sic]—And, perhaps, such is the Vanity, as well as Changeableness of human Estates, in *their* Turns set up for Pride of Family, and despise the others" (258). The vicissitudes of time have the same effect as earthquakes: they serve as reminders that monuments to human glory, accomplishment, or status—whether physical buildings or a family's place in the social hierarchy—do not

---

34. Terry Eagleton notes that a "whole moral metalanguage" is necessary to resist sexual domination in *Pamela*. While he sees the novel as "a sickly celebration of male ruling-class power," he also realizes that it offers a "fierce polemic against the prejudice that the most inconspicuous serving maid cannot be as humanly valuable as her social superiors." Terry Eagleton, *The Rape of Clarissa* (Minneapolis: University of Minnesota Press, 1985), 34, 37.

endure, nor are they intrinsic to personal identity. Grand architectural displays may come and go, but dunghills are always with us.

In *Clarissa*, the Harlowe family fits the description of the kind of upstarts Pamela imagines: willfully oblivious to the limits of temporal glory, they would rather cultivate estates than piety. Indeed, Lovelace dismisses their arriviste pretensions by noting of Harlowe Place, "Like Versailles, it is sprung up from a dunghil within every elderly person's remembrance."[35] In Richardson's fiction, the glory of the French monarchy, the English elites, and the new arriviste bourgeoisie—their extravagant palaces, edifices, and domestic monuments—all totter on the reality of their foundations: dunghills. Richardson was as concerned as Jonathan Swift with the moral consequences of taking at face value "gaudy Tulips rais'd from Dung."[36] Shit, like death and time, just happens. Woe to those who forget or willfully ignore this basic reality. Edifices raised on dunghills are not secure, for dunghills are ever changing according to the natural cycles of physical existence. Mistaking the temporal world for the real one, the Harlowes, by their cruelty (born of crudity), give away their inheritance for a bowl of pottage (Genesis 25:30–34).

This is why, in order to triumph within the narrative—to wrest representational control from Lovelace and the Harlowes—Clarissa must move away from her father's house, established on a dunghill, to her Father's house through death. For Richardson's eternal perspective, as Mary Poovey has pointed out in her analysis of providence in Richardson and Fielding, the "details of formal realism index the emergence of the absolute from the quotidian."[37] Those who don't know

---

35. Samuel Richardson, *Clarissa. Or, the History of a Young Lady: Comprehending the Most Important Concerns of Private Life. In Eight Volumes.* 3rd ed. (London: printed for S. Richardson: and sold by John Osborn; by Andrew Millar; by J. and J. Rivington; and by J. Leake, at Bath, 1750–51), 1:231. All subsequent references in the text are to this edition, unless otherwise noted, and are cited parenthetically within the text. I have modernized all instances of the long *s*.

36. Jonathan Swift, "The Lady's Dressing Room," in *The Basic Writings of Jonathan Swift*, selected and with an introduction by Claude Rawson (New York: Random House, 2002), 873.

37. Mary Poovey, "Journeys from This World to the Next: The Providential Promise in *Clarissa* and *Tom Jones*," *ELH* 43, no. 3 (Autumn 1976): 301. The difference between the tragedy of *Clarissa* and the comedy of *Tom Jones* depends on the latter's "narrative

shit, or who refuse to acknowledge its existence within and outside of themselves, will never get away from it. Clarissa—a woman who chooses to spend her leisure hours in a "Poultry-yard" (I: 52), with all its attendant animals, odors, and material wastes—knows more about the reality of dung than any of her family members. Richardson's providential narrative disavows the stability of the ground, the specificities of time and space, by which that very narrative is rendered probable according to the standards of formal realism. The reminder of the cycle of life—the circulations of bodily materials as well as the instability and decay of monuments—that defecation, earthquakes, and Richardson's socially disruptive heroines represent can only be traumatic for characters whose identities are invested in the temporal world.

For the upper classes—in Richardson's fiction or in the physical locales of London, Jamaica, or Lisbon—earthquakes were an uncomfortable reminder that social distinctions were fragile and heavily dependent on conventions, not based on natural distinctions at all. Pamela's ultimate success in proving her worthiness to be Mr. B.'s wife hinged on her assertion of intrinsic merit, which she had emphasized in pleading to Mr. Williams to help her escape from her imprisonment: "Were my Life in question, instead of my Honesty, I would not wish to involve you, or any body, in the least Difficulty for so worthless a poor Creature. But, O Sir! my Soul is of equal Importance with the Soul of a Princess, though my Quality is inferior to that of the meanest Slave" (158). Pamela may be vain, attracted to money, and less than honest with herself about her feelings for Mr. B., but her narrative is distorted when her willingness to subordinate material gain to the eternal joy of her immortal soul is ignored. The soul is central to Richardson's female characters' resistance to abusive temporal authority. Indeed, Clarissa insists to her friend Anna that if her parents would refrain from forcing her to marry the morally and physically repulsive Solmes, they need not worry about her marrying Lovelace, for, as she says, "If they will signify as much to me, they shall see that I never will be his: For I have the vanity to think my soul his soul's superior" (3:255).

---

interpolations" for "as a true providential surrogate, the narrator guarantees the comic structure of the whole" ("Providential Promise" 312).

Throughout Clarissa's trials, which are often of his invention, Lovelace preserves the unsinkable confidence and humor of the committed libertine. He reminds his friend Belford of part of the rake's creed: "We have held, that women have no Souls: I am a very Turk in this point, and willing to believe they have not" (4:330). Lovelace's point relies on a stringent and sexist soul-body dualism, in which a sexual injury done to a woman ceases to exist as soon as her female body does. Significantly—given the complexity of Ottoman representations in eighteenth-century fiction and also, possibly, Richardson's interest in the Jewish Naturalization Bill[38]—the third and heavily revised edition of *Clarissa* (1750–51) substitutes "Turk" where the first edition had "Jew," thus reassigning the belief in women's mortality from the Jewish to the Muslim faith within a year of the earthquake.[39]

That Muslims were considered beyond the pale of English national identity is also evident in a letter from Carter to Talbot the next year, in which she criticizes Richardson's views of young women as he expressed them in an essay published in Samuel Johnson's periodical *The Rambler* (February 19, 1750). In a letter to Talbot of March 4, 1751, Carter fulminates against what she perceives as Richardson's depreciation of women's spiritual and intellectual dignity: "I cannot see how some of his doctrines can be founded on any other supposition than that Providence designed one half of the human species for idiots and slaves. One would think the man was, in this respect, a Mahometan." Talbot, more

---

38. For the widely divergent representations of Islamic figures in seventeenth- and eighteenth-century literature, see Bernadette Andrea, *Women and Islam in Early Modern English Literature* (Cambridge: Cambridge University Press, 2007). The assertion that Muslims denied women's immortality was commonplace in eighteenth-century literature. Bonnie Latimer made a convincing case for Richardson's interest in the Jewish Naturalization Act of 1753 at the 2010 British Society for Eighteenth-Century Studies (BSECS) conference at St. Hugh's College, Oxford. See Bonnie Latimer, "Samuel Richardson and the 'Jew Bill' of 1753." Though the bill did not pass the House of Lords until 1753, it had been under consideration for several years previously.

39. As for the characterization of Judaic theology, Angus Ross, the editor of the Penguin edition of *Clarissa*, which is based on the first edition, points out that Lovelace's comment is a misunderstanding of the Talmud. Ross refers the reader to Adin Steinsaltz's *The Essential Talmud*. See *Clarissa, or the History of a Young Lady*, ed. Angus Ross (London: Penguin Books, 1985), Letter 219, note 2. For an explication of the Talmud's teachings regarding women, see Adin Steinsaltz, *The Essential Talmud, 30th Anniversary edition* (New York: Basic Books, 2006), 182–83.

sympathetic to Richardson than Carter is, justifies his article in terms of both education and women's potential. She uses his fictional creation as an example:

> I will answer your's [sic] in order, and first for the Mahometan Richardson. Fie upon you! . . . He does not pretend to give a scheme (not an entire scheme) of female education, only to say how when well educated they should behave . . . How can you ever imagine that the author of Clarissa has not an idea high enough of what women may be, and ought to be?[40]

With less complexity in their views of religious others than is evident in the seventeenth-century jeremiads, Carter and Talbot assume that Christianity is better—at least for women—than Islam. The same assumption is evident throughout Mary Wollstonecraft's *A Vindication of the Rights of Woman* (1792), most famously in her reference to Milton as "Mahometan" in his representation of Eve.[41] On one hand, such sentiments indicate the increasingly condescending attitude toward Islam (and other Eastern religions) that would subtend British colonial efforts; on the other, they indicate the continuing importance (and complexity) of religious identity in representations of personal and national identity into the late eighteenth century.

The range of responses to the 1750 earthquakes indicates that individuals in positions of religious and literary prominence were far from feeling, in the period leading into the full development of the British Empire, that England's national morality as it was currently practiced was anything of which to be proud. Indeed, Islamic peoples were often portrayed as having more integrity and being less of a domestic threat than groups who espoused the "wrong" kind(s) of Christianity. This context complicates the notion that proponents of the British Empire had a monolithic and unqualified belief in English moral integrity and this, in turn, complicates assessments of the British understanding of *la mission civilisatrice*, the belief that "natives and their territories" needed

---

40. Talbot to Carter, March 16, 1751, *A Series of Letters*.
41. Mary Wollstonecraft, *A Vindication of the Rights of Men with A Vindication of the Rights of Woman and Hints*, ed. Sylvana Tomaselli (Cambridge: Cambridge University Press, 2001), 87.

the moral guidance of superior Western powers, which Said had identified as the rhetorical engine of the imperial project (*Culture and Imperialism* xix).

This is not to dispute Said's and other postcolonial theorists' criticism of the Christian colonizers' hypocrisy and sense of moral superiority that fueled the colonial project—"white men, seeking to save brown women from brown men," as Gayatri Spivak has put it.[42] It is, rather, to heed Said's warning that no culture is "single and pure," that each is "hybrid, heterogenous, extraordinarily differentiated, and unmonolithic" (*Culture and Imperialism* xxv). Therefore, scholars studying colonialism must not think in terms of a uniform, monolithic Christian attitude; rather, they must be attentive to the spectrum of individual Christian perceptions of the relative morality of Christian and non-Christian populations.

If, as Said argued, England's imperial perspective was developed from the sixteenth century, was incorporated into the novel beginning with *Robinson Crusoe* (1719), and was institutionalized in that genre by the 1840s, what did England's empire mean to those who flocked to Sherlock's sermons, sang Wesley's hymns, or bought providentialist novels? It cannot be denied that atrocities were committed in the name of religion and for the glory of empire, but secular skepticism will only yield a partial understanding of the representational frameworks that supported, among other endeavors, *la mission civilisatrice*. Based on the evidence of popular literature—sermons, hymns, and novels—Britons believed in the existence of their immortal souls and believed that those souls would be rewarded or punished in eternity. These beliefs must be taken into account when evaluating the representation of religious difference at home and in England's colonies.

Theorists of the association between the novel, empire, and the Enlightenment must therefore acknowledge the complexity of English self-representations, especially as refracted through the lens of religious identity. Such an acknowledgment would surely be consistent with Said's own injunction to engage in a "contrapuntal" and "nomadic"

---

42. Gayatri Chakravorty Spivak, "Can the Subaltern Speak?" in *Marxism and the Interpretation of Culture*, ed. Cary Nelson and Lawrence Grossberg (London: Macmillan, 1988), 305.

approach to historiography (*Culture and Imperialism* xxv). And this approach would, in turn, lead to a richer historiography of the British Enlightenment, one attentive to the full narrative power produced by the partnership of faith and reason in popular literature.

# Reading Diderot's *La Religieuse* as an Evangelical Novel

*Muriel Schmid*

> "The 'evangel' died on the cross."
> F. Nietzsche, *The Antichrist* (§39)

Denis Diderot's novel, *La Religieuse*, has traditionally been read as a diatribe against convent life. Diderot's critique is then described as twofold: first, he strongly condemns the common practice of forced vows; and second, he describes life in a convent as fundamentally unnatural, leading individuals to perverse behaviors. Suzanne Simonin, the third daughter of a Parisian lawyer, is the main character of the novel, and her fate illustrates Diderot's critique. As the reader discovers in the course of the narrative, her birth is the result of an affair, and her mother regards her illegitimate daughter as a source of guilt and shame. When she is sixteen, Suzanne is therefore sent to the convent as a way for her parents to safely make her disappear from their life. In a last attempt to escape her fate, Suzanne publicly refuses to pronounce her solemn vows during the official ceremony and begs her parents to spare her from convent life. In response to this public scandal, she is sequestered in her parents' home; under their pressure and lack of compassion, she finally agrees to enter the monastic life. Once Suzanne is trapped in a religious life she did not choose, the novel tells the story of the abuses she suffers at the hands of both her fellow nuns and the

Mothers Superior, ultimately supporting Diderot's argument against the very principle of convent life. Each Mother Superior who takes care of Suzanne's community seems to personify a form of perversion—obsessive mysticism, sadism, and lesbianism—that Diderot attributes to negative religious experiences. Diderot has been credited with using a typology and a terminology in his descriptions that stems from a newly formulated analysis of feminine sexuality on the one hand, and emotional disorders (e.g., hysteria) on the other.[1]

In light of her suffering, Suzanne appeals to the judiciary system to be released from her vows. Monsieur Manouri, the lawyer who takes up Suzanne's case, pleads for her and questions the fundamental justification of convents. His plea sums up Diderot's critique:

> Does God, who created man as a social being, approve of him locking himself away? Can God who created man as such a fickle and fragile being, allow such rash vows? Can these vows, which fly in the face of our natural inclinations, ever be properly observed by anyone other than a few abnormal creatures in whom the seeds of passion have withered and whom we should rightly consider as monsters . . . ?[2]

---

1. On female sexuality and *La Religieuse*, see Lieselotte Steinbrügge, *The Moral Sex: Woman's Nature in the French Enlightenment* (Oxford: Oxford University Press, 1995), 41–53. On the lesbian component of *La Religieuse*, see Jennifer Waelti-Walters, *Damned Women: Lesbians in French Novels, 1796–1996* (Montreal: McGill University Press, 2000), 11–21. And for an analysis of the three "pathologies" described in *La Religieuse*, see Irene Fizer, "Women 'Off' the Market: Feminine Economies in Diderot's *La Religieuse* and the Covent Novel," in *Illicit Sex: Identity Politics in Early Modern Culture*, ed. Thomas DiPiero and Pat Gill (Athens: University of Georgia Press, 1997), 80–108; or Marie-Claire Vallois, "Politique du paradoxe: tableau de mœurs/tableau familial dans La Religieuse de Diderot," *Romanic Review* 76, no. 2 (March 1985): 162–71. In the last convent of the narrative, Suzanne experiences, without fully understanding it, a sexual relationship with the Mother Superior; those scenes have produced a wealth of scholarship and are quoted incessantly. For a more general overview of the history of the novel and its interpretations, see the classic study by George May, *Diderot et 'La Religieuse'* (Paris: PUF, 1954). For a more concise overview, see Vivienne Mylne, *La Religieuse: Critical Guides to French Texts* (Valencia: Grant & Cutler, 1981).

2. . Denis Diderot, *The Nun*, trans. Russell Goulbourne (Oxford: Oxford University Press, 2008), 14. All subsequent quotes of Diderot's novel will be cited from this translation.

Much attention has been given to Diderot's medical, sexual, and anticlerical discourse; little has been said about Suzanne's faith as a potentially positive example for Christian believers. In the pages that follow, I argue that Suzanne embodies a form of faith that is strong, personal, and fully independent from all authorities. What has been read by critics as a Jansenist response to suffering constitutes, as I will show, a Protestant model of faith grounded in the individual's relationship with God and centered on the interpretation of Jesus' death as *evangelion*, or good news—the ultimate revelation of the divine. I want to suggest that Diderot's *La Religieuse* represents a unique genre, what I will call the evangelical novel, which shapes its primary character through the interpretation of early Christian faith.[3]

## Opening Scenes

Published posthumously in 1796, *La Religieuse* is the result of a long gestation; Diderot last revised his manuscript in 1780, four years before his death, but the story began in 1758 when Marguerite Delamarre, a nun from the Longchamp convent, asked the authorities to release her from her vows, arguing that her parents had sent her to the convent without her consent. Diderot drew from this well-known *fait divers* the basic storyline of his novel. Almost forty years elapsed between the actual events on which the narrative is built and the publication of Diderot's novel. Between 1760 and 1780,[4] Diderot actively worked on his text, recounting the misfortunes of Suzanne, Marguerite Delamarre's fictional counterpart.

---

3. The term "evangelical" as it is used throughout this essay refers to the Greek *euangelion*. Both the French *évangile* and the German *Evangelium* still reflect the Greek root of the word and do not have the same political and charismatic connotation as the English "evangelical."

4. Aside from recognizing the overt social and institutional critique, numerous scholars have read Diderot's novel as the product of his avowed admiration for Richardson's novel of sensibility. Indeed, Diderot published his *Éloge de Richardson* in 1762 and writes most of *La Religieuse* while discovering Richardson and the virtues of the novel of sensibility. A partial English translation of his *Eloge* is available on the University of Virginia website: http://graduate.engl.virginia.edu/enec981/dictionary/25diderotC1.html. For a presentation of the parallels between Richardson and Diderot based on *La Religieuse*, see David Marshall, *The Surprising Effects of Sympathy: Marivaux, Diderot, Rousseau, and Mary Shelley* (Chicago: University of Chicago Press, 1988), 84–104.

If the novel encountered wide success in terms of its number of editions and sales between the end of the eighteenth century and the beginning of the nineteenth century, as of the mid-nineteenth century, critics reviewed it negatively and accused it of being poorly written as well as scandalously provocative. The ideological attacks formulated against Diderot's depiction of women's convents focused primarily on its anticlerical and pornographic elements, which were condemned as unrealistic and slanderous. This negative reputation haunted *La Religieuse* throughout most of the nineteenth century and the first half of the twentieth century and led to two official bans on its publication in 1824 and 1826.

In May 1966, the French filmmaker Jacques Rivette released his film *La Religieuse* at the Cannes Festival; it was a screen adaptation of Diderot's novel published almost two centuries earlier. Yet the film was censored at the end of March 1966 under the auspices of the state secretary of information, Yvon Bourges, and its distribution forbidden. Parisians waited until November 1967 to see the movie and it finally made its way to New York's theaters in July 1971.[5] This episode of censorship in the French arts is quite unique and reveals the polemical status of Diderot's novel. Aside from the polemical link between Rivette's film and Diderot's novel, Rivette's cinematographic adaptation of *La Religieuse* provides a useful frame for the argument of this essay.

Due in part to an initial theater adaptation of the novel by Rivette and Jean Gruault in 1963, the film incorporates many elements directly inspired by the experience of the stage. In a recent study on the movie, Kevin Jackson notes:

> In fact, Rivette goes out of his way to signal the theatricality of the enterprise: before the opening credits roll, the soundtrack is filled with the noise of an audience shuffling and murmuring, to

---

5. See review by Vincent Canby, "'Nun' Adapted from 'La Religieuse,'" *The New York Times*, July 9, 1971. For a detailed account of the controversy, see Jean-Claude Bonnet, "Revoir *La Religieuse*," in *Interpréter Diderot aujourd'hui*, ed. Elisabeth de Fontenay and Jacques Proust (Paris: Le Sycomore, 1984), 59–79.

be silenced by the traditional *trois coups* [three knocks] which announce that a play is about to begin.[6]

After the three traditional knocks and other theatrical signifiers that open the scene, a rising red curtain signals to the viewer the actual beginning of the play. However, the curtain uncovers the chapel of a convent with a priest in full attire and nuns ready for the ceremony of a profession. The initial perception of the space shifts immediately: from a theater atmosphere, the viewer moves into the sacred space of a church to witness Suzanne's solemn vows. In its opening scene, the film superposes several conventional forms of representation: the viewer of the movie is also the spectator of a play who is then transformed into a member of a church congregation. In so doing, Rivette's opening scene conveys a clear interpretative choice: "the religious ceremony, in other words, is regarded as a species of staged performance."[7]

Once the viewer has passed through these various levels of representation, he or she has entered the chapel alongside the attendees and becomes a member of the congregation gathered for Suzanne's profession. From this perspective, the camera can introduce another interpretative element in the viewer's field of vision: the physical barrier that separates the congregation and the celebrants. As Fabienne-Sophie Chauderlot aptly describes it:

> The spectators will find themselves within the audience of friends and family having come to attend Suzanne's official vows and symbolic wedding with God. But that is part of the literary story. Visually, the ceremony is re-presented behind vertical bars that force the spectator to grasp it in spatial terms. Clearly evoking a jail, the lines both block the vision of Suzanne and draw the spectators' attention to the film's object of focus: enclosure.[8]

---

6. Kevin Jackson, "'Carnal to the Point of Scandal': On the Affair of *La Religieuse*," in *Eighteenth-Century Fiction on Screen*, ed. Robert Mayer (Cambridge: Cambridge University Press, 2005), 149.

7. Jackson, "'Carnal to the Point of Scandal,'" 149.

8. Fabienne-Sophie Chauderlot, "'Becoming-Image': Deleuzian Echoes in Jacques Rivette's *La Religieuse*," *Eighteenth-Century Life* 25 (Winter 2001): 90.

Throughout the movie, multiple scenes use similar visual images and provoke similar effects on the viewer: grids and lines striate its austere décor and reinforce the strong sense of separation between an outside and an inside. Marc Buffat notes that this visual technique leaves the viewer at a safe distance from the reality being observed:

> La grille du choeur . . . [et] le rideau . . . séparent en somme deux mondes étrangers l'un à l'autre: celui des spectateurs, de ce côté-ci de la grille, celui des personnages, de l'autre côté de la même grille.[9]

> [The grille of the choir . . . and the curtain . . . somehow separate two worlds alienated from each other: the spectators' on this side of the grille, the characters' on the other side of the same grille. (My translation.)]

Unlike the viewer, the reader of the novel crosses these separations. Suzanne Simonin's memoirs, a first-person narrative that cannot be fully reproduced on the screen, allows its reader to enter into the inside space with her. Diderot's textual rendering of the chapel scene is indicative of this perspective: whereas the film leaves the viewer always on the side of the congregation, the same scene in the novel ends when the curtain falls (without any mention of it rising) and forcefully traps the reader behind the scenes with Suzanne:

> As I spoke one of the nuns drew the curtain across the grille, and I realized that it was pointless continuing [appealing to the audience]. The nuns surrounded me and reproached me vigorously; I listened to them in silence. I was taken to my cell and locked in. (*The Nun* 14)

If Rivette's movie captures brilliantly the feeling of entrapment that Suzanne experiences in her convent, Diderot's narrative seeks to implicate the reader in this experience. Rather than inviting the reader to a theatrical performance set in a convent, Diderot's novel takes the

---

9. Marc Buffat, "Pour un Spectateur Distant," *Eighteenth-Century Life* 25 (Winter 2001): 75.

reader behind the walls of the convent, putting him or her in Suzanne's place. As I suggest, this literary device of entrapment forces the reader to question for him- or herself the status of certain forms of religion *as* entrapment. And if Suzanne's role is initially to lead the reader to this interrogation through an intimate engagement with her experience, she equally offers an example of faith that can be understood as a viable alternative to the perversions of institutional Christianity—namely, Catholicism as portrayed in the novel.

In order to develop my argument, I will look at three fundamental concepts that shape Diderot's narrative and its structure. First, I will analyze the role of the veil at the beginning of the novel, which starts well before Rivette's movie does, and demonstrate how this specific piece of clothing introduces an important facet of Diderot's critique of convent life as a hypocritical form of religious experience. Second, I will interpret Diderot's famous literary device of mystification in relationship to the religious notion of mystery and the tension it establishes between truth and religious lies. Third, I will show how the images of the cross and Jesus' crucifixion play an important role in how Suzanne understands her faith and ultimately redefines it for the reader.

## *Veil and Vows*

Sent to a convent at the age of sixteen-and-a-half, Suzanne understands her situation to be temporary and expects soon to be introduced to her future husband just as her sisters had been before her. Her hope is shattered when Father Séraphin, the spiritual director of the family, comes to see her and announces that her parents' fortune has been depleted by her sisters' dowries. She is then left with only one alternative—to take the veil [*prendre l'habit*]. Despite Suzanne's protest that she has "no inclination whatsoever towards the religious life" (*The Nun* 5), her parents' attitude is unwavering. The exchange between Father Séraphin and Suzanne sets the narrative into motion: as of this moment, Suzanne loses her freedom of movement and action and is confined thereafter to an unwanted religious life. The Mother Superior advises her to accept her fate for the time being: "What are you being asked to do? To take the veil? So! Why don't you? What does it commit you to?" (*The Nun* 6). Convinced by the Mother Superior's argument, Suzanne agrees to enter the novitiate, noting "How quickly all the preparations were made! The date was set, my habit made" (*The Nun* 6). The veil, along with the habit, becomes the tangible object that transforms Suzanne into *Sister Suzanne* (*The Nun* 7) and thus functions as a synecdoche for convent life. The definition of "voile" in the *Encyclopédie* refers to this function: "le *voile* ... au figuré, comme chrétien, ... considère l'état des filles qui prennent le *voile*, c'est-à-dire qui se font religieuses [the *veil* ... from a Christian perspective ... refers to the state of girls who take the *veil*, i.e., become nuns (my translation)]."

The description of Suzanne's novitiate follows and opens a new universe to the reader: the hidden reality of cloistered life. Suzanne's depiction of this reality quickly indicates that the reader is about to discover a dark and unknown side of convent life: "I will spare you the details of my novitiate. If one observed all its austerities, it would be unbearable" (*The Nun* 7). Suzanne insists on the "nonsense" of it all and the thorns that accompany such a life. The Mother Superior practices the "dark art" of seducing the young nuns into convent life, constantly fabricating lies. Everyone conspires to "prepare young, innocent girls for forty, fifty years of despair and perhaps eternal suffering" (*The Nun* 8). Despite Suzanne's resistance, the date of her solemn vows is fixed: "Every effort was made to obtain my consent, but when it became evident that these efforts were made in vain, the decision was taken to proceed without my consent. From that moment on I was locked in my cell" (*The Nun* 11). Suzanne cannot but see her future as a useless sacrifice.[10]

Rivette's movie starts after Suzanne's novitiate, on the very day of Suzanne's profession; however, as shown above, Diderot's narrative slowly sets the tone of the novel and introduces the scene of Suzanne's profession with an initial description of convent life as Suzanne herself discovers it, full of hypocrisy and austerities. In this environment, Suzanne's fate corresponds to a death sentence: "Alas, I have neither father nor mother; I'm a poor, wretched girl who's hated and who's to be buried alive in this place" (*The Nun* 5). Diderot's introduction renders

---

10. For a Girardian reading of Suzanne's fate, see Jean Balcou, "A propos de *La Religieuse* de Diderot: la terreur et le sacré," in *Le siècle de Voltaire* (Oxford: Voltaire Foundation, 1987), 47–54.

the scene of Suzanne's forced profession extremely distressful; by this time, the reader, unlike Rivette's viewer, knows what awaits Suzanne behind the convent's walls. Thus, when Suzanne attempts for the last time to protest and escape her fate at the moment of her vows, the fall of the curtain along with the silencing and the entrapment it represents becomes very powerful. In the novel, the curtain of the chapel is not really a reminder of a stage performance, but rather a direct amplification of Suzanne's veil, symbolizing the enclosure that awaits her in the convent. The veil and the curtain hide Suzanne and at the same time reveal the secret reality that exists behind the bars.

## *Mystery and Mystification*

As mentioned above, the story of Suzanne is inspired by real events and the experience of Marguerite Delamarre,[11] who, in 1758, tried to be released from vows she pronounced against her will. When one of Diderot's friends, the Marquis de Croismare, left Paris to live in the countryside, Diderot and several friends exploited his absence to construct an elaborate ruse to bring him back to Paris. Diderot used the story of Marguerite Delamarre to write the fictional memoirs of a nun who appeals to the Marquis de Croismare for help to escape.[12] The entire structure of the novel in its published form depends on this specific context of production: the fictional memoirs written in Suzanne's voice are accompanied by the "Préface-Annexe" which discloses for the reader the epistolary exchange between Suzanne (fictive letters) and the Marquis (revised actual answers). As Herbert Dieckmann notes:

> To be sure, the preface still gives the immediate occasion for the novel, its origin in a trick played on a real person. But soon the trick became part of the overall invention, and as Diderot combined part of the correspondence with the novel and

---

11. For a reconstruction of the events that inspired Diderot's character Suzanne, see May, *Diderot et 'La Religieuse,'* or Jacques Proust, "Recherches nouvelles sur *La Religieuse*," in *Diderot Studies VI* (Genève: Droz, 1964), 197–214.

12. Ultimately, the hoax failed to convince the marquis to come back to Paris; he may have quickly realized that the story was the product of his friends' imagination and played along without being fooled. See Vivienne Mylne, "Truth and Illusion in the 'Preface-Annexe' to Diderot's 'La Religieuse,' " *The Modern Language Review* 57, no. 3 (July 1962): 350–56.

modified the original text, the line could no longer be drawn between the "real" story and the work of art.[13]

Because of this particular frame, *La Religieuse* has been seen as the epitome of Diderot's use of mystification. The word "mystification" appears in French in 1764 and stems from the word *mystères*, a Christian word that refers primarily to the sacraments. As Julia Abramson adds in her study of the form, "To Diderot and the other philosophes who eventually adopted the term 'mystification' and expanded its meaning, this relationship [to the mystery] was of prime importance."[14] The article "mystère" in the *Encyclopédie* illuminates this relationship:

> Ces secrets de la religion étoient appellés des *mysteres*, non parce qu'ils étoient incompréhensibles, ni élevés au-dessus de la raison, mais seulement parce qu'ils étoient couverts & déguisés sous des types & des figures, afin d'exciter la vénération des peuples par cette obscurité.

> [The secrets of religion were called *mysteries*, not because they were incomprehensible, nor beyond reason, but only because they were covered over and disguised behind types and figures, in order that this obscurity might stimulate the veneration of the people.[15]]

Analysis of Diderot's works shows recourse to various forms of practical jokes and hoaxes among which *La Religieuse* constitutes a unique example. Aside from the "Préface-Annexe" and the rhetorical function it plays, the genre of the novel itself complicates the concept of mystification. More than any other genre, the novel allows Diderot to blur reality and fiction in an extensive and radical way. In his study on the phenomenon of mystification in Diderot's works, Jean Catrysse draws a direct parallel between mystification and the novel: "comme la

---

13. Herbert Dieckmann, "The Preface-Annexe of *La Religieuse*," in *Diderot Studies II* (Westport, CT: Greenwood Press, 1971), 31. Dieckmann's essay has become the classic study on the "Préface-Annexe"; it is followed by a reproduction of Diderot's manuscripts.

14. Julia Abramson, *Learning From Lying: Paradoxes of the Literary Mystification* (Newark: University of Delaware Press, 2005), 38.

15. Quoted in ibid.

mystification, le roman est un mensonge, il nous présente une réalité volontairement altérée, sans pour autant cesser d'être vraisemblable" [like mystification, the novel is a lie, it presents a reality deliberately altered, without stopping to be realistic (my translation)].[16] The novelistic writing paired with mystification sheds light on the interplay between reality and fiction, truth and lie, and leaves the reader wondering about the powerful ability of any imaginary narrative to shape his or her reality and belief system. If, as the first reviewers of the "Préface" rightly noted, "to include the preface is to destroy the illusion,"[17] it also inevitably points toward the power of lies, manipulation, and fiction.

Similarly, Suzanne's memoirs recount countless lies and manipulations. *La Religieuse* becomes then a perfect case of mystification and offers a sort of a *mise en abîme* of the phenomenon. Originally initiated as practical joke, the story eventually becomes a work of fiction that denounces the hidden reality of religious lies. In her study, Abramson describes the role of mystification for the *philosophes* as "a cycle that enacts a drama of enlightenment. It is a carefully planned incident that alters reality by means of deception. . . . The cycle of mystification and demystification is thus a secular counterpart to revelation."[18] In this light, rather than being a mere critique of the unnatural conditions of convent life, *La Religieuse* can easily be read as a broader critique of religious mystification, which appears here to be characterized as religious lies.

Elisabeth de Fontenay remarks that, in his treatment of religion, "Diderot is a direct descendant of Spinoza,"[19] and that he formulates a critique of religion as a type of abuse made up of lies, deceit, and secrets that enslave individuals. In the novel, the descriptions of the convent become illustrations of this ongoing critique. After her profession of faith, Suzanne is incapable of recalling what happened during the ceremony, and she describes her state as "physically alienated," similar to a "long illness" lasting several months (*The Nun* 30).

---

16. Jean Catrysse, *Diderot et la mystification* (Paris: Nizet, 1970), 296.
17. Dieckmann, "The Preface-Annexe," 21.
18. Ibid., 26.
19. Elisabeth de Fontenay, *Diderot: Reason and Resonance*, trans. Jeffery Melhman (New York: George Braziller, 1982), 28.

Suzanne's fate exemplifies the effects of organized religion on innocent people: it entraps them, transforms them into either monsters or slaves, tricks them, makes them suffer, and eventually kills them—the deaths of several nuns are recounted in Suzanne's memoirs. It is striking, however, that in spite of this oppressive and hypocritical environment, Suzanne never loses faith, always reads her Bible, rejects all sects, and has no issues "with being called a Christian" (*The Nun* 33). Based on these elements of the narrative, I want to suggest that Diderot represents in Suzanne his vision of an enlightened believer.

### *The Power of the Crucified God*

Despite her suffering and despair, Suzanne's faith never weakens. On the contrary, Suzanne prays constantly, asking God for help and support. Alice Laborde aptly remarks:

> Mais une force plus puissante la guide, sa foi en Dieu, sa croyance qu'Il est là, présent, toujours à ses côtés, seul témoin, bien souvent, de ses malheurs. Cette présence constante de Dieu semble écarter d'elle la possibilité de tout conflit de conscience. On ne la voit jamais tergiverser entre le bien et le mal, point de combat intérieur, elle ne se pose pas de question, elle connaît toujours la réponse. Elle n'est pas une sainte mais elle est à sa manière une privilégiée.[20]

> [A powerful force guides her, her faith in God, her conviction that He is there, always standing by her side, unique witness, often, to her suffering. God's constant presence seems to prevent her from a conflict of conscience. We never see her hesitate between good and evil or suffer internal conflict. She does not ask questions as she always already knows the answer. She is not a saint, yet she is in some sense privileged. (My translation.)]

The very night preceding her profession, Suzanne "cried out to God for help" and "called on him to witness the violence" being done to her (*The*

---

20. Alice Laborde, "Le Paradoxe de La Religieuse," *Pacific Coast Philology* 2 (April 1967): 29.

*Nun* 12). More importantly, at the height of the abuses she suffers at the hands of her fellow nuns, Suzanne declares:

> It was then that I came to feel that Christianity was superior to all other religions in the world. What profound wisdom there was in what benighted philosophy calls the folly of the cross. In the state I was in, how would the image of a happy and glorious lawgiver have helped me? I saw that innocent man, his side pierced, his head crowned with thorns, his hands and feet pierced with nails, and dying in agony, and I said to myself: "This is my God." (*The Nun* 65)

In this passage, the strength of Suzanne's faith emerges: she embodies the believer put to the test who confesses, despite her suffering, the superiority of Christianity. Significantly, the superiority of Christianity is directly associated with the "folly of the cross" and the death of the innocent.

Two biblical echoes shape Suzanne's confession of faith. The first passage is found in Paul's first letter to the Corinthians (chapter 1, verses 18–25), which presents the ultimate paradox of God's revelation through the cross. Suzanne's words about the cross repeat the beginning of this passage with remarkable precision: "For the message of the cross is foolishness to those who are perishing, but to us who are being saved it is the power of God" (NIV). The French translation of the Bible by de Sacy (first published in 1667 and reprinted numerous times during the eighteenth century) renders this verse with the French word "*folie*." This biblical reference would have been impossible to miss for anyone who was educated in Christian theology or who had any knowledge of Paul's letters.

A second passage informing Suzanne's reading of the cross comes from the Passion narrative, here taken from Mark's Gospel (chapter 15, verse 39): "When the centurion, who stood there in front of Jesus, heard his cry and saw how he died, he said, 'Surely this man was the Son of God!'" (NIV). Suzanne repeats the words of the centurion, only able to confess Jesus as the son of God at the very moment of Jesus' death on the cross.

In light of these two biblical references, Suzanne's words represent a reminder that God's ultimate presence is revealed under the most unexpected circumstances; Suzanne's Christian God is a paradoxical figure. If Suzanne is totally misunderstood in her convent, she also directly accuses the *philosophes* who criticize the church of being as much in error as the priests: they promote a "benighted philosophy" that completely misunderstands the "folly of the cross" and its wisdom. *Philosophes* and priests alike have yet to read Jesus' death as the ultimate manifestation of God's paradoxical presence.

George May ends his analysis of Suzanne's meditation at the cross by stating, "Si l'auteur, en effet, n'est pas chrétien, il l'a été et l'héroïne dont il tient la plume ne cesse jamais d'être chrétienne" [If the author is not Christian, he was Christian at some point, and his main character, for whom he writes, never ceases to be Christian (my translation)].[21] May goes as far as affirming that Suzanne's words reflect Diderot's sincerity. However, I want to suggest instead that Diderot formulates a theological paradigm that becomes an alternative to the hypocrisy of the official Christian institution. In opposition to Suzanne's forced profession at the altar of the church, the personal meditation at the crucifix while Suzanne is alone in her cell expresses her true understanding of Christian faith, rooted in a paradoxical understanding of God's manifestation.

## Deus Sub Contrario *and the Theology of the Cross*

Throughout the New Testament, the Greek word for "veil" (*katapetasma*) appears only six times, the most important occurrence of which coincides with the exact moment of Jesus' death in the Passion narrative, originally found in Mark 15:38 (with its parallels in Matthew 27:51 and Luke 23:45): "The curtain [*voile*/veil][22] of the temple was torn in two from top to bottom" (NIV). The traditional interpretation of this passage links the death of Jesus with the opening/unveiling of the Holy of Holies in the Temple of Jerusalem. Customarily closed to common believers and practitioners, the Holy of Holies is the most sacred space

---

21. May, *Diderot et 'La Religieuse,'* 168.
22. The seventeenth- and eighteenth-century French translations of the New Testament use the word "voile" in this passage. See again the translation by de Sacy.

in the Jewish Temple where God himself was said to reside. Priests alone are authorized to enter this space. All three synoptic Gospels indicate that Jesus' death opens this sacred space and gives everyone access to it. Following the tearing of the curtain, the Roman centurion confesses his conviction that Jesus is truly the son of God.

If one interprets *La Religieuse* in light of its biblical allusions and Suzanne's personal creed, God's revelation, according to the novel, is deliberately linked to the cross and the death of Jesus; the whole novel seems then to point to the crucifixion as the only moment of truth set against religious lies and secrecy. By a succession of biblical allusions, the veil/curtain that initially represents Suzanne's entrapment is associated with Jesus' death and the uncovering of God's presence. Moving beyond scholarship that sees in Suzanne a Jansenist nun,[23] I want to conclude on the suggestion that Suzanne professes a theology of the cross inspired by Martin Luther.

Jacques Proust is one of the leading partisans of reading Suzanne's character as a Jansenist nun. In support of his argument, he cites one passage in which Suzanne refuses to pledge allegiance to the papal bull *Unigenitus* issued against Jansenism: "When they asked me if I accepted the Papal Bull, I replied that I accepted the Gospels" (*The Nun* 34). Proust develops his argument further by analyzing persecutions perpetrated against Jansenist nuns as recorded in the *Nouvelles ecclésiastiques*, an underground eighteenth-century Jansenist publication. In his analysis, Proust notices many parallels between the punishments imposed on Suzanne and the ones practiced against Jansenists nuns in convents of that period. Based on his findings, Proust sees in *La Religieuse* a militant novel denouncing the persecutions against Jansenists in France, especially the abuse taking place in convents.

The Jansenist vision Proust suggests is primarily based on these two elements: Suzanne explicitly refuses to recognize the papal bull against Jansenism, and she experiences abuses similar to Jansenist nuns of that period. Yet, Proust does not offer any theological reading of Suzanne as

---

23. The official condemnation of Jansenism, the papal bull *Unigenitus*, was published in September 1713. The controversy between Jesuits and Jansenists became one of the major theological battles of the eighteenth century, especially in France.

a Jansenist nun. Furthermore, Suzanne declares twice that she does not want "to be called a Jansenist or a Molinist" (*The Nun* 33, 34).

If Diderot's novel shows sympathy for the Jansenist cause, the ultimate theological paradigm Diderot puts in Suzanne's words may be closer to an evangelical (i.e., based on a direct reading and interpretation of the gospel) Protestant understanding of God's revelation than a Jansenist vision. Suzanne's faith goes against the one that is imposed on her: she reads the Bible and the Gospels for herself, rejects the authority of the church, and openly professes for the reader a *Deus sub contrario*.

In the Heidelberg Disputation (1518), Luther formulated a distinction between a *theologia crucis* and a *theologia gloriae* (Theses 18–26). According to Luther, the *theologia crucis* is the only Christian theology that truly recognizes God's ultimate revelation at the cross and its unexpected form. In the midst of his demonstration, Luther quotes 1 Corinthians, the same passage that inspires Suzanne's understanding of the folly of the cross. Luther declares: "He deserves to be called a theologian, however, who comprehends the visible and manifest things of God seen through suffering and the cross" (Thesis 20). If one follows Luther's words, Suzanne is a theologian; she can even be seen as a true theologian who understands Jesus' death on the cross as the central manifestation of God's presence. If *La Religieuse* denounces the abuses of convent life and critiques the Catholic Church and its hypocrisy, it also presents Suzanne as a faithful Christian believer, who, despite rejecting the authority of the church, has reached a personal understanding of God's revelation.

Nevertheless, at the end of the novel, Suzanne does not escape her condition. Even though she manages to flee her convent, her life in the real world is riddled with anxiety: she constantly fears for her life as well as her virtue, and she is unable to move freely. Moreover, her old habits are physically trapping her and her spirit is not free— it remains marked in its practice by her experience as a nun: "I was never suited to being in a cloister, and it shows clearly in what I am doing now, but I did become accustomed to certain religious practices which I now repeat automatically" (*The Nun* 151). What then does Suzanne's faith at the end of the novel represent? If the novel contains a critique of convent life and forced vows, it also suggests that the power of religion as an institution is so strong that one cannot fully escape it once he or she has fallen prey to it. At the same time, the novel invites the reader to go back to evangelical Christianity, read the New Testament, and recognize the paradox of God's ultimate revelation in order to discover the true Christian creed. If the novel contains anticlerical and anti-Catholic elements, it is not anti-Christian, but attempts rather to go back to an evangelical reading of God's revelation through the crucifixion.

## *Post-Scriptum*

Suzanne ends her memoirs with a postscript in which she reevaluates the tone of her writing. Having reread her account, she laments that she does not depict herself truthfully. Again, the issue of truth and lies comes up at the end of the novel: What is fiction? What is seduction? What is duplicity? She explains her choice of wording by asking, "Could it be that we believe men to be less sensitive to the depiction of our suffering than to the image of our charms, and do we hope that it is much easier to seduce them than it is to touch their hearts?" (*The Nun* 152) This postscript has led scholars to accuse Suzanne of being falsely innocent and of consciously playing the victim in order to seduce the Marquis.[24] Another way to interpret her words is as a denunciation of readers who are not sensitive to suffering, insofar as Suzanne reveals sensitivity to suffering as the key to understanding God's revelation. At the end of the novel, Suzanne invites her reader to reread her memoirs with this analogy in mind. A very similar literary device has been identified by New Testament scholars at the end of Mark's Gospel (chapter 16, verses 6 and 7): "'Don't be alarmed,' he said. 'You are looking for Jesus the Nazarene, who was crucified. He has risen! He is not here. See the place where they laid him. But go, tell his disciples and Peter, 'He is going ahead of you into Galilee. There you will see him, just as he told you'" (NIV). The last command given to Jesus' disciples is to go back to Galilee, to the beginning of the Gospel's narrative, and retrace Jesus'

---

24. See in particular Pierre Saint-Amand, *The Libertine's Progress: Seduction in the Eighteenth-Century French Novel*, trans. Jennifer Curtis Gage (Hanover and London: Brown University Press, 1994), 50–68. The author reads the novel through the prism of Suzanne's false innocence.

"Que ce jour est heureux, mes sœurs. Oui, les doux noms de mère et d'épouse est bien préférable à celui de nonne, il vous rend tous les droits de la nature ainsi qu'à nous."

[This day is a happy day, Sisters. The name of mother or spouse is preferable to nun; it gives you back your natural rights. (My translation; Image available in the Prints and Photographs division of the Library of Congress under ppmsca-07501. See http://loc.gov/pictures/resource/ppmsca.07501/.)]

steps through the prism of the Passion and the crucifixion. At the end of her memoirs, Suzanne encourages her readers to proceed in a similar way: she asks them to overcome their initial reaction of scandal sparked by the reading of her account, in order to reread religious life and its institution through the prism of Jesus' crucifixion.

At the end of the nineteenth century, the paradox of the crucified God provoked one of the most violent reactions against Christianity: Nietzsche's *The Antichrist*. Published in 1888, Nietzsche's book represents one of the strongest attacks against the figure of the crucified God and Paul's theology of the cross, summed up in the following formula: "*Deus, qualem Paulus creavit, dei negation.*"[25] Citing 1 Corinthians, Nietzsche laments the impact of Paul's theology of the cross on Western culture: "God on the cross—are the horrible secret thoughts behind this symbol not understood yet? . . . Christianity has been the greatest mis-

---

25. Friedrich Nietzsche, *The Antichrist*, in *The Portable Nietzsche*, trans. Walter Kaufmann (New York: Penguin Books, 1976), 627. "God, as Paul created him, is the negation of God" (§47).

fortune of mankind so far."[26] For Nietzsche, the theology of the cross preaches the denial of life and the glorification of the weak and the sick and represents the end of a positive representation of the divine. In light of Nietzsche's critique of Christianity, we can draw a parallel between the fate of Diderot's novel and the fate of the faith that Suzanne incarnates. By the end of the nineteenth century, both were condemned. Not only was Diderot's novel criticized for its anti-Catholic and anti-Christian messages, but Suzanne's model of Christian faith was also philosophically rejected.

Since one of Diderot's main attacks against convent life was the social practice of forced vows, we can assume that Diderot would have rejoiced with the nuns released from their vows when the French Revolution abolished monastic orders on February 16, 1790. Whether Diderot would have agreed with Nietzsche and his strong rejection of the crucified God remains an open question.

---

26. Ibid., 634 (§51).

# Enlightenment Sermon Studies: A Multidisciplinary Activity

Bob Tennant

The past two decades have seen a collective reconsideration of the positions occupied by religion in the eighteenth century, amounting to a fundamental shift in historiography. The revived study of the period's sermon literature seems to contribute to this. The present essay suggests the need for more interdisciplinary cooperation in better defining sermon studies and presents four questions about sermons to scholars working on the British Enlightenment, and, more generally, the Long Eighteenth Century, which will be referred to as "our period": What are the characteristics of the corpus? What is distinctive about the relationship of sermons to theological and doctrinal development? What sort of evidence do sermons offer the historian? What is distinctive about the sermon in critical terms? The essay also offers a specific contribution to discussing the fourth of these questions: the demonstration of a simple but powerful analytical tool.

Sermon studies in our period are helping to highlight the centrality of the liturgy and religious discourse in public space, and this is increasingly accepted within the scholarly mainstream.[1] Both in and

---

1. Thus, the unapologetic tone of Kathryn Duncan's account of the period in her introductory essay to *Religion in the Age of Reason: A Transatlantic Study of the Long Eighteenth Century* (New York: AMS Press, 2009) could hardly have been sustained even a decade previously.

beyond our period the study of sermons seems to be developing into a somewhat discrete area of activity, as the significant and growing body of scholars, for whom sermons are a resource of first resort, exchange ideas. At the same time, it is recognized that the sermon literature of our period seems in some important ways different both from those of the decades from Cranmer to Juxon and those after the mid-nineteenth century, when the genre started its decline.

Sermon readership came to a peak in the eighteenth century in proportion to the total population. In Britain it was statistically the predominant literary form, amounting to perhaps a quarter of all non-ephemeral publications. Preaching gained in prominence in the established church and the printed sermon gained ground in family worship, politics (local and national), theology and philosophy, the human and physical sciences, and nonecclesial public spaces. Increasingly, the sermon, as the focal point of committee life, drove social organization. Sometimes it functioned as an academic research paper and sometimes it included the annual report of charitable and civic societies. One of the chief correctives of perspective achieved recently is the insight that the Enlightenment was a period saturated in exegesis and, increasingly, textual criticism of the Bible.[2]

Sermon studies are no longer confined to the tiny handful of investigators of two decades ago; there are at least a hundred scholars publishing important and innovative sermon-related research on every continent. Although we have not yet created a cohesive enterprise, the research infrastructure is developing quickly. Still useful is Harry Caplan's and Henry H. King's *Pulpit Eloquence: A List of Doctrinal and Historical Studies in English*, a special issue of *Speech Monographs*.[3] Compiled through manual searches of library catalogs, it aimed at comprehensiveness from the sixteenth to mid-twentieth centuries. It was joined in 1996 by the late John Gordon Spaulding's

---

2. For an example of the recent exploration of this penetration of the public space by exegesis and the use and exploration of biblical texts, see Pasi Ihalainen, *Protestant Nations Redefined* (Leiden: Brill, 2005).

3. Vol. 12, no. 4, 1955. My thanks to William Gibson for this rediscovery.

*Pulpit Publications, 1660–1782*,[4] which presents generous listings of sermons, although it is bibliographically unsatisfactory because its chief sources are the collections of two eighteenth-century book buyers (Sampson Letsome and John Cooke).[5] Since the publication of the Spaulding set, the Internet has been a great stimulant. The *English Short Title Catalogue* (ESTC) offers invaluable scholarship, of course, while *Early English Books Online* and *Eighteenth-Century Collections Online* are irreplaceable. For the physical environment there is Lambeth Palace's digitized archive, *Church Plans Online* (sourced from the records of the Incorporated Church Building Society), and for the career structures of authors, and indeed the entire clergy, there is the *Clergy of the Church of England Database* (CCED), which is still under development but promises to be of fundamental importance. The Durham University–based State Prayers project, now moving to a conclusion with a projected publication date of 2012, provides the administrative and ideational environment of sermons on the fasts, humiliations, and thanksgivings of state occasions.

Activity in sermon studies is growing so quickly that a review of its personnel and productions would be invidiously incomplete. Continuing instead the theme of the development of what I have termed the research infrastructure, we will here acknowledge only a handful of collective enterprises in what might be seen as systems-building: these enterprises offer the prospect of healing the fractures inherited from the research priorities of previous generations. Whether the line is drawn in 1660 or 1688, there remains a distinction between early-modern and modern research methods and perspectives, reflecting the better-established scholarly tradition, in the earlier period, of linguistic and textual studies. The later period seems to remain dominated by the nineteenth-century Tory and Tractarian anathema of all things Whig and Enlightenment, if only by reaction against it. It is thus no accident that the colloquium of early-modern sermon scholars currently meeting

---

4. 6 volumes (New York: Norman Ross, 1996). This invaluable work is available from the publisher both in hard copy and on CD.

5. Letsome's work of 1753, *The Preacher's Assistant*, was expanded and updated by John Cooke in 1783. Cooke's collection was to form the basis of the sermon holdings of the King's Collection in the British Library.

in Britain is based distinctively in literary as much as in ecclesiastical studies.[6] It is loosely associated with the forthcoming *Oxford Handbook of the Early Modern Sermon*,[7] which originated in Oxford University Press's literature list. In contrast, another colloquium in Britain, loosely associated with the *Oxford Handbook of the Modern British Sermon, 1689–1901*[8] (which originated in Oxford University Press's religion list), consists largely of ecclesiastical historians of the much-extended eighteenth century.[9] In practice, the two groups are edging toward each other. In the United States it would not be unfair to make a similar observation about the successive volumes of Brill's multivolume *New History of the Sermon*.[10] These volumes' production, too, is strengthening working relationships, while a contributor to both the British and American projects[11] is editing Charles Spurgeon's three thousand sermons for an online database.

Thus, networking facilitated by collective publication is working well, but the map of the corpus still contains much terra incognita. Even the triangulation points are not firmly agreed upon, although we are probably now at the stage of knowing what we don't know and are helped in diachronic studies by the sermon's fairly stable liturgical role. However, only a generation after 1832, and despite the efflorescence that was the phenomenal Charles Spurgeon, the genre began its numerical and cultural decline, being displaced by "material religion": the productions of the visual arts, such as posters, postcards, book illustrations, slides, and, surprisingly early in the twentieth century, film—a subject

---

6. It is convened annually by Mary Morrissey of Reading University and Hugh Adlington of Birmingham University.

7. Ed. Peter McCullough, Hugh Adlington, and Emma Rhatigan (Oxford: Oxford University Press, forthcoming). Hereafter referred to as *OHEMS*.

8. Ed. William Gibson and Keith Francis, with consultant eds. Robert Ellison, John Morgan-Guy, and Bob Tennant (Oxford: Oxford University Press, scheduled for 2012). Hereafter referred to as *OHMBS*.

9. It is convened annually by William Gibson of Oxford Brookes University.

10. *Preachers and People in the Reformations and Early Modern Period*, vol. 2, ed. Larissa Taylor (Boston: Brill, 2010); *Preaching, Sermon and Cultural Change in the Long Eighteenth Century*, vol. 4, ed. Joris van Eijnatten (Boston: Brill, 2009); *A New History of the Nineteenth-Century Sermon*, ed. Robert Ellison (Boston: Brill, 2010).

11. Keith Francis, Secretary of the American Society of Church Historians.

area that now boasts a dedicated and eponymous journal.[12] By contrast, sermon studies do not possess their own narrative of the retreat from the wider public spaces. This poses a theoretical obstacle to discussing any part of the genre; until we have a theory about its decline in relation to religious worship, liturgy, and doctrine, we cannot be confident that we can theorize its rise and apogee.

This essay therefore offers four very broad questions, which, bearing in mind their implications for our various disciplines, might help strengthen our collective enterprise, both theoretically and empirically.

## Question 1: What are the characteristics of the corpus?

This question asks first of all for information about numbers, subjects, occasions, authors, printers, markets, and industrial technology. Unfortunately, while it is the most important and urgent question, we are not in a position to answer it with exactness. The following remarks imply the need for a range of primary research.

The raw numbers are challenging. In the 1660–1832 period, there were published in the Anglophone world, not including the post-independence United States, at least fifty-five thousand sermons, or somewhere around a third of a billion words.[13] With sufficient determination a student could read the entire corpus of fiction, or even poetry, in our period.[14] This is not possible for the student of sermons. A critical assessment must therefore be collective and computer based.

Many sermons, especially provincial publications and those on the far side of Old Dissent, are not held in the major libraries of deposit

---

12. Seminal works of material religion include David Morgan's works, notably *Visual Piety* (Berkeley: University of California Press, 1998), *Protestants and Pictures* (New York: Oxford University Press, 1999), and *The Lure of Images* (New York: Routledge, 2007).

13. The United States is omitted due to sheer personal ignorance. Spaulding lists about 34,000 British sermons for 1660–1782, which suggests about 50,000 for 1660–1832, but allowance must be made for an approximate 10 percent underestimate by him and his sources (which he partly acknowledges).

14. Indeed, with regard to poetry, Hoxie Neale Fairchild, in *Religious Trends in English Poetry*, 6 vols. (New York: Columbia University Press, 1939–68), lamented that he had probably done so.

and research. Moreover, library catalogs exist above all else to enable books to be delivered to the reader's desk and to be used by the institution, not to duplicate parts of the ESTC. Even within Library of Congress protocols,[15] there is a wide scope for variation in cataloging practice and, in our period, there was no stereotyped style of title page. Sermons were indifferently called sermon, lecture, discourse, or homily; others were printed as tracts and not identified as sermons on their title pages or were edited into secularized publications. In one catalog an item may appear as, say, "A Sermon Preached before the Duke of Clarence," in another as "A Sermon Preached in the Cathedral of St. Paul's" (or perhaps "A Sermon on Genesis 1:1"); about 5 percent of holdings common to both catalogs cannot be matched without physical inspection, often extending beyond the title page. Thus, a key edition of a sermon that featured in a project I published in 2009 came to my notice purely by accident. Even with hindsight I could not have discovered it without physically inspecting every sermon, in every library, appearing in tract form in its year of publication. This item, be it said, was not on the face of it obscure: it was preached in Scotland's capital city and issued by a leading publisher. A major challenge, therefore, is to determine what sermons were actually published and to put them in a comprehensive online catalog. Many scholars in the groups mentioned above are associated with, or supportive of, the attempt to launch such a database, *The British Pulpit Online, 1660–1901*.[16] The research infrastructure needs to develop with a degree of, if not synchronism, then at least, in Jung's term, synchronicity. Systematic, quantitative historical research is needed before qualitative research moves beyond speculative plausibility and before we can be confident about approaching this question.

---

15. I would like to thank Françoise Deconinck-Brossard and the following librarians for their patience in discussing relevant aspects of cataloging with me: Sarah Wheale (Bodleian Library), Richard Palmer (Lambeth Palace Library), Rosemary Stenson (University of Glasgow Library), and Helen Vincent (National Library of Scotland).

16. Baylor University Library has designed such a database to the specifications of the group editing the *OHMBS*.

## Question 2: What is distinctive about the relationship of sermons to theological and doctrinal development?

Sermons are exegetical texts delivered in a liturgical context, but this fact seems neglected by theologians, so that a dimension is missing from the narrative of the church's presence in society and its members' liturgical engagement with the object of their worship. It is a question that I am not competent to approach, but it can hardly be denied that the parochial clergy adapted, refined, and promulgated doctrine and pursued theology; contrary to eighteenth-century satire and nineteenth-century sectarian calumny, the parochial clergy weren't exclusively placemen, foxhunters, topers, and magistrates. Sermons exegetically applied the scriptures and doctrine to the experience and circumstances of the congregations so that there was an interpenetration of the two. In the manner popularized by John Tillotson, many sermons tended toward a subdivision of the exegesis, often tripartite, with the parts moving from textual criticism (of God's word) via matters of faith (revealed by the Son) to matters of practical faith (suffused with the Spirit). This should be admitted as a theological activity. But even the exegetical component may not be quite what it seems. For example, Joseph Butler's preaching, or philosophizing, is routinely alleged to have killed off deism. A consideration of the context and rhetoric of his work suggests, however, that his pastoral and philosophical strategy was to argue that deism was inadequately empirical as a contemplation of physical and psychological reality and that it was not to be defeated but, rather, completed by orthodox Christianity—a strategy of continuing inclusiveness rather than decisive conflict.[17] In contrast to his contributions to moral philosophy and psychology, Butler is not generally considered a theological innovator. However, to deploy such a strategy in regard to deism was to make *theological suggestions* about

---

17. Bob Tennant, *Conscience, Consciousness and Charity: Joseph Butler's Thought and Ministry* (Woodbridge: Boydell Press, forthcoming [2011]), chapters 2 and 3. It is there demonstrated that Butler's *Fifteen Sermons*, although heavily revised, remained texts for use in the pulpit and that his anti-deist *Analogy* was assembled from sermons.

the spiritual, metaphysical, and epistemological relationships between God and creation; about questions of empirical verification; and about a "unified field theory" of knowledge.

Sermons were often published "at the request of" members of the ecclesiastical and political hierarchy. Their doctrine, once published, was presented as authoritative, even if sometimes only in a narrow—party—sense. Thus a subsidiary question is, "How did the act of publication change the status of a sermon's doctrine?" This may be approached piecemeal. We are familiar, for example, with examining the relationship between a bishop's own doctrine and the episcopal visitation sermon given by a junior in his diocese: charges and visitation sermons are an inviting area of research. But the question may also be approached not only in relation to its place in the publisher's list, its dedicatees and subscribers, items in market competition, and so on, but also more strategically: when doctrine mediated experience, what resulted theologically? Moreover, publication tended to be a nexus either of acts of conformity—church- and career-building—or of dissent. Was the relationship between doctrine and such acts circumstantially arbitrary, or was it creative? Sometimes, as with the Anglican-turned-Unitarian John Disney, both may be seen in operation at different stages of his ministry.

## Question 3: What sort of evidence do sermons offer the historian?

While the answers to this question might seem obvious, our comments on Question 2 have already shown that at least one dimension of potential evidence—the theological creativity of pulpit preaching—is currently almost entirely neglected.

Very broadly, sermon studies take two approaches. One, the more narrowly historical, is through a process of analysis that identifies smaller, manageable corpora by situation or function; by text or theme, doctrine or political circumstance; or else by the class of occasions: the church calendar, decrees of the Privy Council, annual sermons of the various charitable and church societies, the lecture series, events like the Three Choirs Festival, assizes, and, of course, parochial sermons. The list could be extended enormously, but it must be remembered that, once beyond the objective facts of times and places, this is to hypothesize and thus to invite challenges about verification and underdetermination. Practitioners of critical studies will surely raise such challenges when our studies achieve a powerful impact on historiography.[18]

The other approach is more critical in nature and may be illustrated (with apologies to scores of works here passed over) by titles such as *Veiled Speech: Preaching, Politics, and Scriptural Typology* and *"Dishonest Scars": Holiness, Secrecy and the Problem of Perpetual Peace*.[19] In such works, sermons are used as evidence of religious behavior in society, to reinforce, qualify, or create analyses pertaining to overarching ideational phenomena. Such work uses theoretical methods from critical writing developed for other disciplines and literary genres and thus secures the sermon in the mainstream of literary activity.

Another body of evidence is produced by considering sermons as cultural products—that is, as religious objects received as the production of industrial society rather than of the church specifically. As was implied above, this pursuit is crucially hampered by the lack of information, which remains locked up in inadequately cataloged title pages and volumes scattered inaccessibly around the world's libraries. Colleagues will not take the observation amiss that work like this (including some of my own)[20] has currently the status of a provocative to further research. It seems, however, one of the potentially richest fields of future activity. The numbers (of items and authors) are so enormous, compared to the meager few hundreds of novels, that statistical approaches similar to those practiced by economists and social historians become feasible. Thus, the sermon, although as artful a production as any secular work, has a relationship with society and its dynamics that may be subject to quantitative research.

---

18. The reference, of course, is to engagements with the philosophies of Karl Popper and Bas van Fraassen.

19. Titles by Kevin Killeen (*OHEMS*) and Michael Rotenberg-Schwartz (*Religion in the Age of Reason*), respectively.

20. For example, "John Tillotson and the Voice of Anglicanism," *Religion in the Age of Reason*, ed. Kathryn Duncan (New York: AMS Press, 2009), 97–119.

In particular, research into sermon production is also research into the dominant product of the rapidly developing print manufacturing and knowledge sectors of the Anglophone world's economy. When Joseph Butler preached to London's mayor and aldermen about economics, or to London's merchants about the 1747 Master and Servant Act, he offered a manifesto for Britain's economic development and its ethical implications; readers will recall Adam Smith's acknowledged debt to him. Decisions, like those taken annually by the SPG Board to print and distribute specified numbers of copies in specified outlets, constituted a binding together of an extrovert church, a dutiful state, an aggressive economy, and a paternalist society. Study of the sermon's contribution to industrial productivity, its shaping of the literary retail market, and its competitive relationship with other pamphlet and essay literature promises to open up the important question of how authorial supply of sermons and public demand for them related to each other—a question, in other words, about the dynamic of ideological development and the place of church and theology within it.

It is refreshing that ecclesiastical and theological historians nowadays critically scrutinize the virtually universal repudiation of the Whig church by the early nineteenth-century church, but the historiographical landscape remains dominated by a body of evidence of discontinuity and radical change inherited from the nineteenth and twentieth centuries.[21] Evidence of continuities is not organized so as to assert itself against the evidence of change, so the historiography of our period remains unbalanced.[22]

---

21. Two recent books edge toward a correction of this: Stephen Prickett's *Modernity and the Reinvention of Tradition* (Cambridge: Cambridge University Press, 2009) sketches an account of the strange death and resurrection of the concept of "tradition," and James Pereiro's *"Ethos" and the Oxford Movement* (Oxford: Oxford University Press, 2008) may, for present purposes, be said to describe reasserted continuities with the eighteenth century, for example with regard to the ethics of Joseph Butler.

22. The chosen time frame of *OHMBS* deliberately asserts a thesis of continuity.

## Question 4: What is distinctive about the sermon in critical terms?

The remainder of this essay is concerned with questions of the multifarious world of literary criticism rather than historical scholarship, the sermon being, after all, a literary form. Indeed, perhaps it is necessary that sermon studies become involved in criticism for the benefit of the wider community, for at present literary history is grossly biased toward the minority of secular work without understanding the religious contexts of the poetry, fiction, drama, and essays that are so familiar. Thus, the Christian imagination is exiled from history and consequently from modern society in a way that would be considered intolerable if applied to other religions. The term "literary criticism" may be understood in both senses: the processes of establishing and ordering best texts, and the building of accounts of their meaning and the way they work. This is even more necessary because the English language of our period's preaching looks very much like modern English (of both the British and American varieties) and can therefore flatter to deceive.[23] There is a multitude of critical approaches to texts, of course; we will discuss only one and illustrate it with two examples.

While the sermon is undoubtedly a direct source of historical evidence, it needs to be approached with some caution by the unwary, as it is above all a literary performance text, composed to work effects on its listeners (and readers), seeking to persuade out of its "whole body"[24] rather than merely convince by its arguments. The persuasion of groups of people by rhetoric is as much a historical fact as any other but has traditionally been avoided by historians, presumably because it lies in a zone occupied, and often aggressively defended, by other disciplines. Nevertheless, preachers were professionally required to take many things for granted: however daring their exposition, innovative their exegesis, or radical their application, the starting and ending

---

23. Even philosophers have started venturing into literary criticism. See, for example, William Walker, *Locke, Literary Criticism, and Philosophy* (Cambridge: Cambridge University Press, 1994), and Jay F. Rosenberg, *Accessing Kant: A Relaxed Introduction to the Critique of Pure Reason* (Oxford: Oxford University Press, 2005).

24. William Wordsworth, "Resolution and Independence," XVI.

points were predetermined—the rhetorical journey mattered at least as much as the arrival at an often perfunctory peroration. A sermon's "success" is measured by its persuasiveness and its responsibility as a liturgical and social text. In that sense, sermon literature is practically serious and urgent about questions of ethics and well-being in ways that no other literature, religious or secular, approaches, Shelley and his unacknowledged poetical legislators notwithstanding.

Usefully for the critic, pulpit preaching was (and is) too big-voiced to be fully comfortable in the intimacies of the drawing room; many sermons were published for domestic use, but the gathering of the extended family, including its many servants, could hardly be defined as private space. Its rhetoric, typically intended for an audience of up to two thousand, is architectonic and not always subtle. Critical tools may therefore appropriately be broad-brush, and this makes them peculiarly suitable for computer-based statistical treatment.

Sermons are performance texts, but because of their liturgical function and the architecture of churches, they are also highly directional. They might fruitfully be approached through the body of critical theory developed to discuss theater plays. They are, however, performance texts of a very peculiar kind: *only one of the casts of hundreds or thousands actually speaks.*[25] The congregation's presence is nevertheless palpable. Hence the present author has under development a bundle of critical tools to be applied at the level of grammar and syntax, not semantics. They are intended to combine simplicity and power. Space, unfortunately, permits the demonstration of only one, in isolation from the others.

This particular tool is used to investigate directionality: the lines of sight in the church and the patterns of reference among the various parties in the liturgical situation. It does so by examining the use of personal pronouns.[26] Thus, a sermon may be "me" preaching to "you"

---

25. Jeanne Halgren Kilde is especially stimulating in her exploration of the interactivity and roles of preacher, congregation, and architecture: *When Church Became Theatre* (Oxford: Oxford University Press, 2002), chapter 2, "Redefining Clerical and Audience Authority in the Architecture of Urban Revivals."

26. The power and theoretical safety of this tool are derived partly from the fact that eighteenth-century rhetorical theory depended heavily on classical models. Because Latin and Greek use persons in a way fundamentally different from English, there could be no

about how "he" (God) asks "us" (Christians, humankind) to conduct ourselves toward "them" (some third party). We will call the bundles of words deriving from grammatical persons "families": the "me" family—*I, me, mine, my,* and *myself;* the "you" family—*you, your, yours, yourself,* and *yourselves;* and so on.[27] Results are expressed as "densities" of the occurrence of these families (percentages of the total of words in the sermon or a section of it).[28]

This tool immediately suggests two pairs of critical terms: one comprises *inclusive* (where preacher and congregation are joined in "us") and *exclusive* (where they are not, the preacher emphasizing his otherness); the other pair is God$^{pos}$ (where God, or a person of the Trinity, is represented by a grammatical person—usually "he"), and God$^{neg}$ (where he is not). It would be expected that evangelical sermons would generally be "God$^{pos}$" unless there were some extraordinary exegetical or doctrinal reason.[29]

Thus, the first of our two examples provides a moment as dramatic, and even thrilling, as most in literature. It comes on 7 June 1798, in the ninety-fifth annual sermon to the London and Westminster charity schools, given in St. Paul's under the auspices of the Society for the Promotion of Christian Knowledge (SPCK) by Henry Whitfeld, a

---

critical awareness by preachers of the resource (by contrast, this would not certainly be true of, say, twentieth-century preachers). This means not only that they spoke innocently but also that any prepublication editing could not remove the features to be analyzed. In any case, as the reader may find by experiment, such editing is virtually impossible, as it attacks the deep structures of the grammar and semantics.

27. Ignored are the neuter "it," as it necessarily cannot refer to persons human or divine; the feminine "she," because it generally refers to abstracts and personifications; and "thou" and "ye," archaisms that occur mainly in quotations from scripture (special provision would be made for certain Dissenting forms of preaching).

28. For simplicity's sake, an analytical refinement not deployed here is the arrow symbol, for example, "we→he," where one of the terms is predominantly the grammatical subject of sentences and the other the grammatical object, and "we←→he," where this is not the case.

29. I have given an example of the use of the "God$^{neg}$" concept in "On the Good Name of the Dead: Peace, Liberty, and Empire in Robert Morehead's Waterloo Sermon," *Religion in the Age of Enlightenment,* 1 (2009): 251–77. Although analysts should support results with a reading or inspection of their texts, the WordSmith program has a word-in-context feature, which gives initial assistance in identifying the referents of the grammatical persons.

London rector who served for many years on the Standing Committee of the Society for the Propagation of the Gospel in Foreign Parts (SPG).[30] The nave was packed by several thousand charitable dignitaries, officials, and supporters. Also present were about eight thousand charity school children in specially constructed stands under the dome and in the transepts. Whitfeld's sermon was preached directly and exclusively to the adults, as had been every single word of his ninety-four predecessors. But then, reaching his peroration, he turned physically in the pulpit toward the dome behind his left shoulder: "But as for *you*, My Children, (for on this day, I think, I have some right to call you Mine)." The children, hitherto a spectacle for the adults, were for the first time in ninety-five years drawn into the congregation—a moment of high emotional charge for them and a rare example of "you" being a term of "inclusion." This inclusiveness, embodied by the movement of Whitfeld's body, the abrupt changes in the sermon's line of sight, and in the changed referent of "you," was not the least revolutionary act in a revolutionary decade and brought into the mainstream the child-centered pedagogy of the nascent Sunday School movement.[31]

Our second example is more elaborate, involving a comparison of two sermons: John Wesley's *The Original, Nature, Property, and Use of the Law*[32] and William Romaine's *Upon the Moral Law*,[33] selected because both are products of the evangelical revival and share Romans 7:12 as their text.[34]

Both sermons concern the moral law as revealed by Christ's ministry. Wesley argues that it has superseded the Jewish law, that humankind has faculties that recognize it as a copy of the "Eternal Mind." Its commands are not arbitrary because it is based in God's love.

30. USPG Committee Books (Bodleian Library), e.g., vol. 57, June 9, 1799 *et seq.*

31. Henry Whitfeld, *A Sermon Preached in the Cathedral Church of St. Paul's [Acts 10:38]* (London: Francis and Charles Rivington, 1798), 22. The rhetoric of the series changes quite abruptly from this point. This is the subject of forthcoming work.

32. Text taken from *Works*, 3rd ed., ed. Thomas Jackson (London: Wesleyan-Methodist Book-Room, 1831), 5:433–66, also available on CD-ROM (Franklin, Tennessee: Providence House Publishers, 1995), from which it can be copied into a word processor.

33. Text taken from *Works* (London: T. Chapman, 1796), 3:61–92.

34. Word counts were produced by running Unicode text through the WordSmith program. A more elaborate grammatical and syntactical analysis of these two sermons is at present unpublished; it reinforces the diagnosis given in what follows.

The Holy Spirit convinces us of sin and this conviction keeps us close to Christ and allows us to receive his grace. The Calvinist Romaine agrees that the moral law is a copy of God's mind. But repentance for sin is not enough; salvation is only through holiness and thorough obedience. Yet, he points out, in the Prayer Book's communion service we confess our repeated breaches of the law—our separation from God—and thus condemn ourselves to death. Salvation comes only to those who despair and throw their trust wholly on God.

It is likely that Wesley preached a version of his sermon in the open air near the start of his peripatetic ministry, on about 22 June 1738, at Fishponds, a suburb of Bristol. The ideas contained in it are certainly prevalent in his journal around this time. By contrast, Romaine, the "loyal" Anglican evangelical, harassed physically and at law by rector and churchwardens but supported by the bishop of London,[35] preached his "lecture" after a special and provocative mass act of communion earlier in the day, in St. Dunstan's-in-the-West, near Fleet Street, the home of the printing industry and English trade unionism.[36]

Table 1 records the density of the person families in each section of the two sermons. In both sermons, "he" refers almost exclusively to God and the sermons are both distinctly "God$^{pos}$," as we have hypothesized of evangelical productions. In the Wesley sermon, "he" is clearly the dominant person, and "we" + "he" = 3.87 percent, which is 63.44 percent of all persons. In the Romaine, "he" again predominates, while "you" + "he" = 5.65 percent, which is 67.67 percent of all persons; analysis of a larger but statistically unrepresentative assemblage of texts suggests these to be high figures. Both sermons seem at first sight powerfully bipolar, but the contrast between their rhetorical strategies is remarkable, the Wesley being "we-he" and the Romaine "you-he."

---

35. Richard Terrick, who had beaten off Warburton's campaign for London. Since Romaine was under Terrick's patronage (he succeeded him in the St. Dunstan's lectureship) and had criticized Warburton's theory of church and state, there was probably a political element in the conflict.

36. This is emphasized because to acknowledge Romaine is to enter conflict with the twentieth-century, pseudo-Marxist insistence that trade unionism's origins were in Dissent.

## Table 1: Person "Families" in Wesley's and Romaine's Sermons on Romans 7:12[37]

|            | Me    | We    | You   | He    | They  | Totals |
|------------|-------|-------|-------|-------|-------|--------|
| **Wesley** |       |       |       |       |       |        |
| Exordium   | 0.62% | 1.61% | 0.50% | 1.49% | 0.74% | 4.95%  |
| Exegesis 1 | 0.85% | 0.37% | 0.12% | 3.90% | 2.80% | 8.05%  |
| Exegesis 2 | 0.89% | 1.91% | 0.13% | 1.15% | 0.38% | 4.46%  |
| Exegesis 3 | 0.37% | 1.00% | 0.00% | 2.68% | 0.75% | 4.80%  |
| Application| 1.57% | 1.69% | 0.94% | 3.14% | 0.56% | 7.91%  |
| Peroration | 0.75% | 0.38% | 1.51% | 2.26% | 0.38% | 5.28%  |
| All        | 0.89% | 1.28% | 0.43% | 2.59% | 0.92% | 6.10%  |
| **Romaine**|       |       |       |       |       |        |
| Exordium   | 3.18% | 1.02% | 0.51% | 1.78% | 1.91% | 8.39%  |
| Exegesis 1 | 0.21% | 0.11% | 0.84% | 4.59% | 1.69% | 7.44%  |
| Exegesis 2 | 1.47% | 0.59% | 0.10% | 2.75% | 1.08% | 5.98%  |
| Exegesis 3 | 0.25% | 0.70% | 4.57% | 2.73% | 0.83% | 9.09%  |
| Application| 0.22% | 0.22% | 2.67% | 4.06% | 2.37% | 9.53%  |
| Peroration | 0.00% | 0.00% | 6.67% | 2.67% | 0.00% | 9.33%  |
| All        | 0.68% | 0.41% | 2.17% | 3.48% | 1.61% | 8.35%  |

In the Wesley sermon, however, the "we-he" polarity is undermined by the fact that "me" + "we" ≈ "he."[38] "Me" thus sustains a challenge by "us" for the right to the relationship with God, achieving a narrow dominance toward the end. What is certain is that "they" (the potential locus of a third, corporate party in the relationship with God) and, above all, "you" lack structural significance. The polarity hesitates between an uncertain inclusiveness and, increasingly, an uncertain exclusiveness.

The contrast with the Romaine sermon is definite and twofold. In density the Romaine is 37 percent more "personal" than the Wesley; extraordinarily, in the latter half of Romaine's sermon almost a tenth

---

37. The Romaine sermon has an "Exegesis 4," which is too short for analysis and has therefore been incorporated into Exegesis 3.

38. ≈ means "approximately equal to." When a comparator corpus is available, the range of variation for ≈ to apply can be assigned a value. Currently, ±20 percent is adopted arbitrarily.

of the words are "personal." "Me" and "we" are insignificant, and the rhetorical axis is firmly "you-he," with "you" being the weightier, so that his sermon is structurally less "God$^{pos}$" than Wesley's and distinctly "exclusive." Romaine's peroration must have had an almost physical impact on the members of his congregation ("you" = a grotesquely high 6.6 percent), driving them from the church with specific personal instructions to evangelize ringing in their ears.

Romaine built a fairly stable but dynamic audience through his St. Dunstan's lectures. His sacerdotal authority is projected into the congregation, mobilizing them, leading them into an active politico-religious project within the disciplines of the Prayer Book, which he quotes and lengthily explicates in this sermon. He sends his congregation out of St. Dunstan's as individual components of the evangelical Church of Christ to work in the mêlée of society, supported by the disciplines of his symbolic and rhetorical structures. Wesley's rhetoric, by contrast, is austere and remote. Unable to structure his peripatetic ministry and rhetoric like Romaine, he presents a dynamically more inert theological object to his listeners and then, after editing, to his domestic readers.[39]

Our analysis has suggested that Romaine's sermon was concerned to provoke and give practical shape to his congregation's evangelical awakening, while Wesley's sermon was addressed to an awakening that it could acknowledge but to which he could not at present propose an institutional expression; his diary for this period confirms the improvisatory nature of his ministry. Without this analysis of the use of persons it would hardly have been possible to formulate Wesley's and Romaine's strategies in these sermons, nor to write accurately about how they might be distinguished. If extended into a representative sample of their sermons, or those of the various streams of eighteenth-century evangelical preaching, it might approach the most important thing for these two great evangelicals' ministries—the formulation of theology and effecting of personal motivation in their listeners by rhetoric—and thus supply evidence surely not peripheral to the historian's account.

---

39. The Latin tags in this sermon as published were surely not spoken before illiterate Bristol miners. They do not, however, affect the rhetorical dynamic, but merely reinforce Wesley's claim to intellectual authority.

Moreover, the analysis would be amenable to linguistic research and the results to independent verification. Earlier, we noted the prevalence of the method of analysis by the construction of corpora based on situation or function. We can now see how these "horizontal" categories can be discussed, as it were "vertically," through their rhetorical characteristics and potentially plotted against these two axes. While subjective impressions seem to suggest that functional corpora tend toward norms of style, vocabulary, and content—that there is a likeness between SPCK sermons, for example—we cannot at present objectively establish this or gauge the effect on an individual's preaching style of occupying a particular pulpit or contributing to a particular function. Crucially, however, we have no scientifically constructed comparator corpus to establish norms. Such a resource will not become available until the students of sermons in our period form a strong consensus that it is necessary.

This general, but almost entirely unexplored, assumption that sermons in a functional corpora share a generic likeness conceals an interesting hypothesis about the nature of pulpit preaching's place in the liturgy. Insofar as this is verifiable—and we should not hastily assume that it is—it necessarily assigns a subordinate role to the core feature of the sermon: its existence as a dynamic rhetorical object working effects on its audience. Such a subordination in itself would be interesting to study because all authorized ceremony is valid and, as Milton pointed out, "They also serve who only stand and wait." To loyally occupy a pulpit with a situationally neutral rhetorical and theological object seems theologically valid. It is equally undeniable that others—like Whitfeld and Romaine—with equal validity challenged their assigned functions and parameters. Here, then, is another potential statistical plot of sermons' situational functions. What might have seemed initially to be a purely linguistic question quickly becomes an element in the assessment of the text's value as historical evidence.

Such suggestions barely start to exploit the resources offered to sermon studies by literary criticism. My own tentative answer to my fourth question is that there are many ways of exploring the sermon as a distinctive literary genre and that while critics need historians to anchor their analyses and narratives, historians need critics to produce solid, verifiable evidence which otherwise is inaccessible.

# Reviews

## Heart Religion in the British Enlightenment: Gender and Emotion in Early Methodism

*A review by Dustin D. Stewart*

Problems of agency often materialize as problems of attribution. Early in her remarkable new study, *Heart Religion in the British Enlightenment*, historian Phyllis Mack describes how eighteenth-century Methodists are typically viewed as either "emotionally needy followers or . . . a mob of hysterical worshippers run amok." Such Methodists, Mack contends, "have rarely been viewed as thinkers and actors" in their own right (5). To make amends, Mack delves into the agency of the everyday. She discloses how lay Methodists and leaders, men and women alike, used various forms of writing as tools for the work of emotional self-fashioning. What made that labor so strenuous—and what gives traction to Mack's project—are the complex interrelations between "Enlightenment ideals and Protestant theology." The author argues that these relations, sometimes complementary, sometimes conflicting, "heightened the tension inherent in Christian thought between the desire for passivity and self-abnegation on the one hand, and the urge toward self-transformation and world-transformation, on the other" (14). Mack's effort to take seriously such tension of the heart leads her to the documented emotions and spiritual struggles of early Methodists, which she unstintingly reads as sincere. She reads them so, and, indeed, she writes them so: Mack's book teems with extended quotations drawn from hundreds of published and unpublished manuscript sources. Mack gives ordinary Methodists their say. Thus the printed text, even more than the argument of *Heart Religion*, redresses the problem the historian identifies early on. The study provides an archive of eighteenth-century Methodist feeling, a body of recovered material that, Mack hopes, can enable secular historians "to share, however imperfectly, the struggles of ordinary Methodists and lay preachers" (7).

The book speaks to a number of ongoing scholarly debates. Mack deploys Methodist narratives to dispute the increasingly questioned conflation of modernity with secularization. Drawing at points on anthropologist Webb Keane's recent work, she advances claims for the modernity of the eighteenth-century Methodists, linking their psychological struggles for self-mastery with modernity's premium on "human liberation" (18). Mack's book sorts well with recent attempts by intellectual and literary historians (such as J. G. A. Pocock, B. W. Young, and Jon Mee) to rethink the relationships between enthusiasm and enlightenment. *Heart Religion* should also catch the attention of students of affect. The author demonstrates how Methodist discourse participated in eighteenth-century redefinitions of feeling and sensibility. Especially significant to this line of inquiry is her focus, not on emotion as such, but on Methodists' attempts to analyze and to refine their emotions. Mack crafts a humane history by reading such writings as the authentic, because anguished, attempts of people grappling to improve their lives. A picture emerges of a movement whose lived contours are—as Mack describes its leaders' priorities— "psychological, not theological" (31). Literary scholars exploring life writing in the period will therefore find much of interest. Lastly, and more obviously, the book makes a signal contribution to Methodist studies, transformed in 2005 by David Hempton's *Methodism: Empire of the Spirit*, a major source for Mack. Since the tercentenary of Charles Wesley's 1707 birth, several new studies of Methodism have proceeded to bring the "other" Wesley to the fore. Gareth Lloyd's *Charles Wesley and the Struggle for Methodist Identity* (2007) figures prominently here, and Mack draws upon Lloyd's book and his published essays. However, Mack doesn't adopt one assumption often subtending recent readings of Charles Wesley—namely, that a right reassessment of early Methodism needs some distance from his brother. Mack instead relies a good deal on John Wesley, and specifically on a portrait of John as walking briskly (with or without his tea) through the Enlightenment, forward from Locke. This John cuts a more winningly moderate figure than Mack's Charles, who often appears gloomy and even "extreme" by contrast (181). Some readers may thus find that Mack overemphasizes John's modern virtues, as when she chalks up his support of women's preaching to his "radically democratic view of the ordinary person's spiritual potential" or when she asserts that his refusal to censor Methodists' dreams "encouraged an extraordinary freedom of individual interpretation" (140, 277). The book's sharpest polemical edge consequently cuts through its final chapter, which treats Wesleyan leaders after John Wesley.

To account for these upbeat choices of inflection, accentuating the "radically democratic" over other understandings of John Wesley's leadership, one might consider the book's numerous reactions to historian E. P. Thompson. After making his first appearance on the third page of *Heart Religion* ("It was Thompson who endowed the early Methodists with their unhappy image as apostles of bad sex"), Thompson reemerges at regular intervals thereafter. Most often his antagonistic presence leads to thoughtful clarifications, Mack venturing to take Methodist religion on its own terms rather than as just so much repressed sexuality. But now and again, the specter of Thompson spooks the author into unfortunate and unbidden defenses like this one: "Surely the repressed hunger for genital sex is too narrow an idea to explain the complexity of the desire embedded in these accounts" (78). Near the outset, Mack uses Thompson's influential attack in *The Making of the English Working Class* to introduce two competing historiographies of Methodism: those inside and those against the Methodist tradition. She depicts, in a brilliant stroke, these divergent traditions pictorially. A stained-glass image of Wesley dons the dust jacket, and William Hogarth's scornful print "Credulity, Superstition and Fanaticism" (1762) serves as the frontispiece to *Heart Religion*. Every reader must ask whether Mack's approach tends at times to recapitulate this visual arrangement—concealing Thompson-style blame with the praise that is Methodism's self-image. Yet even if so, it is a wonder that the study so often succeeds in opening up new historiographical space, neither casting early Methodists as mere arms of Wesley nor explaining away their desires and anxieties. (Mack's attempt to do justice to the latter unavoidably pits her against a different group of skeptics, too: those who have long found that Methodist leaders were, in the phrase of theologian John Kent, "overdependent on theological explanations of what people felt that they felt.")

The ground unearthed most fruitfully in the book is the Methodist Archive and Research Centre in the University of Manchester's John Rylands University Library. Her encounters with primary documents from the archive, especially those of women like Mary Bosanquet Fletcher, are enough in themselves to validate Mack's project and establish its importance. The author frequently compares primary texts with later, often quite different, published editions. Rather than lionize the manuscripts as authentic and denigrate the published accounts as constructed, Mack sensibly considers their mutuality. At one point, for instance, she declares that male leaders' public and private texts represent different "pole[s] of the preachers' emotional self-fashioning," and she concludes that their "particular kind of agency" resulted from "the tension between the two" (126). The realization of agency through tension is the theme of *Heart Religion*'s compelling introduction. Seven chapters follow, which, despite their clear unity, may be read discretely. References to earlier chapters are kept to a useful minimum. One consequence is that some chapters repeat previously discussed material. (The reader learns several times about John and Charles Wesley's divergent views of perfection, for example.) Chapter 1, "The managed heart: Educating the emotions in Methodist discourse," aims to establish what Methodist leaders made of emotion and to suggest how their views relate to difficulties faced by laypeople. The chapter focuses on the Wesleys, and its distillation, though necessary, may prove overly reductive for some experts' taste. (No small challenge awaits the scholar who ventures to condense, into a fourteen-page section, "Holy discipline and sacred music" in early Wesleyanism.) After Chapter 1 closes with a discussion of competing perspectives within the movement, Chapter 2 ("'Out of the paw of the lion': First conversion") continues that broadening of vision by uncovering a variety of conversion narratives keyed to the theme of loneliness. Mack shows how, for many Methodists, the experience of justification meant "a vastly increased capacity for love," an outcome "not ecstatic but empathic" (81). This social turn leads to the core of *Heart Religion*: the third chapter, "Men of feeling: Natural and spiritual affection in the lives of the preachers," and a complementary fourth, "Women in love: Eros and piety in the minds of Methodist women." Having introduced gender-related differences marking the narratives in Chapter 2, in this subsequent section Mack develops her argument that "different patterns of friendship and marriage generated a different emotional and imaginative relationship to the divine" for Wesleyan men and women (135). She clinches the point with extended individual case studies, the use of which characterizes Mack's most achieved work. Chapter 5 (titled, with somewhat misleading specificity, "Mary Fletcher on the cross: gender and the suffering body") moves to issues of embodiment and pain, health and healing, culminating in a discussion of "gendered perceptions about the worshipper's relationship to Christ's wounded body" (173). Chapter 6, "Agency and the unconscious: The Methodist culture of dreaming," establishes a suggestive link between accounts of dreams and the paradox of spiritual agency considered throughout. Dreams become a kind of metadiscourse commenting on, and helping to resolve, the crises that appear earlier in the book. The seventh and final chapter, "Methodism and modernity," looks beyond John Wesley's death in 1791. It examines the rise of missions as both an outgrowth of and a solution to early Methodism's problems with agency. Mack concludes the book by assessing a consequence of that solution: into the nineteenth century, proclaiming the good news entailed among Methodists "the muzzling of women as public preachers and published writers" (293). Supplementing the book's revisionist effort to give ear to silenced voices like these, *Heart Religion* includes, by way of appendix, a helpful "Biographical list of Methodists discussed in the text." The book's learning also extends into its expansive bibliography and useful index.

*Phyllis Mack. Cambridge: Cambridge University Press, 2008. Pp. xii + 328.*

# Bodies of Thought: Science, Religion, and the Soul in the Early Enlightenment

*A review by Robin Runia*

Of what does the soul consist? What is the relationship of the soul to the body? What are the implications of the soul's materiality or immateriality for its immortality? Ann Thomson's meticulous examination of these questions and the answers posed by early Enlightenment thinkers sets out to show how previous critical labels have failed to adequately reflect the complexity of the period's debates about the soul.

Thomson's endeavor functions as another example of scholarship that aims to contextualize intellectual and theological debates of the long eighteenth century. In particular, she is intent on exploding the opposition between the material and immortal soul that critics have continued to impose. She insists, "I am arguing for a more complex reading of the intellectual history of the time, which can only be achieved by attempting to understand it in its own terms and not sticking labels on it" (27). The resulting study begins with an analysis of how the "accusations of heresy and irreligion [that] were used as a stick to beat one's political opponents" have resulted in a number of unproductive and overwrought critical examinations that, for Thomson, simply miss the point of the debates in which they were so frequently deployed. The bulk of her project goes on to draw out the lines of the late seventeenth-century theological debates about the soul, their role within the English political climate, their influence in Dutch and French intellectual circles of the early eighteenth century, and their connections to mid-eighteenth-century materialism in France and England.

Thomson's book begins by detailing how the debate on the soul is expressed in Church politics after the Glorious Revolution, specifically the conflict between the latitudinarians and the High Church. Thomson spends much time providing examples of religiously heterodox views of the soul that, upon close examination, prove deeply committed to Christian doctrine, and her discussion of Locke's attempts to incorporate reason into religion and perceptions of these attempts as a denial of revelation and an assertion of atheism proves an especially compelling case. She examines the Cambridge Platonists' acceptance of Cartesian mind/body dualism and their insistence on an immortal/immaterial soul, and she goes on to consider the specific shape such views took in the Boyle lectures. To the political and theological reverberations of debate about the soul, Thomson adds an examination of the contributions of scientific discourse. Offering nonstandard readings of work by figures including Thomas Willis and Francis Glisson, Thomson demonstrates how the contributions of thinkers were distorted and manipulated for arguments on all sides. Thomson also pulls examples from both sides of the Channel to demonstrate how contributors to the debate self-consciously grappled with their contemporary audience's perception of materialism as irreligious.

Eventually, however, Thompson's main focus emerges, in particular, her interest in determining the ways in which the English debate on the soul continued in France and ultimately impacted French thought, a project she admits results in a "vaguer connection, more difficult to grasp" (136). However, here is where Thompson's careful scholarship shines. Tracing the published work of figures including Pierre Bayle, Thomson teases out the connections between English, Dutch, and French intellectuals. Meticulous examination of published extracts and manuscripts referencing English thought as it circulated in Holland and, eventually, in France allows Thomson to link figures including Locke, Hobbes, and Coward to mid-eighteenth-century materialism and to argue convincingly that theologically minded contributors to the debates on the soul's materiality were used to "provide ammunition" for irreligious arguments against the soul's immortality (152).

At the end of the book, Thomson applies her insistence for the need to understand the period's debates about materialism through the lens of seventeenth-century debates on the soul to the mid-to-late eighteenth century, illuminating, once again, the consequences political and theological interests had on scientific conceptions of matter. Highlighting the connections of Maupertuis, La Mettrie, Buffon, and Diderot to materialist determinist debates both religious and otherwise, Thomson suggests that the apparently unresolvable, lingering theological and political tensions surrounding the topic ultimately led to disciplinary distinctions between scientific discussions of matter and theological discussions of the soul.

While Thomson's final gesturing toward the continuation of these fault-lines in the discussions of race, class, and gender as they emerged in debates about human inequality in the late eighteenth and early nineteenth century are extremely interesting, their hectic glossing rehearses the entire book's somewhat fraught attempt to cover ground. In addition, Thomson's ambitious attempts throughout the book to place lesser known figures alongside the more well known fail to provide a clear sense of the relative importance of the contributions of each. Ultimately, however, what is made clear is the *range* of contributions to the debate on the soul in the late seventeenth and early eighteenth century. Ultimately, Thomson reads the contributions she gathers with a compelling insight that functions successfully as a first step in revising our understanding of the relationship between materialism and religion in the early Enlightenment.

*Ann Thomson. Oxford: Oxford University Press, 2008. Pp. viii + 320.*

# Peripheral Wonders: Nature, Knowledge, and Enlightenment in the Eighteenth-Century Orinoco

*A review by Laura Miller*

Margaret R. Ewalt's *Peripheral Wonders: Nature, Knowledge, and Enlightenment in the Eighteenth-Century Orinoco* responds to several essential topics in eighteenth-century studies, including the connections between scientific work and socio-economic forces, the interpenetration of colonial powers and Amerindian populations, the recasting of the Enlightenment, and the variable uses of rhetoric to address print audiences. *Peripheral Wonders* centers on Jesuit missionary Joseph Gumilla's *El Orinoco ilustrado* (1741, 1745), a natural history that offers a narrative in which Catholicism and scientific inquiry mutually engage. In *El Orinoco ilustrado*, natural history remains informed by religious beliefs as well as local and transatlantic intellectual traditions and cultural practices. Ewalt uses Gumilla's text to recast the Spanish Enlightenment as a geographically far-reaching and eclectic movement, which was heavily connected to Catholicism and responded to both Baconian and natural philosophical scientific traditions. In *El Orinoco ilustrado*, the rhetorical use of the concept of "wonder" allows scientific research and Catholic theology to connect, inspiring in readers a desire for colonial expansion, economic investment, and the conversion of souls.

*Peripheral Wonders* is divided into four chapters, excluding its substantial introduction and conclusion. The first chapter contextualizes

Gumilla's volume as a work of Jesuit natural history, as "a textual natural history cabinet" of the diverse curiosities of the Orinoco region (29). Ewalt shows that Gumilla constructs this cabinet by adapting classical rhetoric to a sacred framework, ensuring that the text's rhetorical goals align with Jesuit missionary goals. Both New Granada's biodiversity and its people inspire wonder in Gumilla, and he explores the linked destinies of the land and its people, balancing "pictures bursting with natural beauty and bounty" and "panegyrics of evangelical successes" (52). His wonder, curiosity, and authority intermix to create a narrative that guides readers through the cabinet of textual curiosities. For Ewalt, "Gumilla developed this rhetoric of wonder in order to reach a wide variety of readers who bring diverse approaches to interpreting his natural history," and this diversity plays out in *Peripheral Wonders'* succeeding chapters (63). This breadth of audience is significant to *El Orinoco ilustrado's* missionary and colonial agendas; when a work like Gumilla's reaches a large public, Spain and the Jesuits are perceived to have a strong presence in the Orinoco.

Ewalt's second chapter explores the implications of colonial power by examining the book's maps, arguing that these maps can help scholars understand Spain's transition into modernity. Ewalt integrates the maps of *El Orinoco ilustrado* with its content, finding that together they represent "the region's human and natural resources [as well as] the Jesuits' and Spain's previous successes and future possibilities in New Granada" (65). This "inextricable union of commerce, colonization, and conversions" (65) also served a practical purpose, offering visual evidence of the dangers and rewards of New Granada. In light of this evidence, Spain would be obliged to continue to protect the Jesuits and their missions, who faced very real and violent danger, even from other religious orders. Gumilla, who comments on "domesticating peoples and plants," may be producing "a Jesuit treasure map to commercial exploitation," but he also "exemplifies the dual nature of the Hispanic Enlightenment, which is both spiritual and intellectual" (75, 77, 93).

The third chapter examines the methodologies that underlie Gumilla's natural history, describing its Western influences, which include Baconian scientific inquiry and eighteenth-century natural philosophical practices. Ewalt situates Gumilla among "eighteenth-century Catholic natural philosophers [who] mediated innovations within Christian paradigms instead of divorcing religion from science," as a part of a broader "eclectic Enlightenment' (95, 97). Jesuits previously had mediated relationships with the indigenous populations of colonies and other countries, intertwining natural philosophy with local knowledge. Gumilla responds to other works of philosophical eclecticism, but his contributions remain unique and wondrous on their own because of the uniqueness of the Orinoco. Gumilla's wonder at local turtles' "innate sense of direction" that leads them to the same place, regardless of where they are initially oriented, evokes meditations on Christian faith and the proper path to God (116). Not only flora and fauna offered opportunities to mediate faith and observation, but in his study of humans, Gumilla also "blended his own observations and induction with deductions based on previous authorities, following an experimental approach very much influenced by Spanish Baconianism, yet open to other methodologies" (138).

The fourth chapter returns to Gumilla's rhetoric, breaking down *El Orinoco ilustrado*'s "rhetorical journey from wonder to knowledge" (141). Ewalt identifies "four seemingly contradictory types of rhetorical paths (Christianization, demonization, correction, and validation) that provide alternatives to notions of knowledge in Enlightenment studies" (141). In this section, Ewalt interprets Gumilla's description of El Dorado and its adaptation to a Christian narrative (143). For Gumilla, the myth of El Dorado is a mark of divine providence, its seductiveness calling attention to the region itself as a possible place for colonization and development. According to this narrative, the human souls the Jesuits will convert represent the true golden reward. Gumilla also demonizes Amerindian knowledge, in particular in his descriptions of the poison curare, perhaps because of the biological threat it could potentially pose to Jesuits. Even his units of measurement evoke Christian struggles: "when a man is slightly injured with the tip of a curare arrow, even if it does not make more of a scrape than a pin would make, all his blood coagulates in him and he dies so instantaneously that he can only just say Jesus three times" (147).

The strengths of *Peripheral Wonders* are many. Ewalt defines a vivid eighteenth century where Catholicism, science, violence, colonization, and commerce coexisted and describes a book with an overtly colonizing agenda that remains a valuable historical document of the Spanish Enlightenment, eighteenth-century natural history, and Jesuit history. Possible improvements to *Peripheral Wonders* might include a greater focus on the other inhabitants of the Orinoco region. The people Gumilla, and others like him, aimed to convert and members of other religious orders, such as the Franciscans and Capuchins, are part of the narrative of *Peripheral Wonders* and their perspectives could have enriched it further. Ewalt writes that "studying texts not previously regarded as enlightened can broaden traditional conceptions of the Enlightenment" (95) and in this volume makes a compelling argument for the presence of a Catholic Enlightenment in the Spanish Atlantic, where wonder allowed scientific research and Catholicism to intersect.

*Margaret R. Ewalt. Lewisburg, PA: Bucknell University Press, 2008. Pp. 258.*

# Enlightenment and Modernity: The English Deists and Reform

*A review by Scott Breuninger*

The traditional view of the Enlightenment has often dismissed the study of religion as peripheral to a larger narrative of progress that describes the triumph of reason and liberty over superstition and autocracy. Recent work has begun to correct this impression, as scholars have examined the nature and extent of a "religious Enlightenment" (or more appropriately "Enlightenments") that developed during the long eighteenth century. Although innovations in political and philosophical thought during this period were relatively cosmopolitan, the religious dimension of the Enlightenment typically reflected national concerns and disputes. This was especially true in England, where the loosely defined thinkers known as deists challenged orthodox Protestantism from a position that rigorously examined accepted tenets through the lens of rationality. This important group is the subject of Wayne Hudson's two-volume study, which carefully explicates their thought and locates it within its English context.

In the first volume, *English Deists: Studies in Early Enlightenment* (2009), Hudson explores the conceptual problems facing the study of religion during the early Enlightenment, rejecting the traditional interpretation that deism was a unitary phenomenon in favor of a more nuanced approach that stresses the diversity of "deisms." Tracing the genealogy of these ideas prior to the seventeenth century, Hudson's analysis highlights the important contributions of Herbert of Cherbury and Charles Blount before concluding with a discussion of the religious works of John Toland, Anthony Collins, and Matthew Tindal. In *Enlightenment and Modernity*, Hudson uses Collins and Tindal as a point of departure for a close examination of a number of "constellationally related" thinkers during the first half of the eighteenth century (4). Hudson's work pays careful attention to the public face of these writers during the years after 1721, when the stability of the English political situation created a space for more critical considerations of Christianity. In doing so, Hudson provides an important study of how an assortment of English thinkers problematized revealed religion from an "enlightened" perspective during a key moment in the creation of modernity.

At the heart of Hudson's argument is an appreciation for the diverse nature of Protestant theology during the first half of the eighteenth century. The rational religion advocated by figures such as Collins and Tindal was not necessarily hostile to Protestantism per se, but found its traditional reliance upon revelation to be wanting. These writers approached religious questions from a vantage point steeped in a deep understanding of Protestant scholarship, turning their theological knowledge against their more orthodox opponents. According to Hudson, both Collins and Tindal targeted common justifications of revealed religion for rational scrutiny, but within a context circumscribed by religious debates. For instance, Collin's ire toward revealed religion was exhibited in his contributions to a contemporary debate concerning the nature of prophecies, which he claimed should be read allegorically, rather than being seen as evidence for the literal interpretation of scripture. In a similar manner, Tindal identified those who relied upon the evidence of miracles to justify Christianity as his true foes and argued against them on a priori grounds. In each of these cases, Hudson stresses that both Collins and Tindal were participating in an "inter-Protestant" debate and that both "argued within the Protestant theological culture of the day" (34). Additionally, Hudson notes that Collins and Tindal were not advocating a rationalist theology for the bulk of the English population, but rather sought to carve out a social and political space for freethinking that would allow for further application of reason to religious matters.

In questioning the proofs of Christianity, Collins and Tindal placed themselves near the edge of acceptability by polite English society, but the second pair of thinkers examined by Hudson went further beyond the pale. Thomas Woolston and Conyers Middleton shared a concern for Christian hermeneutics and were well-versed in Patristic scholarship. As Hudson explains, their exploration of Christianity's historical dimension, coupled with their rejection of biblical literalism, often led their contemporaries to view their works as advocating that Christianity was false. Woolston's early religious views were premised upon a form of "apologetical historicism," which held that the rational grounds for the acceptance of revelation—namely necessity, reasonableness, and certainty—were only present during the life of Jesus. Furthermore, Woolston attacked the typological interpretation of scripture and rejected the historical accuracy of the New Testament, going so far as to claim that when considered "as a literal miracle worker, Jesus was a sorcerer and an imposter" (55). Middleton also sought a form of Christianity that was free of miracles and supernatural elements, rejecting literal reading of the scriptures in favor of a more allegorical approach. Hudson carefully recounts how Middleton's work during the 1740s and 1750s marked a logical continuation of the positions of Collins and Tindal, since he attacked the notion of primitive miracles by the Church Fathers and rejected the efficacy of prophecy.

The final trio of thinkers examined by Hudson—Thomas Morgan, Thomas Chubb, and Peter Annet—are linked by their contributions to biblical criticism and harsh attacks on some of the central tenets of Protestant belief. Morgan first gained his reputation for his critiques of the Law of Moses, which were grounded in his scientific background and his conviction that natural philosophy could help illuminate the moral world. Hudson observes that in his notorious *The Moral Philosopher* (1737), Morgan "used counter-histories to subvert the authority of the Scriptures" as part of a larger assault on the institutional authority of the Church (81). One of the first thinkers to emerge from the working classes, the prolific Chubb also drew upon scientific literature to justify a "democratic" view of "Christian deism," which stressed the importance of free will and reason. Finally, Hudson examines the work of Annet, who published the first deist newspaper in 1761 (*The Free Enquirer*) and ended his career as "a propagandist for explicit disbelief" (91). For his efforts, Annet was found guilty of blasphemy and sentenced in 1763 to be pilloried and imprisoned, thus marking the end, according to Hudson, of a relatively open period of discussion within England of the heterodox religious ideas associated with deism.

Surveying the influence of these variants of deism, Hudson argues that their contributions to reforming philosophy and morality within the context of religious thought played an important role in the creation of modernity. Through their efforts to ground religion upon rationality and their equation of reason with natural law, these thinkers hoped to provide "an alternative and more reliable source of guidance than revelation" (105). This desire was sparked by their common assumption that religion posed a serious problem for civilized societies. In response, Hudson contends that these thinkers advocated for a "natural religion" that was founded upon reason, but that also drew upon classical Stoic and contemporary scientific strands of thought. Although diverse in nature, Hudson suggests that the English deists' insights proved to be quite influential in shaping the modern conceptualization of the relationship between religion, politics, and philosophy throughout Europe and the Atlantic worlds. In recovering and contextualizing some of the key figures and issues involved with these debates, Hudson not only broadens our understanding of the English Enlightenment, but also illuminates the wider reach of their work upon later generations in an accessible and insightful manner.

*Wayne Hudson. London: Pickering & Chatto, 2009. Pp. ix + 225.*

# Fellow-Feeling and the Moral Life

*A review by Patrick Mello*

In his *Fellow-Feeling and the Moral Life*, Joseph Duke Filonowicz challenges readers to modify the premises underlying much moral philosophy since Kant by considering with open minds whether human beings possess an innate moral sense. Despite the systematic logical satisfaction achieved by ethical rationalism, Filonowicz argues that the dogged adherence to reason reduces morality to a mere set of anemic thought-experiments having little to do with the actions undertaken by people living emotionally complex lives. Modifying rationalism, Filonowicz finds inspiration from a notion expressed in Henry Miller's *Black Spring*, that "what is not in the open streets is false, derived, that is to say, *literature*" (11). Filonowicz reads Miller as suggesting that the day-to-day actions of people living in the world tell us far more about morality than any theory formulated in a sterile lab of rational speculation. Filonowicz situates his work as reviving the short-lived tradition of the moral philosophy delineated by Shaftesbury, Hutcheson, Hume, and Smith.

Those already familiar with these philosophers will recognize many of Filonowicz's analyses and arguments. For instance, he goes to great lengths in disrupting philosophical assumptions that human action is fundamentally selfish—in other words, morally reprehensible—and to replace these assumptions with the supposition that the day-to-day progress of our lives is better described as a habitual pursuit of our own convenience, morally indifferent to the well-being of others. Morality, in this outlook, surfaces whenever our routines are interrupted in ways that compel us to judge the actions of others. Of particular interest are those moments when one person is confronted by the apparent need of another. Filonowicz believes that all people instinctively approve of actions taken with the intention of mitigating that need. He contends that this approval is experienced as a felt emotion, not as a rational choice, and therefore, only sentimental moral philosophy is capable of adequately accounting for such an emotional response. Like Shaftesbury and Hutchinson, the sentimentalist thinkers whose writings are of most interest to his analysis, Filonowicz contends that "altruism—the actual practice of it, not some alleged rational demand that we take others' interests into account when we 'adopt' intentions—is essential to morality and that what ultimately accounts for it is sentiment, not reason (or normative self-government)" (17).

*Fellow-Feeling* distinguishes itself by being refreshingly at ease with the indeterminacy inherent in its position. After all, Filonowicz is fully aware that what initially derailed philosophical interest in sentimentalism was how it impeded dialectic by undercutting casuistry and instead asserting feelings and sentiments as the only appropriate sources for judging another's action. Since feelings are ineffable by their very nature and philosophy by its nature seeks to explain systematically, what would motivate philosophers to adopt an outlook that would bankrupt their own methodology? Filonowicz bravely answers that whether we currently possess the data or terminology necessary to discuss our innate moral sense is secondary to whether it exists. What he sees on the streets tells him that it does. In fact, he goes so far as to claim, along with Hutcheson, that at the present it is best to acknowledge that the "the whole thing is a mystery" and must remain so until evolutionary psychology, cognitive science, sociology, or some other field comes up with an answer (222). Hutcheson, of course, sought to fill in this blank spot by asserting God as the ultimate source of man's morality. While Filonowicz is unwilling to follow Hutcheson's lead into moral realism, his return to sentimental thought absent the assumptions of post-Kantian moral speculation enables him to justify Hutcheson's occultism as a reasonable response to a salient, though irreconcilable, philosophical problem.

Some readers will find Filonowicz's arguments both nostalgic and willfully naïve. To be sure, the exploratory nature of his project does require him to speculate that his hypotheses are correct more often than he is able to demonstrate. Moreover, his justification for returning to sentimentalist thought—that it gives greater credence to the question of what constitutes reality by deemphasizing reason and focusing on human emotion—is, itself, a somewhat reductive account of the rationalist enterprise. Nevertheless, I would argue that Filonowicz's apparent sacrifice of rationalism is far more ceremonial than actual and that perhaps we should read it as a performative act meant to disrupt the "ritualistic" approach of most contemporary moral philosophy. In this light, Filonowicz is allowed to open his methodology to a provocative mixture of analytical philosophy, intellectual history, and, on occasion, philology—an interaction more familiar to literary critics than to analytical philosophers.

*Joseph Duke Filonowicz. Cambridge: Cambridge University Press, 2008. Pp. xi + 248.*

# Anna Letitia Barbauld: Voice of the Enlightenment

*A review by Robert K. Lapp*

The subtitle of this long-awaited, monumental biography of Anna Letitia Barbauld, *Voice of the Enlightenment*, captures both McCarthy's achievement as a scholarly biographer and the vital relevance of Barbauld's wide-ranging and lucid articulations of Enlightenment values in Britain. McCarthy's twenty years of meticulous scholarship have literally brought to revisionary light what we need to know about a woman of letters uniquely positioned to propagate the impulses of the Enlightenment in education, literature, political debate, and religion. As McCarthy points out in his preface, "[Barbauld's] story is part of the story of Protestant Dissent's campaign for equal political rights, and both belong to the story of reform's struggle against 'Old Corruption'" (xix). McCarthy can thus make a convincing case for the urgent importance of Barbauld's multifaceted liberalism in a twenty-first century of renewed "religious bigotry . . . and predatory war-making" (533).

For readers of *Religion in the Age of Enlightenment*, this work offers a wealth of nuanced and illuminating analyses of the social, political, and religious factors shaping the experience of English Unitarian Dissent under the Test and Corporation Acts. For sixteen years (age fifteen to thirty-one), Barbauld (née Aikin) lived with her family at the Dissenting Academy at Warrington, where her father was a faculty member alongside the likes of Joseph Priestley. Later, after a decade of breaking new ground in pedagogical practice at the Palgrave Seminary for Boys (which established her reputation as an ideal educator among the Victorians), Anna Letitia and her husband, Rochemont Barbauld (a Dissenting minister of Huegenot descent and Universalist beliefs), moved to London in 1787 and participated fully in the hyperactive public sphere of the French Revolution and its reactionary aftermath. For Dissenters, this included the "Church and King" mobs of 1791 and the bitter failure of the movement for the repeal of the Test and Corporation Acts. Perhaps McCarthy's greatest contribution to the study of religion in this period is the way he brings into sharp focus Barbauld's courageous interventions in the debates of the revolutionary era via such polemical essays as "Address to the Opposers of the Repeal of the Test and Corporation Acts" (1790). Indeed, in a kind of prologue to the book entitled "March 1790," this particular essay is singled out as one of Barbauld's defining works. In this prologue, McCarthy sets up the occasion on which the essay "Address" was written, followed by a stirring précis of the essay made up of excerpted key passages. Quite apart from its rhetorical power—with its brilliant command of "genteel irony" and such ringing phrases as, "We appeal to the certain, sure operation of increasing light and knowledge"—this essay is important, in McCarthy's view, because it contains, far in advance of its time, a "structural understanding of discrimination that fully grasps what we now call 'identity politics'" (276, xxiii):

> The distinction [Barbauld] makes between the frame in which a person's identity as a member of a group may matter and the frame in which it ought to be invisible remains alive; it is still urged by advocates of civic equality for minority groups. And her idea that the politics of discrimination is a dialectic set in motion when a majority's hostile insistence on a minority's difference creates defensive reaction in the victim—"If we are a party, remember it is you who force us to be so"—has no doubt been stated more elaborately, but probably never better. (281)

Moreover, when this essay is placed alongside other such interventions in public debate as *Epistle to William Wilberforce* (supporting

Abolition in 1791) and *Sins of Government, Sins of the Nation* (opposing the declaration of war in 1793), McCarthy is able to make a new case for Barbauld's prose as equal in importance to her poetry.

Meanwhile, with respect to her poetry, McCarthy manages not only to recontextualize those poems that are now routinely anthologized but also to expand the canon of her important works. For our purposes, these include such early poems as "Address to the Deity" and "A Summer Evening's Meditation," which appeared in the volume of *Poems* (1773) that established her cultural authority with the British reading public and her canonization as of one of "The Nine Living Muses of Great Britain" (117). "Address to the Deity" is a rich and resonant liturgical expression (in masterly heroic couplets) of both Warrington Dissent and Barbauld's own personal dissent from *within* Dissent, combining Hutchesonian benevolism and rational religion with the tradition of female mysticism and Barbauld's warm "devotional taste"—her "craving to feel a humanlike intimacy with a humanlike God" (158)—which her coreligionists regarded as a dangerous streak of Methodist enthusiasm (149–64 *passim*). It is illuminating to read this poem alongside McCarthy's explication of her 1775 essay "Thoughts on Devotional Taste, on Sects, and on Establishments," where his nuanced analysis of influences and biographical circumstances serves precisely to locate both the poem and the essay in the spectrum of rapidly evolving and hotly contested religious ideas both within and surrounding Dissent. The only gap in McCarthy's analysis of influence is his omission of Edward Young's *Night Thoughts* as a key resource in Barbauld's magisterial contribution to the night poem tradition, "A Summer Evening's Meditation." In addition to the sources for this poem that McCarthy does adduce, such as Milton, Fontenelle, Anne Finch, and Elizabeth Singer Rowe, we can surely add Young's "Night Ninth"; with its imaginative voyage through the planets and outer stars (lines 1714–1849), many lines of this poem are directly echoed in the similar episode in Barbauld's poem.

But this is a very small quibble with a great book. Readers of this journal will be rewarded by reading such chapters as "Devotion," such chapter divisions as "Stoicism and Power," "Talk about God," and "Ministry to Children," and such episodes as Barbauld's 1803 review of

Chateaubriand's *Le Génie du Christianisme*. Richly illustrated, compellingly argued, and elegantly written, McCarthy's biography of Barbauld reminds us that, despite our lip service to postmodern cynicism, the default position of effective, transformative scholarship continues to be fundamentally "Enlightenment" in its values, procedures, and rhetorical forms. Indeed, here is a book that, by recovering Barbauld as a crucial lens through which both religious Dissent and Enlightenment ideas were lastingly refracted, leaves us feeling fortunate that contemporary scholarship has in fact such deep roots in the values that Barbauld strove to embody and to articulate.

*William McCarthy. Baltimore: Johns Hopkins University Press, 2008. Pp. xxiv + 725.*

# Trauma and Transformation: The Political Progress of John Bunyan

A review by Jeffrey Galbraith

In these papers from the Third Triennial Conference of the International John Bunyan Society, the life and writings of John Bunyan assume a less tidy shape than appears in standard biographies. Bunyan braved the consequences of defying the Act of Uniformity of 1662, yet *Trauma and Transformation* does not view the Dissenting author as possessing an identity galvanized by persecution. Nor, on the other hand, do the essays reduce Bunyan's religious sensitivity to a psychological disorder. Rather, the contributors to this collection work to excavate the gaps in the existing record of Bunyan's life. Notably, they address Bunyan's silence concerning the execution of Charles I in 1649, directing attention to his vexed relation with royalism. Along the way, *Trauma and Transformation* also reconsiders Bunyan's connection to libertinism, gender, Puritan selfhood, and his youthful transgressions, revealing a writer more closely tied to the literary and political culture from which he sought to distance himself.

Peter Rudnytsky broadly examines the traumatic effects of Charles I's execution in his opening essay, "Dissociation and Decapitation." At the Restoration of the monarchy in 1660, royalists lamented the regicide as a second loss of Eden. But the silence of their opponents rang just as loudly. Rudnytsky argues that the killing of the king resulted in an Oedipal cultural dynamic, with writers such as Milton, Andrew

Marvell, and James Harrington struggling to repress their guilt for the murder of the "primal father" (16). Citing Freud's *Totem and Taboo*, Rudnytsky examines poetry and prose to show how "the moment of the King's defeat was also his supreme triumph," as the event came to dominate the cultural psyche (19). Curiously, Rudnytsky ties the success of his argument about royalism's continuing significance to T. S. Eliot's thesis that a "dissociation of sensibility" occurred in the period. For him, the traumatic effects of 1649 explain the split between thought and feeling that, according to Eliot, defines literature of the seventeenth century. It is unclear, however, how Eliot's view of an essentialized "mind of England" provides a helpful context for reading Bunyan (34). If dissociation does indeed contain "a kernel of psychoanalytic truth," as Rudnytsky contends, its appearance here reproduces an antiquated definition of culture as an elite, masculine, and absolutist domain (16). In his response essay, David Norbrook cautions that royalism does not reflect an originary order but was itself a dialectical construct, one of several warring political ideologies. He suggests that "Dissociation and Decapitation" suffers from "default-mode thinking, with any variant from Caroline absolutism presented as an equivalent of the primal sin" (39–40). Perhaps Rudnytsky's essay would be more useful if it engaged the work of Slavoj Žižek, which provides a more up-to-date model of cultural psychoanalysis.

The value of *Trauma and Transformation* lies in its precise and often nuanced interventions into existing critical discussions. Several essays refocus the contexts against which critics have viewed Bunyan's life. In "One Soul, One Flesh," Thomas Luxon examines Bunyan's silence regarding the Puritan celebration of marriage. In the seventeenth century, the humanist ideal of close, masculine friendship began to be applied to the marriage relationship. Around the same time, many Puritan preachers hailed the sexual pleasures of married life. Yet Bunyan rejected these Early Modern views of marriage, privileging his marriage to Christ above all other relationships. Only Christ could fulfill the role of Bunyan's most significant other, for which reason Luxon provocatively describes Bunyan's relationship with his Lord as "a Pauline version of Socrates' enlightened pederasty" (99).

In the essay "Bunyan's Women, Women's Bunyan," Margaret J. M. Ezell draws a much different conclusion. She takes issue with assumptions regarding Bunyan's view of women, challenging the critical commonplace that his inability to represent convincing women characters stems from an inveterate misogyny. Ezell examines documentary evidence of a lost tract in which the preacher lent support to a woman accused of being a witch. Though far from conclusive, the tract offers a clue to Bunyan's personal involvement with "transgressive women," exuding enough mystery to call for rethinking the "complex social dynamic" that Bunyan had to negotiate as a young preacher in Bedford (79).

Michael Davies provides the collection's most compelling treatment of sex and gender in "Bunyan's Bawdy." It is difficult not to laugh when, in the prologue to *Pilgrim's Progress* (1678), Bunyan uses a metaphor from the activity of spinning flax to describe his authorial output: "Still as I pulled, it came" (103). Bunyan surely didn't intend such a pun—or did he? Davies examines other potentially licentious passages in the book, concluding that Bunyan does indeed use sexual puns intentionally and, at times, misogynistically. However, Bunyan employs such traits of libertine literary culture in a counterintuitive sense. For Davies, the preacher's puns are "'bawdy' turned inside out." The Dissenting author is didactic rather than indulgent, using wordplay "to relocate [desire] within a discourse of sinfulness and salvation, the end of which, ultimately, is to turn the reader away from sexual transgression and 'back to God'" (118).

It is stimulating to find scholars who can pierce the aura that surrounds Bunyan's life while still respecting its complexities. In "Young Man Bunyan," Vera J. Camden provides the most focused treatment of trauma and royalism in Bunyan's works, as she attempts to uncouple the man who enlisted in the Parliamentary army from the Dissenter who later disobeyed the restored monarchy. Scholars are quick to find psychological difficulty in the mature Bunyan, invoking theories of displacement and indirection to explain, for example, his reasons for professing loyalty to Charles II in *The Holy War* (1682). But what about the young man who first departed his father's house? Was Bunyan a decided Parliamentarian in his early years? Camden notes that there is scant biographical evidence of a young ideologue. She traces Bunyan's enlistment in the army to his "conflicted identification" with his father, who was a royalist sympathizer (61). Bunyan's self-destructive behavior after the war, Camden explains, further evinces a cycle of "displace[d] aggression against parental authority" (51). Alluding to Freud's essay "Remembering, Repeating, Working-Through," she suggests that Bunyan's relationship with his royalist father provided a traumatic foundation that was responsible for the strength of his adult commitment. The conflict with his father forged his struggles as son and subject that Bunyan subsequently mastered by becoming God's dutiful servant. "The neurotic suffering contained in his early life," Camden suggests, "led to psychological 'work' which is foundational to his life's work as author and preacher" (45).

Though significant for the practical-political critique of state religion that marks Nonconformity in the late seventeenth century, the Bunyan that emerges from this collection is both more and less oppositional than readers have previously thought. Demonstrating the qualified rapprochement with royalism that marks the collection, Roger Pooley's "Bunyan and the Antinomians" examines Bunyan's attitude to moral and state laws. Bunyan refused the constraints of both Mosaic law and the established church. However, circumstances changed during the reign of James II (1685–88). At a time when the monarchy was at its most fragile, Bunyan chose to endorse the status quo, avoiding the resistance theory championed by Whigs and fellow Dissenters.

Sharon Achinstein provides a brief but fascinating interpretation of this stage of Bunyan's life in the concluding essay, "John Bunyan and the Politics of Remembrance." The Catholic James II sought to institute policies of toleration, soliciting the help of Dissenters, Whigs, and Quakers to repeal the requirement that state officials had to take communion in the Church of England. Bunyan's support of this campaign, Achinstein suggests, provides an explanation for the fact that the Dissenting community was strangely silent when Bunyan died in 1688. Suddenly, Bunyan's life did not fit the narrative of strength under persecution typically inscribed on Dissenting monuments and lauded at Dissenting funerals. Achinstein asks, "What narrative forms could give shape to a life whose end came when the political circumstances of his nation could yield neither closure nor certainty?" (143). Such a question unites the essays collected here with the Bedford congregation struck by the loss of their preacher. For scholars, this lack of closure presents a welcome contribution to the field of Bunyan studies.

*Vera J. Camden, ed. Palo Alto, CA: Stanford University Press, 2008. Pp. 200.*

# Walls and Vaults: A Natural Science of Morals (Virtue Ethics according to David Hume)

*A review by Christopher Fauske*

David Hume's place among intellectuals of the eighteenth century is at least in part based on the happy circumstance of when he wrote. Hume had the advantage of being in the position to begin to systematize, summarize, and develop the remarkable progress and theorizing that had characterized the period prior to his own contributions. Hume's work stretched from a time in which conjecture and exploration were the hallmark of intellectual activity to one in which it became possible—necessary even—to take stock of what had transpired over the preceding decades.

Hume's earliest work, *A Treatise of Human Nature, Being an Attempt to Introduce the Experimental Method of Reasoning into Moral Subjects* (1739–40), appeared toward the end of that period in which projects claimed to be establishing new foundations (excepting, most noticeably, Immanuel Kant's *Prolegomena to Any Future Metaphysics* [1783], although, despite the title, that work is itself a response to much that had happened in the previous one hundred plus years of European philosophy). *An Enquiry Concerning Human Understanding* (1748) encapsulated an inclusive understanding and critique of the emerging interest in the human mind as a mediator and agent of understanding, and its synthesis of this approach foreshadowed works outside of Hume's immediate area of interest, such as his friend Adam Smith's *Wealth of*

*Nations* (1776), and those perhaps tangentially related, such as Edward Gibbon's *The History of the Decline and Fall of the Roman Empire* (1776) (Hume had published *The History of England, from the Invasion of Julius Caesar to the Revolution of 1688* starting in 1754), as well as those more directly dependent upon his insights, such as Edmund Burke's *Reflections on the Revolution in France* (1790).

It is little surprise, then, that the bibliography of works about David Hume is extensive. Studies of Hume's ideas are also many. Yet Jordan Howard Sobel's *Walls and Vaults* makes a contribution to assisting modern readers in understanding Hume, particularly his thinking about benevolence, virtue, and justice (not always synonyms) that should be welcomed. Rather than considering what Hume said in the context of when he said it, Sobel offers a clear, careful, and comprehensive consideration of how today we can understand what Hume wished his readers to understand based on both the contexts of Hume's time and developments in various fields since he wrote, most particularly in mathematics, logic, and economics. Hume's analyses are tested by Sobel not in relation to themselves but in relation to modern philosophical problems.

For scholars of the eighteenth century, it can be enormously helpful to revisit Hume in a setting other than that with which he is most familiar, and for those less comfortable with Hume's contexts, it can be instructive to grasp why the Scotsman's impact is as profound as it has been.

Sobel writes that "although . . . I do not honor to the letter Hume's request that *An Enquiry Concerning Human Understanding, A Dissertation on the Passions, An Enquiry Concerning the Principles of Morals*, and *The Natural History of Religion* 'alone be regarded as containing his philosophical sentiments and principles,' I have tried to honor its spirit" (xi). He does so most effectively while explaining Hume's arguments and identifying the potential problems either in Hume's ratiocination or in application of those ideas in light of later philosophical and scientific developments.

Particularly helpful early in the book is Sobel's careful delineation of "Illusory Qualities" in his discussion of the nature of virtue. A passage of Hume that promises, and delivers, clarity can still benefit from Sobel's pithy summation, thus:

> The distinct boundaries and offices of *reason* and of *taste* are easily ascertained. The former conveys the knowledge of truth and falsehood: the latter gives us the sentiment of beauty and deformity, vice and virtue. The one discovers objects as they really stand in nature ... the other has a productive faculty, and gilding or staining all natural objects ... raises in a manner a new creation (*An Enquiry Concerning the Principles of Morals*).
>
> We project sentiments of moral approval onto the objects that elicit them and mistake these sentiments for qualities of those objects. And so virtue and vice can *seem* to be *objective conditions* that are not even in part due to the sensitivity of beholders. (50)

After the introductory sections, *Walls and Vaults* develops into a well-designed and (miracle of modern miracles) well-edited philosophy book, readily accessible almost throughout to anyone with a modicum of patience or training in the discipline. Helpfully, Sobel spends time and care on his argument about Hume's understanding of the critical distinction between benevolence and justice. That they are not the same should, presumably, be self-evident from the fact that Hume's *Enquiry Concerning the Principles of Morals* contains one section "Of Benevolence" and one "Of Justice," but this apparent difference would seem to raise a myriad set of complications for the overarching claim that "moral virtues are for Hume social virtues" (148). Sobel demonstrates, while offering a quick and clear-witted tour through modern conjectures about "justice," why the two terms are necessarily different but are both framed by Hume's understanding of moral virtue.

Occasionally, there are sections of the work that might appear unnecessarily dependent upon notational devices such as "Here is why you end up in (Lm, –Ly): At whichever of your two possible decision nodes, ⊠, you found yourself, –Ly would be in your interest" (271), but, even here, there is a helpful visual guide to the decision tree that is the explication of Hume's "corn case" from the *Treatise of Human Nature* wherein he ponders the consequences of two corn growers not collaborating when harvest time arrives for want of mutual "kindness." This conundrum, and others like it that Hume raises throughout his writings, is, of course, now well modeled and understood by game theory, and Sobel's ability to consider Hume not just for what he says but for how what he says both stands the test of and can be illuminated by modern theory reinforces the strength of Hume's work.

Hume is not remembered just because he was a towering figure of the eighteenth century but because, too, what he wrote speaks still to the modern condition.

*Jordan Howard Sobel. Hoboken: Wiley, 2009. Pp. xiii + 414.*

# Art and Religion in Eighteenth-Century Europe

*A review by Karen Bryant*

With publications such as *The French Revolution 1789–1804: Liberty, Authority and the Search for Stability* (Palgrave, 2004), *Christianity in Revolutionary Europe, 1760–1830* (Cambridge University Press, 2002), *Anticlericalism in Britain from the Reformation to the First World War* (Sutton, 2000), *Religion and Revolution in France, 1780–1804* (Macmillan, 2000), and now *Art and Religion in Eighteenth-Century Europe* (2009, Reaktion), Nigel Aston has established himself as an erudite sleuth bent on uncovering in meticulous detail those subjects within eighteenth-century religious scholarship that hitherto have been either ignored or given short shrift. Aston does not disappoint with his latest book in which he writes about what he calls "virtually a non-subject," that is, religious art circa 1700–1800 (7). Due to the lack of other resources on this important topic, Aston's comprehensive and highly readable *Art and Religion in Eighteenth- Century Europe* would be a welcome addition to any eighteenth-century scholar's library.

It is in no small part due to Aston's corrective research that scholars are beginning to recognize that the eighteenth century was still a deeply religious age despite the influence of the Enlightenment. This assertion, aside from squaring with observation, makes a good deal of common sense. Aston asserts that historians and literary scholars have ignored evidence of continued faithfulness in order to prove deductively that the Enlightenment marginalized religion "as a cultural and intellectual force" (45).

Given the lack of attention religious art of this era has garnered, one might be inclined to draw the conclusion that only inferior artists, with the sole exception of Tiepolo, dealt with religious subject matter and that the best artists (such as Boucher, Fragonard, David, Canova, Reynolds, and Constable) turned their attentions solely to secular or mythological subject matter. One might be further inclined to think that only Catholic countries bought religious works of art, while Protestant countries bought only landscapes, portraits, and genre scenes. While these notions constitute a neat and tidy package, they are also utterly wrong. All of the above-mentioned master artists completed major works of religious art, and every European country, whether Protestant or Catholic, avidly collected religious art. Aston notes: "The 'waning of the Baroque' brought no corresponding diminution in the appeal of religious subject matter for artists and patrons alike" (55).

In *Art and Religion in Eighteenth-Century Europe*, Aston strives to show that religious art, like religious sentiment, crosses the entire spectrum during this age and cannot be easily pigeonholed. To this monumental task, Aston brings his usual organization and clarity to bear. The introduction, the first chapter (which lays the foundation of European religious artwork circa 1520–1700), and the second chapter (which reviews the art and religious culture of eighteenth-century Europe) lay the foundations for his argument. The body of his book is divided into nine thematic chapters: "The State and Religious Art," "The Churches and Religious Art," "Religious Art in Public Spaces Outside the Churches," "Elite Private Patrons and Religious Art," "Religious Buildings and their Contents," "Funerary Art and Religious Life," "Popular Religious Art in Europe," "Religious Art and the Influence of the Market," and "Revolution and Religious Art." Some 250 images, many in color, illustrate these chapters.

In these thematic chapters, Aston explores why monarchs, such as Louis XIV and George III, commissioned monumental works of religious art for government buildings and hospitals and how those works were perceived by their countrymen. Those scholars less interested in the movers and shakers will find Aston's sensitive analysis of the prevalence and importance of affordable, popular religious art particularly useful. Of interest to this writer was Aston's exploration of the fine line the Catholic church walked between its basic distrust of popular religious art, rife as it often was with remnants of pagan beliefs and superstitions, and the understanding that curtailing the practice, aside from being logistically difficult, would likely drive away the faithful.

Aston also explores the differing aesthetic tastes Protestants and Catholics had for the artwork that decorated their churches. Aston handily dispatches the notion that Protestants did not buy religious art, and especially not Catholic art, by detailing numerous examples of British nobles who, while on Grand Tour, eagerly bought religious works to decorate their country homes and private chapels. Sometimes these works were bought as mere trophy items to promote the eminence of the collector as a man of taste, style, and wealth, and other times the purchaser responded on a more honest aesthetic or emotional plane. Aston shows that the Gothic imagination found fertile ground in the transplanted, decidedly Catholic works that made their way to England. The mysticism and rituals of storied Catholicism combined with the fact that most Protestants were comfortable with religious art by 1800 to allow religious art to be seen as a vehicle for the sublime.

*Art and Religion in Eighteenth-Century Europe* offers a vital corrective when one considers the degree to which religious art of the eighteenth century is flatly dismissed. As Aston writes:

> It is telling that in his important *A Theology of Artistic Sensibilities: The Visual Arts and the Church* [1986], John Dillenberger does not have a chapter on the eighteenth century. He writes that in Protestant countries, "art continued to remain outside the Church." Such sweeping and misleading dismissals are largely to blame for the neglect of the more positive attitude to the value and uses of art within a Christian context that Protestant polities experienced between 1700 and 1800. (65)

Aston readily acknowledges he is not an art historian and does not attempt to approach this subject from that perspective. He is, first and foremost, a historian. His interests, therefore, do not lie in tracing the stylistic development of art from the Baroque through the Romantic period, nor do they lie in exploring the aesthetics of specific images. What he is interested in showing is how images reflect the eighteenth-century religious zeitgeist. To this point, Aston writes, "Art shows to an extraordinary degree both how contemporaries imagined religion and what its imaginable qualities were" (7).

While aesthetic analyses would have been most interesting, it seems rather trifling to mention this, especially given the book already runs to 292 pages and Aston warns his readers immediately not to expect such a discussion. That complaint, if such it is, is far outweighed by the greatest strength of Aston's book: his equitable handling of the artists. He does not focus solely on the well-known artists about whom much has already been written, such as Tiepolo. Instead, and to prove the pervasiveness and importance of religious art in the eighteenth century, Aston explores lesser-known artists who, through the vagaries of faddish appreciation, have not garnered the fame they perhaps deserve. For this rare glimpse into eighteenth-century religious art, I highly recommend Nigel Aston's *Art and Religion in Eighteenth-Century Europe*.

*Nigel Aston. London: Reaktion Books, 2009. Pp. 344.*

# Revolutionary Spirits: The Enlightened Faith of America's Founding Fathers

A review by Kevin L. Cope

Many years ago, Walter Jackson Bate was asked by a student in a general education class what he thought about "Coleridge, you know, his opium use." Jack Bate, ever the master of the comically surly rebuttal, retorted, "What do you want me to say, well, naughty naughty?" So it is with regard to that band of culturally ambitious yet permanently rusticated idealists and ideologues who once traded under the name "the founding fathers of America." Having lived for decades, even centuries, atop the plinths and amid the applause created by Parson Weems, textbook authors, documentary directors, and special event producers, those gentlemen whose images grace American currency now face calumny and reprobation from contemporary historians and critics eager to draw attention to themselves by discovering the cracks in the finely sculpted images of would-be American idols.

In *Revolutionary Spirits: The Enlightened Faith of America's Founding Fathers*, Gary Kowalski is less inclined to complete the cycle of praise, derogation, and revived appreciation by returning to an idealized account of America's founders than to spiral up to a new level of veneration located high on the metaphysical plane. Although he recognizes some less-than-imitable behavior among the founders, whether Thomas Jefferson's habit of terrorizing slaves with a whip or James Madison's bursts of melancholy, Kowalski presents the founding fathers' faults as part of a spiritual evolution that leads to an elevated, Unitarian-universalist position. A Gnostic in materialist disguise, Kowalski presents his six top early Americans—Benjamin Franklin, George Washington, Thomas Paine, John Adams, Thomas Jefferson, and James Madison—as seemingly diverse, sometimes flawed men who take a practical approach to the world and who evidence mundane needs, problems, and quirks, but who, in the end, all arrive at a refined, liberal, Latitudinarian outlook that Kowalski variously describes as "deist," "universalist," and "Unitarian." The novelty of Kowalski's approach abides in his simultaneous rejection of the sanitized mythology that usually attends the founding fathers at the same time that he lifts these figures to a level of abstraction (and philosophical purity) that they have never before enjoyed, even among the most ardent hand-clappers.

As often happens with books that are proving a point, the strongest chapters occur near the beginning of Kowalski's production, where he lays out his manifesto and plan. Although it is not altogether clear whom Kowalski is addressing—whether he intends his book as a wedging response to both liberal and conservative ideologues who want to hijack the works of the founders for their own purposes, whether he aims to write a genuine scholarly study, or whether he is hoping to upgrade the insights of the educated layperson—Kowalski strikes an academic tone, explaining that early America abounded in religious creeds and that simplistic attempts to render the colonial-to-federalist period as a pageant of Puritanism or as a carousel of Episcopalianism or as a romp through Enlightenment rationalism or as anything else are certain to fail. Diversity and variety reigned among the settlers, planters, and eccentrics who presided over the first wave of American expansion. Kowalski offers nothing that will surprise any scholar of the period or of the history of either religion or ideas, but he does a decent job of presenting, in outline form, the complexity and multiplicity of late colonial speculation. He sums it all up in the concluding paragraph of his introduction, where he announces that "understanding the credo of these revolutionary spirits will help preserve the United States' unique and most valuable attainment—nurturing a people whose faith is at once powerful, varied, and free" (10). This affirmation may not square completely with the evidence presented in the following chapters, where we see that some of the aforementioned sentient six routinely avoided church and occasionally complained of religious despair. Kowalski's statement is nevertheless refreshingly fair and optimistic, announcing as it does an intention to appreciate the accomplishments of colonial American thinkers without prejudice or anachronism and to affirm, against current critical fashion, that early America had more to offer than troubles related to race, class, gender, and oppression.

Kowalski does a decent job of explaining the difference between the classical liberalism advocated by John Locke and other seventeenth- and eighteenth-century thinkers and the "liberal" politics of our day (17–18). Concerned that too many regard Jefferson, Franklin, and their brethren as conventional god-fearing religionists, he reviews their enchantment with science, empiricism, and secularism; he notes their collective concern for the finiteness of human wit; and he proclaims that these gentlemen "worshiped in the Cathedral of Creation" (21) rather than adhering to what professional wrestler and Minnesota governor Jesse "the Body" Ventura dismisses as "organized religion." Kowalski further spices the mix with assorted stories illustrating the prevalence, among the colonists, of belief in witchcraft and of superstitious ideation. These lamentable lapses in the rise of toleration are juxtaposed against steps toward modernization such as Benjamin Rush's studies of the medical origins of insanity (38ff.) or the emergence of almanacs as distributors of astronomical and agricultural knowledge (34ff.). None of this information will amaze professional scholars, yet all of it is presented in a clear, organized, and persuasively genteel fashion that the denizens of Monticello and Montpelier would have admired.

So much for Kowalski's Gnosticism: for his commitment to the redemptive power of knowledge and to cerebration as the first step toward spiritual understanding. Kowalski is somewhat less successful when it comes to detailed study of the six founders for whom he offers individual intellectual character sketches. His push to combine classical liberalism with easygoing Latitudinarianism so as to hint at Unitarianism leads to excessive abstraction. To be sure, Kowalski provides sound if only preliminary biographical sketches of his selected superstars. We meet taciturn and philosophically withdrawn George Washington, with his statesmanlike concern to observe propriety in office but also his ready fatigue with tiresome sermons and preference for outdoor action; we watch the incendiary but ultimately disappointed Thomas Paine, who burns himself out writing bestsellers in Belgian jails only to become a hot potato in the increasingly gentrified early republic; we become slightly annoyed with the hardworking, minimally articulate John Adams, America's first *unpopular* president; we meet Jefferson, Madison, and Franklin in slightly amplified, intelligently supplemented, quietly updated versions of their traditional characters. Kowalski stays both short of and on the far side of caricature, showing the evolution of these public personae and ultimately of the caricatures derived from them. Unfortunately, he bypasses the critical examination of these polished images.

This neglect of critical analysis results from Kowalski's wholehearted desire to discover Unitarian expansiveness and universalist toleration in every last one of these figures, whether the fiery action-figure Thomas Paine or the grumpy Prozac candidate John Adams. Kowalski's universalizing tendencies distance these figures from their own rich and various characters and stories. Instead, Kowalski's muted Unitarian fervor leads him to concentrate on the founders' most abstract beliefs. Individuality disappears. Every last one of these gentlemen is suspicious of religion, harbors secret doubts about the divinity of Jesus, questions the veracity of miracles, scoffs at the preeminence of humanity in the creation, and otherwise commits himself to a coolly monotheistic view of creation that drifts away from the more tangible and practicable ideas of Protestant or Catholic Christianity or, for that matter, of Judaism, Islam, or any other particular creed. The result is a confused blend of personal appreciation—essays showing the lovable, primarily intellectual traits of this or that founder—with a sort of Swedenborgian glow in which everything shines into everything else.

A second difficulty that Kowalski encounters is the reconciliation of his version of the "great man" approach with his abstracted, ahistorical view of early American thought. With the exception of good old Dolly Madison and a few passing parents and friends, these six founding fathers seem to exist in their respective vacuum cells, at best occasionally having dinner with one another. Their ideas emerge from the highest levels of human experience, whether from correspondence with European luminaries or from consultation with weighty tomes or from pure cogitation. We lack any sense that these chaps ever really did anything other than ascend into the high heaven of structuralist analogy. To be fair, Kowalski seems to be writing a short and appreciative book that does a certain amount of debunking. Unfortunately, he somehow loses sight of the fact that these practical as well as philosophical men—and there are only men, it seems—were interacting with the nature and with the society that they so aptly described.

Kowalski's book is refreshing in its forthrightness if somewhat lacking in the diversity that it praises. Scholars have yet to appreciate fully the effect of universalist thought, with its cabbalistic mixture of eclecticism, globalism, cosmology, historicism, and occasional faddishness, on the formation of early America. There is very little in Kowalski's book that could be labeled as an error. It abounds in true information even as it glides over details. Perhaps we can best appreciate *Revolutionary Spirits* as an effort to do what its title suggests, which is to reclaim the spirituality of early American intellectuals at the same time that it foments a revolution in the history of ideas, if only by serving as a limited pilot study of some of the most interesting figures and ideas of eighteenth-century America.

*Gary Kowalski, New York: BlueBridge, 2008. Pp. 215.*

# Index

## A

Abramson, Julia, 312, 313
Achinstein, Sharon, 372, 373
Adams, John, 384, 386
Adams, William, 3
Addison, Joseph, 267, 268
Adorno, Theodor, 137, 151
Adrichomius, Christianius, 201
Aeneas, 127
Aeschylus, 136, 149
Agate, William, 264, 268
Aikin, Anna Letitia. *See* Barbauld, Anna Letitia
à Kempis, Thomas, 185
Aldersey, Laurence, 195, 206
Allen, John, 256, 261
Allestee, Richard, 217
Andrews, Elizabeth, 55
Anne, Queen, 108, 117–18, 120–22
Aristotle, 213
Arnold, Matthew, 132, 148
Arphaxad, 139
Ashley, Rebecca Kellogg, 169, 170, 172
Aston, Nigel, 379, 380, 381, 382
Astruc, Jean, 145
Atterbury, Francis, 105, 109, 110, 111, 226
Augustine, 138, 143, 146
Augustine, St., 209
Aupaumut, Hendrick, 162
Aylmer, William, 229

## B

Bacon, Nathaniel, 223
Ballard, George, 207
Barbauld, Anna Letitia, 365–68
Barbauld, Rochemont, 366
Barclay, Peter, 11
Barlow, Thomas, 220
Barnabas, St., 234
Bar-Yosef, Eitan, 189, 190
Basil, 143
Bate, Walter Jackson, 383
Bauer, G. L., 141, 142
Bauman, Richard, 164
Baxter, John, 99, 100
Bayes, Joshua, 213
Bayle, Pierre, 350
Benedict, Barbara, 193
Benezet, Anthony, 95, 96
Benson, Joseph, 79
Bentley, Richard, 134, 221
Beverley, Thomas, 262
Bhabha, Homi, 281
Biddulph, William, 187, 188, 192, 196, 202, 205
Bishop Colenso of Natal, 136
Bishop of London. *See* Sherlock, Thomas
Blackall, Offspring, 230
Blackmore, Sir Richard, 124
Bland, Lady Ann, 43
"Bloody" Mary, 108. *See also* Mary I
Blount, Edward, 109

Blount, Martha, 108, 109
Blount, Teresa, 108
Bolingbroke, Henry St. John, 1st Viscount, 105, 107, 118, 119, 128
Bolton, Ann, 77
Bosanquet, Mary. *See* Fletcher, Mary
Bossy, John, 87
Boswell, James, 3, 5, 6, 8, 10, 12, 13, 16
Boucher, François, 380
Bourges, Yvon, 306
Boyce, Sarah, 61, 62, 63, 69, 72
Boyle, Robert, 81, 220, 221, 225, 230, 350
Bristed, John, 251
Brooke, Henry, 106
Brooks-Davies, Douglas, 121
Browning, Robert, 144
Brutus, 127, 128
Bryan, Jonathan, 99
Buffat, Marc, 308
Buffon, Georges-Louis Leclerc, Comte de, 351
Bugg, Francis, 231
Bundock, Michael, 6
Bunyan, John, 369, 370, 371, 372, 373
Bunyan, Thomas, 372
Burghley, William Cecil, 1st Baron, 118
Burgon, J. W., 148
Burke, Edmund, 376
Burnet, Gilbert, 228
Burney, Frances, 4
Burns, R. M., 236
Burrel, John, 205
Bury, Arthur, 230
Butler, Joseph, 329, 332
Butler, Samuel, 181, 194
Butterfield, Sir Herbert, 23, 25, 34, 35
Butt, John, 126

C

Caesar, Julius, 376
Cainan, 139
Calvin, John, 147, 210, 216, 218, 220–21
Camden, Vera J., 371, 372
Canova, Antonio, 380
Caplan, Harry, 324
Carlyle, Thomas, 6, 148
Carter, Elizabeth, 282, 290–91, 299–300
Caryll, John, 106, 108, 109, 111, 113, 114, 115
Cassels, W. R., 135
Cassian, John, 146
Catrysse, Jean, 312
Celsus, 237, 238
Chai, Leon, 156, 157
Chambers, Catherine, 6, 7
Chambers, Kitty, 5
Chapin, Chester, 115
Chapin, Chester F., 7
Charles I, 120, 122, 369, 370
Charles II, 103, 104, 120, 122, 124, 371
Charteris-Black, Jonathan, 218
Chateaubriand, François-René de, 368
Chauderlot, Fabienne-Sophie, 307
Churchey, Walter, 79
Churchill, John, 124
Clarendon, Lord. *See* Hyde, Edward
Clarke, Edward Daniel, 187, 207, 208
Clark, J. C. D., 26, 27, 28, 30, 33, 34, 49, 279, 280
Cleland, John, 283
Clement, St., 234
Coleridge, Samuel Taylor, 135, 148, 383
Colet, Dean, 142
Colley, Linda, 269
Collins, Anthony, 134, 235
Conibear, Anne, 62

Constable, John, 380
Cooke, John, 325
Cooper, Anthony Ashley, 212
Copernicus, 141, 142
Cornbury, Viscount, 118
Corns, Thomas, 178
Coward, William, 350
Cranmer, Thomas, 324
Critchley, McDonald, 4
Crookshank, William, 252, 254
Cross, Walter, 262
Crouch, Nathaniel, 258, 262
Culverhouse, Captain, 207–8
Curio, Jacobus, 140
Cyprian, St., 234

## D

d'Alembert, Jean le Rond, 138
Daniel, Stephen, 175
Daniel, Stephen H., 157
Darling, Linda, 285
Darwin, Charles, 139
David, Jacques-Louis, 380
Davidoff, Leonore, 56–58, 66–67, 73
Davies, Michael, 371
Dawkins, Richard, 132, 137, 142, 151
Dean of Chichester. *See* Burgon, J. W.
Defoe, Daniel, 223
de Fontenay, Elisabeth, 313
Delamarre, Marguerite, 305, 311
Delaroche, Paul, 151
Dennis, John, 103, 104, 111, 117, 120
Derrida, Jacques, 180
de Sacy, Isaac-Louis Le Maistre, 315
de Spinoza, Benedict. *See* Spinoza, Baruch
Dickenson, Peard, 90
Diderot, Denis, 303–6, 308–12, 316, 318, 321, 351
Dieckmann, Herbert, 311
Dillenberger, John, 381
Dionysius, 234

Disney, John, 330
Dixie, Sir Wolstan, 5
Dodd, C. H., 152
Doddridge, Philip, 267
Doolittle, Thomas, 257, 287
Doubting Thomas, 197, 198
Drake, Sir Francis, 118
Duffy, Eamon, 87
Duke of Marlborough. *See* Churchill, John
Duke of Newcastle. *See* Pelham-Holles, Thomas

## E

Edwards, Jonathan, 157–60, 162–64
    metaphors, 155–56, 166–69, 175–76, 178
    sermons of, 165–66, 171–74, 177
Edwards, Timothy, 162
Eichhorn, J. G., 135
Eliot, George, 135, 151
Eliot, Thomas Stearns, 370
Elizabeth I, 86, 110, 116–20, 138
Elsner, Jaś, 191
Erasmus, Desiderius, 115, 116, 136
Eusebuis, 234
Evelyn, John, 262
Ezell, Margaret J. M., 371
Ezra, Aben, 144, 145

## F

Felton, Henry, 225
Fielding, Henry, 292, 297
Finch, Anne, 367
Flamsteed, John, 247
Flanagan, Roy, 178
Flaubert, Gustave, 138, 190
Fleming, Robert, 197, 198, 257
Fletcher, John, 59
Fletcher, Mary, 55, 58–66, 68–76, 346–47

Fontenelle, Bernard le Bovier de, 367
Foote, G. W., 139, 150, 151
Foxe, John, 222
Fragonard, Jean-Honoré, 380
Franklin, Benjamin, 384, 385, 386
Frederick, Prince of Wales, 128
Freud, Sigmund, 370, 372
Froude, J. A., 133
Fuller, Thomas, 1, 100, 177, 277, 303, 343, 349, 353, 357, 361, 365, 375

# G

Galen, 141
Galileo, 141, 142
Gatrell, Vic, 33
George I, 120
George II, 170
George III, 380
Gibbon, Edward, 132, 136, 138, 376
Glisson, Francis, 350
Godolphin, Sidney, 121
Goethe, Johan Wolfgang von, 131
Gordon, Thomas, 272, 273, 274
Greenblatt, Stephen, 193
Gregory of Nyssa, 142, 143
Grey, Richard, 209, 212
Gruault, Jean, 306
Guilford, Sir Richard, 184
Gurdon, Brampton, 226

# H

Habermas, Jürgen, 131
Hachicho, Mohamad Ali, 184
Hales, Stephen, FRS, 247, 258, 259
Hall, Catherine, 56, 57, 58, 67, 73
Hall, David D., 158, 175
Hammond, Brean, 282, 292
Hardy, Thomas, 148
Harley, Sir Robert, 113
Harrington, James, 370
Harris, Howell, 48

Hastings, Lady Betty, 46
Hawkins, John, 4
Hawley, Gideon, 170
Haywood, Eliza, 292
Helm, Paul, 156, 157
Hempton, David, 31, 344
Herodotus, 268
Herring, Thomas, 28
Hick, John, 137
Higden, William, 81
Hill, Aaron, 194, 197, 293
Himmelfarb, Gertrude, 279
Hobbes, Thomas, 144, 186, 214, 350
Hogarth, William, 345
Hogden, Margaret T., 93
Homais, Monsieur, 138
Homer, 111, 149
Hooker, Richard, 16
Horkheimer, Max, 137, 151
Howard, John, 92
Howell, James, 202
Hull, Samuel, 250
Hume, David, 81, 132–33, 138, 272, 375–78
Huxley, T. H., 132, 133, 147
Hyde, Edward, 121, 122
Hynson, Leon O., 80, 87

# I

Ingram, Robert, 279
Israel, Jonathan, 227

# J

Jackson, Kevin, 306
James I, 119, 120, 121
James II, 104, 105, 119, 121, 122, 126, 372
Jefferson, Thomas, 133, 383, 384, 385, 386
Jenkins, Sarah, 72
Jerome, 140

Johnson, Samuel, 1–2, 4–10, 12–17, 46, 177–79, 181, 194, 197, 299
Jowett, Benjamin, 136
Judas, 203
Julian the Apostate, 231
Jung, Carl, 328
Juxon, William, 324

## K

Kafka, Franz, 151
Kant, Immanuel, 375
Keane, Webb, 344
Kellogg, Joanna, 169
Kempe, Margery, 207
Kent, John, 346
Kimnach, Wilson, 168
King, Henry H., 324
King Philip. *See* Metacom
Klein, Lawrence, 60, 61, 63, 71
Kowalski, Gary, 383, 384, 385, 386, 387

## L

Laborde, Alice, 314
Lake, Peter, 210, 215
LaMettrie, Julien Offray de, 351
Latimer, Hugh, 222, 240
Laurence, David, 156
Law, William, 14, 212
Lawrance, Sarah, 68
Lee, Sang, 156
Leighton, C. D. A., 211
Leo X (pope), 116
Leslie, Charles, 211, 217, 225, 231
Lessing, Gotthold Ephraim, 135
Letsome, Sampson, 325
Lewalski, Barbara, 178
Lewes, G. H., 133
Lewis, C. S., 218
Lightfoot, John, 140
Lithgow, William, 196, 206
Littré, Émile, 135

Lloyd, Gareth, 344
Locke, John, 156, 220, 345, 350, 385
Lopez, Gregory, 86
Lord Clarendon. *See* Hyde, Edward
Lord Oxford. *See* Harley, Sir Robert
Louis XIV, 90, 108, 280, 380
Lund, Roger, 234
Luther, Martin, 317, 318
Luxon, Thomas, 370
Lyell, Charles, 139
Lynch, Jack, 13
Lyttelton, George, 118

## M

MacDonald, Flora, 87
Mack, Phyllis, 59, 74, 343–347
MacLean, Gerald, 187, 188, 200, 205
Madison, Dolly, 387
Madison, James, 383, 384, 386
Madison, T. W., 94
Maimonides, 138, 141, 145
Mann, Horace, 271
Marchmont, 118
Marlborough, Duke of, 124
Marquis de Croismare, the, 311, 319
Marshall, Peter, 215
Marvell, Andrew, 369
Mary I, 86, 108 119, 222
Mary, Queen of Scots, 86
Matar, Nabil, 187, 189, 285
Mather, Cotton, 167
Matthew, St., 237
Maundrell, Henry, 188, 189, 192, 196, 207
Maupertuis, Pierre Louis, 351
May, George, 316
McCarthy, William, 365, 366, 367, 368
McDermott, Gerald R., 175
Mee, Jon, 344
Metacom, 159
Mill, John, 134
Milner, John, 254

Milton, John, 178, 180–83, 195, 201, 208, 300, 340, 367, 369
Mitchell, John, 265
Montagu, Lady Mary Wortley, 108, 111
Moody, Josh, 156
Moore, John, 40, 50
Morgan, Godwin, 94
Moryson, Fynes, 188, 193
Moses, 141, 144, 145, 150, 234
Moyer, Lady, 225

## N

Napier, Robina, 5
Nerval, Gérard de, 190
Newman, Thomas, 260, 269
Nicholls, William, 230
Nicolas, Armelle, 86
Nietzsche, Friedrich, 320
Noah, 139
Noonan, Thomas, 182
Norbrook, David, 370
Norton, John, 168

## O

Occom, Samson, 162
O'Donnell, Paris, 208
Ogden, Samuel, 15, 16
O'Leary, Father Arthur, 89
Origen, 138, 142, 144, 146–47, 234–35
Orsi, Robert, 158, 159, 161, 175
Otto, Rudolph, 152
Outram, Dorinda, 159

## P

Paine, Thomas, 384, 386
Palmer, Julius, 86
Paul, St., 137, 213, 216, 315, 320
Penn, William, 217
Peter, St., 229
Philip II of Spain, 118
Pilate, Pontius, 201, 202, 234

Pitt, William, 97, 118
Plato, 143
Plutarch, 268
Pocock, J. G. A., 344
Pocock, John, 211, 212, 227
Pointer, Richard W., 159
Pooley, Roger, 372
Poovey, Mary, 297
Pope, Alexander, 104–28
Pope, Alexander, Sr., 105, 112–13, 123–24, 126–27
Pope, Edith, 112, 113, 122, 123
Porter, Elizabeth, 9, 12
Porter, Roy, 33, 51
Potter, John, 47
Pretender, the, 104–5, 121. *See also* Stuart, James Francis Edward
Pretender, the Young. *See* Stuart, Charles Edward
Priestley, Joseph, 47, 365
Prince of Orange, 120
Prince of Wales. *See* Frederick, Prince of Wales
Proust, Jacques, 317

## R

Rabbi Ben Ezra. *See* Ezra, Aben
Racine, Louis, 109
Rack, Henry, 19
Raleigh, Sir Walter, 118
Ramsey, Colin, 167
Regan, Shaun, 282, 292
Reisner, Noam, 178, 182
Renan, Ernest, 135
Rendall, Jane, 58
Renty, Gaston de, 86
Reynolds, Sir Joshua, 380
Rhodes, Catherine, 76
Richardson, Samuel, 278, 279, 282, 292–300
Ridley, Nicolas, 222
Rivette, Jacques, 306–11

Robinson, George, 198, 199
Rogers, Hester, 71, 73
Romaine, William, 336–40
Rosenblatt, Helena, 211
Rousseau, G. S., 256, 274
Rowe, Elizabeth Singer, 367
Rudnytsky, Peter, 369, 370
Rush, Benjamin, 385
Rutherford, Ian, 191
Ryan, Sarah, 64

## S

Said, Edward, 189, 190, 207, 277, 280, 281, 282, 301
Salah, 139
Salusbury, Hester Maria, 5
Sanderson, John, 199, 200, 203, 205–6
Sandys, George, 182, 183, 192, 194, 196
Scaliger, J. J., 139
Schiller, Johann Christopher Friedrich von, 132
Schleiermacher, Friedrich, 152,
Schur, Nathan, 184
Secker, Thomas, 40, 48, 252, 290, 292
Seeley, J. R., 135
Shaftesbury, 3rd earl of, 233, 237, 240. *See* also Cooper, Anthony Ashley
Shapin, Steve, 224
Sharp, Granville, 95, 96, 97
Shaw, Jane, 53
Shaw, Thomas, 197
Sheehan, Jonathan, 179
Shehadeh, Raja, 177
Sherlock, Thomas, 249, 254, 259–60, 264, 268–70, 272–75, 282–86, 289–91, 301
Shower, John, 286
Simon, Richard, 145
Smith, Adam, 332, 375
Smith, William Robertson, 149
Sobel, Jordan Howard, 376, 377, 378

Socrates, 370
Somerset, James, 96
South, Robert, 2, 9, 10, 11
Spaulding, John Gordon, 324
Speck, W. A., 30
Spence, Joseph, 106–7, 110–11, 121, 128
Spinoza, Baruch, 133, 141, 142, 144, 150, 152, 313
Spira, Francis, 223
Spivak, Gayatri, 281, 301
Sprat, Thomas, 270, 271, 273
Spurgeon, 326
Starr, George, 292
Stewart, Charles, 96
Stillingfleet, Edward, 230
Stott, Anne, 69
Strahan, George, 6, 12
Strauss, David, 135, 139, 151
Stuart, Charles Edward, 285
Stuart, James Francis Edward, 128. *See* also Pretender, the
Stukeley, William, 258, 259
Suaraz, M. F., 233
Swift, Jonathan, 109, 111, 118, 279, 297
Sykes, Norman, 38

## T

Taft, Mary Baritt, 65, 66, 69
Talbot, Catherine, 282, 286, 290–91, 299
Taylor, Joan, 200
Taylor, Thomas, 85
Tenison, Thomas, 40
Tertullian, 234
Tetty. *See* Porter, Elizabeth
Thomas, 197, 198
Thomas, Diana, 62, 63, 64
Thompson, E. P., 345
Thompson, Flora, 75
Thomson, Ann, 349, 350, 351
Thorne, Susan, 57

Thrale, Hester, 5
Tiberius, Emperor, 234
Tiepolo, Giovanni Battista, 380, 382
Tillotson, John, 215, 219, 220, 221, 223, 225, 230, 329
Timberlake, Henry, 196, 200, 201, 205
Tindal, Matthew, 134, 148
Toland, John, 51, 133
Tooth, Mary, 62, 70, 72
Townsend, W. J., 22, 23, 30
Trapnell, William, 235
Trueblood, Elton, 6
Trumbull, Sir William, 107
Turner, Edith, 190
Turner, Victor, 190

## U

Ussher, Archbishop, 139

## V

Valenze, Deborah, 67, 68
Ventura, Jesse, 385
Vickery, Amanda, 57
Vikan, Gary, 198
Virgin Mary, 108, 201
Viscount Cornbury. See Hyde, Edward
Voltaire, 52, 279, 288

## W

Wake, William, 40
Walpole, Horace, 250, 265, 271, 272
Walpole, Sir Robert, 104, 105, 117, 119
Walsh, John, 32
Walton, Brian, 140
Warburton, William, 111, 263, 267, 275
Ward, W. R., 39
Warton, Thomas, 182
Washington, George, 384, 386
Watt, Ian, 280, 282

Weber, Donald, 164
Weber, Max, 131
Weems, Parson, 383
Weinbrot, Howard, 113
Wellhausen, Julius, 145
Wells, Samuel, 84
Wesley, Charles, 47, 95, 244, 250–51, 265, 269, 282, 291, 301, 344–46
  beliefs of, 286, 290
  sermons of, 288–89
Wesley, John, 43, 72, 212, 336–39, 344–47
  and his preachers, 41, 46
  as Enlightenment figure, 50–52
  as parish priest, 44–45
  context of, 22, 24, 30, 35–36, 49, 52
  criticisms made by, 37, 38, 40, 48
  era of, 23–24. 28–29, 31–34
  life of, 19–21, 25, 27, 39, 42, 47
  on public and private worship, 61–62, 69–70
  political and social opinions of, 80–101
  use of *Armenian Magazine*, 77–101
Westerfield Tucker, Karen B., 289
Wheeler, Rachel, 162, 163, 175
Whiston, William, 275
Whitefield, George, 48
White, Richard, 154
Whiteley, J. H., 19, 20
Whitfeld, Henry, 335, 336, 340
Wilberforce, William, 97, 99, 100
William I, 120, 121
William III, 103, 104, 119, 124–26, 286
William of Orange. See William III
Williams, Eunice, 169
Willis, Thomas, 350
Winiarski, Douglas L., 159
Wollstonecraft, Mary, 300
Woodman, Thomas, 107
Woolston, Thomas, 232–40

Wyatt, James, 40

# Y

Young, B. A., 344
Young, Brian, 211
Young, Edward, 367
Young Pretender, the. *See* Stuart, Charles Edward

# Z

Zahai, Avihu, 156
Žižek, Slavoj, 180, 370

# Submissions Policy

*Religion in the Age of Enlightenment* (RAE) is an annual, peer-reviewed journal that publishes scholarly examinations of (1) religion and religious attitudes and practices during the age of Enlightenment; (2) the impact of the Enlightenment on religion, religious thought, and religious experience; and (3) the ways religion informed Enlightenment ideas and values, from a range of disciplinary perspectives, including, but not limited to, history, theology, literature, philosophy, the social and physical sciences, economics, and the law.

While the Enlightenment generally refers to an eighteenth-century philosophical and cultural movement that swept through Western Europe, the editors welcome studies that encompass the seventeenth-century intellectual movements that gave rise to the ideals of the Enlightenment—e.g., materialism, skepticism, rationalism, and empiricism—as well as studies that consider later manifestations of Enlightenment ideas and values during the early nineteenth century. The editors likewise welcome studies of non-Western religious topics and issues in light of Enlightenment attitudes. In addition to publishing original research in these areas, *RAE* includes reviews of books that explore topics relevant to the thematic scope of the annual.

Submissions should be aimed at an audience of professional scholars, educated laypersons, advanced undergraduates, and graduate students from a variety of disciplines. Contributors should thus avoid highly specialized language. The suggested length for manuscripts is 7,000–10,000 words, though shorter and longer articles will also be considered. Submissions should adhere to the guidelines of the most recent edition of *The Chicago Manual of Style*. Both electronic and hardcopy submissions are welcome. Contributors should include a cover memo that includes the contributor's name and essay title, in addition to two copies or an attachment of the essay in Microsoft Word with the author's name and other identifying references removed. References should be given as footnotes, rather than endnotes, and should follow the conventions described in *The Chicago Manual of Style* for documentation provided in notes alone, without a bibliography. (For an introduction to this distinction, see section 14.14 of the sixteenth edition of *Chicago*.)

Brett C. McInelly
Editor, Religion in the Age of Enlightenment
Brigham Young University
English Department
Provo, UT 84602
brett_mcinelly@byu.edu

Book review queries should be addressed to the Book Review Editor, Kathryn Stasio (Kathryn.Stasio@saintleo.edu).

Please direct inquiries concerning subscriptions to AMS Press, Inc., Brooklyn Navy Yard, 63 Flushing Avenue–Unit #221, Brooklyn, NY 11205-1073, USA.